Lifelines

jovis

Lifelines

Politics, ethics, and the affective economy of inhabiting

Camillo Boano,
Cristina Bianchetti
(eds.)

jovis

Part 1

Promise and failure of infrastructures

Part 2

Spaces of lifelines and lifelines of spaces

Acknowledgments

Many people have contributed to Lifelines. Since its inception, the research has been accompanied by moments of public dialogue with interlocutors from different fields of knowledge who have addressed issues that can only be indirectly related to the concept of lifelines, contributing substantially to build it. The first cycle of Immune Dialogues, held in late spring 2020, was attended by Emanuele Coccia, Donatella di Cesare, Diane Davis, Carlo Olmo, and Sara Protasoni. A few months later, a second cycle saw the participation of Keller Easterling, Matthew Gandy, and Omar Jabary Salamanca who addressed the politics, ecologies, and violence of infrastructural thinking. Carmen Andriani, Roberta Amirante, Massimo Bricocoli, Isabella Inti, Clare Melhuish, Nina Rappaport, Matteo Robiglio, and Nicola Russi discussed progress by participating in round tables in spring and autumn 2021. We would like to thank all of them for critically feeding our thoughts.
The research has a pronounced empirical character: it was constructed from case study analyses carried out by some twenty researchers from various academic institutions, with different experience and orientation. Thanks to Isabel, Fernanda, Clare, Hoda, Hanadi, Joana, Nina, Nadine, Ramona, Abir, Emanuel, Valentina, Federico, Alberto, Ianira, Antonio, Alberto, Federica, Elisabetta, Maria Teresa, Camilla, Giulia, Lorenzo, Andrea, Marco, Agim, Alessandra, and Lorenza. Luis, in his role as a dedicated researcher, followed the many paths of research more closely, also taking care of substantial aspects of the manuscript submission. Special thanks to Luis Martin Sanchez who worked as research assistant in the project, and to Harriet Hallsop and Richard Lee Peragine for helping with the language revisions.
Finally, it has been possible to conduct this research, intergenerational exchange, and close dialogue with colleagues and scholars thanks to the support from DIST, which financed it and hosted its work. We would like to thank the director, Prof. Andrea Bocco, Stefania Guarini, and Oceane Escobar, who followed the numerous, not always simple administrative steps.

Lifelines: the stakes of life in the project

Camillo Boano

Lifelines are many things. A research project whose results you are about to read in the following pages and whose ambitions include trajectories that are here only imagined.
Lifelines is a research project that has involved researchers from various disciplines, with different experiences, geographies, and interests related to that system of spaces, dispositifs, and relationships that is centered around life, the latter being the focus of space, policies, and projects. It is a research project that revolves around urban and architectural spaces confronted with crises constituted by protection and immunity and that clashes with a new era that many have defined as computational and pandemic, in which spatial tensions between life and death, finiteness and futurity, difference and contingency are recoded and through which it tries to define other trajectories suggesting "kinship of an unexpected nature," as Haraway would say.[1]
Lifelines is a research project born in confinement: shared and conceived during those months of lockdown in the spring of 2020 that made visible and accelerated the awareness of crises – multiple, overlapping, historically determined – whose stake is life itself. But – like all thoughts in confinement – it is in debt of lucidity, it is undisciplined, it is still incapable of tracing the perimeters, the thicknesses. It sees a broader project, but not clearly enough, because it is clouded by unease, despair, the aftermath of the health emergency, the frustration of living on a planet that is irreversibly damaged and in troubled times.
Lifelines is a research carried out using a language that was negotiated in the interstices of the possible. It follows up on previous research, reformulating the centrality of life that was underlying but invisible; it recodes experiences in territories that are no longer accessible due to the pandemic, connecting relationships without defining them too much, leaving space for invention and interweaving. It misses the target, allows shifts and approximations by dressing up with different attributes; it is modelled in the holding capacities of alliances; it is oriented towards reformulating the calculating spectrum of academic impact and frames co-productions, co-writings, and dialogues at the center.
Lifelines is inextricably linked to the contemporary socio-ecological crisis. It mobilizes thoughts and reflections on that present which Achille Mbembe has called "brutalism" in a perpetual struggle against life; a planetary condition, "a time without guarantees or promises, a time obsessed with its own end" and a process of 'exhaustion' that produces "frontier bodies"[2] and "chocking subjects"[3] in a constant dialectic between control and abandonment, entanglement and separation, immunity and exposure.
Lifelines is a way to change the agenda and the way we look for answers in the biopolitical present of architecture. Lifelines refocuses the relationship between life, its protection, and its exposure to death, destruction, and finiteness. In other words, since life is at the center of the making and becoming of cities, space, and collective existence, the current conditions force us to think about what the biopolitical project behind the pandemic imaginary might be. Life at the crossroads of the political and economic practices of space, to paraphrase Esposito, in the

light of the risk of a completely immunized society, the need for an investigation into those peculiar characters in which politics unfolds and infrastructures organizing them, spaces in which life and death, health and suffering, exile and capture, proximity and distance, solidarity and abandonment, freedom and dependence are constantly at stake.
Lifelines are not solutions. Their usefulness certainly does not lie in producing a formula or a product that will save us. Instead, they claim the necessity of life at the center, of the politics of space and its projects without settling for the consolatory tones of care. They think of their own process through an industriousness capable of building, maintaining, and repairing their living space without internal integrity – only fractured. They let us glimpse the possibility of a new living space, destabilizing the affective cartographies of exception and leaving lines of flights, contamination, and failure.
Lifelines are those spaces where the world and life intertwine, mingle, twist in a constant resistance – awkward and fragile – to the mechanisms of capture, exploitation, and creation of social and environmental precariousness that characterize the violent techno-capitalist present. A scenario in accelerated transformation where the assumptions of progress, of modernity have determined forms of 'coexistence without relationships,' generating an indifferent subject who is not interested in his own life. Generating an indifferent subject, spectator, and consumer forces us to reconsider our relationships "with technology, with bodies and with the spaces we live in."[4]
From here, lifelines become those spaces that resist abandonment and carelessness, the true generators of precariousness and exhaustion, while offering the possibility of protection "from the specter of self-destruction."[5] Not only spaces and procedures, mediums and relations that settle in to make some form of life possible or impossible; not only the impacts and effects on mobility and immobility of human and other-than-human life but a re-appropriation of protection in space and design. Living is not a question of survival but a process of continuous adaptation between protection and freedom, between care and control; and this adaptation is a struggle, it is finding ways to escape, degrees of freedom; a struggle to transform the existing by coming to terms with vulnerabilities.
Lifelines are nothing more than inhabiting the meanders of adversity, of coming to terms with life, vulnerable and collective, resisting the adversity of what is there by creating space for maneuvers, support, operations of liberty.

Life at the center of death's games

Achille Mbembe argues that the spread of Covid-19 appears as a continuation of the war modernity wages against life, a life that was already threatened by suffocation, by lack of air, before the virus.[6] A planetary condition that is "a time without guarantees nor promises, a time obsessed with its own end."[7] For Mbembe, the planetary exhaustion

– which he calls brutalism – is caused by processes that include "fracturing and fissuring," "emptying," "drilling," and "expelling"[8] organized around the impending ecological crisis, the ever-present techno-molecular forms of colonialism, and spatialized in the dialectic between entanglement and separation.[9] Here, life is at stake.
The dialectic relationship between entanglements and separation is defined by the perceived risk posed by proximity and exposure on the one hand, and by the practices of partitioning space to slow-down, to control, and to increase distance to carceral and violent spaces, on the other. Such "borderization"[10] leads to "the creation of a segmented planet of multiple speed regimes."[11] The paradigm of protection is where life is at stake in spaces that are separating those who are insured from those who are not. These latter, *uninsured* bodies are "bioavailable,"[12] and in "[...] a relation of *radical inequivalence*"[13] with the insured bodies, following a bifurcation between life and bodies; a bifurcation that definitively co-implies politics and life.
Such an overwhelming reality of the terrestrial condition stirs and disrupts the very ground of human existence. Terrestrial beings cease to be a stable and passive background for human activities to the point that they threaten human existence itself. Chakrabarty claims that "with the crisis of anthropogenic climate change coinciding with multiple other crises of planetary proportions – of resources, finance, and food, not to speak of frequent weather-related human disasters,"[14] both the future of humans and the one of earth are threaten. Franco 'Bifo' Berardi calls this "a society that is on the brink of an environmental, financial, but also psychic collapse" and a "landscape of anxiety."[15]
With this scenario, the project manifests the inconsistency of life and its inherent contradiction: the immanence of death in life. It gives itself to life, to protect it, to improve it, to cure it, even though it knows it must die and therefore fail. It imagines a future that escapes like the world itself, and is at the same time incapable of excess. Today's alternative, beyond the rhetoric, does not lie in the possibility of reversing the course of things or securing ourselves on the edge of the abyss. This is now too late. We are left only with the awareness that today it is a matter, perhaps, of succeeding in slowing down the catastrophe by opting for different gradations of ecological hell instead of its extreme consequences: the end of the species. Current events disturb and paralyze us because they show scientific projections that scan the future as an evolutionary dead end: an absence of future. The future comes to us from the IPCC scenarios, any dystopic Netflix series, and with the vanguard of the scientific community: in the comfortable techno-green salvation and the consolation of the community and the reuse of spaces.
To survive, we must return to all living things – including the biosphere – the space and energy they need, which recalls Mbembe again: "in these conditions, one of the possibilities is to worry about the death of others, from a distance. Another is to become immediately aware of one's own putrescibility, to have to live in proximity to one's own death, to contemplate it as a real possibility."[16]

This seems to be the real point of lifelines: the exhaustion of a life in constituent proximity with death. In this, the architectural project cannot be simplified to a requalification, a functionalist infrastructure to extend life, to renaturalize it, to open a natural system. Rather, we must reframe its biopolitical essence as a question of inhabitation. For Agamben, questioning inhabitation from such spaces means revealing that "the very possibility of living and inhabiting is indissolubly intertwined with death."[17]

We can maybe, audaciously, suggest that the project today should be less consolatory and seen more as "a creative process through which they withdraw from death in order to escort it [...]. And yet if human communities are not destined, as so many today seem to suggest, for simple disintegration, if human life is an inhabitable life, men will necessarily have to try to rediscover and reinvent a way of inhabiting their city, their land."[18] What seems to be important to think, therefore, is an inhabiting life, which we know to mean "to be in what one holds dearest, one's own and at the same time common. That is, to be and to enjoy one's own nature. It is certainly a way of resisting, of staying, of preventing oneself from being dragged elsewhere but also," Agamben continues, "a way we have to protect (sheltering) life from its devastating fury."[19]

The inadequacy of project disciplines to read and to understand the present is evident. Design faces an epistemic debt towards the intersectionality – and therefore the complex articulation of causes, effects, and spatial figures – of great planetary changes and technological hegemony just because they are anachronisms that distort the image of the present and because they are incapable of any prognostic thought if not the constant production of simplified, momentary, conceptually impoverished utopian models. Design thoughts are linked to the privilege of position, negation of otherness, negationism of various kinds that paint an exhausted world, to be cured, rehabilitated, and mended, but always centered on an anthropos so powerful that it stands for a geological era – the Anthropocene.

The precariousness and margins of the lifelines game

Lifelines have emerged from the intersection of different dimensions: one of greater precariousness that defines living as a result of the crises we are experiencing (1), a dimension of vulnerability that is no longer just of the individual but of the species, both in bodies and in nature, of life, bodies, and the political paradigms that derive from them (2), a dimension of defense, protection, care with their implications of subjugation, capture (3) and submission, thus making protection itself one of the greatest risks. This constellation serves to illuminate and redefine a discourse on contemporary living at the crossroads of all practices, political, social, economic, technological, and cultural, and therefore of living and its space.

As Anna Tsing says, precariousness is a life without the promise of stability.[20] Living in the burning house, in the burning world, and in its relative impossibility of breathing and of redemption, in the refusal of any messianic adjustment, correction, or redemption implies not only analyzing the processes of privatization, oppression, extractivism but at the same time refusing its immunitarian dimension. Inhabiting not as having, disposing, infrastructuring, organizing but as our way of being in the world consists in weaving relationships, incorporations, knotting, taking distance, "[...] inhabiting is something vacillating."[21] One inhabits in a continuous 'failure,' in a "ruin of plans, of ideologies, of possibilities, in a perpetual dysfunctionality."[22]

Late capitalist imperialism, misogyny, racism, climate change, all the debilitating conditions of planetary life have foregrounded the pandemic and its urban imaginaries. Precarity takes differently gendered, historicized, embodied, geopolitical manifestations and challenges the project in its being burned-out, incapable of imagining dehumanization, the inhumane, the inhospitable: "precarity is first and foremost the form of life in the age of crisis as art of government," Dario Gentili reminds us.[23] Lifelines are those spaces in which protection is deployed in forms and spaces that are configured more as a margin of play, a possibility, between support and coercion, between abandonment and taking charge, between contamination and immunization, between community and immunity.[24] Lifelines are not the form, pure, purified or not, of the synthesis between the power of the project and the capacity of the body but the effect of the compositions of space that grapples very urgently with forces that are always co-apparent with their own opposite, in the irreducibility between protection and negation of life.

Immunity, as Esposito reminds us of in the reflections we are proposing, "is always a protection against an absolute evil through a lesser evil [...] a medicine that is also a poison,"[25] is thinking about ecologies, or rather an ecological difference, capable of observing not only the different ways of living and inhabiting space but the proliferation of "alliances between creatures beyond the creator,"[26] an openness to the acting out of consequences, when protocols of experience are established within a constant interweaving of activity and passivity, power and vulnerability in their continuous coming to terms with its surroundings. Surroundings, then, not simply as territories or spatial objects but as places where the impossible and the possible, protection and exposure, community and immunity converge in a mysterious entanglement, in a subtle enigmatic convergence. A non-peaceful unity, a synthesis "that does not save the human from its natural fragility but makes this its strength."[27]

Inevitable pandemic imaginaries

The pandemic – the inevitable background to this work – has once again brought life into the orbit of politics. It is not that *biopolitics* – because that is what it is – has lost any relevance. It is not an exception, generated by the health crisis, but a normalization where power functions automatically, invisibly, and along the perfect ordinary. An inhabiting life, made up of lines of tension between inside and outside, between control and resistance, between economization and mutualism, production and reproduction, exclusion and inclusion, where bodies and spaces, as in the discipline described by Foucault, are no longer regulated in their gestures and times by perimeters and forms but broken down, recombined, and reprogrammed through a profound reconfiguration of the boundaries between death and life and their relative forms of politics.

This redefinition leaves a void at the center, that of planetary destruction, border violence, and the abandonment of the human as a paradigm. A void that gives way to contamination, coexistence, hybridization in a new composition. The virus, a paradoxical being that constantly mediates the interstices of the borders between life and death, is an important prism for thinking about the present and its lifelines. Why? Because, as Elizabeth Povinelli suggests, the virus is "one of the figures that challenges the rigid division between life (bios) and non-life (geos)."[28] Povinelli calls the government of this division "geontopower,"[29] and its mode of government is geontology, a power that divides life and death and a regime of government that decides what is valued as life and what is disvalued as death.

The virus is an ungovernable entity that disrupts the conventional way we have known since Foucault, based on the clear differentiation between life and non-life. In its constant oscillation between life and non-life, the virus has no fixed and given place in the world, no sense of belonging or attachment, and this makes it vulnerable to expulsion and therefore "to live in the vicinity of the virus is to inhabit an existential crisis."[30] Therefore, as an ungovernable entity, the virus becomes a paradigm, introducing crisis in the existing order of governability and in its lifelines because it challenges the established distinction between life and non-life and, thus, exposes dependency and vulnerability by limiting protection, but at the same time, being a danger to human lives, its existence is fought with increased protection.

A crisis that has generated "pandemic imaginaries," to use Christos Lynteris'[31] words, as an instituting force of the social that originate from a pervasive anxiety about loss of control, about the inevitable failure to achieve total protection from some forms of external threat, even if it stems from the ecological contradictions generated by modernity. If, on the one hand, the pandemic imaginary reduces the power of the project as master of human-non-human relations, it delineates, on the other hand, a biopolitical imperative of control, preparation, management protocols, and reformulation of distances. The paradigm of protection in its immunitarian dimension[32] returns to the center in these pandemic imaginaries, both in their dystopian version of techno-controlled futures and in the consolatory version of the fifteen-minute city.

Inhabiting the burning house: holding lifelines

The climate crisis makes large parts of the planet uninhabitable; the patina of colonialism as well as the health crisis displace bodies in their own ways in physical space, in social space, in the space of control and limitation of freedom; they shape forms of protection, spaces of immunity across scales, and immobility around secured borders. While around us it is disintegrating at such a dizzying speed that any description of its physical, social, economic, or political makeup yields to the image of the "burning house" that Giorgio Agamben used as the title of one of its recent books.[33]

Exhaustion, extinction, proximity of death, ashes are all evident in front of us, but the response of the architectural and urban project is the same: "aimed at relaunching economic growth at all costs, we will enter a spiral of violence, racism and war. Instead, we must accept the reality of exhaustion and face reality on egalitarian terms: share frugally what knowledge, solidarity and technology can provide. Redistribution of wealth, egalitarianism, frugality: this is the recipe for survival, and possibly for a new pleasurable social life."[34]

A living and a life are therefore not qualified by norms, conventions, dispositifs but delineated by forces of friction. Paraphrasing Anna Tsing, who researches into matsutake mushrooms, Lifelines has allowed us to explore the ruins which we all now inhabit, opening "the possibility of coexistence within environmental disturbances"[35] and revealing a "tangible example of collaborative survival,"[36] and "ecologies born of perturbations in which many species coexist without harmony or conquest."[37] Precariousness is the condition in which we are vulnerable to others. A precarious world is a world without teleology. Indeterminacy is frightening, but thinking through precariousness shows that indeterminacy makes life possible.[38] When reaffirmed through the dimension of precariousness, the spaces of the project and of simply living become defined by the "strength of what they unite as much as of what they disperse"[39] and by the indetermination between ineffability and presence.

If Lifelines has at its center a sort of affective economy of precariousness, inhabiting this condition is what we seem to have glimpsed in the folds of Lifelines: the urgency of questioning oneself on one's way of being on and in the earth "on one's way of being, taking care of this very being, and, precisely for this reason, leaning towards the other, open to something else, to the possibility of a not yet."[40]

It is text that, perhaps with a little risk, would like to build up a lexicon that helps to outline a project for our political-existential condition of all inhabiting, of being in a world with a time limit, a space that is being compressed and eroded, a condition of residence, but with the new aggravating factor of the deprivation of the future, and suggested even more strongly by the pandemic crisis. A temporary inhabitant in the complex system of conventions and immune devices, based on the fear of contagion, of sharing, of abandoning the privilege of thinking oneself universal and indestructible.

Lifelines and its articulations: lifelines as a form of holding

What follows, organized in three different sections and preceded by a reflection by Cristina Bianchetti, is an investigation, discovery, and representation of those capacities that establish practices and spaces in order to compose the contemporary stakes of life, which allows us to think about "vulnerability and contamination"[41] as outcomes of a thought, with its fears, uncertainties, and tribulations.

Promise and failure of infrastructures constructs the argument on the basis of the most obvious dimension of lifelines: they being infrastructures, i.e., spaces that "structure contacts"[42] in economic, cultural, and political material conditions. Things and spaces, assemblages and devices that organize human social order but also more-than-human ontologies.[43]

The second part, *Spaces of lifelines and lifelines of spaces*, organizes reflections on the multiplicity of vital spaces, of worlds, as they configure themselves and become space. It is not a question of celebrating life or vitalism but of creating a thought about space; of its becoming but as a continuous renegotiation of limits, boundaries, possibilities beyond the reach of the thought of capturing the future, of governing the species, of nature, but also of its regressive dimension of renewed naturalism. Lifelines are then seen as spaces of embodiments, movements, and relationships. The space of living is something that lies between the problematic instances raised by the environment – its necrotization – and the capacity for openings and, at the same time, constrained responses. The spaces of the city are configured in a field of tensions between the urgencies of the environment and the practical capacity of living and coming to terms with the project.

The third and last part of the book reflects on the structural ambivalence of lifelines, on what has been called *The dark side of protection* to complete the shift from the notion of otherness to the one of difference, understood as what can neither be expelled nor eliminated. Coming to terms with the idea of contamination makes it possible to think of "vulnerability and contamination"[44] as outcomes of a metamorphosis and to resist the positive vitalist, immanent definition of lifelines. Frictions that make visible a power exercised over social bodies and their ecologies. Forms of solidarity, of credit, of collaborations, which make visible a dark side that controls social positions, access, acceptance, and empowerment, where life and death overlap, undifferentiating, as Agamben would say. Protection that becomes control, that leaves room for perverse effects of risk and protection, while manifesting itself in spaces of immobility and informality. Living is not a question of survival but of coming to terms with the scandalous joy of being vulnerable, of collective life by resisting adversities.

Lifelines, like all research in times of crisis, does not only ask difficult questions about the stakes of life but embraces what Denise Ferrera da Silva calls "the incompleteness of the prevailing mode of thinking."[45] Lifelines is the impossibility of composition around those zones of contact that build places, make the world; capture but at the same time

sustain; allow many ways to exist without anyone taking over; draw uncomfortable but familiar presences; trace forms of exile and resistance almost leaning on what exists, what one would like to exist.
An agenda that becomes a project of critique of the present, capable of creating an additional meaning to the triumph of death and neglect in those tensions between consolation and care, exile and escape, calculation and poetics.

Holding on to Lifelines

Lifelines, like all collective and transnational research, was conceived and written in several languages, punctuated by translations and approximations. Thinking about lifelines, about their being such ambivalent supports of the central issue of protection, we came across the verb 'to hold.' Hold in English means to take and hold something in the hand or in the arms, to support, to hold someone in a place so that they cannot leave; but, when used in the gerund, it also means to maintain, to support, to create spaces of maintenance: Winnicott would say[46] of caring about the environment that a parent creates for their child and the therapist for the patient.
A membrane that allows the suspension of treatment in order to increase the safety and independence of the patient, without exposing them too much. Spaces of transition, places of rest, of pause to catch one's breath; Aradau and Tazzioli[47] would say thinking about migration routes and border violence; again, with Winnicott,[48] between parent and child, analyst and analysand, for the individual engaged in keeping internal and external reality separate but interconnected.
A space of relationship but of control, of protection, of care but also, as Christina Sharpe says, of the hold – in reference to the place of the slave ships where "in the midst of so much death and the fact of Black life as proximate to death, how do we attend to physical, social, and figurative death and also to the largeness that is Black life, Black life insisted from death?"[49] – a life inhabited by death but to its own possibility of survival, to "survive the holding."[50] Containment, regulation, quarantines, camps, capture, imprisonment, expulsion, invisibility, as "symbols of the death sentence of (black) bodies" without succumbing and resisting, while thinking of ways "in which the hold cannot contain and does not contain" but becomes "womb, and elsewhere," embodied work of caring, supporting, and inhabiting this time of waiting, says Sharpe.
Given these premises, the answer that Lifelines helps us to give is that of a future and of protection as paradigms of the project.

Endnotes

1 Haraway, *Chthulucene. Sopravvivere su un pianeta infetto*, 17.
2 Mbembe, "Il diritto universale a respirare," 249.
3 Tazzioli, "'Choking without killing': Opacity and the grey area of migration governmentality."
4 Fadini and Villani, *Eco/Logiche. Politiche, saperi, corpi, ambiente*, 7.
5 Pulcini, *La cura del Mondo. Paura e Responsabilità nell'età globale*, 277.
6 Mbembe, "The Universal Right to Breath."
7 Mbembe, "Il diritto universale a respirare," 249.
8 Mbembe, *Brutalisme*, 9–10.
9 Mbembe, "Futures of Life and Futures of Reason."
10 Ibid, 21.
11 Ibid.
12 Ibid, 23.
13 Ibid, 23.
14 Chakrabarty, "New Literary History," 3.
15 Berardi, *The Third Unconscious. The Psycho sphere and the viral Age*, 16.
16 Mbembe, "Il diritto universale a respirare," 252.
17 Agamben, "Introduzione," 11.
18 Ibid, 11–12.
19 Ibid.
20 Tsing, *Il fungo alla fine del mondo. La possibilità di vivere nelle rovine del capitalismo*, 24.
21 Ibid.
22 Ibid.
23 Gentili, *The Age of Precarity. Endless crisis as an art of government*, 11.
24 Esposito, *Immunitas. The protection and negation of Life.*
25 Spina, "In dialogo con Roberto Esposito."
26 De Fazio, *Ecologie del Possibile. Razionalità, Esistenza, Amicizie.*
27 Iofrida, *Per un Paradigma del Corpo: una rifondazione filosofica dell'ecologia.*
28 Povinelli, *Geontologies. A requiem to late liberalism*, 13.
29 Ibid.
30 Ibid, 32.
31 Lynteris, *Human Extintion and the Pandemic Imaginary.*
32 Esposito, *Immunitas. The protection and negation of Life.*
33 Agamben, *Quando la casa brucia.*
34 Berardi, *The Third Unconscious. The Psycho sphere and the viral Age*, 193.
35 Tsing, *Il fungo alla fine del mondo. La possibilità di vivere nelle rovine del capitalismo*, 22.
36 Ibid, 27.
37 Ibid, 29.
38 Ibid, 48.
39 Ibid, 79.
40 Petrosino, *Lo Spirito della casa. Ospitalità, intimità e giustizia*, 12.
41 Pulcini, *La cura del Mondo. Paura e Responsabilità nell'età globale*, 22.
42 Amin and Thrift, *Seeing like a City.*
43 Barua, "Infrastructure and non-human life: A wider ontology," 1467–1489.
44 Pulcini, *Tra Cura e Giustizia. Le Passioni come risorsa sociale*, 22.
45 Ferrera da Silva, "Forewords," 6.
46 I am indebted to Jane Rendell who introduced me to Winnicott's work, suggesting reading his 'hold' in a symposium titled "Neoliberalism, globalization and the ecological crisis" organized at the LAU School of Architecture in Beirut on September 29, 2021, with further reference to her text entitled "Seven Studies for 'a Holding'," available at https://www.pirammmida.life/jane-rendell.
47 Aradau and Tazzioli, "Biopolitics multiple: migration, extraction, subtraction," 198–220.
48 Winnicott, "The Theory of the Parent-Infant Relationship," 585–595.
49 Sharpe, *In the Wake: On Blackness and Being*, 35.
50 Ibid, 38.

Bibliography

Agamben, Giorgio. *Quando la casa brucia*. Macerata: Giacometti e Antonello, 2020.

Agamben, Giorgio. "Introduzione." *Civita. Senza Aggettivi e altre specificazioni*, edited by Giovanni Attili. Macerata: Quodlibet, 2020.

Amin, Ash and Nigel Thrift. *Seeing like a City*. Cambridge: Polity Press, 2017.

Aradau, Claudia and Martina Tazzioli. "Biopolitics multiple: migration, extraction, subtraction." *Millennium. Journal of International Studies*, Vol. 48(2) (2020): 198–220.

Barua, Maan. "Infrastructure and non-human life: A wider ontology." *Progress in Human Geography, Vol. 45, Issue 6 (2021): 1467–1489.*

Berardi, Franco. *The Third Unconscious. The Psycho Sphere and the Viral Age*. London: Verso, 2021.

Chakrabarty, Dipesh. "Postcolonial Studies and the Challenge of Climate Change." *New Literary History*, Vol. 43, No. 1 (Winter 2012): 1–18.

De Fazio, Gianluca. *Ecologie del Possibile. Razionalità, Esistenza, Amicizie*. Verona: Ombre Corte, 2021.

Esposito, Roberto. *Immunitas. The Protection and Negation of Life*. Oxford: Wiley, 2011.

Fadini, Ubaldo and Tiziana Villani. *Eco/Logiche. Politiche, saperi, corpi, ambiente*. Rome: Manifestolibri, 2021.

Ferrera da Silva, Denise. "Forewords." *All Incomplete*, edited by Stefano Harney and Fred Moten. New York: Minor Compositions, 2020.

Gentili, Dario. *The Age of Precarity. Endless crisis as an art of government*. London: Verso, 2021.

Haraway, Donna. *Chthulucene. Sopravvivere su un pianeta infetto*. Rome: Produzioni Nero, 2019.

Iofrida, Manlio. *Per un Paradigma del Corpo: una rifondazione filosofica dell'ecologia*. Macerata: Quodlibet, 2019.

Lynteris, Christos. *Human Extinction and the Pandemic Imaginary*. London: Routledge, 2020.

Mbembe, Achille. "Il diritto universale a respirare." *Environmental Humanities Vol.1, Scienze Sociali, politica, ecologia*, edited by Daniela Angelucci, Marco Armiero, Daniele Balicco, Ilaria Bussoni, Dario Gentili, and Federica Giardini. Rome: DeriveApprodi, 2020.

Mbembe, Achille. "The Universal Right to Breath." *Critical Inquiry*, April 13, 2020. https://critinq.wordpress.com/2020/04/13/the-universal-right-to-breathe/ (last accessed: December 12, 2021).

Mbembe, Achille. *Brutalisme*. Paris: La Découverte, 2020.

Mbembe, Achille. "Futures of Life and Futures of Reason." *Public Culture*, Vol. 33, Issue 1 (93) (2021): 11–33.

Petrosino, Silvano. *Lo Spirito della casa. Ospitalità, intimità e giustizia*. Verona: Il melangolo, 2019.

Povinelli, Elizabeth A. *Geontologies. A requiem to late liberalism*. Durham: Duke University Press, 2016.

Pulcini, Elena. *La cura del Mondo. Paura e Responsabilità nell'età globale*. Turin: Bollati Borlinghieri, 2009.

Pulcini, Elena. *Care of the World. Fear, Responsibility and Justice in the Global Age*. Dordrecht: Springer, 2012.

Pulcini, Elena. *Tra Cura e Giustizia. Le Passioni come risorsa sociale*. Turin: Bollati Borlinghieri, 2019.

Rendell, Jane. "Seven Studies for 'a Holding'." July 8, 2020. https://www.pirammmida.life/jane-rendell (last accessed: December 12, 2021).

Sharpe, Christina. *In the Wake: On Blackness and Being*. Durham: Duke University Press, 2016.

Spina, Salvatore. "In dialogo con Roberto Esposito." *Immunitas e Persona. La filosofia di Roberto Esposito*, edited by Salvatore Spina. Pisa: Edizioni ETS, 2021.

Tazzioli, Martina. "'Choking without killing'. Opacity and the grey area of migration governmentality." *Political Geography*, Vol. 89 (August 2021). https://www.sciencedirect.com/science/article/abs/pii/S096262982100072X (last accessed: December 12, 2021).

Tsing, Anna. *The Mushroom at the End of the World: On the Possibility of Life in Capitalist Ruins*. Princeton NJ: Princeton University Press, 2021.

Tsing, Anna. *Il fungo alla fine del mondo. La possibilità di vivere nelle rovine del capitalismo*. Rovereto: Keller, 2021.

Winnicott, Donald W. "The Theory of the Parent-Infant Relationship." *The International Psycho-Analytical Library*, 41 (1960): 585–595.

Cartographies of protection

Cristina Bianchetti

The sixteen cases of Lifelines that constitute the empirical work of this research have little in common. Except for two characteristics: they reveal some form of protection, and they are situated in physical and social territories that are interstitial, lateral, negligible. The second condition can be easily recognized: even when it comes to Berlin or Milan, the processes unfold in the cracks in the lines of transformation. On the contrary, the link with protection is controversial.
What is meant by the term lifelines is explained by Camillo Boano in the introduction. Here we can add that lifelines is also a space of protection with an active and productive character of social ties. A complicated, extended space, difficult to handle.

Extension of the concept: protection of life

We are living in a moment marked by the convergence of a double crisis, health and climate, both of a radical nature that we could hardly have imagined living through. We have talked about this for a long time and will continue to do so. In a time like this, any idea of the future (any plan, policy, action, project, hope, image or projection of the future, any lifelines) cannot but have the protection of life at its heart. And since life (like death) is kept within the confines of the body, it is the body that protection is concerned with, an encumbrance body, active in space. Not an abstract, smooth, polished body, or an incorporeal body. But a body that is individuated, sexualized, marked by race, age, ungrammaticalities, capacity, incapacity, misunderstandings, scars, grafts, technical manipulation, complicity with technological regimes. An encumbrance body in space: with its weight, posture, intonation. Putting the body under protection reveals the deception of universalism, the deception of any forced recomposition of a humanity united in vulnerability and fear.
Therefore, the protection of life is first and foremost the protection of bodies. Bodies of individuals, animals, plants, air, water, and soil. Protection is a broad concept, extended to the multitude of bodies that enable our bodies to sustain themselves. This is not a statement taken from one of the many texts that can be traced back to posthuman studies, it is almost a new successful literary genre. It refers to a well-known passage in *The Ethics*, where Spinoza writes that "to preserve itself the body needs a great many other bodies."[1] Any idea of the future, therefore, calls for an extended dimension of protection which, in wanting to protect life, is above all protection of bodies.
It could be argued that in dealing with cities, landscapes, villages, and rural areas, urban and architectural design (which is the specific field in which this research is positioned) has always dealt with bodies: healthy, sick, dead bodies; bodies to be removed, hidden, rescued; bodies fragile due to deprivation, suffering, exile, remoteness, solitude, abandonment, and dependence. Or emancipated, liberated bodies, hedonistic bodies, bodies of pleasure, of enjoyment. It has dealt with bodies but on the rebound, so to speak, without placing the body at the center of its critical

reflection and design tension. Then came the pandemic to dramatically bring the body back to the center of everything. The pandemic was a terrible experiment, displacing bodies in the physical space of our homes, schools, squares, and parks. In the social space of our emotional, educational, and working relationships. In the space of control and limitation of certain freedoms. The pandemic has generated an enormous dislocation and a progressive marginalization or emptying of the individual and social body. It has asked us to rethink the whole relationship between bodies and space, to conceive a body that wants to protect itself and which, in order to protect itself, deprives itself of the most important faculty, that of touching – other bodies, surfaces, objects. This dimension, which in my opinion could be described as solitude, imposed the idea that bodies, surfaces, and objects had to exist without being touched. It is the *noli me tangere* of the Gospels: the moral prohibition that becomes a taboo.

Repositioning protection at the center of an idea of the future implies adopting an open, extended concept that is at the same time a metaphor, an objective, a political instrument, a mystical constraint, a model of the relationship between humans, taking shape, in the wake of Karl Polanyi,[2] as a utopian alternative paradigm in terms of production and distribution. In a subordinate way, repositioning protection at the center of an idea of the future implies tackling in the city, in the territories, the great themes of the body: vulnerability, porosity, real, affective, and psychic distance – making these themes the subject of design.

Breaking the concept: the fall of horizontal planes

In a phase of great economic and social differentiation such as the one we are experiencing, in which the city is itself a mechanism of differentiation, no protection can be thought of as a horizontal plane that runs through everything in the same way: a sort of great process of medicalization extended to the entire sphere of social interaction. The interweaving of the problems is very complicated. It is no longer as it was in the past when the problem of protection could be taken to one corner and raised. And the corner took everything else with it.

Protection, from a certain moment onwards, becomes even more plural. To discuss such a statement, let us think of how protection was understood in the 1970s, within the field of urban and territorial studies. There, one theme, that of the house (not the dwelling), could characterize the entire protection action because what this theme held together was sectorized and segmented aspects of an overall design: workers' claims; incongruities of the production cycle; technological and normative aspects; commodification of the urban; mystifications of a political design that opposed enlightened capitalism and archaic rent. Then, over time, this has not lost importance, but it has lost the power to qualify. The theme ceased to be unifying. The example of the house helps to understand the plural character of protection because it highlights the fact that from a certain point onwards there are no longer any themes that can be taken as central, capable of nourishing and characterizing the whole of urban research. It is as if the latitude of the theme has narrowed. Once, protecting the homeless meant dealing with different categories. Today, this is no longer the case. It is difficult to construct horizontal planes. Vulnerability itself is not a horizontal plane. Nor are safety or health. In this research, we have tried to explore the plural and decomposed plane of protection in which we find the deep sense of lifelines. Here is what we have understood.

Firstly, we have understood that protection can coincide with small everyday utopias, within a semantic horizon that has to do with relationships between individuals and social forms. Small utopias that oppose the neglect and carelessness of neo-liberal policies that make life (and not only human life) increasingly precarious. And if those speak of an autonomous, sufficient, free, and independent individual, opposing them means at first repositioning such individual within a relational, embodied, situated dimension that abandons the idea of one's own sovereignty and comes to terms with openness to the other. Here, protection activates mechanisms and devices of proximity even against established supply chains (as Nina Rappaport writes): mechanisms and devices that have direct implications for environmental, social, economic, political, and racial issues.

Secondly, looking at the nature of the protection bond, we have understood that it is activated by strategies that are not always frontal oppositions to vulnerability but rather reaction mechanisms. Rather than a univocal force of protection, it is a backlash, counterforce, rebound. It is a continuous coming to terms with what is there. A form of resistance.[3] Something to do with *mētis*, tricks, a do-it-yourself protection that brings actions in resonance with the contexts that host and reflect them. Not a strategic orientation but something that exists to the extent that it is practiced, expressed, interpreted, and disseminated in the various places where it is given. Such seems to be the protection offered by the interstitial, provisional, cynical, and opportunistic dwelling that survives in the niches of the hyper-financed real estate markets of European capitals, in Berlin more than elsewhere. Or the do-it-yourself that lurks in the hostile contexts of Suzhou in China. Or in the unstable territories of the Caquetá region in Colombia, where cattle breeding and coca cultivation define mobile borders, closely intertwined between what is legal and what is not. These are offstage protections: social spaces created and defended by some form of resistance.

We have realized that protection is not just an acquired good but a limited evil. To be protected is to consider a condition that cannot be completely remedied. Like the one concerning the great territorial and digital inequalities converging in the Italian Alpine territories. Along this line, protection can be read as damage reduction, in the conviction that there is not much more to be done. A position exposed to the risk that mitigation of damage for some will result in a more critical condition for many.

Finally, we realized that sometimes protection is itself part of vulnerability. In extreme situations such as Borgo Mezzanone, inhabited

predominantly by African migrant farm laborers and built on the disused NATO airstrip in the Foggia countryside in southern Italy, what does the '*caporalato*'[4] do? In its own way, it provides housing, work, mobility, bureaucratic assistance, services, and money at usurious rates: a terrible paradox interrupted by periodic, inconclusive police operations. This is a very delicate matter. One must be careful. In extreme situations such as those of Borgo Mezzanone or the refugee camps near *Tell* Serhoun in Lebanon (both territories exhausted by the absence of a future), there is a terrible ambiguity fueled by forms of protection that, in their own way, protect and at the same time nurture mechanisms of exclusion. This is the opaque side of protection.
The spatial expression of protection, in its various forms, is what interests us: it takes the form of a desire to cross a border, to limit distances, to mark old and new proximities, as in Milan's San Siro neighborhood. Or, on the contrary, it underlines separations and distance, as in the necrotized spaces of Taranto. If, as Elias Canetti writes, "the origin of freedom lies in breathing,"[5] then in the city cannibalized by the factory it is freedom, as well as life, that is missing, alongside breathing. In this manner, the traditional concept of protection is touched upon: to protect, to repair, to defend places and bodies in order to shelter them from what could harm them. Things do not change if the protagonist is the community called to contribute to the Housing Monitor in Beirut, or a patriarchal or religious power of some *Beik* or 'master' as in Sawfar. Taken together, the cases show how that protection (extensive, plural, fragmentary, partial, parochial) is, in practice, an operational space that has lost the transparency, luminosity, and univocality of the past; and, in a certain sense, also its strength. It fights neglect, carelessness by discrete points, not by great objectives. It is embodied in practices, habits, traditions, and in more or less historically and culturally determined reasons in identity. Something that sheds light on the social and spatial practices of contemporary territories. And which, to use the closing words of Mauss' essay on *The Gift*, "illuminates our morals."[6]

Relational cartographies

Let us return to the lifelines and their concrete, minute, and plural mechanisms of protection. Do-it-yourself mechanisms, backlash, resonant actions are, in the worst cases, themselves part of dispossession. Protecting, as they seem to do, another body, not only human, brings the themes of interdependence and vulnerability back to the center of a value dimension, sometimes in a dramatically contrasting way. Protection is not only formal. It is driven by interests and above all by responsibilities that can be linked to emotions, moral feelings, and passions. If protection work is a job of repairing life, the issue it raises is not private but public. We must avoid institutionalizing or, on the contrary, naturalizing protection.
The semantic horizon of protection observed in Lifelines is very close to that of care, reinterpreted in an anti-capitalist and anti-liberal way

in the international feminist debate by Joan Tronto, Marta Nussbaum, Brunella Casalini, and Elena Pulcini. However, it is not to this debate that we want to refer directly. What is more important is to understand if and how it is possible to deal with the spatialization of this opposition to neglect and carelessness. If and how it is possible to do so according to the current lexicon and postures in urban studies. Not directly on the level of moral psychology and ethics but on the level of architecture and urbanism. Without denying the transdisciplinary character of the questions posed by Lifelines but without making an alibi out of it.
So, what we can say is that the Lifelines' cases, empirically observed in their disorder, construct an initial embodied, affective, relational cartography that looks at the territories it deals with, renouncing reading them along the consolidated paths of morphology, history, and the institutional processes that regulate them. Starting from bodies, not arriving at bodies, their needs, requirements, and requests, as has always been the case. Cartographies that trace the places and ways of moving, of the many vulnerabilities that observe the exposing and withdrawing of bodies within protective mechanisms (minute mechanisms, do-it-yourself, backlashes, rebounds, resonant actions). They observe places that are generated by the density or particularity of protective relationships between bodies: exhibitions, attractions, repulsions, pushes, grabs, abandonments, possessions, and dispossessions. As in Borgo Mezzanone, where the vicious circle of debt chains and fixes migrant bodies to places. Starting from an idea of protection of life that is extended and attentive to bodies leads to imagining affirmative practices and policies that are not morphological or topological but existential and relational. It leads to rethinking spatial protection policies that no longer have the broad ambitions of the past but are redefined in micro-projects of civil economy in space (if we can call them that), around problems left open by market mechanisms and institutions. Within a cultural and normative dimension aimed at reconstructing horizons for the protection of life. Weak connections, one might object, bearing in mind the powerful protection of welfare. The counter-objection is that weak ties have their own implicit strength since they almost always generate less resistance. To what extent do micro-projects of civil economy open spaces for new territorial policies? To what extent can the project continue to deal with bodies, rethinking them in their materiality and immanence? These are questions that challenge a design that is quite different from that of the modern project. The end of that project is marked by new boundaries drawn by uses, histories, anthropologies, and archaeologies. Boundaries which in some cases are no longer physical, as Carlo Olmo argues, nor even juridical, even though they dictate rules for the use of space which mark values and identity. These boundaries are as fragile as the authorities that promote them, but they draw complex and interwoven cartographies "really far from confirmation [...] on the existence of a possible unique and uniform space of exchange [...], far from the homologous and abstract space of a mythical democratic society of equals."[7] Here, the conflicts and values linked in different ways to the protection of life mark that paradigm shift that this research has tried to map.

Endnotes

1 Spinoza, *Ethics*.
2 Polanyi, *The Great Transformation*; Polanyi, Arensberg, and Pearson, *Trade and Market in the Early Empires: Economies in History and Theory*.
3 Scott, *Seeing like a State: How Certain Schemes to Improve the Human Condition have Failed*; Scott, *Domination and the Arts of Resistances: Hidden Transcripts*.
4 An illegal intermediation of (migrant) job placement in which the "caporale" finds someone a job in exchange for a percentage of the salary or a sum of money.
5 Canetti, *Appunti*. 1942–1993, 18.
6 Mauss, *Saggio sul dono*, 277.
7 Olmo, *Architettura e Novecento*, 54.

Bibliography

Canetti, Elias. *Appunti. 1942–1993*. Milan: Adelphi, 2021.

Mauss, Marcel. *Saggio sul dono*. Turin: Einaudi, 1965.

Mauss, Marcel. *The Gift. The Form and Reason for Exchange in Archaic Societies*. London: Cohen & West, 1966.

Olmo, Carlo. *Architettura e Novecento*. Rome: Donzelli, 2010.

Polanyi, Karl. *The Great Transformation*. Boston: Beacon Press, 1944.

Polanyi, Karl, Conrad M. Arensberg, and Harry W. Pearson, eds. *Trade and Market in the Early Empires: Economies in History and Theory*. Detroit: The Free Press, 1957.

Scott, James C. *Domination and the Arts of Resistances: Hidden Transcripts*. New Haven: Yale University Press, 1990.

Scott, James C. *Seeing like a State: How Certain Schemes to Improve the Human Condition have Failed*. New Haven: Yale University Press, 1990.

Spinoza, Baruch. *Ethics*. London: Penguin Books, 1951.

Part 1
Promise and failure of infrastructures

Lifelines are first and foremost those objects that create the terrain on which other objects operate; they structure contact under particular material, economic, cultural, and political conditions. They are an operational space. Through lifelines, sociality, governance and politics, accumulation and dispossession, institutions and aspirations hovering between promises and their own failure and rupture are formed, reformed, and manifested.

Broken distribution logistics inspire a shorter ecological supply chain

Nina Rappaport

Infrastructures, or as we call them lifelines, have an essential place in the history of the built environment and our social, political, and economic organization. First, from the intensity of "hard" infrastructures of physical movement from highways, bridges, train systems (including the underground railroad), tunnels, sewage and water treatment centers, dams, and roads to "soft" rhizome-like networked infrastructures of housing, social welfare, health services, and the increasingly invisible digital, augmented realities, and biologically enhanced systems – all of which have their own economic underpinning through financial flows and their contingent physical and virtual systems. *Infra*, a prefix meaning 'below,' combined with *structure*, meaning a supportive element, connotes the underlying framework of a physical or organizational element that allows activities. To be supportive both politically and economically without social disparities, distribution infrastructure, and local production centers can be enhanced through numerous funding and policy directives but needs to include and focus on social equity and the environmental values, what I have called "multitasking infrastructures," Multitasking infrastructures, inspired by concepts of "inhabitable infrastructures" mix the hard and the soft systems both in terms of community and physical forms.[1] It could be deduced that anything that supports humanity is an infrastructure as long as all people have access to it, no matter their economic status or background. However, infrastructures have flaws and vulnerabilities that usually favor the corporate and political leaders in a colonial control over space and land use. The transit infrastructure also limits where people can go. Think of the fact that the white community voted down a subway connection to Georgetown, Washington, D.C. or that people of color have been banned from what are called redlined communities in cities such as Detroit and Baltimore.[2] Sustaining the lifelines, especially when something unpredictable, unexpected happens, exacerbates the social infrastructural issues as much as the physical systems, particularly in disadvantaged communities.[3] We need to direct our energies towards developing the sustainable configurations of the future, with an eye to alleviating and perhaps even curing the systemic racial, ecological, social, and economic problems we now face. A new concept of this multitasking infrastructure would offer amenities and connect essential civic needs to become more transparent especially in times of crisis.

Production infrastructure

Turning to industrial infrastructure of flows, manufacturing, and goods movement leads to a spatial organization that includes long and short supply chains that are also hard and soft, physical, and digital. The vulnerability of long and globally extending supply chains was recently illuminated during the Covid-19 pandemic, which prompted manufacturers and entrepreneurs to turn to more local manufacturing and shortened supply chains to source and produce things.

A scenario of a production downtime / scarcity

About two years before the coronavirus pandemic was even predictable, when the world was abundantly overflowing but also filled with labor abuse in hidden factories and unsustainable production, I was trying to imagine a scenario of the impact of putting production on hiatus in the United States for a year. Could we survive on what already existed in the world? So much food wasted, so many clothes sent to landfills, so many electronics built for obsolescence; could a pause in manufacturing activities make the world ecologically sustainable? We would use fewer resources; we would recycle, repair, reuse. Thrift shops would boom; fashion designers would fail. We would burn less fuel and coal, resulting in a cleaner environment and a more sustainable ecosystem, breaking down the continuous circulation of goods of the neoliberal capitalist rollercoaster.

And then the answer struck me: of course it would devastate the economy, employment, wages, and well-being! However, as an economic modelling exercise, it could lead to growth being measured not as GDP but in the Gross National Happiness index.[4] But ... then it happened like a futuristic dystopia – Covid-19. Around mid-March 2020, many factories and businesses, especially in China, where the pandemic originated, closed their doors due to a lockdown. People lost jobs or were furloughed; supply chains halted because there were not enough goods to fill the cargo ships, so shipping fleets shrunk.[5] Governments initiated economic stimulus packages, such as the Paycheck Protection Program (PPP) in the US in April. Supermarket shelves emptied, people scavenged, hoarding basics such as toilet paper and pasta, and raw material production stalled. The workers, often people of color, who were deemed as 'essential,' including supermarket staff, nurses, caregivers, public transit, sanitation, and delivery workers, were on the frontlines even as the infection rates of Covid-19 increased. Their lifeline was, to say the least, precarious.

Emergency supplies like personal protective equipment (PPE), normally used to protect against workplace hazards, quickly became identified as essential protective gear against Covid-19 – hospital gowns, gloves, masks, cleaning products, and hand sanitizer – and then disappeared. This foregrounded the knowledge gap and lack of foresight regarding the disturbances in the supply chain unimagined by the industrialized West with its production stoppages;[6] trade regulations and shipping controls falsely appeared to be seamlessly continuous, and everyone struggled. Basic parts such as computer chips and semiconductors, produced in just few factories in Taiwan and China to feed other assembly lines, including automotive production, became precious goods. By relying on few producer countries – China, Vietnam, and India – the capitalist world was in a shaky situation. We have known for decades that China's cheap labor and freer economic policies have influenced manufacturers' migration away from their own shores, all for the sake of capital growth.[7] Raw materials such as lumber, steel, cooper, and aluminum became scarce or inflated in price.[8] Just as during the 2003 SARS crisis

Fig.1
Empty supermarket food shelves. Photograph by Nina Rappaport, March 2020.

and other natural disasters such as floods and fires, companies that had adopted just-in-time and lean manufacturing methods to eliminate warehousing had to increase their supplies, which requires capital. Scarcity brought to light the fragility of the industrial commons, which was no longer a common.

Returning to local production

On the other side of the production ecosystem, it is now evident that slowness – slow food, slow fashion, local production, additive manufacturing, and artisanal craft – is beneficial not just in times of crisis but at all times. Localized production, of course, has its own productive history. During the second industrial revolution when trade was opening borders, French sociologist Le Play and Russian sociologist Peter Kropotkin considered that decentralized industries benefited from regional competition. The idea that villages should produce the goods they need themselves created a self-sufficiency model with a local supply chain.[9] Following this concept, if today we produce things locally, on site, and self-sufficiently, whether in the city, village, or territory, there could also be a positive impact on the global economy, as every place would be synchronized. In a new sustainable production paradigm, it would create

enhanced local infrastructures and less waste, less pollution, and include other social impact programs with education and health benefits for local workers. While some may think this cries 'protectionism,' it is not to limit trade but to be more self-reliant, especially in times of environmental and economic crises.

During the initial months of Covid-19, supply chains shortened and that compactness became a new lifeline. Manufacturers' lack of industrial flexibility for emergency production came as a surprise. Those manufacturers who thought that they were nimble turned out to be mistaken and had to learn to reconfigure their production lines to make new items on-demand, like in wartime. Companies retooled and were innovative in ways that had not been tested in decades in new, networked spaces. An energy and willingness developed to nourish the industrial commons through sharing of machines and workers, in an all-out effort not normally seen in competitive capitalism; all hands were on deck and local companies produced necessities from masks to ventilators and home goods.

WFH (Working From Home) is not for all

At first, when factories closed in the US, the idea of neo-cottage industries and making things from home seemed to be possible. In this Fourth Industrial Revolution and Industry 4.0, the factory is more flexible and mobile due to the shrinking scale of technologies, including the use of not only computers but robots, CNC automated machines, 3D printers, and additive manufacturing for on-demand production in micro-factories or neo-cottage spaces.[10] Working from home, or WFH, the new moniker, has existed centuries before the current pandemic. In the eighteenth and nineteenth centuries, workers produce from home. Family members of all ages became productive citizens. The "electronic cottage" – a computer in every home – as Alvin Toffler and John Naisbitt presaged in the 1970s, became a reality for all but the disadvantaged poor.[11] We, in turn, have decentralized the workplace, as they predicted, away from the central business districts back into our homes.

However, blue-collar workers could not really work at home in the way that the more privileged white-collar workers could, except for smaller products and those related to the crisis – PPE equipment including masks, gowns, face shields. For example, at the start of the pandemic, many garment manufacturers scrambled to keep their businesses afloat and send people home with textiles to sew gowns and masks in an autonomous process. Bill Mountain of Mane Neckwear in Queens, New York, at first sent his workers home but realized that "working from home was not very productive because our employees' household sewing machines were much slower than the industrial ones in the factory." He then qualified as an "essential" business and could reduce the number of workers on the factory floor for the required 6-foot distance as well as receive the Paycheck Protection Program (PPP) grants to pay the

Fig.2
Miguel at Brooklyn Tile and Stone. Photograph by Nina Rappaport, January 2021.

workers he had furloughed. They produced a large order of fabric masks for nurses to wear over the mass-produced N95 masks.
Wing and Weft, the last glove manufacturer in New York, had their staff complete some work from home because they couldn't fully start up in their workshop until Phase 2 of the reopening. As part of the then newly formed Costume Industry Coalition, they made masks to protect people from Covid-19, including everyday masks, that were more elegant than the standard surgical ones. Then they switched to fashionable masks they call Face Gloves to maintain their cash flow. However, for efficient production, the team must work face-to-face, as Katie Sue Nicklos, the company's owner, points out. "The process is holistic with constant communication and feedback," plus, she emphasizes, "working alone from home takes away the fun of making things together."[12] At Timberlake Studios, a costume company, they switched production to masks, purchasing wholesale bolts of fabric, which they divided, washed, and cut into ten-yard pieces that were sent to staff at home. They made over 2,000 masks that they donated to groups like Doctors Without Borders and the Navajo Nation Health Center in Arizona. Nevertheless, Zoe stressed that producing at home was a "great stop gap, but not a long-term solution [...]. The whole reason to work in this business is the camaraderie; in our workshop, we place our machines in a pinwheel shape so everyone can talk to each other."[13]
The community was also essential to Tidal, a flip-flop producer owned by Tim and Tommy Gibbs in New Rochelle, who halted production at their first knowledge of Covid-19. They couldn't convert to making PPE products because their machines are product specific. Instead, through the New York State, a subcontractor contacted Tidal to make straps and foam padding for face shields. In their 10,000-square-foot premises with machines generously spaced out and PPP funds to pay their workers, the Gibbs used their production line downtime to research ways to retool the company for future crises. The automated large-scale machinery meant that workers could not produce from home, but they gained a stronger realization that their factory, located in a residential neighborhood, was a community. Tim Gibbs recognized that the workers and the employers need each other. Working together towards common goals created a support system since "the factory builds and stabilizes community,"[14] relying on consistent alliances between workers and employers.
Adaptability and flexibility during this time prompted the Boyce Electronics company to shift from subway electronic safety machines to producing tens of thousands plastic face shields, and to invest in the design and construction of a fully automated five-robot mask-making machine. When the critical ventilator shortage occurred in New York, they teamed up with investors, the city, entrepreneurs, and technology specialists from MIT. They created a new design for ventilators by bringing in Partsimony, a supply chain sourcing company, to identify local suppliers and develop the product based on the materials available. As Rich Mokulou said, "one of the key things we saw was that we could identify local capacity to manufacture the ventilators. We had to look at

Fig.3
Container ship Evergreen stuck in the Suez Canal, Egypt, March 24th, 2021. Source: Wikimedia Commons.

critical engineering decisions in the product and the supply chain, including redesigning and changing the specifications to adapt. With new technologies like additive manufacturing, products can be made locally, or the design of circuit board can be customized to leverage the ability of available electronic components."[15] This way, the product design cycle can be tighter based on local material supply and sustainable through local sourcing, resulting in a smaller carbon footprint. The FDA approved the ventilators quickly, showing how a company can be nimble for emergency response and produce locally in a more efficient and resilient way.

Breakdown of the global supply chain

However, a product's distribution either by the public postal service or a private global shipping company broke down during Covid-19. Many post offices reduced staffing of their "essential" workers; some countries didn't even accept packages during the first six months of 2020.[16] Shopping in person became a dramatic experience. However, with consumers already accustomed to fast delivery times, their expectations shrunk at both a global and a local level. Private delivery companies, normally the lifelines when governmental services fragment, had their own infrastructure entangled in bottlenecks because of the reduction of air and shipping cargo at a global scale.

As has been recounted, consumer spending on household products increased in 2021, but the goods could not get to the homes and piled up as the price of shipping a container increased tenfold, and the ports experienced congestion, in part because of an increased number of workers with Covid-19. Often, Chinese cargo ships arrive in the US fully loaded and leave empty, but this happened around the world, causing a container shortage as well.[17] To make the situation even worse, a container ship got stuck in the Suez Canal for 106 days, amplifying poor navigation and inadequate infrastructures – ships too large and canals too small. While not related to the pandemic, it further strained international trade because of the vast amounts of goods stuck at sea that people had purchased to increase their happiness quota since they were unable to shop in person. The disaster magnifies that, as in the example of PPE production, if we can source locally and produce locally, we can shorten the supply chain, releasing dependence on the already broken global logistics and distribution system, and have resilience both economically and environmentally.

A sustainable last mile

With the rise of e-commerce and instant gratification capitalism, not only is the global chain strained, but so is the last mile – the distance goods have to travel after arriving in a city or village to reach the consumer. The pandemic served to exacerbate the already existing issues as people relied on urban delivery services so as not to risk going to a store or even have contact with delivery people. However, delivery trucks only have narrow unloading spaces especially in dense cities, even if the streets have designated unloading zones. Goods move from truck to hand truck or vans so as to be able to navigate narrow streets, but truck drivers often operate dangerously in the middle of the street. Delivery drones, a potential alternative, are just receiving permit approvals from the FAA and will still take time to be standardized.[18]

As we imagine future distribution alternatives, a new typology of the local "goods hub" can instead evolve as a new multitasking infrastructure, a mix of movement, flows, and production. Some of these have started incrementally as local centers and have the potential to be a mixed use of warehouse combined with light industry. With new technologies and digital and cleaner production as mentioned earlier, making things can be returned to cities, which makes sense in terms of costs, materials, space, and flexibility in a time of crisis. Because of the shorter distances between warehouse and place of delivery, electric vehicles can distribute goods in the urban centers; train lines combined with metro systems could bring the goods to the urban core, which in turn would reduce pollution caused by trucks.

Informally, some bodega shops have been accepting deliveries for those who are less advantaged, often in neighborhoods of people of color, so that their parcels are not stolen from their front doors. The company Amazon more formally created storage areas at new Whole Foods supermarkets with shelving for parcels that people can pick up or have delivered via its cargo bike fleet. These bikes have become ubiquitous along with electric bikes. Some new companies have gone further, renting the numerous vacant neighborhood stores to start supermarkets without consumers, called "dark" stores. They can use all the space for shelving and don't need cash registers, nor do they rely on foot traffic. They guarantee delivery by bike couriers within 10 minutes to locations in the neighborhood within a one-mile radius. Only delivery workers enter the store, and they are given cell phones, bikes, and a paycheck. However, we need to seriously question our global economic systems as to why it takes a pandemic to revive and even discern the essential infrastructure of local urban manufacturing and local logistic services. While the pandemic is devastating the world, strange opportunities have percolated from previously disregarded ideas that are more socially and locally based, including a refocus on urban manufacturing, building communities, climate change awareness, exposing systemic racism and job inequality, and increasing sustainable sourcing and production methods with resilient infrastructures. A lifeline is a secure, resilient, sustainable supply chain, both long and short, local and global. Otherwise, we will no longer have a connective tissue – politically, economically, and socially – for a shared multitasking infrastructure during or after the pandemic.

Endnotes

1 This was the topic of an unpublished paper that I gave at Harvard Graduate School of Design symposium in 2004, *Inhabited Infrastructure*, in relationship to an exhibition I curated called *The Swiss Section*, Van Alen Institute, 2003.
2 Taylor, *Race for Profit: How Banks and the Real Estate Industry Undermined Black Homeownership.*
3 These activities can include collapses of coal mines, bridges, roadways, and dams; the destruction of the physical engineering relied on.
4 See: https://sustainabledevelopment.un.org/partnership/?p=2212.
5 Haren and Simchi-Levi, "How Coronavirus Could Impact the Global Supply Chain by Mid-March."
6 Author's discussion with Rich Mokulu of Partsimony, October 25, 2021.
7 Midler, *Poorly Made in China: An Insider's Account of the Tactics Behind China's Production Game.*
8 Spence and Durisin, "The Price of the Stuff That Makes Everything Is Surging."
9 Kropotkin, *The Industrial Village of the Future.*
10 Rappaport, *Vertical Urban Factory*, 2015.
11 Toffler, *Future Shock*; Naisbitt, *Megatrends.*
12 Author's discussion with Katie Sue Nicklos, summer 2020.
13 Author's discussion with Zoe of Timberlake, summer 2020.
14 Author's discussion with Tim Gibbs, summer 2020.
15 Author's discussion with Rich Mokulou of Partsimony, October 25, 2021.
16 I tried to send a box of books to a colleague in Port Elizabeth, South Africa and was told to wait 6 months to send it.
17 Goodman, "How the Supply Chain Broke, and Why It Won't Be Fixed Anytime Soon."
18 See: https://about.ups.com/us/en/newsroom/press-releases/innovation-driven/ups-flight-forward-cvs-to-launch-residential-drone-delivery-service-in-florida-retirement-community-to-assist-in-coronavirus-response.html.

Bibliography

Goodman, Peter S. “How the Supply Chain Broke, and Why It Won’t Be Fixed Anytime Soon.” *The New York Times*, October 23, 2021. https://www.nytimes.com/2021/10/22/business/shortages-supply-chain.html (last accessed: December 14, 2021).

Haren, Pierre and David Simchi-Levi. “How Coronavirus Could Impact the Global Supply Chain by Mid-March.” *Harvard Business Review*, February 28, 2020. https://hbr.org/2020/02/how-coronavirus-could-impact-the-global-supply-chain-by-mid-march (last accessed: December 14, 2021).

Kropotkin, Peter. *The Industrial Village of the Future*. 1884.

Midler, Paul. *Poorly Made in China: An Insider’s Account of the Tactics Behind China’s Production Game*. Hoboken: John Wiley & Sons, 2009.

Naisbitt, John. *Megatrends*. New York: Warner Books, 1984.

Rappaport, Nina. *Vertical Urban Factory*. Barcelona: Actar, 2015.

Spence, Eddie and Megan Durisin. “The Price of the Stuff That Makes Everything Is Surging.” May 1, 2021. https://www.bloomberg.com/news/articles/2021-05-01/the-price-of-the-stuff-that-makes-everything-is-surging (last accessed: December 14, 2021).

Taylor, Keeanga-Yamahtta. *Race for Profit: How Banks and the Real Estate Industry Undermined Black Homeownership*. Chapel Hill: University of North Carolina Press, 2019.

Toffler, Alvin. *Future Shock*, New York: Bantham Books, 1970.

Coca, cattle, and cities: fluid lifelines in the frontier of Caquetá, Colombia

Isabel Peñaranda Currie

The Colombian Amazon frontier has historically been associated with images of remote and isolated villages amidst the expansive jungle. However, recent events – among them the pandemic, which hit many of these Amazonian territories particularly hard[1] – are signaling the need to better understand the relationships that constitute the Amazon and other such frontier regions, particularly the forms of spatial structuring and interconnections between rural and urban spheres. This paper aims to contribute to understanding some of these connections by tracing how they have historically crystallized into what is understood in this collective research as lifelines: the hard and soft underlying infrastructures which supports the reproduction of life in these territories. What emerges is that the lifelines which maintain the frontier are as fluid as the frontier itself, endlessly adapting and reconstituting themselves according to the shifting borders of these liminal spaces.

In this text, I will study the lifelines in the frontier territories of Caquetá, in the Amazonian region of Colombia. Caquetá has historically been both in the center of the armed conflict, as a historic stronghold of the Armed Revolutionary Forces of Colombia (FARC), and one of the primary producers of coca and, more recently, cattle. Drawing on previous research in the region over the last ten years, I make use of fieldwork from different works to present a new argument about the production of space in this territory and the implications for infrastructure and, in particular, the lifelines of the region. In the first section, I start by positioning this conversation on lifelines within the existing literature on frontiers and infrastructure. Secondly, I describe their dialectic relationship mediated through credit, liquidity, trust, and debt. This leads to the third section, in which I explore roads, rivers, and other fluid infrastructure and end with some conclusions that connect back to the present pandemic situation.

Lifelines and infrastructure on the frontier

Existing literature on borderlands, peripheries, margins, and frontiers often call attention to the unstable and relational qualities of these liminal spaces; not only are they cast as spaces of disorder,[2] but they do in fact challenge the existing binaries which operate in the "core."[3] To the degree that they are defined vis-à-vis this center, frontiers have to be continuously produced in ways that are specific to their spatial and temporal contexts; as Ramussen and Lund[4] point out, frontiers do not exist but are produced through the dual processes of breaking up existing territorial logics in what they term "frontier moments," and then reconstituted again through what they term "territorializations." What is worth highlighting – and what is particularly true for illegal commodity frontiers and those within armed conflicts – is that this is not a linear process but one which is constantly redefined not only spatially but within the fluctuating logics of sovereignty and legality defined by state and non-state actors alike.[5]

Different kinds of infrastructure have proved highly productive sites for understanding the broader social and political contexts, representing sites where the state co-produced and made legible discursive and material practices, including the ordering of territory.[6] Increasingly, infrastructure has also become a site to identify the contradictions and cracks of power, representing sites of conflict and contestation.[7] This has been a prevalent theme in studies of infrastructure on the frontier.[8] Infrastructure becomes a site to study the dynamic nature of the frontier, insofar as it is both a reflection and a medium for the constant change and instability which characterize frontier regions. Understanding the lifelines of these territories requires developing an eye for the transient and unstable, and for the logics underlying these changes.

Fig.1
Cattle farm in Puerto Camelias, a former coca producing hamlet in Cartagena de Chairá, Caquetá. The lands pictured here were cleared for coca and have since been converted to cattle ranching. Photograph by Isabel Peñaranda Currie.

Fluid economies and the commodity frontier

The coca and cattle economies are usually understood to occupy two different sides of the legal/illegal divide. Cattle ranchers have historically made up the backbone of much of the economic and political elite,[9] and the dairy industry attracted the only multinational – Nestlé – to have set up operations in the state. Coca, on the other hand, is an illegal crop, has been promoted and supplied to traffickers by the FARC, and its cultivation has been persecuted by the state in Caquetá in an open war against civilians that has few parallels in the country.[10] However, coca and cattle have been entwined since their origins. Together, I argue, they represent the economic lifelines which have constantly (re)structured the frontier in Caquetá.

Between the late 1950s and 1970s, the Cold War developmentalism seized Latin America, and in Colombia, geopolitical and internal factors alike led to this state being one of the main sites for experimentation with diverse state-led efforts to promote national and regional development, particularly in the countryside.[11] One of the primary schemes of this era were state-directed colonization programs, the biggest of which was implemented in the Amazonian state of Caquetá. One of these, led by the National Colombian Institute for Agrarian Reform (INCORA) and starting in 1962, extended credit to "spontaneous" *colonos* – those already settled in the area –, primarily in order to promote cattle ranching.[12]

Many of those *colonos* who did not qualify for these programs, or were displaced by the growing cattle ranches, pushed deeper into the rainforest frontier. As in other Latin American countries, the limitations of the state-directed colonization programs had a strong correlation with the emergence of coca frontiers.[13] The first coca plants in Caquetá were planted around 1978 along the Caguán River, which ran from Puerto Rico – a town which switched from growing rice to cattle in the 1970s – into the Amazon plain. Those who did not venture deeper into the jungle opted instead to settle in the existing urban nodes, primarily Florencia, the capital of Caquetá, whose population more than doubled from 28,056 in 1973 to 65,783 residents in 1985. There was, therefore, a clear spatial dialectic in the constitution of these three economies and models of occupation on the frontier.[14]

There were still significant differences between coca and cattle ranching as forms of production, which in turn were linked to the social and economic structure of those who worked within in. Cattle ranching requires larger areas of land, a minimal labor force, and a degree of accumulated capital, and therefore it did not favor either the urban nodes or the most precarious classes – poor settlers and rural workers – on the agrarian frontier. Coca, on the other hand, is a high-value commodity, could be cultivated in small lots, and required significant manual labor, thus sustaining a high population of coca harvesters, or *raspachines* and other day laborers, cooks, and a vibrant commercial sector which flourished amidst the rapid monetization of the economy.

However, there is a reason that these two economies have dominated in Caquetá since the 1960s. Given that these territories are populated by *colonos* who have been reliant on market economies since their settlement, the coca and cattle economies enable an insertion in the market despite the considerable distances and physical challenges which render most commodities financially unviable. These include the acidic and nutrient-poor soil of the Amazonian region, the expensive and unpredictable transportation costs and routes, and the fluctuations in market demand. Amidst these difficult conditions, access to liquidity and credit becomes one of the only ways to weather the constant shocks for a *colono* family trying to live in the frontier. This fact was observed by scholars of the frontier, who noted that intermediaries who could provide credit to *colonos* to buy necessary supplies exercised an almost unchecked control over them. In the words of Molano,[15] "the instrument of the crisis [of colonization] is generally credit. We are not talking here about the habitual usury of institutional credit. The *colono* seeks credit because he knows that it is the only exit of the vicious cycle and because he has made improvements on his land and possesses pastures or permanent crops, which constitutes a kind of saving or, if you will, the only possible form of accumulation."[16] These frontier social systems have been interconnected by lifelines – often in highly asymmetrical contexts – of market relations and debt on the threshold of subsistence. In this context, coca and cattle navigate these challenges, and suggest why the line between these two economies is porous. One of the most defining features is that both coca and cattle can subsist despite the acidic and nutrient-poor soil of the Amazonian region. Their production is decentralized, given that their inputs are few and do not rely on a stable chain of supply. Just as important is that these are not perishable items; once processed, coca can keep for long periods of time, and cattle has no 'harvest' time; so in both cases it is possible to withstand fluctuations in market demand. Relatedly, coca and cattle – as well as salted cheese blocks, produced from the 'double-purpose' (dairy and meat) cows – have relatively high values compared to their weight and can be transported even when road infrastructure is poor or absent.

The deeper one lives in the frontier, the more vital a secure access to liquidity is, even if this is not the most lucrative form of livelihood. The most important aspects of coca were that it had a reliable buyer, a steady price, a point of sale in the territory itself, and could provide a steady – even as it diminished over the years – source of monetary income. This dynamic is repeated almost exactly with cattle ranching and milk sales: Revelo in his analysis of the success of Nestlé noted that "the company quickly became the first large-scale buyer in the region because it offered regular payments, consistent prices, and stable milk collection. Small and mid-size cattle farmers were offered an efficient and predictable way to sell their product at local collection points, thus avoiding the trouble of transporting heavy containers of perishable milk to urban centers, where prices were uncertain and demand limited."[17]

The conditions of the coca and cattle ranching economies enabled both of them to constitute the primary economic lifelines of the region. These similarities all point to a shared resilience to risk and a fluid adaptability.

It was for this same reason that the FARC themselves, when sensing a decline in the coca market as it shifted towards the Pacific coast, helped finance the transition to cattle ranching. The coca tax paid on every gram of coca paste sold was in part used to launch the *Fondo Económico Social* (Social Economic Fund), which was used to create a micro-credit scheme for raising cattle, run by the local community action boards. Furthermore, according to a former FARC intelligence commander, the

Fig.2
Puerto Camelias is a hamlet on the Caguán river founded during the peak of the coca economy in the 1980s as one of the markets where coca was bought and sold in this period. Now, its main "export" is cattle and salty cheese, pictured above. Photograph by Isabel Peñaranda Currie

FARC also invested in cattle ranching themselves as a form of storing their "savings" and as a form of controlling strategic territory, and controlled cattle sales with similar taxes as they had with coca.[18] In later years, the FARC were reported to also have entered into the milk and cheese market.[19]

The centrality of liquidity and the access to markets on this (il)legal commodity frontier necessarily implicated the urban sphere. As Hough[20] noted, the commodity chains of this frontier are difficult to analyze to the degree that the crops or cattle raised in the Caguán basin are embedded in global commodity chains and domestic markets alike, which often bypass local geographies (and urban nodes like Florencia) as well as conventional actors. However, the local urban-rural connections continued to be vital. The supplies to produce coca paste – which included petrol, sulfuric acid, and ammonia – required supply chains along the rivers and roads. According to a local merchant, the provision of consumer supplies – everything ranging from beer, dried goods, and rubber boots – were the result of commercial chains between Florencia, municipal heads, and the small villages, chains which often required high levels of trust and debt as a result of the fluctuations in the coca market.[21]

Under cattle ranching, urban nodes assumed new roles. Specialized labor comprised veterinaries; special supplies focused on medicine, salt, and equipment for cattle. With the shift to cattle ranching, local and regional markets became more important than under coca, and intermediate urban nodes in turn reflected that. When the Nestlé plants were bombed by the FARC, local cheese factories sprouted in its place. Florencia also absorbed many of the rural inhabitants and workers who were displaced in the transition from coca to cattle ranching. This migration was accelerated by the forced displacement generated by paramilitary, guerrilla, and state violence, but it cannot be disassociated from the shifts in the modes of production occurring at the same time. However, this population shift tends to be flexible as well; families are often split between the urban and the rural, frequently shifting back and forth between their homes in the cities or towns and their farms.[22] These fluid urban-rural settlement patterns also contribute to the resilience of the population, providing work possibilities, educational and health needs, and, in particular, present women with new kinds of labor opportunities, access to education, and financial independence.

As I have argued until this point, coca and cattle ranching represent the economic lifelines of Caquetá because of the particularities of their modes of production, which can adapt and respond to the needs of the inhabitants of the frontier. They provide access to liquidity and markets despite a costly and erratic transportation system, which gives producers enough fluidity to adapt within a risky margin as they negotiate the blurry line between the legal and illegal. As I will argue in the next section, the transportation infrastructures that emerged from these two economies reflect these characteristics and are themselves part of the assemblage of the fluid lifelines of the frontier.

Roads, rivers, and fluid infrastructure

Infrastructure – particularly roads – has been associated with being a rigid spatial order imposed by the state to render certain subjects and territories legible.[23] Indeed, the state-directed colonization also restructured space through the construction of infrastructure, while the *Marginal de la Selva* – the major artery that runs alongside the Andes range – is the single biggest piece of infrastructure in the department[24] and also part of the Initiative for the Integration of the Regional Infrastructure of South America (IIRSA), a transnational project so vast it is auguring a new form of "infrastructure-led development" and radical re-structuring of the Amazonian territory.[25] However, analyzing the development and characteristics of the infrastructure on the frontier destabilizes this narrative by showing the existence of a constantly changing infrastructural network which, like the economy it maintains, blurs the line between the legal and illegal, the structural and fluid.

The cattle regions of Caquetá predated the road infrastructure and the state-directed colonization programs. The Lara family – owners of the biggest single cattle ranches in the region – would drive their cattle from their farm near the piedmont to the vast plains of Yarí to fatten them, before transporting them back by foot or even by plane to the

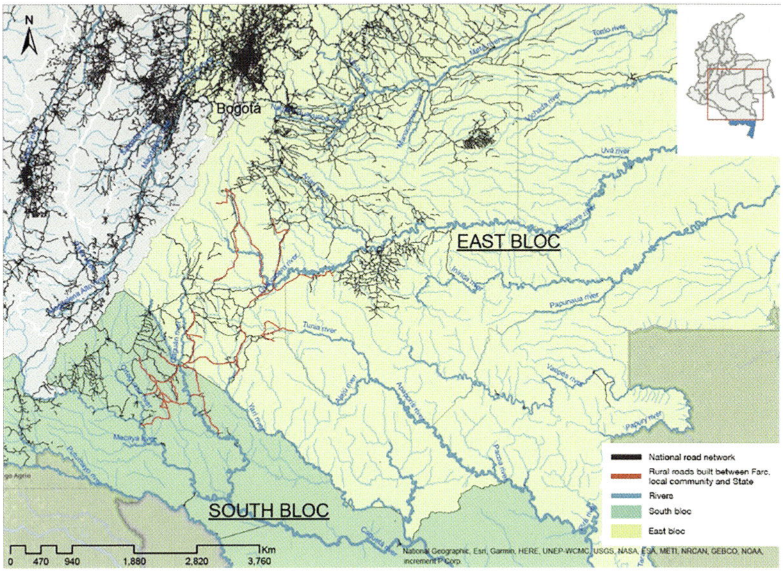

Fig.3
FARC community road network. Source: Otero, Uribe and Peñaranda, 2020.

departmental capital of Huila, Neiva.[26] These migratory geographies of cattle accompanied a culture of vast cattle *haciendas* in the Yarí planes which were interconnected by small aircraft.[27] The settlement of the Lower Caguán basin – where the coca economy originated – unfolded alongside the river Caguán. The dense jungle, as it did in other spontaneous colonization fronts, encouraged a 'linear' colonization along the river, which was the only channel of transport or communication.[28] One of the few forms of state presence along the Caguán river was the *Instituto de Mercadeo Agropecuario* (Institute of Agrarian Markets) boat, which would come down the river every six months to exchange corn for supplies.[29] Transportation of coca and consumer supplies continued exclusively along the river in the 1980s and 1990s.

In both territories, these geographies were complemented by the creation of dense community road networks, different from those built by the state. In the 2000s, when the FARC began to implement a strategy defined two decades before, namely the construction of extensive road infrastructures in their rearguard territories, they focused on the Caguán and Yarí regions. Although these roads were in many cases originally proposed by the FARC, they were constructed primarily by the local communities themselves and often with material support from the local state. As with other infrastructures, the roads are the crystallization of social relations between FARC, community, and the state, operating as the mediums, products, and preconditions for processes of state formation on the coca frontier.[30]

From the point of view of infrastructure and space, there were two characteristics that defined these roads and distinguished them from big state-built infrastructure projects like the *Marginal de la Selva*. The first is the kinds of connections that they enabled. The infrastructure found in FARC frontier strongholds tended to be structured like a web rather than the hierarchical road infrastructure of the state. As such, it connected peripheries with peripheries – specifically providing connective tissue in the north-south direction between rivers. This web-like nature connected the frontier 'from below' for the insurgent actors seeking to mobilize troops and supplies, but it also enabled coca and cattle farms to reach urban nodes and markets without having to do so via the river. This kind of infrastructure was not unique to the insurgent-inspired road networks. In fact, its morphology replicated the community-built road networks constructed to connect farms to the milk market. Given that milk requires refrigeration, a capillary network of roads was required for motorized vehicles to reach the farms.

A second characteristic of frontier infrastructures is that they are more fluid and dynamic than their state-built and more central counterparts. The most extreme example of the flexibility of this infrastructure was its use by the FARC, for whom the road network was only one part of a constantly changing multimodal transportation network known as *mobility corridors* which included rivers, roads, all-terrain vehicles, and footpaths.[31] To move troops or individual guerrilla members from one point to another was a process of constant recombination that responded to weather conditions, the presence of enemy state troops, territorial control, and other contingencies.

Roads used by civilians are also defined by constant mutability. The roads themselves are made by clearing the forest cover, revealing a clay-like mud underneath. Given that rocky material (*balastro*) used for drainage and traction is unavailable in the jungle, the clay paths are uncovered and exposed to rain most of the time and sometimes held together by tree trunks laid perpendicular to the road to allow for drainage (*empalizado*). This makes for a highly unstable infrastructure, whose very materiality reflects the contingencies of the frontier, from the weather conditions, the community's social cohesion and its ability to pay for repairs, the presence of the local state, and the state of the armed conflict.

The transition from coca to cattle ranching partly weakened these road networks because coca – which generated higher coca tax revenues, sustained higher population densities, and was associated to a stronger presence of the FARC, who often coordinated tax collection and road construction – had generated conditions for road construction and maintenance. However, the transition from coca to cattle ranching starting in the mid-2000s and the disruptions to Nestlé operations at the same high point of the armed conflict resulted in a proliferation of new commercial linkages to local cheese factories and cattle buyers for domestic markets that were reflected in new transport systems. A new and fluctuating frontier spread through the Caguán region – between the territories that could sell milk (those connected to the better maintained roads and the river) and those that could sell only salted cheese. At the time of the fieldwork, new roads were penetrating the jungle, this time not associated to coca but rather to the expanding cattle frontier.

Where do Florencia and other urban nodes fit into all of this? As noted before, the change from coca to cattle ranching promoted a shift from a more epicentral form of occupation of the frontier, sustained by a relatively dense rural population, towards one which tended to be concentrated in Florencia, the departmental capital. The concentration of the population has advantages in terms of service provision and access to infrastructure. However, for those who stay in rural regions, the disinvestment continues to be further aggravated as schools and public services close, families move away, cattle ranches expand, and the cycle is reinforced. This is not a purely bureaucratic process but also responds to the unforgiving logics of clientelism that has historically been a strong determinant of public and specifically infrastructure investment.

Conclusion

Lifelines are physical and social spaces that sustain the reproduction of life in a given context. In frontiers – particularly (il)legal commodity frontiers caught in an armed conflict – these lifelines operate in a complex and constantly changing context. The frontier continues to change: coca production expanded almost 50% after the signing of the 2016 peace agreements with the FARC,[32] while cattle ranching in turn is being criminalized in a militarized (and politicized) effort to stop deforestation in former FARC strongholds, supported by a new proposed law that would criminalize these small ranchers.[33] As Stein and Sandwell[34] observe, illegal commodity frontiers are not exhausted but rather remade, particularly when the boundary between the legal and illegal blurs against the background of the constant adaptations which characterize the frontier's productive and spatial forms, as well as the state's constant redrawing of legality and reproduction of the frontier.
In this context, the lines between the legal and the illegal are blurred, modes of production constantly shift, which is also reflected in the production of space on the frontier. The forms of infrastructure spaces which connect the urban and the rural areas are constantly changing, being created and destroyed in a reflection of the social and political context surrounding them. Far from being isolated and static territories, a look at the lifelines that connect frontiers from within and to the rest of the country reveal the dynamic nature of these territories. A form and medium of resistance, of the resilience of life amid war and state neglect.

Endnotes

1 González, "Estudio de seroprevalencia reveló que Leticia alcanzó un nivel de infección de 60% y Barranquilla 55%."
2 Serje, *El Revés de la Nación: Territorios salvajes, fronteras y salvajes y tierras de nadie.*
3 Anzaldúa, *Borderlands/La Frontera: The New Mestiza;* Browder and Godfrey, *Rainforest cities: Urbanization, development, and globalization of the Brazilian Amazon*; Das and Poole, *Anthropology in the margins of the state.*
4 Rasmussen and Lund, "Reconfiguring Frontier Spaces: The territorialization of resource control," 388–399.
5 Stein and Sandwell, "Illicit Crop Frontiers: Colonialism, Commodification, and Countermovements," 24–32.
6 Appel, Anand, and Gupta, "Introduction: The Infrastructure Toolbox"; Harvey, "The Materiality of State Effects: An Ethnography of a Road in the Peruvian Andes," 216–247; Scott, *Seeing like a State: How Certain Schemes to Improve the Human Condition Have Failed.*
7 Acevedo-Guerrero, "Light is like water: Flooding, blackouts, and the state in Barranquilla," 478–494; Larkin, "The Politics and Poetics of Infrastructure," 327–343.
8 Uribe, *Frontier Road. Power, History and the Everyday State in the Colombian Amazon.*
9 González Trujillo, Ramón Mahe, and Torrijos Rivera, *Caquetá: Tradición y Vocación Ganadera.*
10 Vásquez Delgado, *Territorios, Conflicto Armado y Política en el Caquetá: 1900–2010.*
11 Florián Guzmán, "Reforma Agraria y Alianza Para el Progreso en Colombia 1960–1967"; Hormaza Jimenez, "La reforma agraria como ejercicio de planificación: Experiencias de los proyectos de colonización del INCORA en el Caquetá entre 1964–1974"; Martinez Basallo, *Encuentros con el Estado: Burocracias y colonos en la frontera amazónica (1960–1980)*; Montenegro Helfer, "Pensando el campo colombiano: La política del desarrollo, las tierras y la vida del campesino en el diseño de la Reforma Social Agraria."
12 Centro Nacional de Memoria Histórica (CNMH), *La Tierra No Basta: Colonización, Baldíos y Organizaciones Sociales en el Caquetá.*
13 Gootenberg and Dávalos, *The Origins of Cocaine: Colonization and Failed Development in the Amazon Andes.*
14 Explored in detail in Peñaranda Currie, "L'eredità spaziale del fallimento. Un'analisi dei programmi di colonizzazione statale nel dipartimento di Caquetá, Colombia (1959–1981)."
15 Molano Bravo, "Región, Violencia y Democracia, algunas consideraciones sobre la colonización y la violencia," 31.
16 A similar conclusion was reached by the FARC, who controlled the presence and operation of these intermediaries, and checked their usurious practices as a form of defending their *colono* bases (Cubides et al., 1986). This was also made clear when they became the intermediaries in the purchase and sale of coca paste, which provided them almost exclusive territorial control by way of controlling the access to cash.
17 Revelo-Rebolledo, "The Political Economy Of Amazon Deforestation: Subnational Development And The Uneven Reach Of The Colombian State."
18 Personal conversation, October 2019.
19 Arias Ortiz, "Cambio institucional y conflicto armado: El caso del mercado de la leche en San Vicente del Caguán."
20 Hough, "Disarticulations and commodity chains: Cattle, coca, and capital accumulation along Colombia's agricultural frontier," 1016–1034.
21 Personal interview, December 2019.
22 Ciro Rodriguez, "Cultivando Coca en el Caquetá: Vidas y Legitimidades en la Actividad Cocalera."
23 Scott, *Seeing Like a State: How Certain Schemes to Improve the Human Condition Have Failed.*
24 Palau and Arias, *Balance de la Política Nacional de Consolidación Territorial.*
25 Kanai and da Silva Oliveira, "Paving (through) Amazonia: Neoliberal urbanism and the reperipheralization of Roraima," 62–77; Kanai and Schindler, "Getting the territory right: Infrastructure-led development and the re-emergence of spatial planning strategies," 40.
26 Brücher, *La colonización de la selva pluvial en el piedemonte amazónico de Colombia: El territorio comprendido entre el río Ariari y el Ecuador*; Hormaza Jimenez, "La reforma agraria como ejercicio de planificación: Experiencias de los proyectos de colonización del INCORA en el Caquetá entre 1964–1974."

27 Carlos, former pilot, personal interview, December 2019.
28 Guhl Nimtz, *Colombia: Bosquejo de su Geografía Tropical Vol I y II.*
29 Rodrigo, early *colono*, personal interview, August 2019.
30 Peñaranda Currie, Otero-Bahamon, and Uribe, "What is the state made of: Coca, roads and the materiality of state formation in the frontier."
31 Otero-Bahamon, Uribe, and Peñaranda Currie, "Seeing like a Guerrilla: The logic of infrastructure in the building of insurgent orders."
32 United Nations Office on Drugs and Crime (UNODC), *Colombia: Monitoreo de Territorios Afectados por cultivos ilícitos 2016.*
33 Mojica Flores, "El Proyecto de Ley que Criminaliza el Campesinado Colombiano."
34 Stein and Sandwell, "Illicit Crop Frontiers: Colonialism, Commodification, and Countermovements," 24–32.

Bibliography

Acevedo-Guerrero, Tatiana. "Light is like water: Flooding, blackouts, and the state in Barranquilla." *Tapuya: Latin American Science, Technology and Society*, Vol. 2, Issue 1 (2019): 478–494.

Anzaldúa, Gloria. *Borderlands/La Frontera: The New Mestiza*. San Francisco: Aunt Lute Books, 2012.

Appel, Hannah, Nikhil Anand, and Akhil Gupta. "Introduction: The Infrastructure Toolbox." *Society for Cultural Anthropology*, September 24, 2015. https://culanth.org/fieldsights/introduction-the-infrastructure-toolbox.

Arias Ortiz, Gerson Ivan. "Cambio institucional y conflicto armado: El caso del mercado de la leche en San Vicente del Caguán." PhD diss., CIDER, Universidad de los Andes, Centro Interdisciplinario de Estudios sobre Desarrollo, 2008.

Browder, John O. and Brian Godfrey. *Rainforest cities: Urbanization, development, and globalization of the Brazilian Amazon*. New York: Columbia University Press, 1997.

Brücher, Wolfgang. *La colonización de la selva pluvial en el piedemonte amazónico de Colombia: El territorio comprendido entre el río Ariari y el Ecuador*. Bogotà: Instituto Geográfico Agustín Codazzi, 1974.

Centro Nacional de Memoria Histórica (CNMH). *La Tierra No Basta: Colonización, Baldíos y Organizaciones Sociales en el Caquetá*. Bogotà: Centro Nacional de Memoria Histórica (CNMH), 2017.

Ciro Rodriguez, Estefania. "Cultivando Coca en el Caquetá: Vidas y Legitimidades en la Actividad Cocalera." PhD diss., Universidad Nacional Autónoma de México, 2016.

Cubides, Fernando, Jaime Eduardo Jaramillo, and Leonidas Mora. *Colonización, coca y guerrilla*. Bogotà: Alianza Editorial Colombiana, 1986.

Das, Veena and Deborah Poole, eds. *Anthropology in the margins of the state*. Santa Fe: School of American Research Press, 2004.

Florián Guzmán, Jhon Heiver. "Reforma Agraria y Alianza Para el Progreso en Colombia 1960–1967." Master diss., Universidad Nacional de Colombia, Facultad de Ciencias Humanas Departamento de Historia, 2013.

González Trujillo, Héctor Eduvin, José Francisco Ramón Mahe, and Rafael Torrijos Rivera. *Caquetá: Tradición y Vocación Ganadera*. Florencia: Comité Departamental de Ganaderos del Caquetá, 2003.

González, Ximena. "Estudio de seroprevalencia reveló que Leticia alcanzó un nivel de infección de 60% y Barranquilla 55%." *Diario La República*, November 26, 2020. https://www.larepublica.co/economia/estudio-de-seroprevalencia-revelo-que-leticia-alcanzo-un-nivel-de-infeccion-de-60-y-barranquilla-55-3094727 (last accessed: December 14, 2021).

Gootenberg, Paul and Liliana M. Dávalos, eds. *The Origins of Cocaine: Colonization and Failed Development in the Amazon Andes*. London: Routledge, 2018.

Guhl Nimtz, Ernesto. *Colombia: Bosquejo de su Geografía Tropical Vol I y II*. Bogotà: Biblioteca Básica Colombiana, 1976.

Harvey, Penelope. "The Materiality of State Effects: An Ethnography of a Road in the Peruvian Andes." *State Formation. Anthropological Perspectives*, edited by Christian Krohn-Hansen and Knut G. Nustad, 216–247. London: Pluto Press, 2005.

Hormaza Jimenez, Ingrid Carolina. "La reforma agraria como ejercicio de planificación: Experiencias de los proyectos de colonización del INCORA en el Caquetá entre 1964–1974." Master diss., Universidad Nacional de Colombia Facultad de Artes, Maestría en Ordenamiento Urbano-regional, 2016.

Hough, Phillip A. "Disarticulations and commodity chains: Cattle, coca, and capital accumulation along Colombia's agricultural frontier." *Environment and Planning A: Economy and Space*, Vol. 43, No. 5 (2011): 1016–1034.

Kanai, J. Miguel and Rafael da Silva Oliveira. "Paving (through) Amazonia: Neoliberal urbanism and the reperipheralization of Roraima." *Environment and Planning A: Economy and Space*, Vol. 46 (2014): 62–77.

Kanai, J. Miguel and Seth Schindler. "Getting the territory right: Infrastructure-led development and the re-emergence of spatial planning strategies." *Regional Studies*, Vol. 55, No. 1 (2021): 40.

Larkin, Brian. "The Politics and Poetics of Infrastructure." *Annual Review of Anthropologist*, Vol. 42 (2013): 327–343.

Martinez Basallo, Sandra Patricia. *Encuentros con el Estado: Burocracias y colonos en la frontera amazónica (1960–1980)*. Cali: Universidad del Valle, 2017.

Mojica Flores, Jhenifer. "El Proyecto de Ley que Criminaliza el Campesinado Colombiano." La Silla Vacía, May 27, 2021. https://www.lasillavacia.com/historias/historias-silla-llena/el-proyecto-de-ley-que-criminaliza-al-campesinado-colombiano/ (last accessed: December 14, 2021).

Molano Bravo, Alfredo. "Región, Violencia y Democracia, algunas consideraciones sobre la colonización y la violencia." *Colombia: Democracia y Sociedad* (1988).

Montenegro Helfer, Laura. "Pensando el campo colombiano: La política del desarrollo, las tierras y la vida del campesino en el diseño de la Reforma Social Agraria." Master diss., Departamento de Historia, Facultad de Ciencias Sociales Universidad de Los Andes, 2014.

Otero-Bahamon, Silvia, Simón Uribe, and Isabel Peñaranda Currie. "Seeing like a Guerrilla: The logic of infrastructure in the building of insurgent orders." *Geoforum* (2021).

Palau, Juan Carlos and Gerson Arias, ed. *Balance de la Política Nacional de Consolidación Territorial*, Informes Fundación Ideas para la paz, 2011.

Peñaranda Currie, Isabel. "L'eredità spaziale del fallimento. Un'analisi dei programmi di colonizzazione statale nel dipartimento di Caquetá, Colombia (1959–1981)." *La Differenza Amazzonica*, edited by Antonio di Campli. Siracusa: Letteraventidue, 2021.

Peñaranda Currie, Isabel, Silvia Otero-Bahamon, and Simón Uribe. "What is the state made of: Coca, roads and the materiality of state formation in the frontier." *World Development*, Volume 141 (May 2021).

Rasmussen, Mattias Borg and Christian Lund. "Reconfiguring Frontier Spaces: The territorialization of resource control." *World Development*, Vol. 101 (2018): 388–399.

Revelo-Rebolledo, Javier. "The Political Economy Of Amazon Deforestation: Subnational Development And The Uneven Reach Of The Colombian State." PhD diss., University of Pennsylvania, 2019.

Scott, James C. *Seeing Like a State: How Certain Schemes to Improve the Human Condition Have Failed.* New Haven: Yale University Press, 1998.

Serje, Margarita. *El Revés de la Nación: Territorios salvajes, fronteras y salvajes y tierras de nadie*. Bogotà: Ediciones Universidad de los Andes, 2005.

Stein, Serena and Katie Sandwell."Illicit Crop Frontiers: Colonialism, Commodification, and Countermovements." Commodity Frontiers, Issue 2 (Spring 2021): 24–32.

United Nations Office on Drugs and Crime (UNODC). *Colombia: Monitoreo de Territorios Afectados por cultivos ilícitos 2016*. 2017. https://www.unodc.org/documents/colombia/2017/julio/CENSO_2017_WEB_baja.pdf (last accessed: December 14, 2021).

Uribe, Simón. *Frontier Road. Power, History and the Everyday State in the Colombian Amazon*. Hoboken: John Willey and Sons, 2017.

Vásquez Delgado, Teófilo. *Territorios, Conflicto Armado y Política en el Caquetá: 1900–2010*. Bogotà: Ediciones Uniandes, 2015.

Ecological lifelines

Giulia Ravera,
Lorenzo Rabagliati,
Andrea Sanguedolce

The reality that surrounds us, which significantly influences our ways of thinking, has led us to reflect more carefully on how we are currently facing the climate context and how we can best prepare ourselves for future climate phenomena. But which climate are we adapting to? Turin is included in the vision of an entirely distinctive territory, both geographically and climatically.[1]
The interpretation of this territory through its morphological elements, closely interconnected with the climatic ones, has led to a contradictory synthesis, based on the shape of the soil, on the materials; a paradox that shows an ambivalent city, which presents a changing and multiform image of itself, difficult to understand and resolve. On the one side, Turin is known to be one of the cities with the highest levels of pollutants, on the other, it is considered one of the greenest cities in Italy, in which natural material is, however, confined to a rigid zone; a spatial definition of use that potentially eliminates others, conforming to its clear syntax, made up of repeated grammatical figures, delineated boundaries, a rigid road system that spreads to its metropolitan borders. The same differences defined by the fixed meanings of tradition are flattened, made opaque, by the same climatic factors that constitute their interpretation. Thus, the values indicating the temperature and its increase are spatialized in a homogeneous way, cancelling the geographical characteristics of Turin, and the classical dichotomy between organic and inorganic, natural and artificial. The climatic perspective opens meanings, makes them incomplete and, therefore, subject to investigation at other scales and by other stakeholders.
The territory has proved to be non-obvious and capable of leading to new knowledge. It requires a deeper investigation of its materials, of which it is composed, presupposing stories and descriptions. Instead of obscuring the readings, this opacity actually allows one to see.[2]
The elimination of the boundaries between urban and non-urban and the flattening of the differences between organic and inorganic, the annulment of the great figures of production for which Turin is known, shows an unprecedented vision of this territory and, at the same time, the imperative to go down in scale for the description of what we can define as a more intimate opacity. Climate change, in this case global warming (and the case study of Turin), reconfirms the multi-scalar and heterogeneous vision of this theme.
The image of the water is the only one that creates more interference than the opaque cast, it is therefore shown as the element that carries an effective microclimate, annulled at the edge of its natural borders. As in water, the organic element is also seen in the trees and large islands of parks and hills, where it loses its power; its climatic benefit is not eliminated, but in comparison with the surroundings, the difference is minimal.
Other is all that surrounds these spaces composed of natural, organic presences, other no longer assumes the role of a different component, the climatic condition brings the rest under the same scrutiny. Temperature therefore allows us to overcome the nature-artifice dichotomy in a disenchanted coexistence with climate change.

Fig.1
Contrast between green habitat and solid areas of the metropolitan city of Turin, pp. 58–59. Source: Giulia Ravera, Lorenzo Rabagliati, Andrea Sanguedolce.

Fig.2
Temperature opacity of Turin, pp. 60–61. Source: Giulia Ravera, Lorenzo Rabagliati, Andrea Sanguedolce.

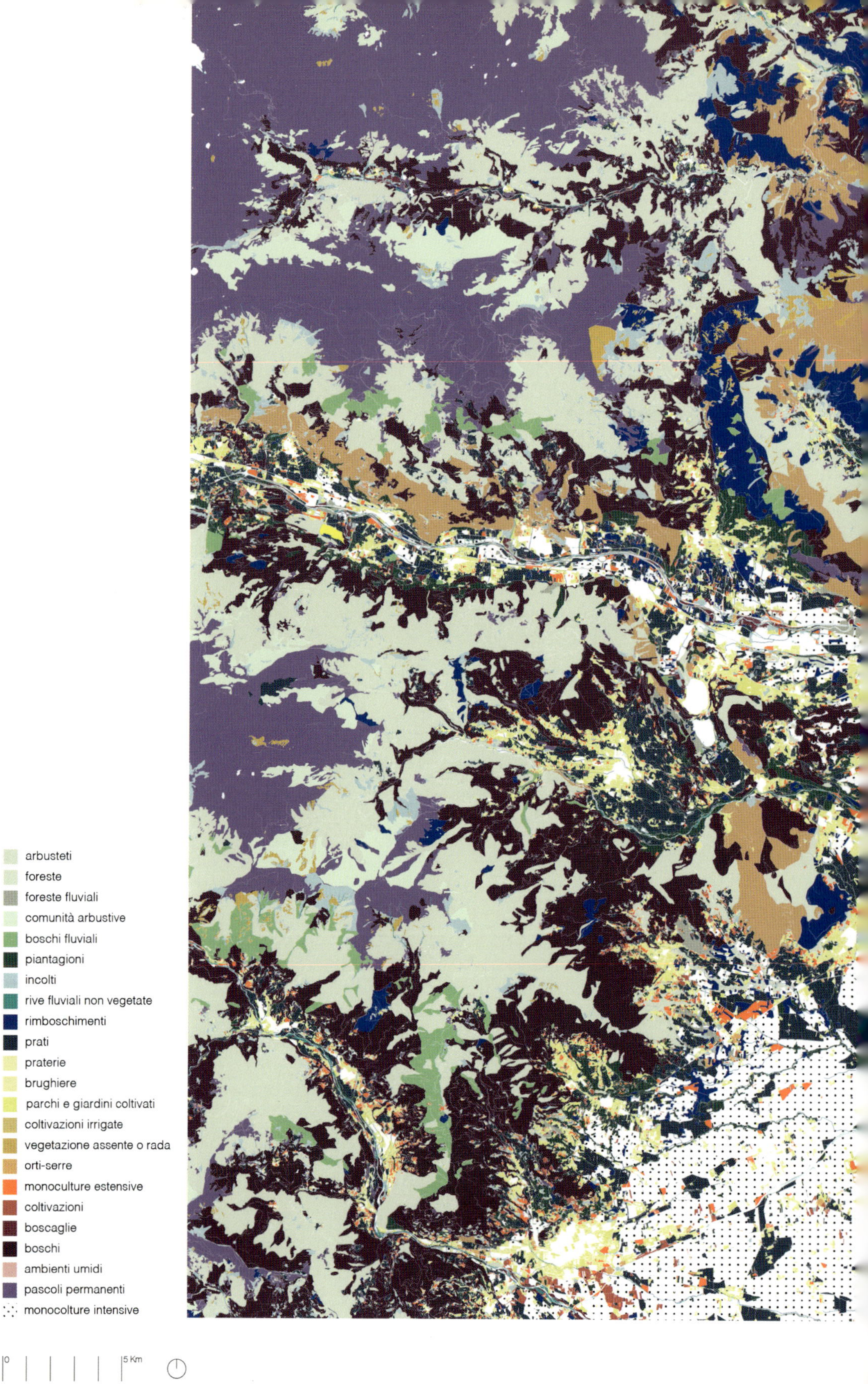
arbusteti
foreste
foreste fluviali
comunità arbustive
boschi fluviali
piantagioni
incolti
rive fluviali non vegetate
rimboschimenti
prati
praterie
brughiere
parchi e giardini coltivati
coltivazioni irrigate
vegetazione assente o rada
orti-serre
monoculture estensive
coltivazioni
boscaglie
boschi
ambienti umidi
pascoli permanenti
monocolture intensive
0
5 Km

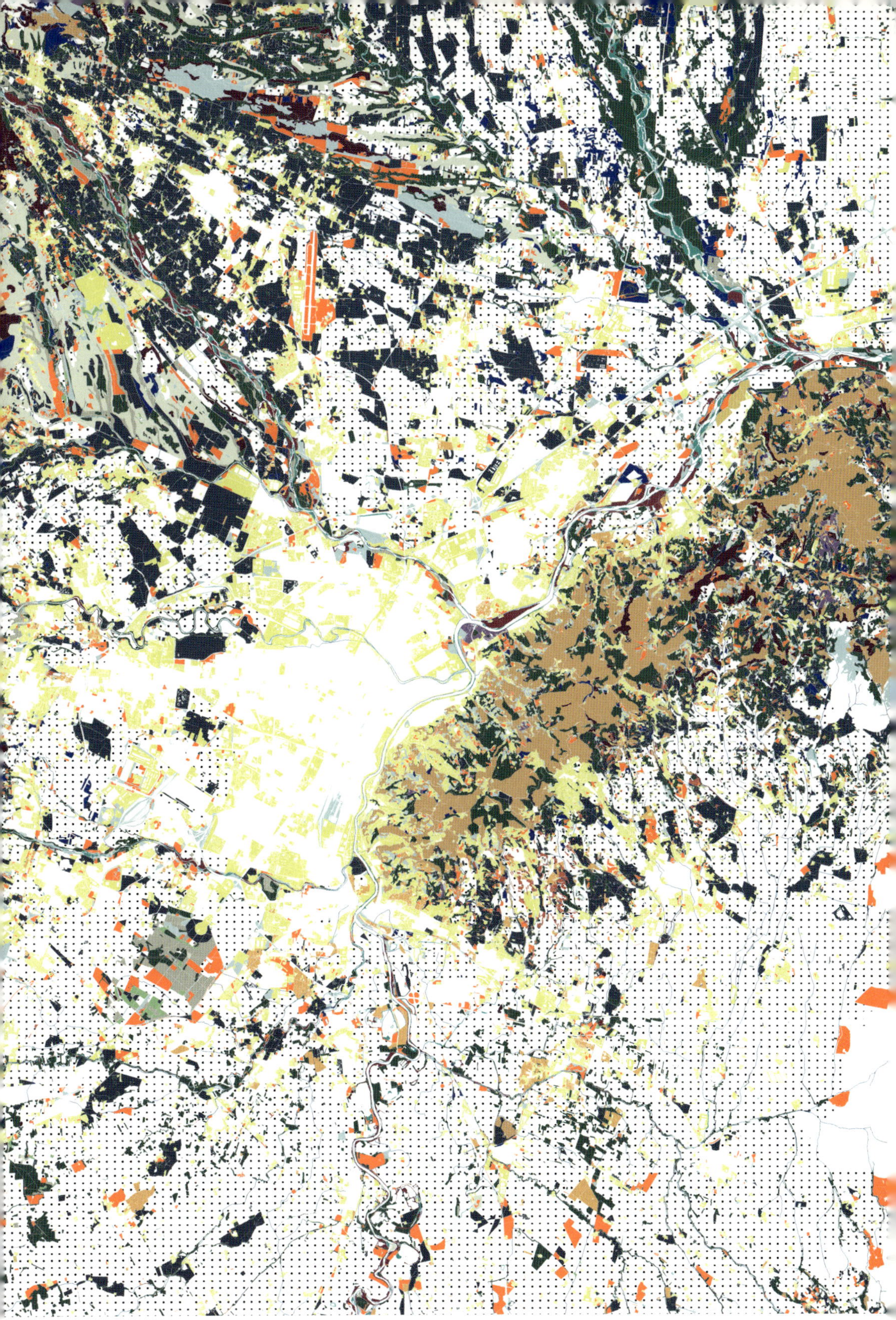

Max. Min. °C

What becomes a field of intervention, in which the resonance of this outdated bipartition can be felt, is the open space that surrounds the built, public, and private; it is that space extending in all directions. The characteristic of this fabric around things is that it is represented by the void, that it lacks thermal heterogeneity, and is therefore homogeneous. The open spaces of the voids, "of an 'obvious landscape,' banal and ordinary,"[3] are charged with a double value, that of repetition. Repetition, in fact, has a double and ambiguous nature.

Referring explicitly to Paola Viganò, it is both "repetition as power, which can reinforce the sense and meaning of the context in which it manifests itself," and "repetition as 'disintegration of the semantic identity of a sign,' for example, within heterogeneous communicative contexts or as a result of changes in the internal discursive structure."[4]

In this plural perspective, the climate issue constitutes the conceptual background of reflections that redefine the classical readings, involving numerous scales of reflection and intervention, in which the open space of the city, the intermediate spaces, whether organic or inorganic, become subjects of investigation and potential. So, can the open space of the city be rethought in its constituent elements? Can the natural elements of gardens, parks, courtyards, and urban areas interact in new ways with the rigid elements of mineral soils?

This paper investigates what kind of protection is provided in an urban context by the spaces occupied by vegetation, and it looks at one of the commonplaces that recurs in the discourse on cities and climate. To do this, it shifts the focus from functional and purely morphological elements to a reading oriented by the cold/hot categories.

Fragments and fragments

The tension between the identification of different open spaces and the climate issue takes on the role of a strategic opportunity for the city of Turin. The mapping of these places has made it necessary to make a choice regarding the space with which we can relate. The void is seen as a place where we can intervene, taking into consideration those urban materials defined as no-name spaces. "The urban materials touched by this theme are some of the most widespread and the least investigated: walkways, car parks, parking areas for vehicles and the loading and unloading of goods, unnamed spaces along a market street, but also gardens, parks, playgrounds, meeting places subject to rarefaction of the built-up area, the soil containing parts of the city."[5]

The urban materials discussed in *La Città Elementare* also assume the role of the first potential devices used to experiment with the design tension between the climatic problem and the intrinsic rigidity of a climatically opaque city.

The different materials of the city are composed in sequences of scales. By performing this task of spaces in between, the voids are entrusted with the role that the garden once had: to be the place where new ideas are experimented.[6] Indeed, the spatial quality of the city's materials must also correspond to the need to make them suitable for hosting the practices of contemporary society linked to climate change. The investigation of these places leads us to cross them, to thematize their reflections.

"The individuation of the ways of acting goes in parallel with the study of the instruments to recognize the minimum units of the composition of the space, through a form of individuation of all its parts, highlighting phenomena that are not immediately noticeable and potentially hidden."[7]

The void investigated becomes that of pauses, of intermediate space, almost isolated from the rest that surrounds it, like cuttings within a defined fabric of streets, buildings, in repetition, like fragments.

Common places, charged with their nominal meaning, their function, lose their ritual role when reviewed. The homogeneity of the climate crisis allows the use of the habitual syntax by which gardens, open spaces, squares, marketplaces, pavements, the free space between buildings at ground level, called "zero architecture,"[8] have to be identified as fragments of a climate project, thus, not abandoning them as singular elements in the city but rather letting the latter recognize itself again in its new grammar. The alteration of the climate reduces material differences, making opacity a factor in the identification of obvious spaces, revisited and filled with value for their repetitiveness.

A structural problem such as climate change can and must be approached in a rigid context, through an inter-scalar dimension. Each piece plays a role, telling different narratives of the same climatic episode. Beyond the assembly of the individual pieces, what is emphasized is their juxtaposition and their possibility of adaptation. The fragments are considered possible operations with which to increase the resilience of the city, giving importance to the molecular. This cellular vision allows for the metaphor of the multiform, multi-scalar, discontinuous city, in which multiple identities are present, in other words the image of an archipelago, a figure that reverses the traditional logic.

The space between the fragments becomes like the extracellular liquid, allowing the discovered pluralities to be grouped together, like cells, reunited in a tissue that, as Foucault states, is relevant from the point of view of becoming, is becoming "other."[9]

Going over the spaces, all the same but each one different, we identify fragments with different scales; it is no longer the difference in materials that matters in deciding whether to implement an intervention but only their proximity and potential adaptability, becoming the translation of possible operations.

These voids thus become the active subject of the project, and a dimensional filter is used to establish relationships of size and agglomeration. The large pauses correspond to the surfaces of the parks, which in an overall vision, assume the role of catalysts; their climatic strength is increased in relation to the remaining fragments, from small spaces to those of medium scale. It is precisely this latter intermediate dimension that becomes the filter for selecting and studying the new practices to be known and applied, as a support for the adaptation of the city,

Fig.3
Playlist of fragments, pp. 64–65. Source: Giulia Ravera, Lorenzo Rabagliati, Andrea Sanguedolce.

Fig.4
Climatic interference of fragments, pp. 66–67. Source: Giulia Ravera, Lorenzo Rabagliati, Andrea Sanguedolce.

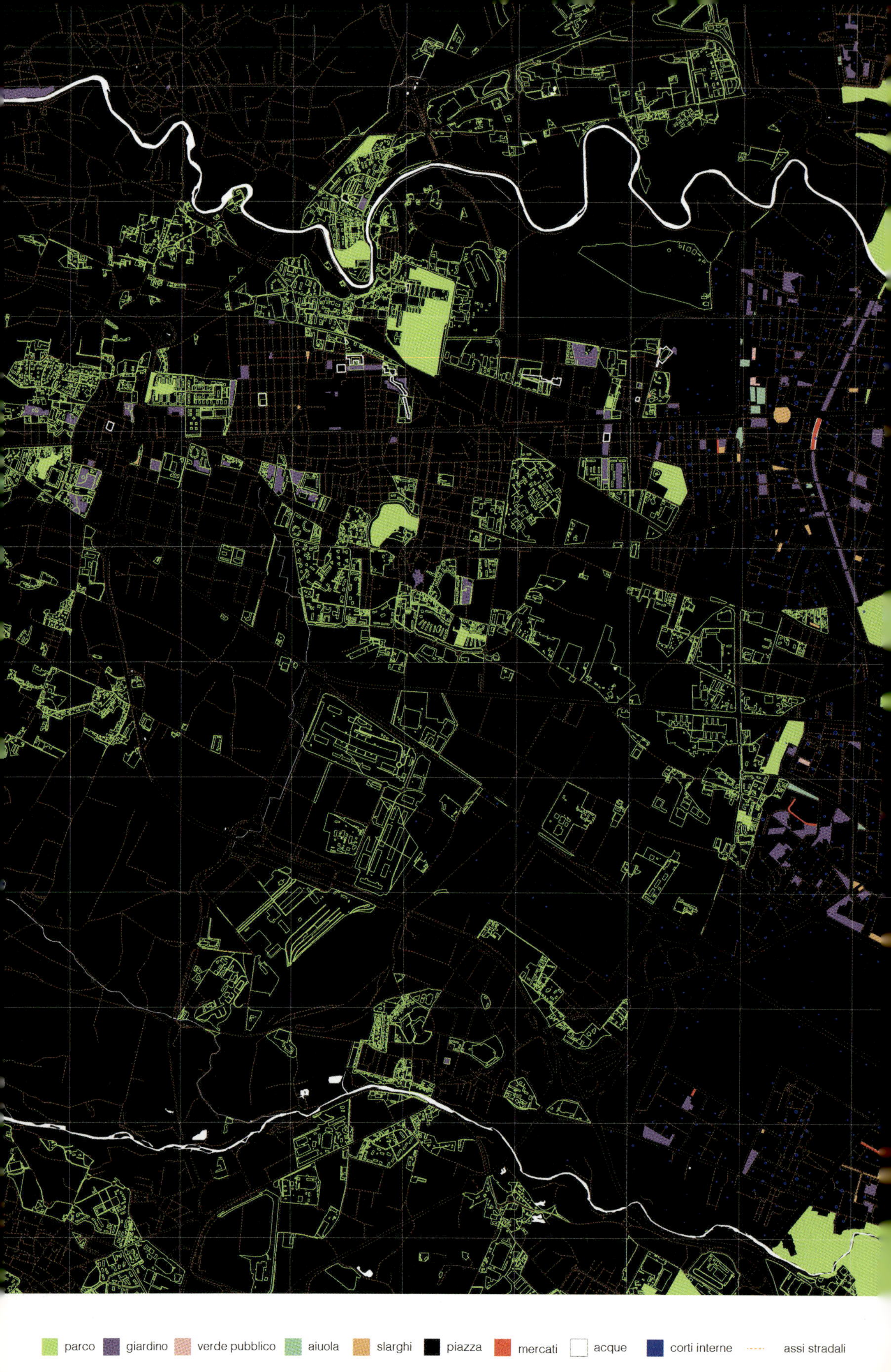
parco
giardino
verde pubblico
aiuola
slarghi
piazza
mercati
acque
corti interne
assi stradali

-0,255
-0,246
-0,254

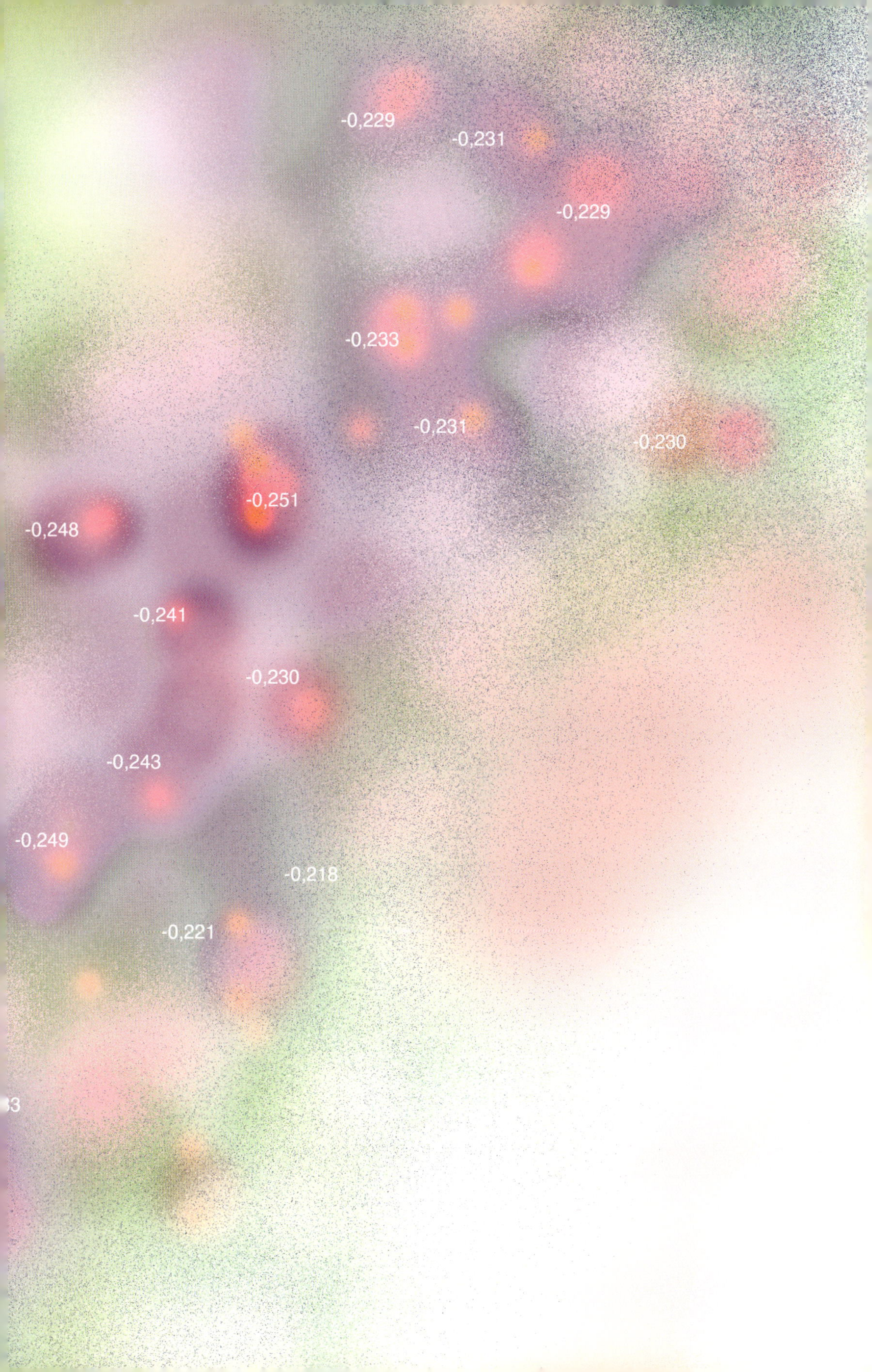
-0,229
-0,231
-0,229
-0,233
-0,231
-0,230
-0,251
-0,248
-0,241
-0,230
-0,243
-0,249
-0,218
-0,221

in programmatic and environmental terms, as a driving force for new ecologies.
The infrastructural strength of the large parks effectively becomes such when combined with that of the open space, developing protective ribbing that dissolves the classic vision of the city of Turin, making it softer, rougher, open to a scenario of climatic coexistence.

Climatic relations

Overcoming the modern narrative also implies bringing our relationship with nature, minerality, and climate to the different scales of a dialogic discourse.[10]
Thus, can the open space of the city be rethought in its constituent elements? Can the natural elements of gardens, parks, courtyards, and urban areas dialogue in new terms with the hard elements of mineral soils? The role of open space is to support new practices linked to climatic conditions and, therefore, to be a surface that must adapt. Similar to the French Support-Surfaces movement,[11] the void between the built-up area becomes itself an open surface capable of autonomously occupying space and not just projecting a function.
"*Un air rose*" is what Bernard Lassus called his 1965 experiment: by inserting a strip of white paper into the calyx of the flower, he shows how the air glows red, without any physical change, making a principle of minimal interference evident. Air, taken as the 'ancient' definition of climate, is what surrounds us and penetrates not only our bodies but also our minds, souls, and societies. Since ancient times, weather events and seasonal patterns have been the epitome of what cannot be controlled by humans but marks the imprint of nature on culture.[12]
The physical space of the city seems like an empty container in relation to climatic agents that cannot be intercepted but is instead filled with invisible material. The relationship with climate is thus highlighted through the medium of the body that traverses air and space, triggering or describing climatic relationships.
Picking up on Elizabeth Gordon, climate is the impalpable and invisible entity that, as the first being in everything, influences our actions within our environment.
The contribution of a perceptive vision, which translates the vision of what surrounds us and allows us to give attention to the senses, recounting Zardini,[13] raises the question of how climate change can be reread, no longer analyzed only as the materialization of a given set of values but also read through multiple sensory modalities, together with the city.
Bernardo Secchi, in his description of Piazza del Campo in Siena,[14] clearly brings out the importance of the perceptive sphere capable of relating what is body and what is space.[15]
The materiality, the consistency of the ground, takes on power when seen in relation to the way it is perceived, even though its organic difference in large-scale climatic terms is depreciated.

Overcoming the dichotomy between natural and unnatural, or rather talking about organic and inorganic, leaving aside the polysemy of the term nature, brings new knots to the surface; among many, that of the role of the contemporary meaning of ecology. However, the term ecology should be recounted in its definition as the study of the interrelationships between organisms and their environment, and in its widely debated meaning. In fact, the term was introduced by E.H. Haeckel in 1866 to denote the part of physiology that studies the functions of relationships of organisms with their environment and with each other, and which finds its mechanical explanation in the theory of the adaptation of living beings as they change because of the struggle for existence, the medium, parasitism, and competition.[16] It is the science of conditions of existence, or environmental biology. Guattari argues that we have a limiting conception of ecology: only by broadening its meaning and our vision could we think of lasting changes.[17] Ecology is something to do with coexistence, it imagines interconnectedness. As in a fabric, in a weave, there are no single, separate entities. Differences persist, or the harmoniously opposed prevails.
Ecological thinking is linked to an ethic that we might call "coexistentialism," in which interconnectedness must admit differences, separations, and blurring, unlike environmental rhetoric that is all too often affirmative and safe.

Lifelines

Observing the city from the inside, in the encumbrance of our bodies, we re-read its materials, its surfaces, affected by the climate, perceived by the body. Climate change brings to the fore the collective practices that take place in the space of the city. This space is experienced by light, water, wind, shade, and sun; it is a sensorial space. What we need to overcome, leaving aside the purely analytical and scientific reflections on global warming, is to understand what actions can switch this relationship between the incorporeal and the non-incorporeal.
The figure of infrastructure needs to be re-read in the ecological sense of the term, no longer in its ritual role but by assuming the role of a device that lives with the climate, endures it, and relates to it, in sequence and in continuity in the fragments of an unprecedented Turin.
But how should this continuity be read?
The question of delineating figures and references is the ritual of defining a function, thus excluding others, reducing the complexity of a given space, removing all ambiguity from its configuration. However, it is precisely in the ambiguity that the climatic space takes shape and relates. Open space is no longer seen as a waste space, cut off by superstructures, but empty space itself becomes an infrastructural force for contemporary practices. It expands, contracts, relates.
These spatial breaks are cells that are not considered as 'sectors,' separated from each other by traffic routes of a higher order, but seen to-

gether as a succession of external elements that make collaboration possible in a diffuse vision.[18]

The opacified Turin shows spaces of interference that give the possibility to re-read reference figures in the territory, exposed as analogies that allow reflection on new rules. The value of the fragments as single devices lies in their ability to create proximity that is not physically continuous but is interfaced in a spatial and climatic resonance.

The grammatical hierarchies of Turin's traditional grid are weakened, reinforcing instead the weight of the resulting fragments. They turn out to be ecological opportunities, partly tracing the existing empty space, partly expanding it, becoming the new climatic centralities, coupled, closed, interconnected, related by their latent potential.

The scenario of a Tropical Turin envisages a proliferation of these operable places, which take on the new guise of interior spaces, approaching what is already present and rooted. Pursuing the meaning of climatic oases, they are immersed in a space in which budding can and will persist, in a composing through attraction and accumulation.

What is a climate infrastructure? An operable space made of different things (soil, water, fog, etc.) that exceeds the project space in the sense that it replaces static projects (the park, the neighborhood) and waives active materials. The interaction between these materials provides a kind of balance between differences in a manner other than that of protection, or in a special ecological protection made of differences and fluxes.

These intercellular climatic prototypes overlap the classical grammar, becoming episodes, promoting visions in which coexistence involves adaptation, not only of man and his body but also and above all the language of the city.

The latter must provide for the inclusion, or rather the reinterpretation, of a climate infrastructure: a system of spaces, devices, and relations that allow or guarantee a certain degree of livability within the future urban scenario. The climate problem therefore raises questions that help broaden our view of the city, the way of it is narrated, allowing the concept of infrastructure to expand, becoming physical, material, fragile, and not afraid to be ambiguous.

Fig.5
Grammatical possibilities of Turin. Source: Giulia Ravera, Lorenzo Rabagliati, Andrea Sanguedolce.

Endnotes

1 Research carried out by Giulia Ravera, Lorenzo Rabagliati, and Andrea Sanguedolce for their Master's thesis project in the Architecture City Construction course at the Politecnico di Torino. Tutor: Nicola Russi; co-tutors: Cristina Bianchetti and Paola Viganò.
2 Agamben, *L'uso dei corpi. Homo Sacer. Vol. IV\2.*
3 Viganò, *La Città Elementare*, 21.
4 Ibid.
5 Ibid, 181.
6 Secchi and Fini, *Il futuro si costruisce giorno per giorno: riflessioni su spazio, società e progetto.*
7 Russi, *Background: il progetto del vuoto*, 28.
8 Viganò, *La Città Elementare.*
9 Foucault and Vaccaro, *Spazi altri. I luoghi delle Eterotopie.*
10 Graham, Blanchfield, Anderson, Carver, and Moore. *Climates: Architecture and the Planetary Imaginary.*
11 Valensi, "Extrait du catalogue Été 70," 67.
12 Graham, Blanchfield, Anderson, Carver, and Moore. *Climates: Architecture and the Planetary Imaginary.*
13 Zardini, *Sense of the City: An Alternate Approach to Urbanism.*
14 Secchi, *La città del ventesimo secolo.*
15 Bianchetti, *Bodies, Between Space and Design.*
16 Haeckel, *Generelle Morphologie der Organismen.*
17 Guattari, *The Three Ecologies.*
18 Viganò, Fabian, and Secchi, *Water and Asphalt: The Project of Isotropy.*

Bibliography

Agamben, Giorgio. *L'uso dei corpi. Homo Sacer. Vol. IV\2.* Vicenza: Neri Pozza Editore, 2014.

Bianchetti, Cristina. *Bodies, Between Space and Design.* Berlin: JOVIS, 2020.

Foucault, Michel and Salvo Vaccaro, eds. *Spazi altri. I luoghi delle Eterotopie.* Milan: Mimesis, 2001.

Graham, James, Caitlin Blanchfield, Alissa Anderson, Jordan H. Carver, and Jacob Moore. *Climates: Architecture and the Planetary Imaginary.* Zurich: Lars Müller, 2016.

Guattari, Félix. *The Three Ecologies.* London: Bloomsbury, 2014.

Haeckel, Ernst. *Generelle Morphologie der Organismen.* Germany: Reimer, 1866.

Ravera, Giulia, Lorenzo Rabagliati, and Andrea Sanguedolce. "Agenda tropicale. Synthesis of urban practices for climate coexistence in Turin." Master diss., Master Degree Architecture Construction City, Politecnico di Torino, 2021.

Russi, Nicola. *Background: il progetto del vuoto.* Macerata: Quodlibet, 2019.

Secchi, Bernardo. *La città del ventesimo secolo.* Rome-Bari: Laterza, 2005.

Secchi, Bernardo and Giulia Fini. *Il futuro si costruisce giorno per giorno: riflessioni su spazio, società e progetto.* Rome: Donzelli Editore, 2015.

Valensi, André. "Extrait du catalogue Été 70." *Supports–Surfaces*, edited by Jean Marc Poinsot, 67. Paris: Limage 2, 1983.

Viganò, Paola. *La Città Elementare.* Milan: Skira, 1999.

Viganò, Paola, Lorenzo Fabian, and Bernardo Secchi, eds. *Water and Asphalt: The Project of Isotropy.* Zurich: Lars Müller, 2016.

Zardini, Mirko, ed. *Sense of the City: An Alternate Approach to Urbanism*, Zurich: Lars Müller, 2005.

Production lifelines: Suzhou's resistive lifelines and mutual support

Luis Martin Sanchez

The current pandemic crisis, like the economic one that began in 2007, has had the paradoxical effect of bringing manufacturing back to the center stage of public debate. While in the early 2000s, in Italy as in the rest of the West, the emphasis was on the transition from industrial to intangible economies – financial, creative, knowledge, etc. –, after the 2007 crisis, and again during the current health one, manufacturing has been once again celebrated as a guarantee of concreteness and security. This is a phenomenon that acquires particular importance in Italy due to the weight that the manufacturing sector still exerts within its economic system but also because of its particular vitality and ability to create and redistribute wealth and jobs. Within the complex system of Italian manufacturing in the context of "disorganized capitalism"[1] – made up of crises and excellences –, a particular type of enterprise has emerged in the last thirty years or so, which is the driving force behind the entire national economic system and which scholars define as the fourth Italian capitalism, hidden champions, pocket-sized multinationals, etc.[2] This type of enterprise, despite being closely linked to local industrial district systems, has already taken on distinctive characteristics since the 1990s, growing and becoming strongly internationalized, in contrast to the carefully studied and celebrated hyper-territorialization of Italian district enterprises.[3]
This paper[4] attempts to investigate how a "diasporic community"[5] of producers linked to Italian industrial districts rewrites its ways of living and producing in a profoundly different context such as that of China, specifically in the metropolitan area of Suzhou in the Yangtze River Delta. The internationalization of district enterprises and their relations with distant and different territories is an understudied topic. The research observes which support networks and life support measures are implemented in a radically different and, in some ways, rigid and hostile context such as that of Suzhou, and how this diaspora modifies strongly homologated production spaces such as those of Chinese compounds, adapting them to its particular characteristics and needs.
The main emphasis is placed on the question of how – in a purely extractive context where incentives and exemptions form a compound understood as a juridical and economic instrument, in which authority marks a state of exception that puts the "atomized man" at the center – networks and life-supporting ties, or lifelines, are set up without being strictly linked to economic aspects. Of how production in this case goes beyond the mere notion of infrastructure as "supply and transmission machine of capture, fluidification, organization" and is reconfigured as something more opaque and ambiguous in support of being-in-common as a peculiar human trait. This is done by trying to observe what production does when it does not produce and how an apparently autonomous and self-sufficient individual repositions himself "within a relational, embodied, situated dimension that abandons the idea of his presumed sovereignty and comes to terms with openings, conflicts and vulnerabilities."[6]

Suzhou. YRD workshop

In 1985, the Yangtze River Delta – a territory on the Yangtze River where some of China's most important cities such as Shanghai and Suzhou are located – was designated by the Chinese central government as a Special Economic Zone (SEZs),[7] with the intention of attracting foreign investment. This move was part of the wider process of economic reform of the People's Republic of China (改革开放, literally 'Reform and Opening-up') initiated in 1978 by Deng Xiaoping, which envisaged the progressive opening up of Chinese economy to the free market.[8]

After years of isolation, Suzhou opened up once again to the 'world economy,'[9] and from that moment on experienced robust economic and demographic growth that radically changed local society and the territory. The city's economic, demographic, and urban growth accelerated again in 1992, when the Pudong New Area[10] – an area with special economic powers – was established in nearby Shanghai (just 80km away), China's economic engine and financial center. In these years, a substantial spatial division of labor emerged between Shanghai – the financial center – and Suzhou – the manufacturing workshop[11] – in the Yangtze River Delta.

Suzhou, a very ancient city and capital of the State of Wu, has always been central to Chinese national imaginary. The territory of Suzhou, located between Lake Tai (*Tai Hu*, literally 'Great Lake') and the Yangtze River Delta, is characterized by the pervasive presence of water. Its history is marked by the presence of the Grand Canal, a very important trade route, which connects Beijing to Hangzhou, covering some 1,800 km. The historical structure of the city and its territory remained practically unchanged until the 1990s, during which the territory experienced rapid economic[12] and demographic growth,[13] due above all to the arrival of new technologies, mainly linked to foreign investment (FDI),[14] which also led to profound changes in the spatial structure. In those years, two industrial parks were established to the east and west of the historic center, in continuity with the master plan drawn up a few years earlier and known as 'One body, two wings.' The reference is to the historic center ('the body') and the two areas of future expansion of the city ('the two wings'), which reinforced the east-west axis of the city in conjunction with the Shanghai-Nanjing railway, to the detriment of the traditional north-south axis of the Grand Canal.

The most important of these industrial parks, known as SIP (Suzhou Industrial Park, formerly Singapore-Suzhou Industrial Park), is located to the east of the old city center and was established in 1994 by a cooperation agreement between the Chinese and Singaporean governments.[15] On the other hand, to the west of the city, the SND (Suzhou New District or Suzhou New & Hi-Tech Industry Development Zone) expansion area was established in 1990 by the local government with the aim of nurturing the hi-tech sector. From the outset, the two industrial parks were imagined as integral urban areas, albeit with a marked manufac-

Fig.1
Suzhou waterscape. Source: Luis Martin Sanchez.

turing focus. In this way, in the 1990s, Suzhou reinvented itself as a modern *'ville industrielle,'* even from its urban structure.

SIP Songlines. An infinite modern

The Suzhou Industrial Park began as an intergovernmental collaboration project between the governments of China and Singapore. Deng Xiaoping, a major protagonist of Chinese economic reforms, looked favorably to the Singaporean experience of 'authoritarian capitalism,' carried out by Lee Kuan Yew – Singapore's prime minister from 1959 to 1990 – as an alternative to Western liberal governments. The Chinese administration was interested in learning about Singapore's policies and strategies for attracting foreign direct investment, while Singaporeans were looking for investment and development opportunities abroad, given the country's small size. In these years, the Singaporean government built industrial parks in Vietnam, Indonesia, India, Thailand, and China based on the famous model of the Jurong Industrial Estate, celebrated by Rem Koolhaas' *Singapore Songlines*:[16] an industrial park that brought the urban renewal model into play as an economic growth strategy, with a history of remarkable success in attracting foreign investment since its opening in the 1960s.
SIP's plan, which strongly favored industrialization as a development model, outlined a hierarchical organization of the city, following Clarence Perry's Neighborhood Unit planning model,[17] as was already the case in Singapore's Jurong Industrial Estate and other Chinese new towns.
As in Perry's model, four levels of spatial organization (region, district, neighborhood, and cluster) structured SIP. In SIP (the 'region'), each of the three districts, developed respectively in three different phases, was designed to accommodate between 33,000 and 100,000 households. Each district was planned to accommodate 8,500 households, arranged around a center with public facilities serving a 400-meter radius. In turn, each cluster was designed to accommodate about 700 families and was equipped with cluster-scale public facilities. The initial plan predicted a population of 600,000: an essential workforce for the massive foreign investment that was being envisaged.
Today, SIP sees the contamination of modernist models – from neighborhood units to the extensive use of zoning – a few years too late, and the characteristics of contemporary Asian metropolises. In SIP, neighborhood units, imagined by Perry as porous, walkable facilities, become extended private compounds on the model of the gated community, built for the growing Chinese middle class. Although it refers, at least in appearance, to the principles of continuity of Modernism, these are denied at the root; and where one would expect a public and porous city, one finds instead a city made up of fenced-off and privatized fragments. The case of SIP, although in some respects peculiar (especially because of the strong Singaporean influence), is exemplary of how the territory has become the central resource of Chinese administrations for

promoting economic growth and how, in order to organize it for unprecedented purposes, they resort to classical models (the neighborhood unit in this case) that have been stiffened and emptied of meaning in an act of almost 'cultural cannibalism.'

Made in Italy, Made in China. Lifelines and "*appaesamenti*"

Between the end of the 1990s and the early 2000s, the first Italian companies[18] began to arrive in Suzhou, attracted by the low labor costs and the proximity to Shanghai's metropolitan area. The majority of these were medium-sized manufacturing firms based in Northern Italy, which can be traced back to the fourth Italian capitalism model.[19]

This model has its roots in Italian industrial districts but differs from them mainly in terms of the growth in size and the degree of internationalization of companies, which is unheard of in district areas. Today, in a radically changed context due to the end of "Cheap China"[20] and the start of Xi Jinping's 'Blue Sky' policy, the establishment of Italian companies in China depends less and less on low labor costs and more on easy access to the Chinese and South-East Asian markets. This system of companies that has taken root in Suzhou over the years – and which, according to local entrepreneurs, is now the largest Italian industrial cluster outside Europe[21] – has been set up as a 'diasporic community of producers' that has not only successfully re-proposed a hitherto very territorialized business model, but at the same time it is attempting to rebuild emotional ties and networks of support and backing for life within the rigid Chinese context.

In 1991, the Italian Chamber of Commerce in China (ICCC)[22] was established in Beijing and progressively opened branches in other Chinese cities, including Shanghai and Suzhou. Within the Chamber of Commerce there are various Working Groups that "bring together representatives of companies operating active in the same sector or located in the same geographical area" in sectors recognized as significant and strategic for business opportunities and that aim to "share information, resources and ideas, organize relevant activities for the companies; build sectorial expertise within the CICC in order to attract interest both in China and in Italy."[23]

The Suzhou Working Group or Suzhou Chapter (SCH) is active in Suzhou, bringing together Italian manufacturing companies based in the city's industrial parks. Members of the group insist on the importance of the Suzhou Working Group – which, due to the tightening of measures against freedom of association in Xi Jinping's China, was set up as an informal group rather than a formalized association – as a platform for sharing information among Italian entrepreneurs in the city. The group aims to be a more pragmatic alternative to the Chamber of Commerce, more related to service and tertiary enterprises, for Italian manufacturers based in the Suzhou area who have specific needs regarding manufacturing. Local entrepreneurs point out that, despite the importance of this association in recent years, there has been a reduction in

Fig.2
Location of investigated companies in Northern Italy (left) and Suzhou (right), pp. 80–81. Source: Luis Martin Sanchez.

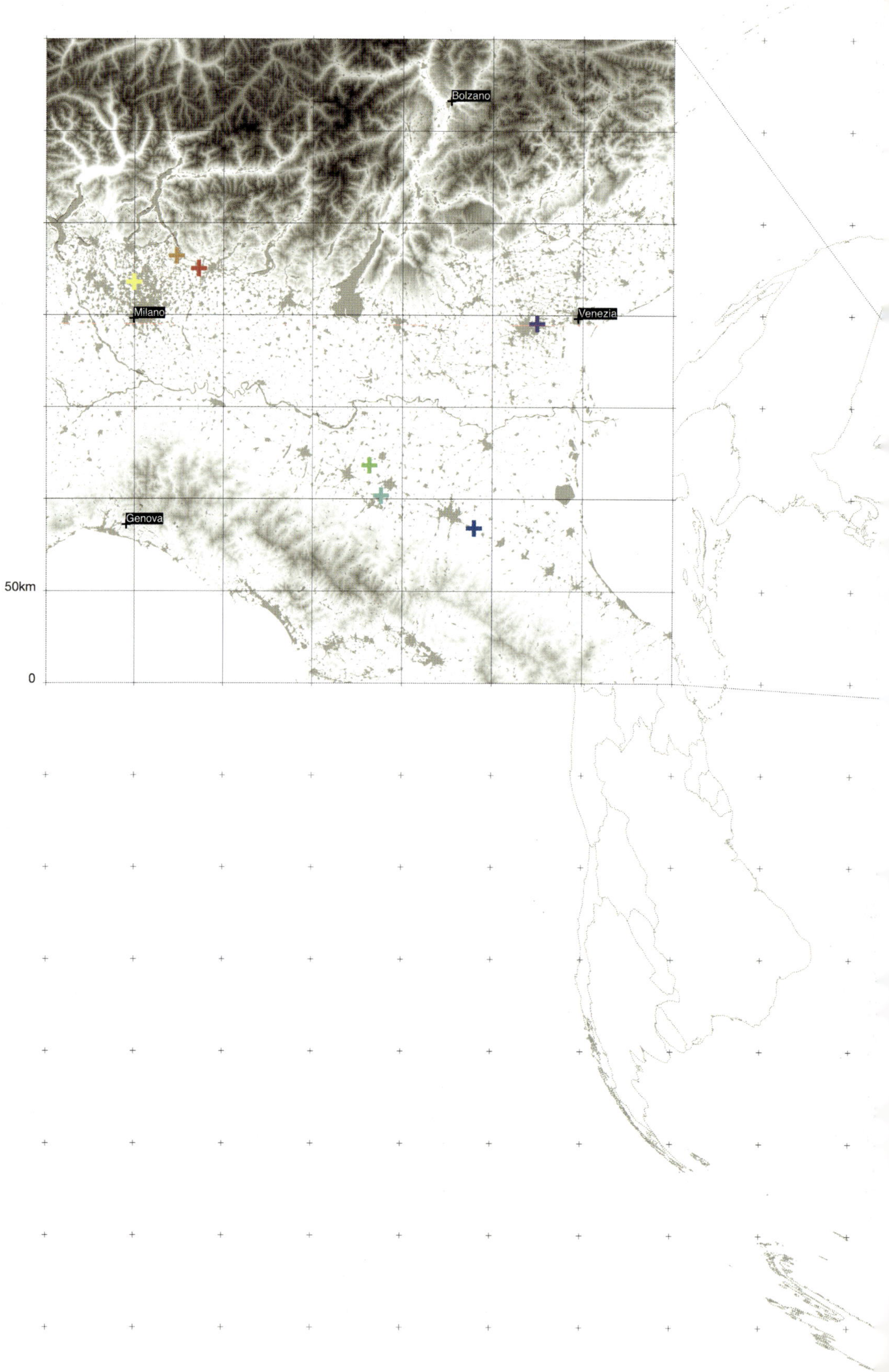
Bolzano
Milano
Venezia
Genova
50km
0

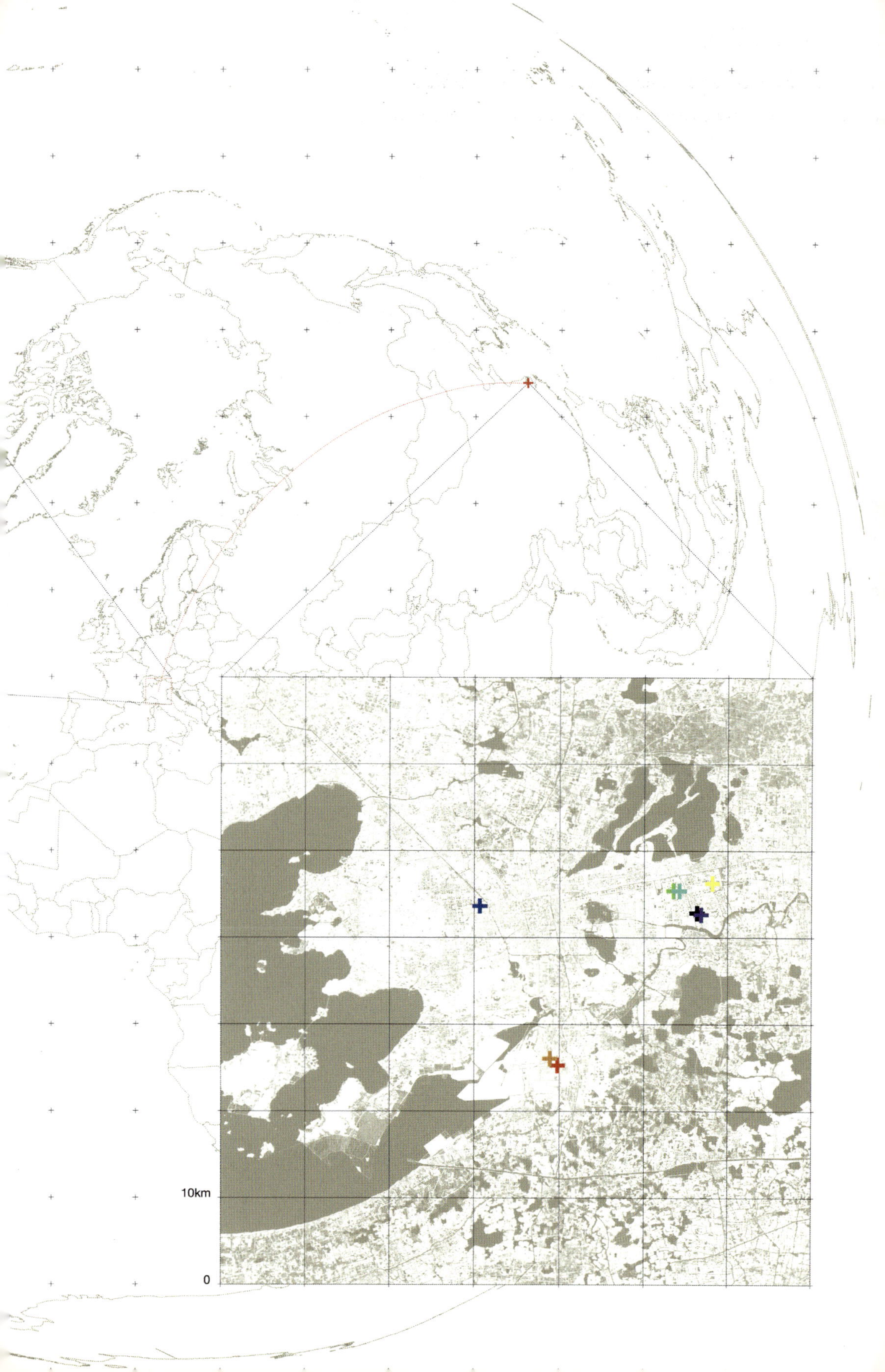
10km
0

Fig.3
System Ceramics SpA spaces in Suzhou. Photograph by Elena Longhin.

its active members. The causes are to be found in the recent exodus of many Italian companies based in the area, mainly those most dependent on low labor costs or with very polluting practices, due to the progressive repositioning of the local economy in the high-tech sectors, which has penalized many Italian companies concentrated mainly in low and mid-tech sectors.

Another support group linked to the Italian community operating in Suzhou is the 'Veneti di Cina'[24] association set up in 2014. Despite its name, the association is open to all Italians based in the area, although most of the entrepreneurs come from north-eastern Italy. The main purpose of the association is to bring together and represent Venetians living in China, both in Italy and in the People's Republic of China. In Suzhou, the group is particularly active (Suzhou – the Venice of the East in the Chinese imaginary – has been twinned with Venice since 1980) as many of the Italian companies based in the area come from the Veneto region. The association constitutes an initial infrastructure of relational and bureaucratic support for new Italian immigrants arriving in the area. Moreover, it promotes a series of social and cultural initiatives, which are essential for the diaspora in a particularly closed context such as that of China. The association is a catalyst for social and cultural life and an effective support for the life of the Italian community in the Suzhou area.

These associations have the merit of constructing "*appaesamenti*" in a harsh context such as that of China, marked by profound cultural, linguistic, social, and political differences. By "*appaesamento*" Ernesto De Martino[25] means a condition in which the individual – or a group of individuals – is rooted in the world and to some extent builds it, appropriates it, constructing a "being-in-common," thus making sharing easier. Within De Martino's reflection, "*appaesamento*" is thus an activity that consists in the construction of a domestic reality, known and obvious, which can respond positively to the Heideggerian "*unheimliche*" (uncanny), a loss of the self. The originality of this case lies in the fact that here the apprenticeship is carried out by a community that somehow always places production at the center. The recombination of rules and products exercised through tricks, ingenuity, and cleverness – their tactics of resistance, De Certeau[26] would say – is in Suzhou primarily aimed at manufacturing. And yet, despite this extractive logic, this community of producers also builds devices and spaces of care, custody, and protection "where protection does not follow univocal, frontal directions, as in classic welfare scenarios. It often acts in a roundabout way. It works through discrete points, indirect logics that work by deviation, subtraction. It is a different 'protective response' from that of the past."[27]

Rewriting the compound. The spaces of Italian enterprise in China

How does this community of producers rewrite and adapt to the rigid manufacturing spaces provided by the local government? Manufacturing spaces in SIP are also marked by the strict zoning of the neighborhood unit. Production, like living, is organized in precise monofunctional compounds. Homogeneous and typical manufacturing spaces are designed for large companies, generally multinationals linked to hi-tech sectors such as Samsung, Huawei, L'Oréal, and Bosch, all based in the Suzhou metropolitan area. On the other hand, the model of Italian companies in the territory, generally of medium size and linked to the mid-tech and high-range sectors, needs different, more contained, and characterized spaces. This difference generates, through cunning and cleverness, strategies for rewriting and adapting to the characteristics of the Italian fourth capitalist enterprise in the rigid spaces provided by local players.

In the case of Carimali, a coffee machine manufacturer based in the Province of Bergamo that has been in Suzhou for ten years, the large warehouse where the company is located is only partially used, while it waits for local production to increase in the hope of establishing itself on the Chinese and South-East Asian markets. The case of Ponzini, a company that produces toothbrushes and opened its headquarters in China because it is part of the L'Oréal supply chain (which has a plant in Suzhou), is in some ways similar, although in this case the remaining space has already been almost entirely occupied given the massive growth in production in recent years. System, a company based in Modena producing machines for the manufacturing of ceramic slabs, and Modula, a company based in Bologna producing horizontal storage systems, share the same production area, thus rationalizing not only the large spaces, which would otherwise be underused, but also various services, from the canteen to logistics. Another case is that of Satek, a company founded by two Italian entrepreneurs in Suzhou, with no headquarters in Italy, which deals with high-quality hydraulic pumps. In this case, given the new company's limited space requirement and the fact that the activity is not polluting or logistically cumbersome, it was decided to locate the production plant in a tertiary compound rather than a manufacturing one. The consequent advantages lie in the lower rental price and in having a space that symbolically reflects the company's position in high-end segments.

Lifelines

In Suzhou, a territory that is both desirable and hostile, the business model of fourth capitalism demonstrates its ability to build "locality" (in Appadurai's view) in contexts that are foreign to Italy. And in some ways, it repudiates the rhetoric that sees globalization as a process of flattening local, deep-rooted models. On the contrary, in the case of Suzhou, it is evident how the strength of the model is capable of rewriting spaces, networks, and practices of living and producing in new ways, even in a context of world economy. It constitutes an original diasporic and mestizo way of living and producing, starting from the model of Italian fourth capitalism and combining district and modern, Western and Eastern features.
In Suzhou, production allows to build 'new alliances' – albeit ambiguous – towards an imaginary of cohabitation in the contingency of unity, in the ephemerality of form and in the intensity of affection, substantial constraints of being-in-common that establishes a series of constraints without obedience, of aims without purpose. The lifelines in Suzhou act in the narrowness imposed by the surroundings and occasions of a hostile environment and therefore in a perpetual ambiguity.

Endnotes

1 Lash and Urry, *The End of Organized Capitalism*.
2 Turani, *I sogni del Grande Nord; Bonomi, I capitalismo molecolare. La società al lavoro nel Nord Italia*; Colli, *Quarto capitalismo. Un profilo italiano*; Berta, *Che fine ha fatto il capitalismo italiano?*
3 Becattini, *Dal distretto industriale allo sviluppo locale. Svolgimento e difesa di una idea*; Becattini, Ritorno *al territorio*; Becattini, *La coscienza dei luoghi. Il territorio come soggetto corale*; Magnaghi, *Il soggetto locale. Verso la coscienza dei luoghi;* Magnaghi, *Il principio territoriale*.
4 This paper reports the results of a research conducted between March and June 2019 during a PhD visiting experience at Tongji University in Shanghai and is part of a doctoral research (Iuav University of Venice) on the territorial and spatial changes produced by the emergence of the Italian medium-sized enterprise ('enterprises of the fourth Italian capitalism') as the engine of development in the country.
5 Appadurai, *Modernity at Large. Cultural Dimensions of Globalization*.
6 Bianchetti, "Cartographies of protection."
7 The term 'SEZs' (Special Economic Zones) covers a wide range of situations: free trade zones, export processing zones, industrial parks, economic and technological development zones, high-tech zones, science and innovation parks, free ports, enterprise zones, and others. In China, since the 1980s, SEZs have been used as a test bed for the transition from a planned economy to a market economy.
8 Easterling, *Extrastatecraft. The Power of Infrastructure Space*.
9 Braudel, *Civilization and Capitalism, 15th–18th Century. Vol. III: The Perspective of the World*.
10 In 1993, one year after the establishment of the Pudong New Area, the city's GDP growth rate was 70.4%.
11 Manufacturing is the main sector of Suzhou's economy. Since 1980, its contribution to the city's GDP has stabilized at around 60%. However, its centrality has been challenged by the gradual growth of the tertiary sector, whose expansion has been greatly encouraged by the municipal government. The GDP contribution of the tertiary sector exceeded 40% in 2011, while that of the secondary sector is gradually shrinking. This trend is likely to continue as Suzhou moves forward with its economic repositioning program. Meanwhile, the primary sector has steadily shrunk. As of 2012, it contributed only 1.6% of Suzhou's GDP due to the loss of arable land as a result of significant urban growth in recent years.
12 From 1980 to 2012, the average annual economic growth rate of the municipality was about 19.83%.
13 In 1980, the municipality had a population of around half a million. In 2019, the population was close to 7 million.
14 Cumulative FDI (foreign direct investment) between 1990 and 2012 reached USD 101.97 billion. Since 2003, the city has surpassed Shanghai in terms of FDI inflows and consistently ranked among the top three FDI destinations among Chinese cities.
15 The China-Singapore Suzhou Industrial Park (CS-SIP) was established on February 26, 1994 when the Chinese Vice-Premier, Li Lanqing, and the Singaporean Prime Minister, Lee Kuan Yew, signed the joint development agreement for the Suzhou Industrial Park.
16 "As it stands, the Singapore model – sum, as we have seen, of a series of systematic transubstantiations which make it, in effect, one of the most ideological of all urban conditions – is now poised to metastasize across Asia. The sparkle of its organization, the glamour of its successful uprooting, the success of its human transformation, the laundering of its past, its manipulation of vernacular cultures present an irresistible model for those facing the task of imagining – and building – new urban conditions for the even more countless millions. More and more, Singapore claims itself a laboratory for China, a role that could lift its present moroseness. [...] Singapore represents the exact dosage of 'authority, instrumentality, and vision' necessarily to appeal. In numerous architectural offices in Singapore, whose names few of us have ever heard, China's future is being prepared. [...] After the iconoclasm of communism there will be a second, more efficient Ludditism, helping the Chinese toward the 'desired land': market economy – but minus the decadence, the democracy, the messiness, the disorder, the cruelty of the West. [...] Projecting outward from Singapore, an asymmetrical epicenter, there will be new Singapores across the entire mainland. Its model will be the stamp of China's modernization." In: Koolhaas, "Singapore Songlines," 1087.
17 Perry's idea represents an important American community planning principle for medium-density suburban neighborhoods organized around schools and bounded by vehicular roads, with houses arranged within a quarter mile from the center of the neighborhood.
18 At the end of 2014, there were 10,708 Italian multinationals (industrial groups and autonomous companies) operating abroad and almost three times as many subsidiaries: 29,073. More than 1.4 million

employees are employed outside Italy, generating a turnover of 531.7 billion euros. It is worth noting that the foreign subsidiaries of Italian companies have a relatively greater weight in manufacturing than other European countries (Agenzia ICE 2017a).

19 Turani, *I sogni del Grande Nord*.

20 Rein, *The End of Cheap China: Economic and Cultural Trends That Will Disrupt the World*.

21 In terms of concentration index, the city of Suzhou is considered the location of the main 'Italian industrial district' outside the national borders. About 150 Italian companies operate in the Suzhou Greater Area. In the first quarter of 2017, the total value of Italian investments in Suzhou reached USD 524 million, with already three new investment projects. In 2016, trade between Italy and Suzhou reached $2.56 billion (Agenzia ICE 2017b).

22 The Italian Chamber of Commerce in China (CCIC) is the only association of Italian entrepreneurs and professionals officially recognized by the Italian State (Ministry of Economic Development, MiSE) and the People's Republic of China (Ministry of Civil Affairs, MoCA), which works to foster the internationalization of Italian companies and promote Made in Italy in the PRC. CCIC's members (546 in 2018) include the main Italian businesses (state-owned enterprises and Italian multinationals), manufacturing and commercial SMEs, service companies, etc.

23 See: https://www.cameraitacina.com/it.

24 See: https://www.venetidicina.com.

25 De Martino, *Il mondo magico. Prolegomeni a una storia del magismo*.

26 De Certeau, *The practice of everyday life*.

27 Bianchetti, "Cartographies of protection."

Bibliography

Agenzia ICE. *Le partecipazioni italiane all'estero*. 2017. https://www.ice.it/it/sites/default/files/inline-files/IM%202017%20Capitolo%203%20-%20Le%20partecipazioni%20italiane%20allestero.pdf (last accessed: November 26, 2021).

Agenzia ICE. *Presenza economica Italiana a Suzhou*. 2017. https://www.ice.it/it/sites/default/files/inline-files/Scheda%20Suzhou.pdf (last accessed: November 26, 2021).

Appadurai, Arjun. *Modernity at Large. Cultural Dimensions of Globalization*. Minneapolis: University of Minnesota Press, 1996.

Becattini, Giacomo. *Dal distretto industriale allo sviluppo locale. Svolgimento e difesa di una idea*. Turin: Bollati Boringhieri, 2000.

Becattini, Giacomo. *From Industrial Districts to Local Development. An Itinerary of Research*. Cheltenham: Edward Elgar, 2003.

Becattini, Giacomo. *Ritorno al territorio*. Bologna: il Mulino, 2009.

Becattini, Giacomo. *La coscienza dei luoghi. Il territorio come soggetto corale*. Rome: Donzelli, 2015.

Berta, Giuseppe. *Che fine ha fatto il capitalismo italiano?* Bologna: il Mulino, 2016.

Bianchetti, Cristina. "Cartographies of protection." *Lifelines. Politics, ethics, and the affective economy of inhabiting*, edited by Cristina Bianchetti and Camillo Boano. Berlin: JOVIS, 2022.

Boano, Camillo. "Lifelines: the stakes of life in the project." *Lifelines. Politics, ethics, and the affective economy of inhabiting*, edited by Cristina Bianchetti and Camillo Boano. Berlin: JOVIS, 2022.

Bonomi, Aldo. *Il capitalismo molecolare. La società al lavoro nel Nord Italia*. Turin: Einaudi, 1997.

Braudel, Fernand. *Civilization and Capitalism, 15th–18th Century. Vol. III: The Perspective of the World*. Berkeley: University of California Press, 1992.

Colli, Andrea. *Quarto capitalismo. Un profilo italiano*. Venice: Marsilio, 2002.

De Certeau, Michel. *The practice of everyday life*. Berkeley: University of California Press, 1984.

De Martino, Ernesto. *Il mondo magico. Prolegomeni a una storia del magismo*. Turin: Einaudi, 1948.

De Martino, Ernesto. *The World of Magic*. Seattle: Pyramid Communications, 1972.

Easterling, Keller. *Extrastatecraft. The Power of Infrastructure Space*. London/New York: Verso, 2014.

Koolhaas, Rem. "Singapore Songlines." *S, M, L, XL*, edited by Rem Koolhaas and Bruce Mau, 1009–1089. New York: The Monacelli Press, 1995.

Lash, Scott and John Urry. *The End of Organized Capitalism*. Cambridge: Polity Press, 1987.

Liu, Tao and George C.S. Lin. "New geography of land commodification in Chinese cities: Uneven landscape of urban land development under market reforms and globalization." *Applied Geography*, 51 (2014): 118–130.

Magnaghi, Alberto. *Il soggetto locale. Verso la coscienza dei luoghi*. Turin: Bollati Boringhieri, 2010.

Magnaghi, Alberto. *Il principio territoriale*. Turin: Bollati Boringhieri, 2020.

Martin Sanchez, Luis A. "Producing Italy. Territori della nuova produzione." PhD diss., Università Iuav di Venezia, 2020.

Rein, Shaun. *The End of Cheap China: Economic and Cultural Trends That Will Disrupt the World*. Hoboken: Wiley, 2014.

Turani, Giuseppe. *I sogni del Grande Nord*. Bologna: il Mulino, 1996.

Wang, Lei, Jianfa Shen, and Calvin King Lam Chung. "City profile: Suzhou – a Chinese city under transformation." *Cities*, 44 (2015): 60–72.

Beyond the transport infrastructure: the paradigm of accessibility

Federico Cavallaro,
Alberto Dianin

From transport infrastructures to mobility lifelines

Deborah Tall argued that mobility and individualism are at the heart of our identity. Public transport, active and shared mobility seek to erode that combination, offering an alternative to the private vehicle and to all implications described so well by Roland Barthes in reference to the *Citroën DS*.[1] These forms of mobility have achieved appreciable results in some contexts known for the widespread network of public transport or cycle/pedestrian infrastructures: here, private vehicles are no longer a necessity and the problem seems to be the opposite, namely dealing with the increasing demand for alternative solutions. *Mobility as a Service*[2] represents the latest paradigm for rethinking in this direction the set of infrastructures, vehicles, and traffic regulations, namely the transport system. According to the *MaaS* vision, this system is established as a service available to users in the ways, and at the times that most suit them, thereby discouraging private vehicle ownership and contributing to reducing traffic costs and negative externalities.

The deviation between transport systems and vehicle ownership remains an issue within the transport discipline, albeit similar to other reflections on the relationship between the individual and the community, which are typical of our globalized era.[3] When referring to lifelines linked to mobility (*mobility lifelines*), it is worth changing our perspective to include a broader reflection on living and on the relationships that it involves. After the spread of Covid-19, it was clear to see how simply overhauling the infrastructure and/or the vehicular component of transport was unsatisfactory for providing an adequate response to mobility requirements.[4] The number of users allowed on transport was mostly restricted, but without truly rethinking the nature of the service. Mobility lifelines relate only partially to the infrastructure or the vehicles of which it consists. We must move beyond the ontological concept of infrastructure, recognizing their role as things and the relationship between things.[5] Noting that lifelines are seen here as spaces of support to life, mobility lifelines are responses to the need for a *relationship* rather than responses to the need for *movement*. Therefore, they are concentrated not only on the actual materialization of movement, but also on the reasons that make it necessary in contemporary living. The search for the meaning of mobility lifelines must be focused on two aspects, complementary to each other. On one side, it is a matter of understanding how the infrastructure can contribute to redefining the need for mobility and which forms the latter can take in an altered context. On the other side, it is important to understand which measures – not necessarily linked to transport – may be included in their correct planning. It is not a question of diminishing the role of transport but, rather, of accepting that means of transport alone cannot resolve all aspects of mobility linked to today's needs.

Fig.1
Mobility infrastructures in Northern Italy, pp. 90–91. Source: Luis Martin Sanchez.

This step can be translated into the deviation that exists between transport, mobility, and accessibility. Mobility can be defined as the capacity to move, while accessibility is the ability to obtain what one needs.[6] Planning focused on increasing one may be significantly different from

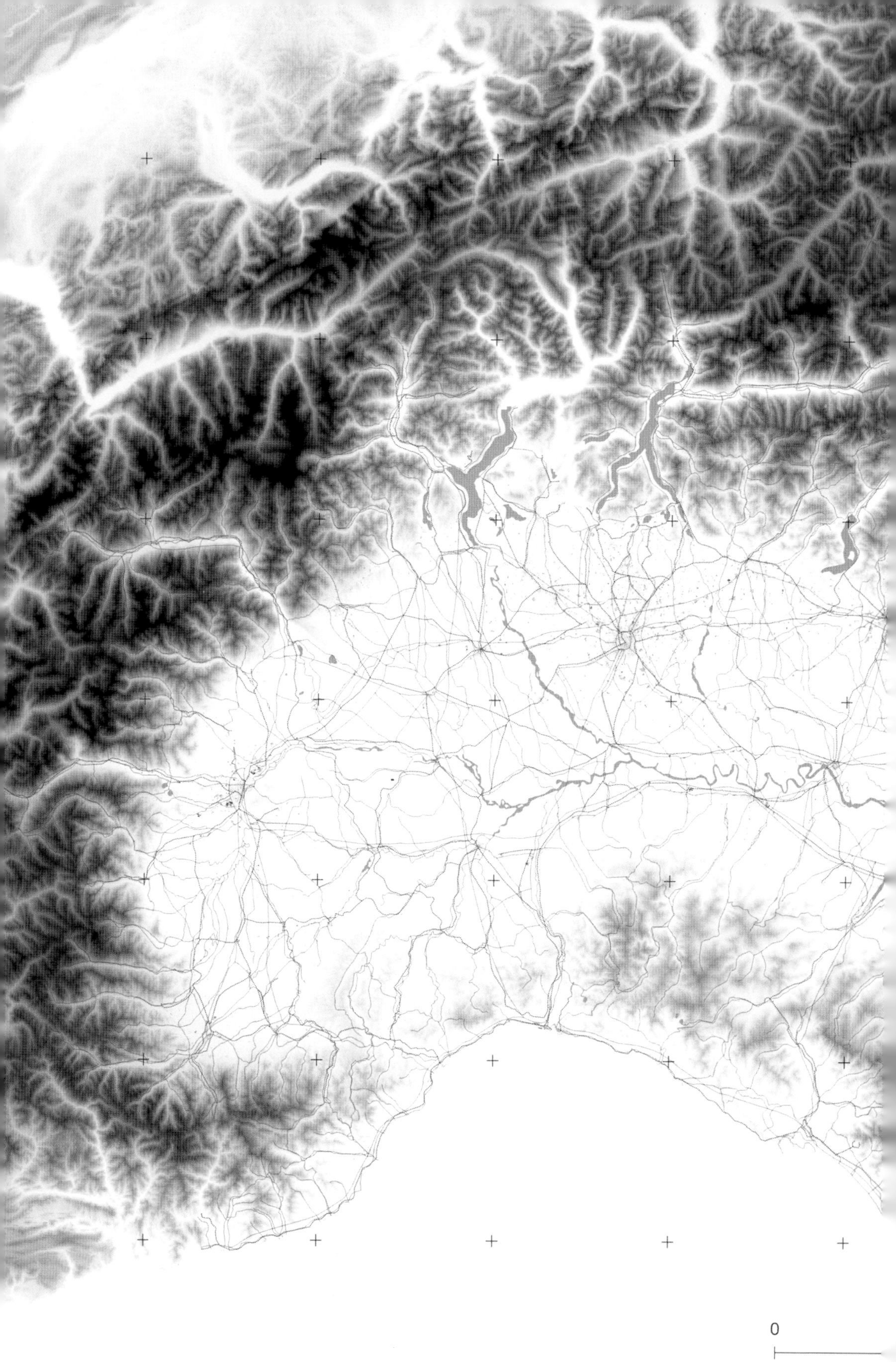
0

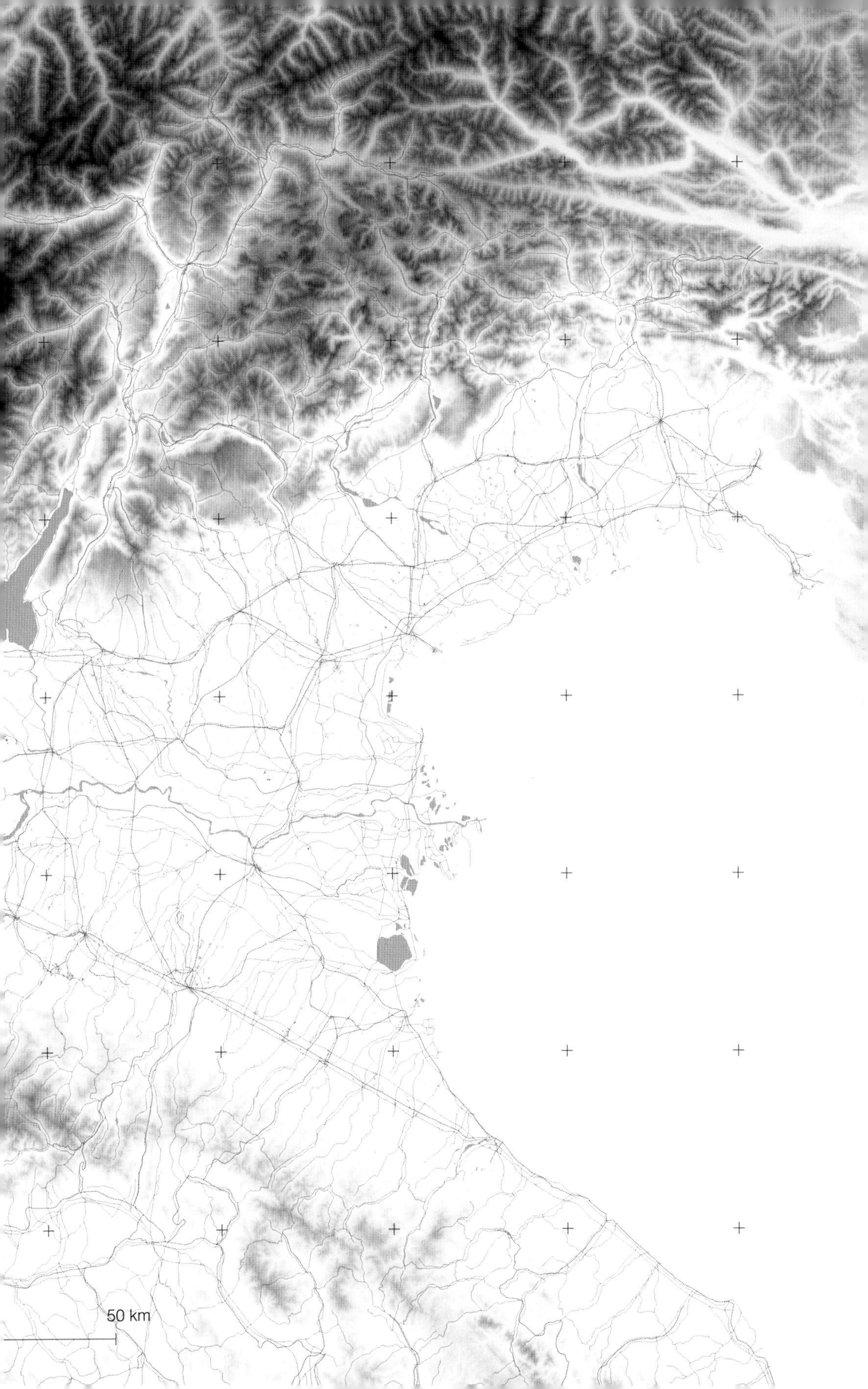
50 km

the other. For example, building a new road between a residential and an industrial area increases the capacity of residents to move towards that area, but it does not alter the need to use the car. Conversely, developing residential areas that include numerous employment activities within them allows residents to reach the workplaces more easily, without the need for high mobility. Therefore, a high level of mobility does not necessarily involve high accessibility, just as high accessibility can be achieved even with a low level of mobility.

Mobility lifelines can therefore be defined as a system of services, policies, and/or measures aimed at meeting needs that produce mobility, rather than the need for mobility itself. Their ultimate aim is accessibility and not movement. In this research, lifelines is used as a very broad and open term. In the case of mobility lifelines, they only coincide partly with the infrastructural, technological, and vehicular substrate of transport; however, they cannot be ignored. For example, the introduction of flexible working hours may be considered a measure that is part of mobility lifelines as it avoids movements at peak times or allows other urgent activities to be carried out at those times. This measure is not actually focused on transport planning, but it can increase accessibility, namely the ease with which people can perform their activities.

Digital infrastructures and digitalization of work as mobility lifelines

Information and communication technologies (ICT) are facilities not directly related to mobility which are able to provide benefits in terms of accessibility.[7] They depend on the development of adequate digital infrastructures but also the dissemination of digital activities in the world of work, education, or services,[8] along with the skills of persons who are to use these technologies. All these elements mean that ICT are an important component of mobility lifelines, as they facilitate a rethinking of individual mobility, reducing its systematic component, and at the same time encouraging the relational dimension (so-called "rebound effect").

ICT can increase accessibility in two ways:[9] (1) by giving access to opportunities such as workplaces, universities, or health services without physical mobility; (2) by streamlining mobility through detailed information on public transport and road traffic or by improving the time spent on board. There are few studies that address the relationship between ICT and accessibility, yet this relationship represents one of the greatest challenges in the industry.[10] In focusing on accessibility to workplaces, *digital infrastructures and the digitalization of work* are essential for the functioning of ICT as mobility lifelines: in fact, their absence or limited application may hinder digital work accessibility.

Digital infrastructures: in order to make video calls, access servers, and use remote programs, infrastructures with adequate standards are required. The European Commission indicates the *Next Generation Network* (NGN), a network that must guarantee a minimum download speed of 30 Mbit/s as the basic infrastructure for teleworking.[11] When

the speed is higher than 100 Mbit/s, this is known as a *Very High Capacity Network* (VHCN) and it is the optimal standard. Infrastructures with download speeds of between 2 and 30 Mbit/s are, however, acceptable solutions. According to the goals of the *Digital Agenda for Europe*[12] and the *Strategy on Connectivity for a European Gigabit Society*,[13] the entire European population should have had access to an NGN by 2020, while at least 50% should have had access to a VHCN. Furthermore, by 2025, the entire European population should have a VHCN available.
Digitalization of work: digital infrastructures can only be fully exploited if employers permit forms of teleworking. At European level, teleworking is, however, still an uncommon and non-homogenous practice: in 2019, only 5.4% of workers of the EU-27 regularly worked remotely.
In 2020, Covid-19 changed this picture: 48% of employees in Europe worked digitally at least on a partial basis, while 34% worked digitally almost exclusively.[14] There are substantial differences depending on the sector involved and the size of the enterprises. In Italy, during 2020, 90% of enterprises with more than 250 employees adopted forms of digital work. This percentage dropped to 73% for companies with 50–249 employees, to 37% for 10–49 employees, and to 18% for 3–9 employees.[15] Italian companies dealing with sectors such as the supply of electricity and gas, IT services, financial and insurance activities, real estate activities, professional and scientific activities, and education (corresponding to Ateco codes D, J, K, L, M, and P) tend to offer greater opportunities for teleworking. These data suggest that the composition of the market has a great effect on an area's level of work digitalization.
In this study, we focus on the percentage of workers/companies that enjoy/offer digital work opportunities. Furthermore, the number of companies with sector and dimensional characteristics compatible with teleworking is observed and compared with the total number of companies.

ICT in areas with low demand: Italian Alpine Regions

Areas with low demand may experience significant work accessibility benefits thanks to ICT. In fact, these areas are generally poorly served by transport infrastructures due to a lack of demand that can justify large investments. Transport planning, based upon logics of efficiency and operating with economic constraints, in many cases tends to overlook those areas or to provide limited public transport services or on-call transport services. They are not able to compete with private means of transport. ICT can offer a valid alternative to the need for movement in the face of a job opportunity.
Among the areas with low demand, the Alpine macro-region[16] holds a central role. It is made up of the set of regions, departments, cantons, and *Länder* which include within them a part of the Alpine territory. In an Alpine region, therefore, there may be both lowland areas – with metropolises, large cities, and rural areas – and hilly areas, as well as mountainous areas. It is therefore an articulated territory, useful for identifying the potential aspects and the limitations of ICT as mobility

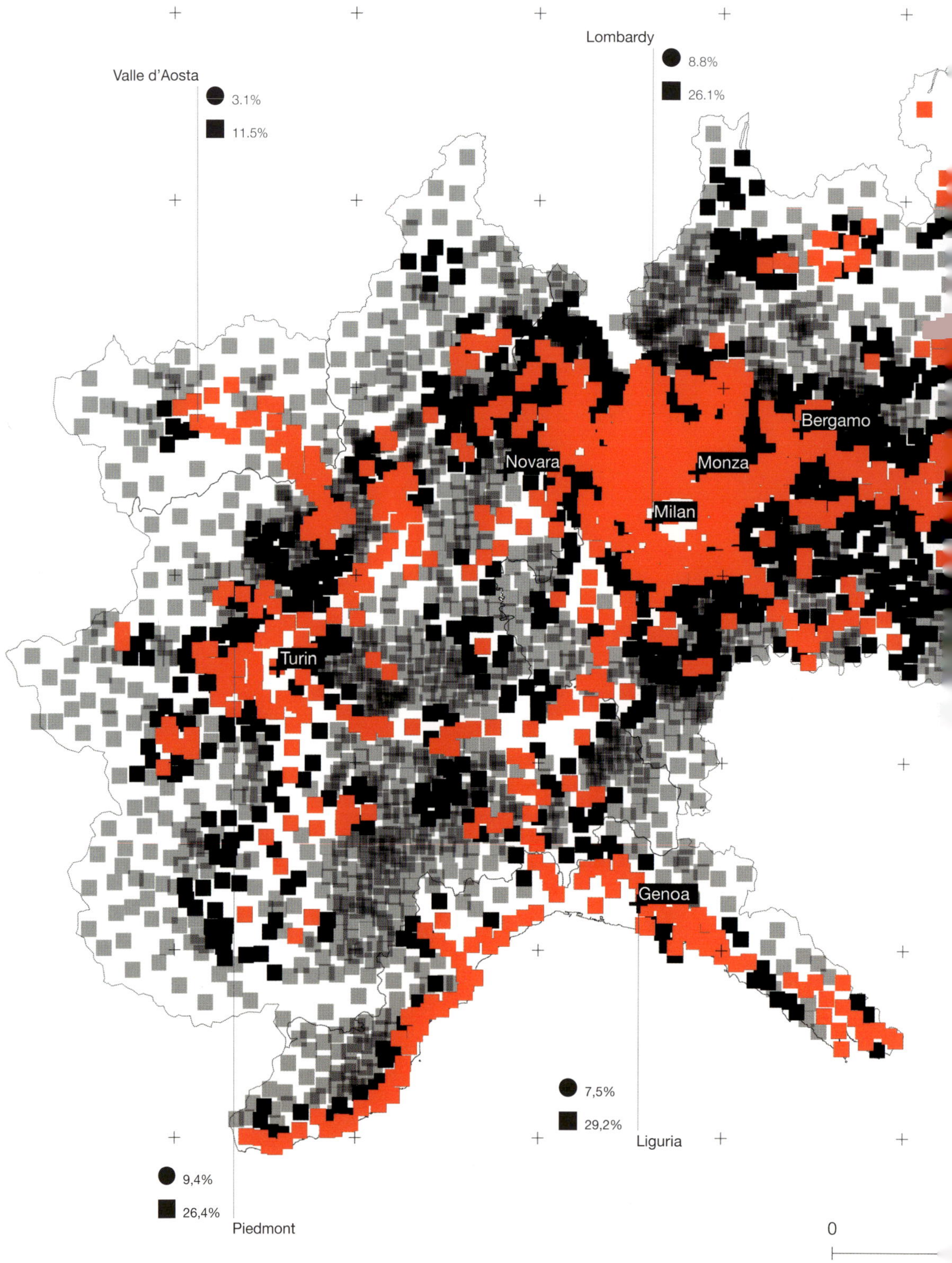

Lombardy
8.8%
26.1%
Valle d'Aosta
3.1%
11.5%
Bergamo
Novara
Monza
Milan
Turin
Genoa
7,5%
29,2%
Liguria
9,4%
26,4%
Piedmont
0

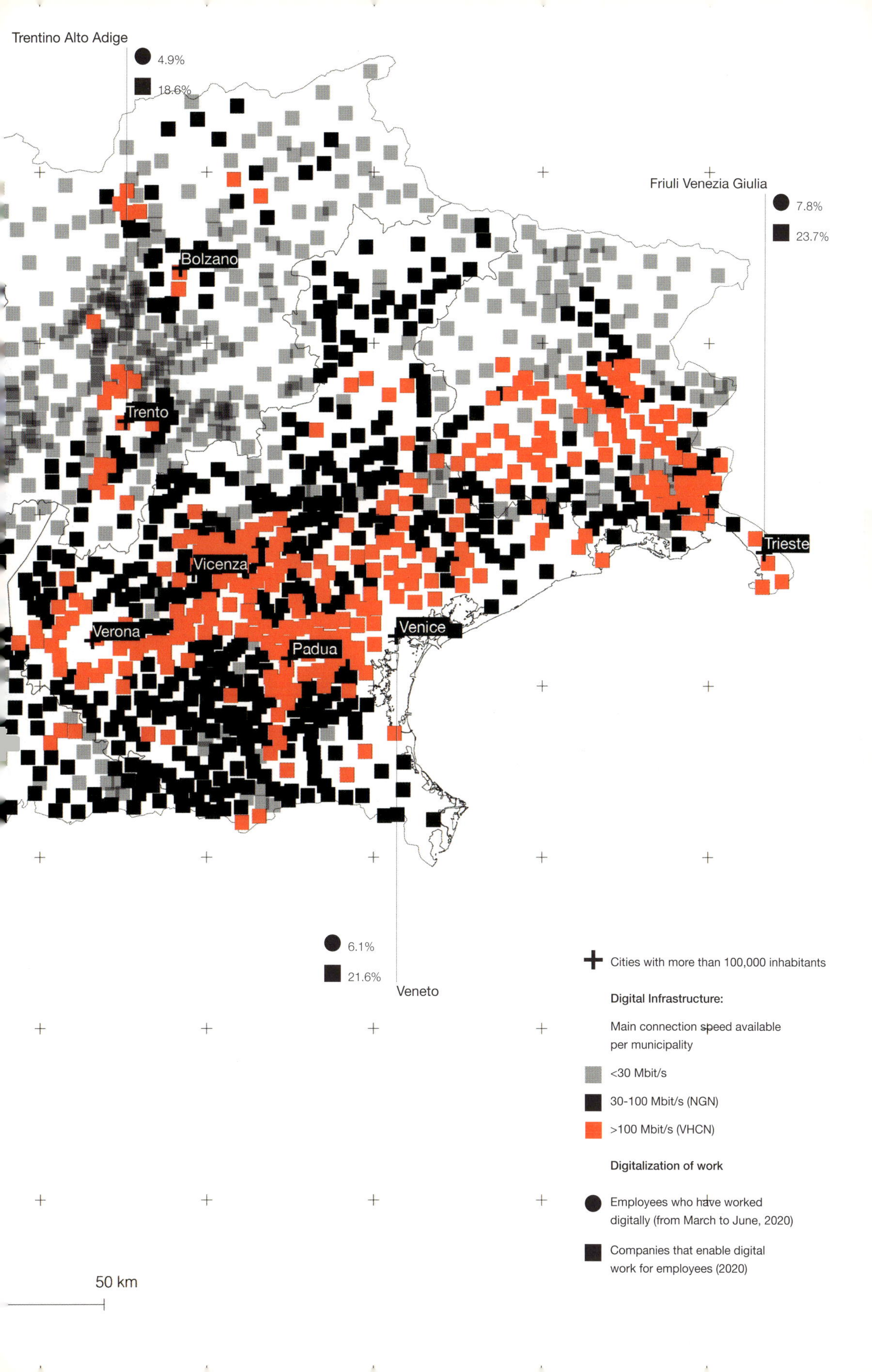
Trentino Alto Adige
4.9%
18.6%
Friuli Venezia Giulia
7.8%
23.7%
Bolzano
Trento
Vicenza
Verona
Padua
Venice
Trieste
6.1%
21.6%
Veneto
Cities with more than 100,000 inhabitants
Digital Infrastructure:
Main connection speed available per municipality
<30 Mbit/s
30-100 Mbit/s (NGN)
>100 Mbit/s (VHCN)
Digitalization of work
Employees who have worked digitally (from March to June, 2020)
Companies that enable digital work for employees (2020)
50 km

Bergamo
Novara
Monza
Milan
Turin
Genoa
0

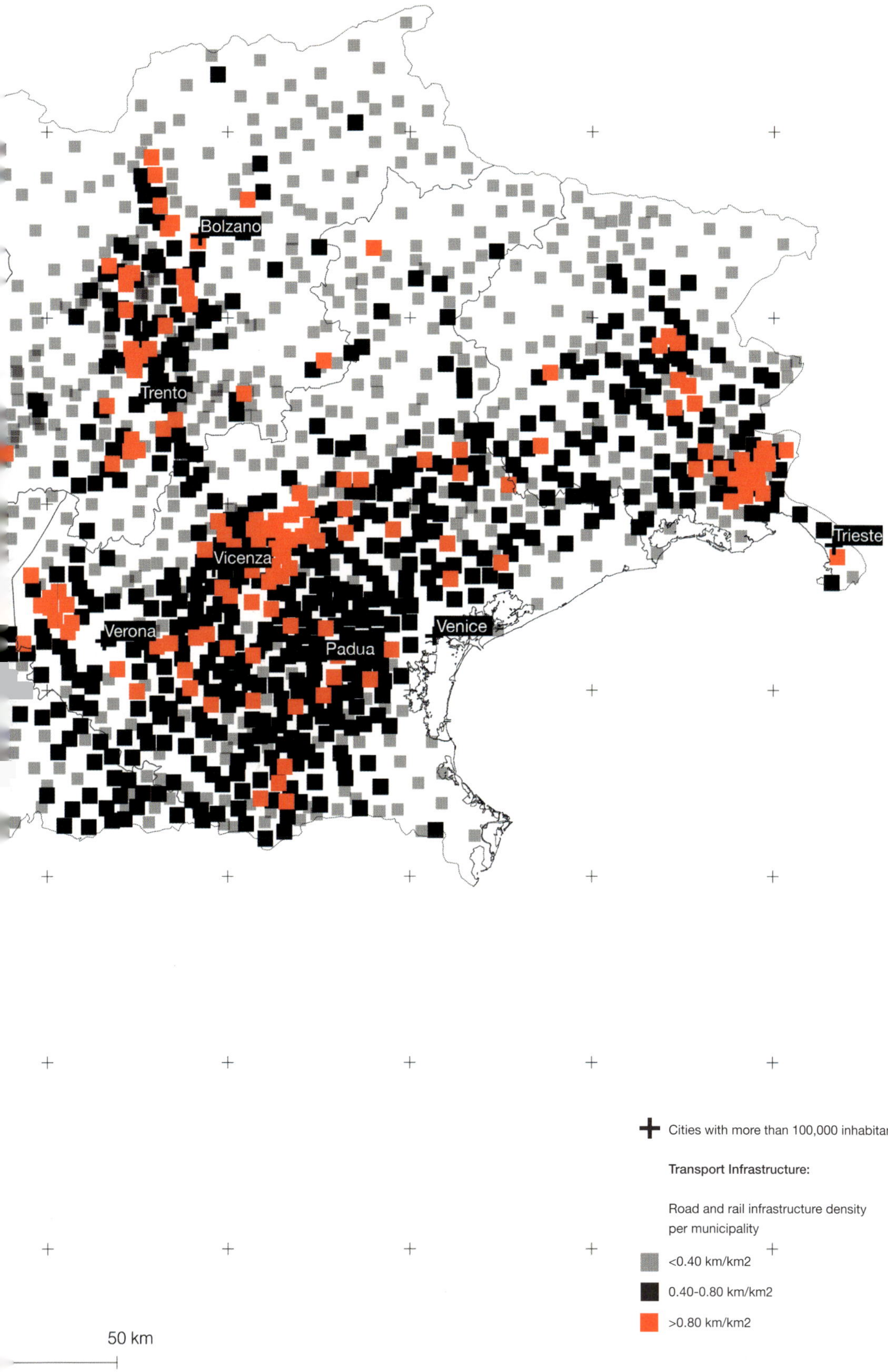

Cities with more than 100,000 inhabitants

Transport Infrastructure:

Road and rail infrastructure density per municipality

<0.40 km/km2

0.40-0.80 km/km2

>0.80 km/km2

lifelines. The urban/rural settlement difference often translates into an accessibility difference[17] caused by strong disparity of job opportunities and services, along with distances and supply of transport.
Potentially, ICT may represent a key factor for changing those urban/rural relationships and reducing their disparities. However, the urban/rural settlement difference largely coincides with the availability of digital infrastructures. The more urbanized areas of the Po Valley and the Ligurian coast are those where the VHCN is most available – areas shown in red in Figure 2. In confirmation of this, all 14 urban areas with over 100,000 inhabitants are served by this type of infrastructure. In addition, the VHCN also reaches the more urban areas along the Brenner axis between Trento and Bolzano, the Friulian pre-Alpine area, the Piedmont urban centers of Cuneo and Alessandria and their immediate surroundings, and the main centers of the Valle d'Aosta. Overall, the VHCN covers 26% of the municipalities of the Italian Alpine regions and 70% of the population, a value higher than the European goal (50% by 2020). The NGN coverage – areas shown in black in Figure 2 – which is considered the minimum network standard for those aiming to carry out teleworking, is not as widespread. 54% of municipalities, accommodating 89% of the population, are served by an NGN. The remaining 11% of the population not yet reached by this infrastructure – areas shown in gray in Figure 2 – represents a gap compared to the European goal of 100% coverage. This gap mostly involves rural areas classified as white areas in the *Ultra-Wide Band Strategic Plan*,[18] namely areas where private operators were unwilling to invest but which, for accessibility reasons, should be equipped with an adequate internet connection. In that regard, approximately 74% of the municipalities with fewer than 2,000 inhabitants and 52% of those with 2,000–10,000 inhabitants are not served adequately by an NGN. Alto Adige is emblematic, as 92% of the municipalities with fewer than 2,000 inhabitants suffer from this deficiency.
The improved availability of digital infrastructures in urban areas and their simultaneous absence in rural areas partly reflects the geographical distribution of transport infrastructures. Figure 3 shows the average road and rail infrastructure density in the municipalities of the Italian Alpine regions. Similarly to what is seen in Figure 2, the most urbanized areas also record the highest level of infrastructure density (>0.80 km/km^2). Conversely, the mountain areas close to the border, along with the Ligurian and Piedmont Apennine areas, record the lowest values. In this case, the percentage of municipalities with fewer than 2,000 inhabitants and a transport infrastructure density of less than 0.40 km/km^2 – shown in gray in Figure 3 – is equal to 52%. This highlights that the digital infrastructure currently tends to widen rather than bridge the gap between urban and rural areas.
As for the digitalization of work, it is worth comparing the 2020 data with those prior to the pandemic (2015–2019). Between 2015 and 2019, Italy saw a slight increase, despite still remaining below the European values. The percentage of employees working occasionally or daily from home increased, respectively, by 0.1% and 0.2% (against a European

Fig.2
Digital infrastructure and digitalization of work in the Italian Alpine regions, pp. 94–95. Source: map elaborated by Federico Cavallaro, Alberto Dianin, and Luis Martin Sanchez. Borders and administrative data: ISTAT; Digital infrastructure data: AGCOM, 2020; Infratel Italia, 2020; Digitization of work data: ISTAT, 2020a, 2020b.

Fig.3
Transport (road and rail) infrastructure in the Italian Alpine regions, pp. 96–97. Source: Map elaborated by Federico Cavallaro, Alberto Dianin, and Luis Martin Sanchez. Borders and administrative data: ISTAT; Transport infrastructure (road and rail): EuroGlobalMaps 2019, road and rail.

average of 0.6%[19]), reaching approximately 3.6% (daily) and 1.1% (occasionally) of Italian employees. In 2020, the situation drastically changed: between March and June 2020, approximately 7% of Italian employees worked from home, with a peak of 8.8% in March and April 2020.[20] The more urbanized regions recorded higher values. In particular, Piedmont, Lombardy, and Liguria reached values of 9.4%, 8.8%, and 7.5%. Conversely, in the more rural regions, this practice was less widespread, as in the case of Valle d'Aosta and Trentino-Alto Adige (3.1% and 4.9%, respectively). These figures are linked to the number of enterprises that allowed their workers to work remotely, which is, in turn, influenced by the size of the enterprises and the most widespread work sectors. For example, in Piedmont, Lombardy, and Liguria, approximately 27% of enterprises have promoted digital work, while in Valle d'Aosta and Trentino-Alto Adige the percentage dropped to 15%. This suggests that there are a series of factors which affect the spread of digital work in a certain location, also depending upon the labor vocation of some areas (for example, tourism or manufacturing).

ICT in Piedmont

Among the Italian regions of the Alpine macro-region, Piedmont presents a strong heterogeneity of urban and rural areas, thus being useful for gaining a better understanding of the role of ICT as mobility lifelines. On one side, the Metropolitan City of Turin is the fourth largest Italian province by number of inhabitants (over 2,200,000) and records a population density of 324 inhabitants/km^2. On the other side, the provinces of Vercelli and Verbania-Cusio-Ossola (with 167,000 and 155,000 inhabitants and a density of 80 and 69 inhabitants/km^2) occupy 89th and 101st place, respectively, among the 107 Italian provinces. In reference to the development of digital infrastructures, Piedmont (Figure 4-A1-2) is the Italian Alpine region with the highest percentage of municipalities involved in the *Ultra-Wide Band Strategic Plan* (BUL) (94%). Despite this, currently, only 57% of Piedmont households are reached by an NGN, mostly concentrated in 10% of the most urbanized municipalities.[21] Conversely, 75% of municipalities are entirely without NGN infrastructures. In terms of geographical distribution, the greatest infrastructural availability is focused in the eight provincial capitals, where over 80% of households are served by an NGN (Figure 4-A2). This condition also involves the peri-urban areas of Turin and the more populous municipalities on the Turin–Cuneo axis. The less populous municipalities have very little coverage: among those with fewer than 5,000 inhabitants, only 6.8% of households are reached by an NGN; a percentage that drops when considering only the municipalities with fewer than 2,000 inhabitants (0.5% of households). Currently, the NGN is not an evenly spread standard in Piedmont, particularly in the rural areas. Many Piedmont households (92%) rely upon infrastructures with speeds of between 2 and 30 Mbit/s (Figure 4-A1), which do not, however, provide optimal performances. Furthermore, 187

(A1)

<20% 20-40% 40-60%
60-80% >80% + Provincial capitals

(A2)

<20% 40-60% >80%
20-40% 60-80% + Provincial capitals

(B1)

<25 25-100 100-300
300-500 >300 + Provincial capitals

(B2)

<2% 2-4% 4-6%
6-8% >8% + Provincial capitals

municipalities, mostly located in the border areas with France, Liguria, and Valle d'Aosta, have poor coverage that reaches less than 40% of the resident households. These municipalities have fewer than 2,000 inhabitants (70% of them fewer than 500) and in total number approximately 70,000 inhabitants.

With regard to the digitalization of work, the majority of digital work opportunities in Piedmont are concentrated in the urban areas. Figure 4-B1 shows strong similarities with what is seen in Figure 4-A2. Five of the eight provincial capitals record the highest number of digital work opportunities: 7,284 in Turin, 729 in Novara, 536 in Alessandria, 462 in Asti, 450 in Cuneo, and 439 in Biella. These municipalities alone offer 43% of all digital work opportunities in Piedmont. The majority of the other digital opportunities are concentrated in the suburban municipalities surrounding Turin and Cuneo, while the more remote mountain communities record on average fewer than 25 opportunities. This geographical distribution plays a particularly important role when considering the dissemination of digital work as a practice exercised a few days a week or a few hours a day. The physical accessibility of the workplace remains an important factor, although it is partially balanced by the possibility of working remotely. Together with the number of digital opportunities, it is also interesting to note the ratio to the total ones (Figure 4-B2). Nationally, 6% of work opportunities can be considered digital. Piedmont stands below this average, with less than 5%. In addition, 85% of municipalities with more than 300 digital opportunities also have a strong digital vocation (higher than 6%); the same applies for 86% of municipalities with 100–300 digital opportunities, for 38% of municipalities with 25–100 digital opportunities, and for 18% of municipalities with fewer than 25 digital opportunities. This suggests some correspondence between the quantity of opportunities offered in a certain community and its predisposition to digital work. Similarly to what is noted for digital infrastructures, there is a non-negligible urban/rural gap also with regard to the digitalization of work.

The results presented so far have some implications on mobility lifelines. Firstly, the inequalities recorded within the Italian Alpine regions demonstrate that the urban/rural accessibility gap typically produced by transport infrastructures is exacerbated by the uneven dissemination of digital infrastructures and by the digitalization of work. To overturn this relationship, the development of digital accessibility policies even in areas with low demand must be accelerated. In addition, traditional accessibility analyses must be extended to include other areas that better reflect mobility lifelines. Some studies[22] integrate physical and virtual accessibility, but these are exceptions in a landscape in which physical accessibility still plays the predominant role.

Fig.4
(A1-2) Percentage of households per municipality served by a network with speeds >2 and >30 Mbit/s; (B1-2) number of digital work opportunities by municipality and percentage of digital work opportunities out of the total. Source: Map elaborated by Federico Cavallaro, Alberto Dianin, and Luis Martin Sanchez. Digital infrastructure data: AGCOM, 2020; Infratel Italia, 2020; Digitization of work data: ISTAT, 2020a, 2020b; Community Research & Analysis, 2020; Number of enterprises: ASC Atlante Statistico dei Comuni ISTAT.

Conclusions

The analysis of the Italian Alpine regions and the focus on Piedmont have demonstrated that ICT represent a key component of mobility lifelines. However, their geographical distribution is highly uneven. *Digital infrastructures* record the highest concentration and the highest performances in more urbanized areas, while rural areas – and mountain areas in particular – suffer from disparity both in terms of transport and digital infrastructures. This condition exacerbates the urban/rural accessibility gap,[23] which, together with other factors, fuels the progressive depopulation of marginal areas.[24] This gap is also partly confirmed by *digitalization of work* processes and by the nature of the labor market. As noted in Sections 3 and 4, some areas, including the more rural areas of Piedmont, demonstrate a low percentage of employees who practice remote working and enterprises that offer this working method. Therefore, the larger centers remain not only the cornerstones of commuting but also the heart of the new digital work offer.

This unbalanced condition in favor of urban areas may seem obvious, but a comparison with other Alpine states such as Austria and Switzerland reveals that it is a political choice, along with the result of economic and cultural conditions.[25] With regard to digital infrastructures, both in Austria and in Switzerland, almost all NUTS3 regions are broadly served by NGN (over 65% of households[26]). In the majority of Swiss cantons (excluding Graubünden, Valais, Uri, Schwyz, and Jura), the coverage is even higher at 95%. In addition, only 9% of the Austrian and Swiss NUTS3 regions classified as rural by Eurostat present NGN coverage of less than 65%. This condition characterizes, on the other hand, 70% of the Italian NUTS3 regions. Digital work is also more widespread in Austria and Switzerland, albeit in two different ways.[27] In Austria, there is a balance between employees who regularly and occasionally work remotely: 9.9% and 12.1%. In Switzerland, on the other hand, occasional remote work is more widespread than regular remote work: 27.7% against 3.9%. In both cases, the total percentages (22% and 31.6%) are significantly higher than that of Italy (4.7%). This confirms that there are possible new policies for promoting digital work, particularly among smaller companies that involve approximately 35% of the country's entire workforce.[28]

Mobility lifelines shift the goal of transport from satisfying the need for mobility to satisfying the needs that make mobility necessary. In other words, they make *accessibility* and not *mobility* the ultimate aim. In this perspective, mobility lifelines are not merely limited to transport infrastructures ("infrastructuring infrastructures," in the words of Keller Easterling,[29] capable of facilitating the actual act of movement) but also other interventions that go beyond the limits of the 'transport system'. The use of ICT and the spread of digital work activities are two examples of how transport planning can be extended beyond its traditional borders. By making systematic movements on a daily basis no longer essential, mobility lifelines open up new opportunities in terms of interpersonal relationships and, in the broad sense, relationships of living. This change may lead to the establishment of a new relational dimension, key for more complex ecology, thereby favoring those practices "of living capable of establishing affective relationships aimed at strengthening that living intensity that binds fellow beings together through difference."[30] At the same time, this could allow the condition of "coexistence without relationships" identified by Pulcini[31] as a characteristic of contemporary society to be overcome. However, this belongs to other lifelines and confirms their inexhaustible intertwining: a very condition of contemporary living, which makes it so complex to define but so rich in possible interpretations.

Endnotes

1 Barthes, *Mythologies.*
2 Liljamo, Liimatainen, Pöllänen, and Utriainen, "People's current mobility costs and willingness to pay for Mobility as a Service offerings."
3 Pulcini, *Care of the World. Fear and responsibility in the Global Age.*
4 European Commission, *Telework in the EU before and after the COVID-19: where we were, where we head to.*
5 Larkin, "The Politics and Poetics of Infrastructure."
6 Handy and Niemeier, "Measuring Accessibility: An Exploration of Issues and Alternatives."
7 van Wee, Geurs, and Chorus, "Information, communication, travel behavior and accessibility."
8 Muhammad, de Jong, and Ottens, "Job accessibility under the influence of information and communication technologies, in the Netherlands."
9 van Wee, Geurs, and Chorus, "Information, communication, travel behavior and accessibility."
10 van Wee, "Accessible accessibility research challenges."
11 Ministero dello Sviluppo Economico, "Piano Strategico Banda Ultralarga – Tecnologia."
12 European Commission, *Digital agenda for Europe. European Commission Directorate-General for Communication Citizens information.*
13 European Commission, *Shaping Europe's digital future.*
14 Eurofound, *COVID-19 series: Living, working and COVID-19.*
15 Istat, "Situazione e prospettive delle imprese nell'emergenza sanitaria Covid-19."
16 European Commission, *An EU Strategy for the Alpine Region.*
17 Moseley, *Accessibility: the rural challenge.*
18 Ministero dello Sviluppo Economico, "Piano Strategico Banda Ultralarga – Tecnologia."
19 Eurostat, "Employed persons working from home as a percentage of the total employment, by sex, age and professional status (%)," last modified September 10, 2021, https://appsso.eurostat.ec.europa.eu/nui/show.do?dataset=lfsa_ehomp.
20 Istat, "Situazione e prospettive delle imprese nell'emergenza sanitaria Covid-19."
21 AGCOM and ESRI Italia, "AGCOM Broadband map."
22 Such as Muhammad, de Jong, and Ottens, "Job accessibility under the influence of information and communication technologies, in the Netherlands."
23 Farrington and Farrington, "Rural accessibility, social inclusion and social justice: Towards conceptualization."
24 Velaga, Beecroft, Nelson, Corsar, and Edwards, "Transport poverty meets the digital divide: accessibility and connectivity in rural communities."
25 Amin and Thrift, *Seeing Like a City.*
26 IHS Markit Ltd, OMDIA. and Point Topic, *Broadband Coverage in Europe 2019 - Mapping progress towards the coverage objectives of the Digital Agenda.*
27 Eurostat, "Territorial typologies manual – urban-rural typology."
28 Istat, "ASC Atlante Statistico dei Comuni."
29 Easterling, *Extrastatecraft. The Power of Infrastructure Space.*
30 Boano, "Lifelines: the stakes of life in the project."
31 Pulcini, *Care of the World. Fear and responsibility in the Global Age.*

Bibliography

AGCOM and ESRI Italia. "AGCOM Broadband map." http://maps.agcom.it/agcomapps/bbmap/ (last accessed: June 10, 2021).

Amin, Ash and Nigel Thrift. *Seeing Like a City*. Cambridge: Polity Press, 2017.

Barthes, Roland. *Mythologies*. Les Lettres Nouvelles, 1957.

Boano, Camillo. "Lifelines: the stakes of life in the project." *Lifelines. Politics, ethics, and the affective economy of inhabitation*, edited by Cristina Bianchetti and Camillo Boano. Berlin: JOVIS, 2022.

Easterling, Keller. *Extrastatecraft. The Power of Infrastructure Space*. London: Verso Books, 2014.

European Commission. *Digital agenda for Europe. European Commission Directorate-General for Communication Citizens information*. Luxembourg: Publications Office of the European Union, 2014 (last accessed: June 10, 2021).

European Commission. *Shaping Europe's digital future*. 2016. https://ec.europa.eu/digital-single-market/en/connectivity-european-gigabit-society (last accessed: June 10, 2021).

European Commission. *Telework in the EU before and after the COVID-19: where we were, where we head to*. 2020. https://ec.europa.eu/jrc/sites/default/files/jrc120945_policy_brief_-_covid_and_telework_final.pdf (last accessed: June 10, 2021).

European Commission. *An EU Strategy for the Alpine Region*. 2021. https://ec.europa.eu/regional_policy/it/policy/cooperation/macro-regional-strategies/alpine (last accessed: June 10, 2021).

Eurofound. *COVID-19 series: Living, working and COVID-19*. Luxembourg: Publications Office of the European Union, 2020.

Eurostat. "Territorial typologies manual – urban-rural typology." https://ec.europa.eu/eurostat/statistics-explained/index.php/Territorial_typologies_manual_-_urban-rural_typology#Classes_for_the_typology_and_their_conditions (last accessed: June 10, 2021).

Eurostat. "Employed persons working from home as a percentage of the total employment, by sex, age and professional status (%)." https://appsso.eurostat.ec.europa.eu/nui/show.do?dataset=lfsa_ehomp (last accessed: June 10, 2021).

Farrington, John and Conor Farrington. "Rural accessibility, social inclusion and social justice: Towards conceptualisation." *Journal of Transport Geography* 13 (2005): 1–12.

Handy, Susan L. and Debbie A. Niemeier. "Measuring Accessibility: An Exploration of Issues and Alternatives." *Environment and Planning A: Economy and Space*, Vol. 29, No. 12 (1997): 1175–1194.

Istat. "Situazione e prospettive delle imprese nell'emergenza sanitaria Covid-19." *Statistiche Report*, June 15, 2020. https://www.istat.it/it/files//2020/06/Imprese-durante-Covid-19.pdf (last accessed: June 10, 2021).

Istat. "Situazione e prospettive delle imprese nell'emergenza sanitaria Covid-19." *Statistiche Report*, December 14, 2020. https://www.istat.it/it/files/2020/12/REPORT-COVID-IMPRESE-DICEMBRE.pdf (last accessed: June 10, 2021).

Istat. "ASC Atlante Statistico dei Comuni." http://asc.istat.it/ASC/ (last accessed: June 10, 2021).

Larkin, Brian. "The Politics and Poetics of Infrastructure." *Annual Review of Anthropologist*, Vol. 42 (2013): 327–343.

Liljamo, Timo, Heikki Liimatainen, Markus Pöllänen, and Roni Utriainen. "People's current mobility costs and willingness to pay for Mobility as a Service offerings." *Transportation Research Part A: Policy and Practice*, Vol. 136 (2020): 99–119.

MISE – Ministero dello Sviluppo Economico. "Piano Strategico Banda Ultralarga – Tecnologia." https://bandaultralarga.italia.it/strategia-bul/tecnologia/ (last accessed: June 10, 2021).

Moseley, Malcom J. *Accessibility: the rural challenge*. London: Methuen and Company Ltd, 1979.

Muhammad, Saim, Tom de Jong, and Henk F.L. Ottens. "Job accessibility under the influence of information and communication technologies, in the Netherlands." *Journal of Transport Geography* 16 (2008): 203–216.

Pulcini, Elena. *Care of the World. Fear and responsibility in the Global Age*. Dordrecht: Springer, 2012.

Van Wee, Bert. "Accessible accessibility research challenges." *Journal of Transport Geography* 51 (2016): 9–16.

Van Wee, Bert, Karst Geurs, and Caspar Chorus. "Information, communication, travel behavior and accessibility." *Journal of Transport and Land Use*, Vol. 6, No. 3 (2013): 1–16.

Velaga, Nagendra R., Mark Beecroft, John D. Nelson, David Corsar, and Peter Edwards. "Transport poverty meets the digital divide: accessibility and connectivity in rural communities." *Journal of Transport Geography*, Vol. 21, Social Impacts and Equity Issues in Transport (2012): 102–112.

Public Works' Housing Monitor: digital lifelines for urban advocacy in Lebanon

Nadine Bekdache,
Abir Saksouk,
Camillo Boano

Public Works' Housing Monitor is a community housing tool to protect and advance housing rights in Lebanon. The tool is used by residents from various marginalized social groups to report on housing vulnerabilities and eviction threats. Public Works Studio (PWS) provides individualized legal and social support, mobilizes tenants around shared grievances, and identifies any trends in housing injustices to then advocate reform. In doing so, it employs evidence-based research to support city dwellers in claiming their housing rights, while recognizing that housing is more than a shelter, as it is deeply rooted in social, economic, and neighborhood-based networks. Accordingly, the Housing Monitor raises attention over detrimental housing and urban policies in Lebanon that have led to inadequate housing, gentrification, displacement, and evictions. It is a project that tackles social inequity in Lebanese cities by shifting power into the hands of tenants (and dwellers in general), by defying illegal eviction practices by some landlords, and fighting existing laws and urban policies that overlook, marginalize, and abuse city dwellers. It serves all social groups, with an effort to represent refugees and migrants who are systematically abused by the country's existing laws and decisions. By entitling previously marginalized groups to housing support services, the project helps build social equity around the right to housing.

By reflecting on the monitor's practices considering the complex urban tensions of Beirut, the chapter addresses the experience of the platform as an infrastructure of knowledge where data gathering, community engagement, mapping, visual narratives, and academic research can reframe the space of publicness in a permanent set of crises.

The extensivity of violence in Beirut, (the 1975-1990 war, the 2006 Israeli bombing, the 2019 uprising and the financial crisis, the port explosion on August 4, 2020, and, of course, the pandemic) cannot be simply framed with the notion of crisis, even if incremental, connected, overlapping, and structural. What is emerging there is an exhausted territory, predated by the absence of the public, brutalized by the fragility of the common, and vandalized by the preclusion of a thinkable and imaginable future. Lebanon is living in a catastrophic present. Catastrophe is not a violent event that happens once and for all, that then goes away after having accomplished its gruesome work of leaving a world of ruins, to be fixed, restored, and recomposed with the limited resources of its people. Catastrophe in Lebanon has been a cumulative process, that erodes the vitalist and progressive message of those who are working to advocate reclaiming publicness, justice, and equity. Violence is not a linear production of events but a manifold and longitudinal overlapping force of dispossessions, explosions, removal, separation, excavation, and evictions that produce complex and contradictory spatial implications.

Public Works Studio's involvement in housing research started with a multi-disciplinary participatory project focused on the impacts of market-driven developments and policies on residential rights in Beirut and the creation of spatial injustices. Seven residential neighborhoods in Beirut were taken as case studies,[1] where we tried to understand how its history, its social fabric, economic relations, and the presence of political

parties played a role in the financialization process. By investigating such localized processes that produce spaces alongside claims and contestations vested by residents, a formulation of counter-strategies to neoliberal policies could possibly be activated. The absence of a social movement and strong public opinion on housing rights,[2] despite a growing housing crisis, can be traced back to post-civil-war (1975–1990) reconstruction of historic downtown Beirut. Damaged buildings in need for renovation were hastily levelled to the ground by Solidere – a publicly owned, privately managed real estate company. The Solidere project turned Beirut's former historic core into a high-end commercial center, causing radical demographic change under the banner of building a future world-class capital city.
The explosion in Beirut's port on August 4, 2020 brought back the concerns of a reconstruction process involving predate properties, that capitalizes on destruction and creates displacement and evictions for the benefit of real estate investments. The model of urban destruction that started with Solidere has continued to haunt the rest of the city. Since the mid-1990s, several waves of demolitions, ruinations, and destructions have targeted and are still targeting each neighborhood in the city, replacing its old fabric with new constructions that are believed to testify to the vibrancy of economic liberalism and a booming real estate market. Not only do these constructions reduce the significance of spatial production to economic profit maximization, but they also prioritize profit over the social dimensions of the city.[3] Such neo-liberal projects – initiated with the Hariri mandate in Lebanon 1995–2005 – aimed to establish Beirut as a global destination for international capital and investors, in line with other neo-liberal urban interventions in the Arab Middle East and elsewhere. The question of 'how it came to be the only option' is undeniably a crucial thread in understanding what alternative options are possible for the city's urban future.
Following that question, PWS focused on investigating rent arrangements in Beirut's neighborhoods and the implications of evicting residents under rent control through both market forces and a new rent issued in 2014 to deregulate all rent-controlled units in the city.
The dismantling of regulatory structures to boost investment in housing and speculation in the property market have been widely discussed in the literature on housing policies as drivers of inequality.[4] At the core of this inequality lies the dispossession of homes and commonly owned property. In the name of 'redevelopment,' privatization is facilitated, consequently producing expensive private homes for richer residents, rather than improving the conditions of the existing building stock. Moreover, particularly in the case of Beirut, the existing tenants have become victims of growing attempts to demonstrate the failure of rent control, as well as their personal failure for not 'owning' a house.
The structurally driven escalation in real estate speculation has increased pressure on housing markets, making informal construction and habitation the only affordable shelter options for low-income families. Studies conducted before the influx of the Syrian refugees (in 2011) state that 53% of the urban population live in informal areas. Housing

legislation issued since 1943 and their relationship with the social, economic, and political developments show that the state's housing interventions have followed three trends in three distinct phases that, when read in its complexity, depict a complex legal infrastructure of dispossession and precarization.

1943–1962: Sporadic laws to control rent or respond to crises

During this period, Beirut witnessed enormous growth. With economic activity centralized in the capital city, many rural residents migrated to the cities. Renting was a key means of accessing housing, and ownership was uncommon among city residents. The laws of this phase came in response to earthquakes and floods and aimed to control rent, but they did not address more comprehensive housing policies that model people's diverse needs and regulate urbanization in inclusive ways. Hence, the only housing solution available to low-income groups often seemed to be to build on public properties or private properties not registered in their name or rent or purchase properties from non-registered holders of the property. Consequently, during this phase, informal settlements spread in all Lebanese cities, most notably in Beirut, Tripoli, Tyre, and Sidon.

1962–1992: A marginal housing policy

During the 'Chehabist phase,' the authorities adopted a new policy based on strengthening the role of the central state and reinforcing its institutions. The existing governmental institutions were regulated and new ones were established. The state created one housing institution after another, the most prominent being the Ministry of Housing and Municipalities in 1973 (which was abolished in 2000). It gave them certain roles in providing housing to some underprivileged groups, albeit without any comprehensive and integrated vision for achieving universal access to adequate housing. Between 1950 and 1975, the population of Beirut rose from 300,000 to 1.2 million, and the number rose further following the Israeli occupation of Southern Lebanon and the subsequent displacement of inhabitants to Beirut and its suburbs. The absence of a national policy for affordable land contributed to the expansion of informal settlements, especially in Beirut. The disintegration and undermining of the central state during the civil war years led to the near-terminal collapse of the state institutions, including those concerned with housing. In the wake of the war, the institutions needed to provide adequate, accessible, and safe housing for all were not re-established. Instead, the above situation was exploited to strengthen private sector interests at the expense of public interest and to exempt the state from its responsibility to foster the right to housing.

1992–2020: A policy serving capital

When the Lebanese civil war ended, a wide-scale neoliberal phase set in and witnessed enormous investments to re-establish Beirut as a center for regional services. Successive governments worked to ease conditions for local and foreign property investors, and the ratios restricting the portion of a property that can be built upon were relaxed. An institutional framework for property investment that provided incentives to investors and lowered investment taxes was established. With the increasing demand for buildings and the surplus liquidity in the banks, a policy based on lending for homeownership arose. The central bank's status as custodian of this policy reduced the state's housing policy to fulfilling the interest of banks and investors under the pretext of the sanctity of private property. The rent control system ceased applying to new contracts and was replaced with an investment-based rent system characterized by contractual freedom. Leases signed before 1992, which became inconsistent with the insane rise of property prices, were converted [to follow the new system] in accordance with the needs of the property market and interests of developers. Hence, the rate of evictions from the city to remote suburbs escalated in the absence of public transport, vacant high-rise buildings replaced historical neighborhoods, and miserable and inadequate housing arrangements proliferated in cities' neighborhoods and suburbs. In the end, after successfully transforming the struggle for – and common interest in – access to housing rights into individual battles, the national housing policy, having been reduced to a policy of bank loans, collapsed.

With the outbreak of Covid-19 and the state's lockdown measures, threats of evictions to tenants renting informally in the capital, mainly refugees – who represent 1/6 of the population – and migrant workers, increased exponentially due to their inability to cover rental fees. As threats of evictions and insecurity of tenure became a principal and everyday manifestation of the state's failure to secure basic housing needs, we developed a platform called the Housing Monitor that prompts residents of all backgrounds and nationalities to report housing discrimination, insecurity, inadequacy, threats of evictions, transfer of property ownership, and vacant units and empty buildings. Reporting is a form of confirming the act of abuse associated with infringement of housing rights, which is mainly absented when tackling urban rights and more associated with other forms of physical abuse. After the port explosion in 2020, in addition to the monitor, a hotline and a campaign to report eviction were launched with the development of a legal task force to support city dwellers but also to develop strategies for litigation.

The Housing Monitor, as a platform, is a site that consolidates the multifaceted dimensions and outputs for housing-related research and actions. Besides reporting forms that users access through the site, we publish periodical reports related to monitoring and investigative long reads that unpack forces of evictions and which are grounded in research on space and property relations. The Housing Monitor also acts

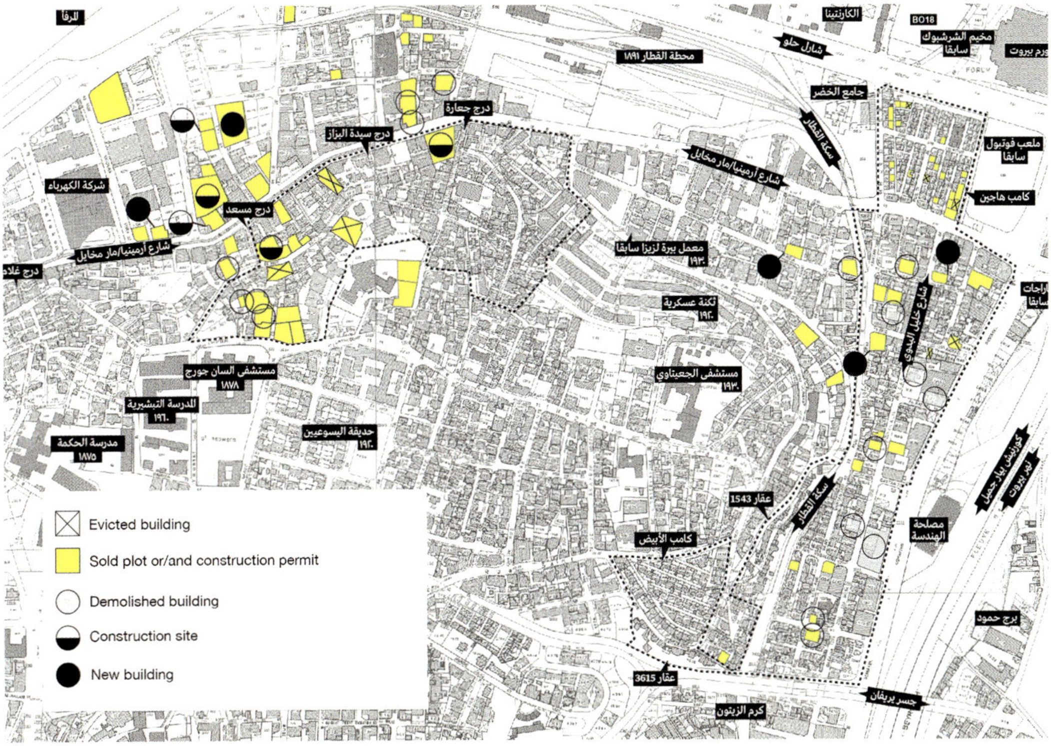

Fig.1
Mapping the transfer of property ownership in Beirut. The neighborhoods of Roum, Mar Mkhael, and Badawi (2007–2017). Source: PWS.

as resourceful platform for building a rights-based approach movement to fighting housing violations and advancing housing rights. With the uprising of October 17, defaulters of housing loans became vocal. We launched a call to defaulters to report. In less than 48 hours, we received more than 180 reports. A few months later, with the lockdown due to Covid-19, the Anti Racism Movement approached us as migrant workers and refugees started contacting them to report threats of eviction. PWS collaborated on developing the monitoring process that would allow us to analyze the data according to spatial readings and the conditions that set forth tenants/landlords' relationship.

Between October 2020 and May 2021, affected individuals were from 15 different countries, most being from Ethiopia (84), closely followed by Syria (45) and Sudan (23). Between January and May 2021 alone, 36 of the reporters were single mothers, all from migrant and refugee communities, while 142 reporters were under 18. Lebanese tenant reports account for just under on-in-ten (9%) of total cases assessed, while the remaining (91%) represent non-Lebanese communities. A legal task force of five lawyers and two law students was formed to provide strategic litigation, legal housing advice, and conduct case interventions. A total of 265 cases were submitted directly by individuals, 196 of which were provided with consultations, legal advice, field visits, and landlord negotiations. Of the migrant cases submitted, 53 evictions have been deterred so far with other cases underway. 131 households have been successfully referred to renovation (five) and social support services (126), the latter of which provides cash for rent, medical aid, and food distribution to beneficiaries.

The reporting mechanism is a basis for mobilizing. PWS started forming partnerships to grow and consolidate data, while seeking and training a network of volunteers in neighborhoods and cities to monitor housing injustices. Accordingly, the counter-mapping we engage in is by itself a political act. Along these lines, we see great value in unpacking neighborhood's spatial production and producing new representation with the communities that inhabited and continue to inhabit them, as an effective means to counter speculative real estate imaginaries. We delved into visualization as a terrain of struggle.

Since the uprising on October 17, 2019, spurred by an economic collapse, followed by Covid-19 lockdown measures, up until the port explosion, this has indeed been a year marked with 'exceptional circumstances,' with food, health, labor and housing security being threatened for the vast majority of the population. On August 4, 2020, explosions rocked the port of Beirut, causing widespread destruction to homes, businesses, and infrastructure within five kilometers of the site of the explosion. The disaster left more than 200 people dead, more than 6,000 injured, and around 300,000 displaced. The detonations destroyed the country's largest port, one of the busiest in the Middle East, and most of Lebanon's grain reserves. The city's dense residential and commercial areas were severely damaged. The damage is huge; of the 3,200 buildings in the affected areas, 1,575 were surveyed, 144 of which are at risk of a partial or total collapse, 57 buildings are at risk of non-structural component's failure, and 245 buildings revealed internal and external cracking. However, the losses are not limited to physical damages. In fact, we find ourselves, and all those around us, picking up the remains of our homes, our neighborhoods, and our lives.

The political battle is especially significant in the context of the damaged neighborhoods, which had been subject to a process of fierce financialization and real estate speculation during the past fifteen years. Today, the percentage of the tenants in the old fabric of Mar Mikhael reaches around 64%. Since 2006, the neighborhood has attracted investors, restaurants and bars began to populate the area and replace old industries and crafts. The investors were attracted to the neighborhood's low rental costs and its unique architectural and social character. In 2014, the area witnessed the opening of 50 new spaces for designers and artists, in addition to more than 70 art galleries, bars, and restaurants. Soon, those spaces were bustling at night with bar and restaurant users. As a result of this economic transformation, the cost for residential apartments increased from 2,100 $\$/m^2$ to 4,000 $\$/m^2$ between 2007 and 2015.[5] The increase in the land prices hugely affected the housing situation in the area and affected the residents' eviction process. PWS survey also documented the complete transformation of 11 buildings (out of a sample of 221 old buildings) from residential into commercial, mainly bars and restaurants, as well as 24 emptied buildings, amounting to 11% of the housing stock sample.

"We cannot stay. It is all dirt, grit and cockroaches coming in. There are no windows or doors. There is nothing. I clean three or four times a day, as if I did never clean. This wall in front of you is very scary. Three engineers came and told us that the wall will collapse, that we need to tear it down and build a new one. The repair works will take lots of time. And when will my turn come? In a year or two? We do not have the money to repair. The owner of the house we live in also lost her own house and moved out of the city, especially after the death of a lady residing with her in the same building. How can we stay here?"

Those were the words of Martine, informing us that she and her family will leave the house forever; the house they rented for more than forty years. To the other side of the heavily damaged wall resides Farah. She lived in the house for two years after renting it without signing a contract with the owner. She was also carrying her belongings and leaving the neighborhood after being told by the owner the following: "Do not come back, I will not renovate the house." Next to Martine and Farah's building, Zuzu resided with his family in a three-story building since the 1990s. He lived on the ground floor and used to work as a security guard at some bank but recently lost his job due to the financial crisis. Because of the blast, his son was injured in the head and needed 17 stitches; the family was unable to raise enough money to renovate the house and moved back to their village in the eastern part of the city of Sidon. Alia, the girl who moved in five years ago and lived on the third floor of the same building, left as well. The residents of the first and the second floor repaired their houses at their own expense.

The ability to repair and restore a house, and consequently move back to one's neighborhood, is directly linked to multiple factors, mainly the family income, whether their housing arrangement provides security of tenure, and the extent of their existing ties to political, religious, or even NGO support networks.

Across the street from Martine and her neighbors, a ground floor apartment was rented by Syrian workers who left due to the collapsing of the apartment's walls. They decided not to come back, especially after suffering from physical injuries. Sarah, Ababish, and Elsa are three Ethiopian workers among 5 workers who lived in the same building. Their apartment's walls did not collapse; however, it was left with no windows or doors. Even after a month since the blast, the Ethiopian workers were not able to fix the openings. They tried to repair the damages as much as possible using an amount of 50 thousand liras donated to them. One of them kept her job, while the others lost theirs due to the country's financial crisis.

In a nearby building overlooking a primary road, a 70-year-old woman sits in her apartment amidst the destruction. She is a lonely widow who rented her apartment under an old lease agreement forty years ago and intends to stay.

In the same building, there are four more apartments; two remain empty while the other two are rented to two old ladies. Before the blast, the owner of the building traveled and sold his building to a big company. The latter demanded the tenants to evict, they refused and asked for a five-year grace period. Now the company is repairing only one of the empty apartments. One of the old ladies living in that building is originally from Tripoli. Some acquaintances from her city visited her and helped her fix the broken windows of the apartment. As for her widow neighbor, no support was offered.

Conclusion

Between September 2020 and June 2021, the Housing Monitor received 127 reports of eviction threats from neighborhoods affected by the port explosion. 58% of reporters came from migrants, refugees, and different nationalities, while the rest came from Lebanese. This testifies to a clear exploitation of the explosion, where dwellers already anxious about their housing and their future in the neighborhood are being taken advantage of. In the aftermath of the explosion, Law 194 was issued that included an article prolonging rent agreements for one year. Besides being insufficient in providing the needed protection of housing, the article never became known by the dwellers themselves, nor was it enforced in any way to halt evictions post blast. A few days following the explosion, and under the pretext of cracked buildings, residents faced eviction pressures from landlords on the one hand and from security forces implementing the governor's decisions on the other. Large numbers of tenants resisted these pressures. No guarantees were provided for their return, and no housing alternatives were offered until the reconstruction was completed. However, the security forces exerted even additional pressure forcing those residents to sign documents that would hold them liable for refusing to evacuate.

Fears of permanent displacement are due to previous practices of the authority regarding the right to housing. They are exacerbated by catastrophic scenarios of previous reconstruction experiences. Beirut and its suburbs have been destroyed several times before. We have witnessed the destruction of other Lebanese cities, villages, and camps. They were rebuilt in a way that reproduced the same causes that initially led to their destruction, in the sense that reconstruction fostered class and other societal division or served specific interests. As a result, an additional population was displaced. The local economy was destroyed, and a large gap was created between the past and the present.

Dispossession in Beirut is a reality. It "works as an authoritative and often paternalistic apparatus of controlling and appropriating the spatiality, mobility, affectivity, potentiality, and relationality"[6] but in here becomes a "language to express experiences of uprootedness, occupation, destruction of homes and social bonds, incitation to "authentic" self-identities, humanitarian victimization, unlivability, and struggles for self-determination," but it also works as a relational dispossession from the world, from themselves, and from alterity in general that "can become the occasion not only of subjugation but also of resilience, courage, and struggle."[7] Dispossession can help to describe the relationship between the body and space in the dimension of power. And this helps us to move (sideways, but perhaps also forward) the traditional way of dealing with the problem of inhabitation, or better the camp as the possibility (or impossibility) of inhabitation.

That being said, the process of rehabilitating and reviving the neighborhoods of Karantina, Mar Mikhael, Gemayzeh, Jeitaoui, Roum, Fasouh, and Badawi will constitute a real political struggle. The authority will try to exploit the destruction to trigger a network of interests linked to the real estate and construction sectors while leaving inhabitants in a permanent state of precarity. According to Butler, precariousness is induced and produced by specific modes of political, economic, and social organization of life with the "promethean hybris and narcissistic indifference"[8] between who is worthy of living a good life and who is not.

If Butler's precariousness is the constitutive condition of existence, a general, common condition, experienced as a sort of "slow death, an irreversibly compromised time, as an ungovernable and arbitrary exposure to loss," the Housing Monitor becomes a "micro-political" lifeline, making life and its negation become "micro-political," "objects of ecology [...] spheres of existence [...] vital environments."[9]

"The opposite of precarity," Butler writes, "is not so much security rather the struggle for an egalitarian political and social order in which livable interdependence becomes possible."[10] The Housing Monitor for us is a way of imagining a cohabitation and re-establishing a correct relationship between life, space, and production that implies a commitment to the defence of the equal right to inhabit the earth, and thus a commitment to equality as such. The Housing Monitor, with its production, dissemination, and activation of knowledge, becomes a support of being-in-common, a fragile one, but one that includes everything that is opposed to the neglect and carelessness of the present. Fragility as an ethical resource in the making, to take up Butler, is capable of rendering fallibility and ambivalence as a source of responsible action capable of "taking care of the world"[11] to take charge of the future and therefore without "exempting oneself from the task of thinking a form of the world,"[12] The legal and communal support structured around the reporting mechanism of the Housing Monitor equipped many residents with the knowledge and courage to resist the injustices they felt. The establishment of a possible framework of a people-centered recovery process with legal and social support was further strengthened by organizational efforts at the neighborhood and building level. One such example is the recent establishment of the Association of Residents of the Neighborhoods Affected by the 4th of August Explosion organized in nine committees representing seven different neighborhoods and two minority groups (refugees and migrants).

Besides providing a social infrastructure, an 'alliance,' the efforts and process in building the association establish a new imaginary of spatial justice where those concerned are active agents in creating a new reality, while confronting and negotiating the multiplicity in needs and aspirations that arise.

Endnotes

1 Between 2015 and 2017 and through a series of workshops and guided fieldwork, Public Works Studio researched the neighborhoods of Bachoura, Tareek el Jdeide, Badawi, Hayy el Roum/Mar Mkhael, Mousaitbeh, Chiah, and Ras Beirut. More information can be found under the project: Public Works Studio, "Mapping Beirut Through its Tenants Stories."

2 The struggle for housing rights was reduced to negotiations over monetary compensation to clear land for real estate development despite individual and communal efforts to remain in place.

3 Makdisi, "Laying Claim to Beirut: Urban Narrative and Spatial Identity in the Age of Solidere," 660–705.

4 For example: Harvey, *A Brief History of Neoliberalism and Glynn, Where the Other Half Lives: Lower Income Housing in a Neoliberal World.*

5 Mediterranean Cultural Network to Promote Creativity in the Arts, Crafts and Design for Communities Regeneration in Historical Cities – MEDNETA, *Report on the Arts, Crafts and Design Sector and Urban Change in the Beirut District of Mar Mikhael.*

6 Butler and Athanasiou, *Dispossession: The Performative in the Political*, 24.

7 Ibid, 28.

8 Pulcini, *La cura del Mondo. Paura e Responsabilità nell'età globale*, 277.

9 De Fazio, *Ecologie del Possibile. Razionalità, Esistenza, Amicizie.*

10 Butler and Athanasiou, *Dispossession: The Performative in the Political*, 50.

11 Pulcini, *La cura del Mondo. Paura e Responsabilità nell'età globale*, 277.

12 Ibid.

Bibliography

Boano, Camillo. "Lifelines: the stakes of life in the project." *Lifelines. Politics, ethics, and the affective economy of inhabitation*, edited by Cristina Bianchetti and Camillo Boano. Berlin: JOVIS, 2022.

Butler, Judith and Athena Athanasiou. *Dispossession: The Performative in the Political*. Cambridge: Polity Press, 2013.

De Fazio, Gianluca. *Ecologie del Possibile. Razionalità, Esistenza, Amicizie*. Verona: Ombre Corte, 2021.

Glynn Sarah, ed. *Where the Other Half Lives: Lower Income Housing in a Neoliberal World*. London: Pluto Press, 2009.

Harvey, David. *A Brief History of Neoliberalism*. Oxford: Oxford University Press, 2007.

Makdisi, Saree. "Laying Claim to Beirut: Urban Narrative and Spatial Identity in the Age of Solidere." *Critical Inquiry*, Vol. 23, No. 3, Front Lines/Border Posts (Spring, 1997): 660–705.

Mediterranean Cultural Network to Promote Creativity in the Arts, Crafts and Design for Communities Regeneration in Historical Cities - MEDNETA. *Report on the Arts, Crafts and Design Sector and Urban Change in the Beirut District of Mar Mikhael*. 2015. http://www.enpicbcmed.eu/sites/default/files/medneta.pdf (last accessed: December 20, 2021).

Public Works Studio. "Mapping Beirut Through its Tenants Stories." https://publicworksstudio.com/en/projects/mapping-beirut-through-its-tenants-stories (last accessed: December 20, 2021).

Pulcini, Elena. *La cura del Mondo. Paura e Responsabilità nell'età globale*. Turin: Bollati Borlinghieri, 2009.

Pulcini, Elena. *Care of the World. Fear and Responsibility in the Global Age*. Dordrecht: Springer, 2012.

Culture and heritage infrastructure as 'lifelines' in east London

Clare Melhuish

As cities start to emerge from the worst phases of the Covid-19 pandemic, at variable rates, the theme of cultural infrastructure has come to the fore in the context of discussions around recovery, healing, and future resilience in east London – cultural infrastructure understood as lifelines for local populations who have suffered great losses of livelihood, family, and friends, and often regard government-led and top-down interventions with distrust and suspicion. The London Borough of Newham (location of the Queen Elizabeth Olympic Park) has suffered one of the highest rates of illness and death in the UK and has a low vaccination take-up rate. Here and elsewhere, the pandemic has disproportionately affected the poorest urban populations, consolidating embedded experiences of marginalization and leaving many questions to be asked about the intersection of public health, economic precarity, and improvisation, and a wide range of urban inequalities. In this example of an urban context defined by high levels of economic deprivation, lack of social mobility, ethnic super-diversity, and rich cultural variation embedded in histories of industrial activity and global migration to the city, it is important to understand how culture and heritage is recognized and operationalized as social and material infrastructure.

As the framing for the Lifelines project has indicated, the discourse in urban studies around infrastructure(s) has shifted significantly from a more technical and material understanding of systems (technologies in relation or relational technologies) which, following Larkin, are designed *to make things move*, enhance mobility, and bring modern economic and social systems into being.[1] An aerial view of east London clearly reveals the impact of this kind of infrastructure on the material conditions, spaces, and territories of urban areas. Actor-network theory has enlarged the discussion of technical agency to incorporate human and non-human actors within heterogeneous, entangled, and extended infrastructural systems, while Simone, for example, explores infrastructure as "a mentality or way of living in the world,' based on precarity, improvisation (or *bricolage*), and inside knowledge of how things work at both a technical and social level in poor marginal neighborhoods.[2] Larkin further explores the ideas that have developed around infrastructures as producers of embodied experience, through "the ambient conditions of everyday life"[3] which they create and points to the intersection with theories of aesthetics (understood as sensory, not solely visual experience) and affect, which have influenced understandings of contemporary and historical urban space and experience.

These perspectives, along with material culture studies' emphasis on the *social agency of things*,[4] have also shaped thinking in critical heritage studies. As a disciplinary field, critical heritage positions cultural heritage as affective sociocultural infrastructure, in comparison to the field regulated by conservation theory, authorized material science interventions, and top-down (often state-led) management processes. In Waterton, Tolia Kelly, and Watson's 2017 volume,[5] "memory is posited as an affective tool for the co-constitution of embodied, political narratives,"[6] and "the politics of affective memory [...] attends to the power of memory not to translate cultural objects, but to acknowledge their power to

Fig.1
Stratford Shopping Centre. Photograph by Clare Melhuish.

articulate pasts, identities, events and create atmospheres of experience and creative heritage."[7] They challenge the 'universalizing' thrust of theories of affect and emotion in the field of cultural geography, insisting on the recognition of 'other' and different ways of seeing, being, feeling, and remembering embedded in history and politics, based on principles of bottom-up participation.[8]

This perspective challenges the traditional positioning of heritage, focused on monuments, buildings, and sites of national significance, as an infrastructure of elite power and privilege *mobilizing* narratives of national identification, political cohesion,[9] and modernity within a linear historic frame of development. But it also acknowledges the critique by de Cesari and others of ways in which the capacity of heritage to produce "strong affect and place attachment"[10] is exploited as a tool of urban governance and political resource "to create good, affective citizens who care about their neighbourhood and its 'social cohesion'" while simultaneously producing "social cleavages by generating a remainder of people who feel that they do not truly belong because they are disconnected from (that particular) heritage."[11] Likewise, affective cultural and heritage infrastructure has been mobilized by urban policy-makers, developers, and investors as a strategic approach to urban regeneration and re-branding – urban renewal through heritage – marketing place attachment to incoming, gentrifying, urban communities and maximizing land values in prime urban areas, at the expense of existing, disenfranchised populations.

Defining the territory

This produces inherent tensions between the capacity of cultural infrastructure both to sustain social resilience and to drive de-stabilizing urban change, which is exemplified in the case of urban change delivered by the Olympic Legacy in east London, and the policy framework which has supported it. In the 1990s, east London was already defined as "the gateway to regeneration"[12] following the decline of the docks and manufacturing which accompanied the financial boom and positioning of London as a global "command and control centre."[13] The London Docklands Development Corporation (LDDC) was created to drive redevelopment in an area in which unemployment was disproportionately high (long-term unemployment at 63% in 1994 compared to 35% in London as a whole), and parts ranked "alongside the poorest areas of western Europe," with Newham ranking first in deprivation in the UK,[14] and second highest in proportion of ethnic minority residents at 42%. Whyatt's account notes that "vast areas of [...] derelict land were to become the key venues for industry, commerce and tourism for the 21st century,"[15] but that little value was attributed to the area's character as "one of the most culturally diverse in Europe with a distinctive history and heritage base."[16] She refers to an 'improving education infrastructure' at that time, but "a need to consolidate and maximise the collective potential of the heritage and tourism attractions in the area,"[17] including heightening attention to "East London as a main focus for ethnic minority culture in London," since "the depth of the activities promoted by these communities are not really seen or appreciated in London."[18]

At this point, the potential of proposed Millennium festival activities at Greenwich was regarded as a catalyst for change in east London, but the staging of the 2012 London Olympics had not yet been envisaged. When this opportunity was granted in 2005, it was grasped by the Labour government and eagerly embraced by the Conservative Mayor of London, Boris Johnson, on his election three years later. A new development corporation, the Olympic Delivery Authority, was created to oversee the radical transformation of the identified site in Stratford into the Olympic Park with its venues, athlete's village, and new infrastructure for the Games. Following the Games, the ODA was replaced by the London Legacy Development Corporation tasked with delivering the legacy use and community regeneration pledged for the park area and its environs, under the so-called Convergence Action Plan, which highlighted the high levels of disadvantage represented in the host boroughs in comparison to the rest of London. The policy was based on a broad commitment to the post-industrial transformation of east London from London's original industrial powerhouse into a new focus for the growth of the knowledge economy powered by a range of new cultural anchor institutions, alongside retail, business, and new housing, building

on earlier visions outlined in the 1990s. Today, these offers are embodied in the huge Westfield shopping center opened in advance of the Olympic Games; the Stratford International business quarter linked to HS1 and the Eurostar link; East Village, the conversion of the Olympic Athletes Village into the first of the new residential neighborhoods with its new postcode, E20; and the development plans for East Bank cultural and education quarter.

The LLDC's planning jurisdiction covers the park and its environs at the intersection of the four 'Olympic' boroughs, although it is due to be replaced by a new authority in 2025. The LLDC's five-year strategy or Local Plan declared a commitment to "a dazzling new arts and culture cluster"[19] representing a radical transformation of the historic and existing cultural and heritage infrastructure of east London to drive economic change. This vision was strongly supported politically, by Boris Johnson, then Mayor of London and leader of the Greater London Authority. The LLDC's plan set out a series of 'place-based policies' describing how its four key sub-areas were expected to change over time through the introduction of new forms of social, cultural, and economic activity. Each side of the park has historically been marked by a distinctive topography, demographic and socio-cultural landscape, and these areas have now changed radically through the development leading up to and following the 2012 Summer Olympics.

Stratford on the east of the park is the main shopping center for the surrounding area, with large swathes of small-scale residential streets extending east and south-east towards the old docklands from the old and new retail clusters. A significant number of new large-scale housing developments have been constructed around the Olympic site. It is also the home of the original University of East London campus, and a number of colleges established to provide further and higher education with a vocational focus for the local community. In addition, the famous Theatre Royal, established by Joan Littlewood, and the neighboring cinema have provided a focus for established local cultural life over many years, now designated Stratford Cultural Quarter. Stratford has been the focus of intensive redevelopment promoted by Newham Council since 2012, and the new high-rise housing developments along the edge of the Olympic Park form an effective physical, visual, and cultural barrier between old and new communities.

Hackney Wick and Fish Island now host the largest concentration of artists' studios and affordable workspace in Europe in canal-side warehouses that once accommodated extensive small-scale industry, but which are rapidly being gentrified and redeveloped as new housing. In 2018, the area was designated a Creative Enterprise Zone (CEZ) by the Mayor of London – the first in what was described by the GLA as "a bold new initiative for London to secure our future as a cultural capital and ensure artists and creatives continue to call this place their home"[20] and part of the cultural infrastructure policy initiative which Khan has developed during his Mayoralty since 2016. South of the park, a 26-acre residential and workspace development will transform the historic industrial network of canals and rivers carving up a landscape formerly

Fig.2
Aerial view of Queen Elizabeth Olympic Park looking north-west. Courtesy of UCL East.

dominated by tidal mills. These environs are of great historic and continuing importance to the capital in terms of everyday cultural infrastructure and creative production, as well as being rich in terms of ethnic and cultural diversity, notwithstanding the 'long-term deprivation' they have suffered; however, this significance has been under-acknowledged in debates about the future of locally embedded communities.

Universities and lifelines

The development of a new university campus for UCL, UCL East on the South Lawn of Queen Elizabeth Olympic Park, forms part of the extended cultural and educational program originally launched as '*Olympicopolis* by Johnson in December 2013,[21] and re-branded the Cultural and Education District, now East Bank, under his successor, Labour Mayor Sadiq Khan in 2016. This new designation, made up of a number of national profile cultural institutions, is distinct from well-established local destinations such as Stratford Cultural Quarter, and the existing and historical transport infrastructure – systems to make things move, as defined by Larkin[22] – around this site represents a further hard edge of material development segregating it from the immediate local neighborhoods south and east of the park.

In considering the question of the lifelines that transcend such material interventions, generating alternative kinds of complex spaces and urban imaginaries, the contribution of the university and its partners to sweeping away the cultural infrastructure and local heritage that have developed over time in response to the needs of the diverse local populations must be interrogated. 'Cultural infrastructure' has been defined at metropolitan level in London as an important element of what Mayor Khan called "good growth," enshrined in his intention to produce "the world's first cultural infrastructure plan, giving an overview of all the city's cultural requirements to inform spatial and transport planning up to 2030."[23] This document defined the capital's cultural infrastructure assets as including "all manner of venues and institutions including theatres, cinemas, music venues, pubs, skate parks, busking pitches, fashion studios and much more," and emphasized the importance of using the new London Plan "to protect creative workspace, heritage and the night-time economy" in London from development.[24]

But in 2017, a new report from the London Assembly Regeneration Committee, *Creative Tensions: optimising the benefits of culture through regeneration*, argued that while "culture helps boost communities,"[25] the dangers of gentrification stemming from culture-led regeneration were very real. It stated that "more data on culture is needed for developing strong evidence-based policies and spending," and criticized the government's survey *Taking Part* (DDCMS), running quarterly from 2005 onwards, in which cultural participation is defined only in relation to six key fields: arts, museums and galleries, archives, libraries, heritage, and sport. It recommended that "the Mayor should develop better quality data establishing the location of venues, artistic groups and cultural

Fig.3
New development, Fish Island. Photograph by Clare Melhuish.

events,"[26] which has resulted in an online, searchable 'Cultural Infrastructure Map' of London as a public digital resource.

These definitions of cultural infrastructure can be compared with the statement published in Newham Council's earlier *Community Infrastructure Study*, which declared, "'Culture' can have a number of definitions, covering the arts, culture, media and sport. For the purposes of this report [...] cultural activities in Newham include museums, galleries, heritage, theatres, cinemas and town centre festivals and markets."[27] In 2012–13, Newham's adult participation in library services and arts events or activities dropped to an all-time low of 18%, compared to London borough averages of 46.2% and 62.1% respectively. Of the four Olympic boroughs, Newham's participation rates in all areas were consistently the lowest between 2008 and 2013, with the exception of visits to museums or galleries in 2012–13 and use of public libraries in 2011–12.

Viewed from a critical heritage perspective, aligned with an affective aesthetics of social identity, there are very evident contrasts and tensions between policy-driven assessments of cultural infrastructure and criteria for participation, bottom-up perspectives on local heritage and culture, and the transformative interventions in the cultural infrastructure driven by the LLDC and GLA, initiated by Mayor Johnson, as part of a place-based regeneration approach designed to attract new

Fig.4
Declining canalside industry, Hackney Wick. Photograph by Clare Melhuish.

investors and more affluent communities to east London. Firstly, the rhetoric used to describe the Olympic Park site and environs as an "industrial wasteland" or a "fridge mountain" was not recognized by many local people, for whom it provided an infrastructure supporting livelihoods and social relationships. Around 600 businesses and 1,000 residents were evicted to make way for the Games, while most of the evidence of the site's multi-layered industrial heritage has been swept away through the remediation and decontamination process. A great visual resource for understanding the pre-existing material and social fabric of the site in detail, documenting 60 of these small businesses, is the publication by Davies, Davies, and Rapp.[28]

Between 2007 and 2011, this radical transformation largely erased the existing cultural identity of the place and the wealth of "affective memory"[29] it hosted to create a tabula rasa for a new kind of cultural life. This included the removal of all the archaeological remains. Since 2019, a site-interpretation project called *Groundbreakers*, run by Living Maps and funded by the Heritage Lottery, has endeavored to reinstate some elements of the collective memory, which has been lost in the process of remediation and redevelopment, through a trail of digital 'hotspots' across the park that will allow visitors to 'beam up' demolished landmarks, such as the Clarnico Sweet Factory, and listen to local people's accounts of their significance in their lives.

Secondly, a large number of local organizations, including Newham Council's own community neighborhood team, which have for many years provided small-scale, low-key opportunities for local people from different ethnic and cultural backgrounds to participate in the arts, including dance, photography and film, art, poetry, literature, music, and heritage, have been deprived of resources and physical space since the Games due to the pressures of surrounding redevelopment, resulting in a strong cultural and geographical divide between the park and surrounding neighborhoods. Local organizers say they have witnessed a diversion of resources to new 'big players,' the cultural institutions with national profiles, re-locating to the park; they threaten the survival of bottom-up cultural networks and infrastructures, or lifelines, which sustain local 'resilience': collective affective memory, social relationships, and identities embedded in locality. 1,500 languages or dialects are spoken in LB Newham, reflecting a diversity of cultures and customs, but the cultural divide between these residents and the new, more affluent E20 residential community in East Village is said to be bigger.
The framework for the new LLDC-led interventions transforming the cultural infrastructure in the Olympic boroughs, especially Newham, is its arts and culture strategy published after the Games, which highlighted the need to "build on the heritage of the area by enlivening our public spaces and connecting with local communities"[30] and was shortlisted in 2013 for the UK's Placemaking Awards. In 2014, following the mayoral decision to create a new cultural quarter on the park, Olympicopolis, the corporation's new Arts and Culture Strategy again underlined the significance of culture and creativity "at the heart of Queen Elizabeth Olympic Park" (in the shape of new permanent artworks and architectural icons) and its importance for transforming the area into a cultural destination: "The Park is already emerging as a dynamic hub for east London's creative economy and a fantastic setting for festivals and celebrations."[31] However, in the same year, arts participation in Newham, assessed according to formal criteria based on museums, gallery, and library attendance, was once again reported as among lowest in the UK over the previous five years. An LLDC report of 2014 further reveals the relatively low significance of the formal arts and culture sector within the local economy, as well as in the spatial landscape of the area, highlighting the predominance of workshop-type spaces with small, local work forces of less than 5 people; of these, manufacturing and printing businesses occupied far more built space than arts and culture enterprises.
These insights prompt a further interrogation of how local 'cultural infrastructure' might be conceived of in relation to the formal arts and culture sector, as it is defined within urban policy and economic analyses. It also prompts a review of what is to be understood by 'prosperity' in non-elite neighborhoods, where thriving informal cultural infrastructures, independent of top-down arts and culture initiatives, may make a bigger contribution to perceptions of wellbeing and opportunity than conventional household income surveys would recognize. The challenges faced by small-scale local community organizations sustaining

that infrastructure are to a great extent embodied in the promises made around the regeneration of the Olympic Park and its environs – the concept of East Bank as a billion-pound 'culture powerhouse' or 'culture boost' bringing a huge influx of new people into the area, particularly university staff and students.

Fig.5
The material and technical infrastructures of industrialization around the perimeter of the Olympic Park are displaced by the arrival of new institutions, in a re-writing of the area's urban heritage. Photograph by Clare Melhuish, 2017.

Conclusion

Many in those surrounding local communities have objected to LLDC's and UCL's re-writing of the area's urban heritage, the erasure of its industrial past, and the effects of gentrification which they fear will define its future identity and lead to their own exclusion. The processes of urban change in east London over the last two decades reveal a lack of engagement with the diverse histories and identities of the local area, embedded across transnational networks of migration and under-acknowledged, under-represented cultural infrastructures. Instead, a different and monolithic vision has been promoted by policymakers in the wake of the grand Olympic project, that endeavors to smooth over, homogenize, and improve a messy urban landscape and social fabric – Robert Park's "mosaic of little worlds" percolating unevenly through urban space – within a global system of commercial comparability, valuation, and exchange of space.[32]

Universities are entrenched in this game of commercial comparison and evaluation more than ever before, both institutionally and spatially. Yet there is great potential for the institutions involved as actors in the transformation of urban landscapes to work towards the recognition and reinforcement of existing networks and connections on the ground, cultural infrastructures that offer lifelines to local communities that desperately need them in the building of resilient futures after the pandemic, and the complex multi-scale spaces and contact zones which host them. As Boano writes in the introduction to this volume, "Lifelines [...] capture but at the same time sustain; allow many ways to exist without anyone taking over; draw uncomfortable but familiar presences; trace forms of exile and resistance almost leaning on what exists, what one would like to exist."[33] Holston[34] points to a comparable idea in the "concept of the possible" located in "spaces of insurgent citizenship," defined by informal practices of architecture, urbanism, and 'bricolage' which regeneration practices in European cities strive to flatten and empty out; while Simone's definition of infrastructure as "a mentality or way of living in the world" further underpins a re-evaluation of urban space and the diverse cultural heritage it hosts as a field of embodied experience, social contact, memory, and affect. Here in east London, where the old embedded material and technical infrastructures produced by industrialization are fast disappearing, new institutions have a significant role to play in recognizing and making visible the lifelines that will sustain the emerging urban landscape as the infrastructures of the future.

Endnotes

1 Larkin, "The Politics and Poetics of Infrastructure," 330; Graham and Marvin, *Splintering urbanism: networked infrastructures, technological mobilities and the urban condition.*
2 Simone, *Improvised Lives: Rhythms of Endurance in an Urban South.*
3 Larkin, "The Politics and Poetics of Infrastructure," 336.
4 Gell, *Art and Agency: An Anthropological Theory*; Miller, *The Comfort of Things.*
5 Waterton, Tolia-Kelly, and Watson, *Heritage, Affect and Emotion: Politics, Practices and Infrastructures.*
6 Ibid, 3.
7 Ibid.
8 Ibid.
9 Hall, "Un-settling 'The Heritage', Re-imagining the Post-nation," 3–13; Shore, "Introduction."
10 Beeksma and De Cesari, "Participatory heritage in a gentrifying neighbourhood: Amsterdam's Van Eesteren Museum as affective space of negotiations."
11 Ibid.
12 Whyatt, "Prospects and interventions. London east: gateway to regeneration."
13 Sassen, "The Global City: Introducing a Concept."
14 Whyatt, "Prospects and interventions. London east: gateway to regeneration," 267.
15 Ibid, 268–269.
16 Ibid.
17 Ibid, 280.
18 Ibid, 284.
19 London Legacy Development Corporation, *Queen Elizabeth Olympic Park and the surrounding area. Five year strategy: 2015–2020*, 2.
20 GLA, *Creative Enterprise Zones*: Prospectus, 2.
21 Evening Standard, "Boris Johnson: The Olympic park will be the Albertopolis of the east."
22 Larkin, "The Politics and Poetics of Infrastructure," 336.
23 GLA, *A city for all Londoners*, 27.
24 Ibid.
25 London Assembly Regeneration Committee, *Creative tensions: Optimising the benefits of culture through regeneration*, 20.
26 Ibid.
27 LB Newham, *Newham Community Infrastructure Study, Culture and Regeneration*, 1.
28 Davies, Davies, and Rapp, *Dispersal: Picturing urban change in east London.*
29 Waterton and Watson, eds., *Heritage, Affect and Emotion: Politics, Practices and Infrastructures.*
30 London Legacy Development Corporation, *Eyes, and minds, and dreams, and tongues. Arts and Culture Strategy*, 5.
31 Ibid, 3.
32 Lefebvre, *Le droit a la ville*; Lefebvre, *The urban revolution*; Ambasz, *The Universitas project: solutions for a post-technological society*, 466–467.
33 Boano, "Lifelines: the stakes of life in the project."
34 Holston, "Spaces of insurgent citizenship."

Bibliography

Ambasz, Emilio. *The Universitas project: solutions for a post-technological society*. New York: MOMA, 1996.

Beeksma, Anne and Chiara De Cesari. "Participatory heritage in a gentrifying neighbourhood: Amsterdam's Van Eesteren Museum as affective space of negotiations." *International Journal of Heritage Studies*, Vol. 25, No. 9 (2018): 1–18.

Davies, Marion, Juliet Davies, and Debra Rapp. *Dispersal: picturing urban change in east London*. London: Historic England, 2017.

Department for Digital, Culture, Media & Sport. "Taking Part Survey." Last updated June 24, 2021. https://www.gov.uk/guidance/taking-part-survey (last accessed: July 12, 2021).

Evening Standard. "Boris Johnson: The Olympic park will be the Albertopolis of the east." *Evening Standard*, December 5, 2013. https://www.standard.co.uk/comment/comment/boris-johnson-the-olympic-park-will-be-the-albertopolis-of-the-east-8982871.html (last accessed: July 12, 2021).

Gell, Alfred. *Art and Agency: An Anthropological Theory*. Oxford: Oxford University Press, 1998.

GLA. *A City for all Londoners*. London: GLA, 2016. https://www.london.gov.uk/sites/default/files/city_for_all_londoners_nov_2016.pdf (last accessed: July 12, 2021).

GLA. *Creative Enterprise Zones: Prospectus*. London: GLA, 2017. https://www.london.gov.uk/sites/default/files/creative-enterprise-zones_prospectus-2017.pdf (last accessed: July 12, 2021).

Graham, Steve and Simon Marvin. *Splintering urbanism: Networked infrastructures, technological mobilities and the urban condition*. London; New York: Routledge, 2001.

Hall, Stuart. "Un-settling 'The Heritage', Re-imagining the Post-nation." *Third Text*, Vol. 13, Issue 49, (1999): 3–13.

Holston, James. "Spaces of insurgent citizenship." *Architecture and anthropology*, edited by Clare Melhuish. London: Academy Editions, 1996.

Larkin, Brian. "The Politics and Poetics of Infrastructure." *Annual Review of Anthropologist*, Vol. 42 (2013): 327–343.

LB Newham. *Newham Community Infrastructure Study, Culture and Regeneration*. London: LB Newham, 2010.

Lefebvre, Henri. *Le droit a la ville*. Paris: Editions Anthropos, 1968.

Lefebvre, Henri. *The urban revolution*. Minneapolis: University of Minnesota Press, 2003.

London Assembly Regeneration Committee. *Creative tensions: Optimising the benefits of culture through regeneration*. London: London Assembly Regeneration Committee, 2017.

London Legacy Development Corporation. *Eyes, and minds, and dreams, and tongues. Arts and Culture Strategy*. 2014. http://www.queenelizabetholympicpark.co.uk/~/media/qeop/files/public/lldc_artculture-strategy_webhigh.pdf (last accessed: July 12, 2021).

London Legacy Development Corporation. *Queen Elizabeth Olympic Park and the surrounding area. Five year strategy: 2015–2020*. 2015.

Mayor of London. *A City for all Londoners*. London: GLA, 2016.

Miller, Daniel. *The Comfort of Things*. Cambridge: Polity Press, 2008.

Sassen, Saskia. "The Global City: Introducing a Concept." *The Brown Journal of World Affairs* 11, No. 2 (2005): 27–43.

Shore, Cris. "Introduction." *Elite Cultures: Anthropological Perspectives*, edited by Stephen Nugent and Cris Shore. London: Routledge, 2002.

Simone, AbdouMaliq. *Improvised Lives: Rhythms of Endurance in an Urban South*. Cambridge: Polity Press, 2019.

Waterton, Emma, Divya P. Tolia-Kelly, and Steve Watson, eds. *Heritage, Affect and Emotion: Politics, Practices and Infrastructures.* London: Routledge, 2017.

Whyatt, Anna. "Prospects and interventions. London east: gateway to regeneration." *Rising in the East: The Regeneration of East London*, edited by Tim Butler and Michael Rustin, 265–287. London: Lawrence and Wishart, 1996.

Part 2
Spaces of lifelines and lifelines of spaces

Lifelines are a movement, a dynamic, and a thing. A disambientation, as Morizot would say, which can see the different emergence of multiplicity, of vital spaces, of worlds as they configure themselves and become space. It is not a question of celebrating some form of vitalism but of creating a thought about space and its making. It is about grasping the spatial expression of sociality, of politics, of dispossessions and protections. To make these spatialities occasions for reflection and action within design tensions.

Bodily knowledges and spatial production practices in the Ecuadorian Amazon: a decolonial analysis

Fernanda Luzuriaga Torres

The foothills of the Ecuadorian Amazon are inhabited by a multiplicity of border peoples and social groups, which can be described as 'threshold dwellers,' characterized by an extreme diversity of dwelling practices and forms of spatial production. In this interaction, diverse colonizing, extractive phenomena, along with powerful fictions such as gender and race play a central role. In this sense, there is a pending task here.

In this context, it is important to go beyond making use of conceptual tensions, dualisms, irreducible epistemic pairs, theoretically obsolete, as almost emblematic devices that have managed to categorize the Amazonian territory. My aim here is to map and locate spatial patterns and logics, when assuming specific postures, practices of relationship and care in the face of the various threads of 'colonialities of power,' which are here woven into the 'other,' and that Aníbal Quijano[1] would call "colonial difference."[2]

How to distinguish these logics of spatial production, how to identify spaces of care, protection, lifelines supporting lives and ecologies in an environment transformed by extractive logics on a large scale? How to make visible this heterogeneous set of resistance practices in urban planning analytical tools and design practices? How to identify practices of the relationship and relate them to socio-spatial structures given or to be configured?

Observing the Tena Canton, located in the territories of the Ecuadorian Amazon, it is possible to identify liminal spatial devices, nested ecologies, inhabited by a multiplicity of border peoples and social groups. The supported hypothesis is an investigation into possible lifelines as forms of relationship between different environments and framing them as properly 'decolonial,' innovative, ecological strategies for the Ecuadorian Amazon, far from Western paradigms. A decolonial lens to read lifelines can be a productive approach allowing a relational perspective that emphasize certain practices of care and relationship of the body with the territory.[3]

In this framework, the practices of the relationship between bodies and the spaces of the Ecuadorian Amazon embody a 'thinking-doing' in defense of the territory, which makes coexistence possible, giving rise to regenerative spatial logics, forms of relationship, lifelines.[4] Here, I suggest lifelines as a break in the face of territorial logics imposed by contemporary discursive scenarios, focused on extractive and environmental problems organized chronologically in a timeline.

Borders

The Tena Canton has around 61,000 inhabitants.[5] The economic system of this territory is largely based on oil extraction activities and on a network of tourist infrastructures managed in some cases by local communities.[6] The urban system is defined by a series of centers arranged along the E45 Troncal Amazónica road, highway 436, where the parishes of Pano, Talag, Tena, Puerto Napo, Misahuallí, Ahuano, and Chontapunta are located.[7] Along the road artery, the settlements tend to

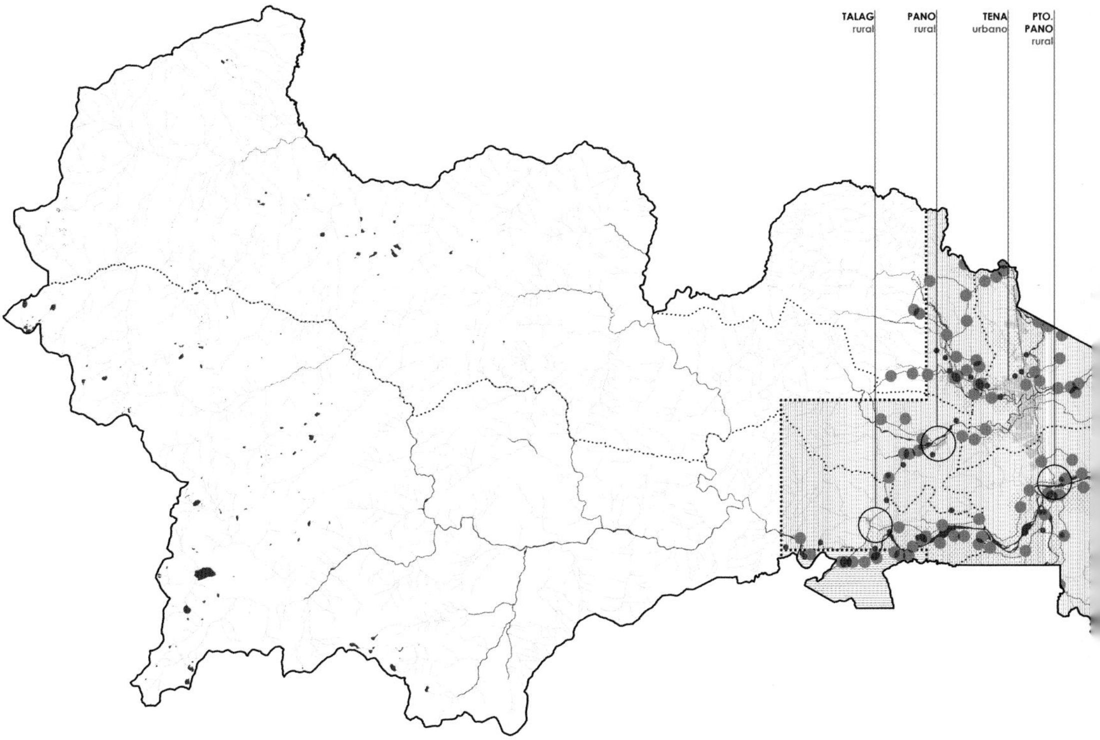

grow according to logics of linear extension, with low density, articulating in the densest parts in comb structures. Tena Canton is inhabited by a variety of populations, marked by a diversity of dwelling and spatial production practices. On the one hand, there are the *mestizos* (colonists), who mainly inhabit urban centers in a strictly western way, on the other, there are indigenous populations settled essentially in the forests, rural areas, and peri-urban areas of the main population centers.[8] This second group is largely made up of the Kichwa, an Andean population transplanted already in the sixteenth century to the Andean foothills by the Spanish colonizers and later attracted by the processes of *Agrarian Reform and Colonization*, carried out by the State in the 1970s through the *Ecuadorian Institute for Agrarian Reform and Colonization* (IERAC);[9] and, to a lesser extent, of native communities of indigenous peoples, in this case the Waorani.[10]

Fig.1
Tena Canton. Urban-rural matrix. Source: Fernanda Luzuriaga Torres.

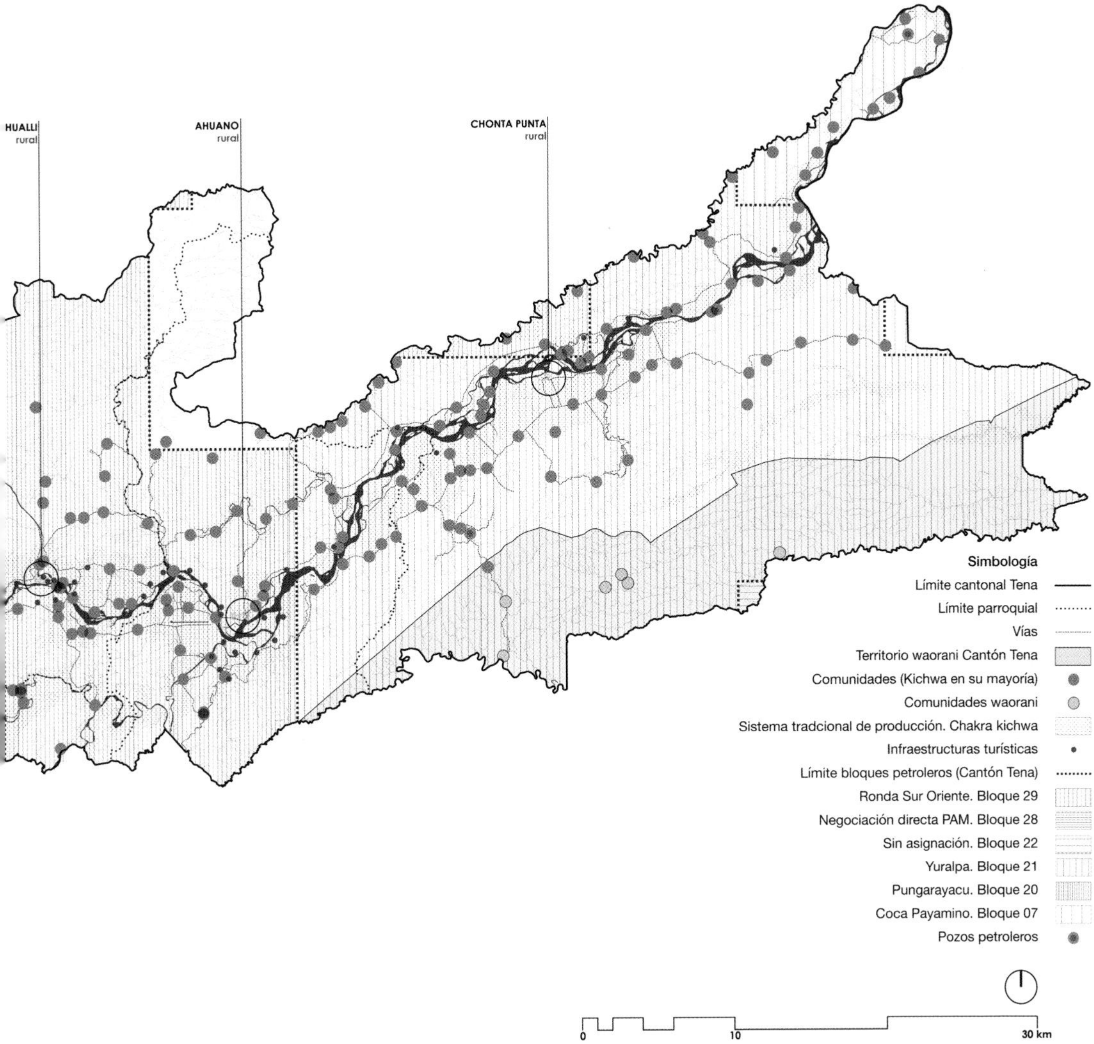

Now, the Agrarian Reform and Colonization requires us to stop and inquire about its premises.[11] This process developed between the end of the nineteenth century and the first half of the twentieth century and it was opposed through the constant and firm actions of the indigenous movements of the Andes led by women.[12] For local indigenous peoples and nationalities, the expropriation of their lands in the process of Spanish colonization also represented a destruction of their bodily knowledge, not only that of the man but also that of the woman, since the whole family was obliged to comply with the stipulated jobs on the farm.[13] This enclosure of indigenous men and women, according to Quijano, was marked at the beginning by a systematic repression that "*recayó, ante todo, sobre los modos de conocer, de producir conocimiento, de producir perspectivas, imágenes y sistemas de imágenes, símbolos, modos de significación; sobre los recursos, patrones e instrumentos de expresión*

Fig.2
Tena Canton. Spatial colonization pattern promoted by the IERAC. Source: Fernanda Luzuriaga Torres.

formalizada y objetivada, intelectual o visual."[14] This aimed to continue the imposition of colonial socio-spatial models and patterns, additionally impressing a notion of mystification on local knowledges and spatial production practices.[15] Therefore, the struggles led by women also demanded the liberation of their bodily knowledge; and although the recovery of their lands was not achieved, these struggles managed to dismantle the *hacienda* system.[16] According to Silvia Federici,[17] this enclosure of bodily knowledge did not annul the resistance of the colonized people, essentially due to the struggles of women and the bond they maintained with the land.

In this context, for Kichwa communities of the Andes, the colonization process in the Amazon meant a way of re-existence, a vindication of their knowledge about the land, an opportunity to connect with the territory, a reactivation of a bond contrary to the colonial/modern project this time developed in tropical lands. For the State, the process of colonization of the Amazonian lands, and of its fringes with the mountains considered as "wastelands,"[18] was an escape valve since it represented an area equivalent to 23% of the national surface, in view of the failed agrarian reforms proposed in coastal and Andean territories. On

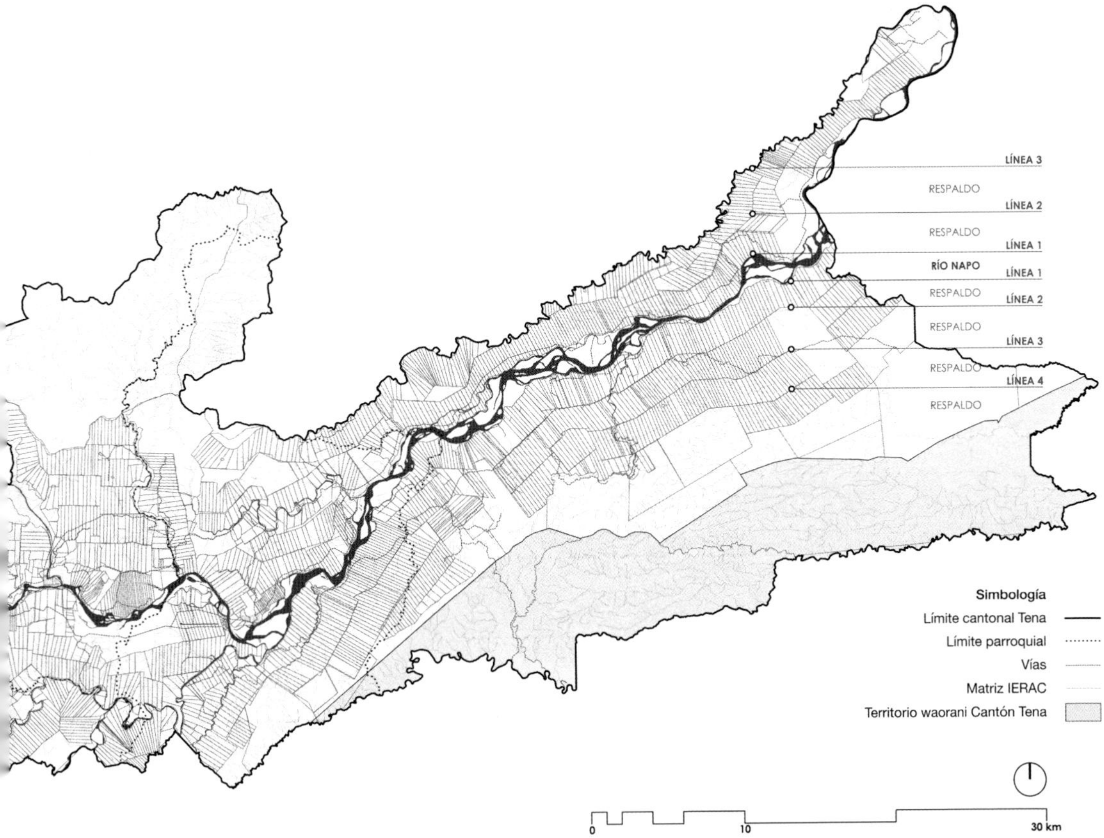

this occasion, the objective of redistributing land was also linked to the expansion of the agricultural and demographic frontier.[19] It should be noted that, in the case of the northern Amazonian area, colonization not only served as a substitute for the agrarian reforms of the untouchable large estates and highland and coastal haciendas, but that it mainly had the purpose of forming an aggregate of workforce willing to meet the needs of the oil project.[20]

This is how the Amazonian territory, subject of the agrarian reform and colonization processes, was structured in a spatial system of bands that are grafted onto the road arteries, planned for the needs of the oil companies, thus giving way to the layout of a succession of lines, from primary to quaternary (fundamentally). Each line articulates narrow, long plots of 40/50 hectares,[21] measuring between 200 to 250 meters in width by about 2 to 2.5 kilometers in length. Each lot was called a farm. This band-based colonization model had previously been implemented in rural areas of Brazil.

On this spatial structuring, the establishment of the Kichwa communities was mainly carried out along the Napo River and its tributaries and, in some cases, along secondary road arteries.[22] While the colonists

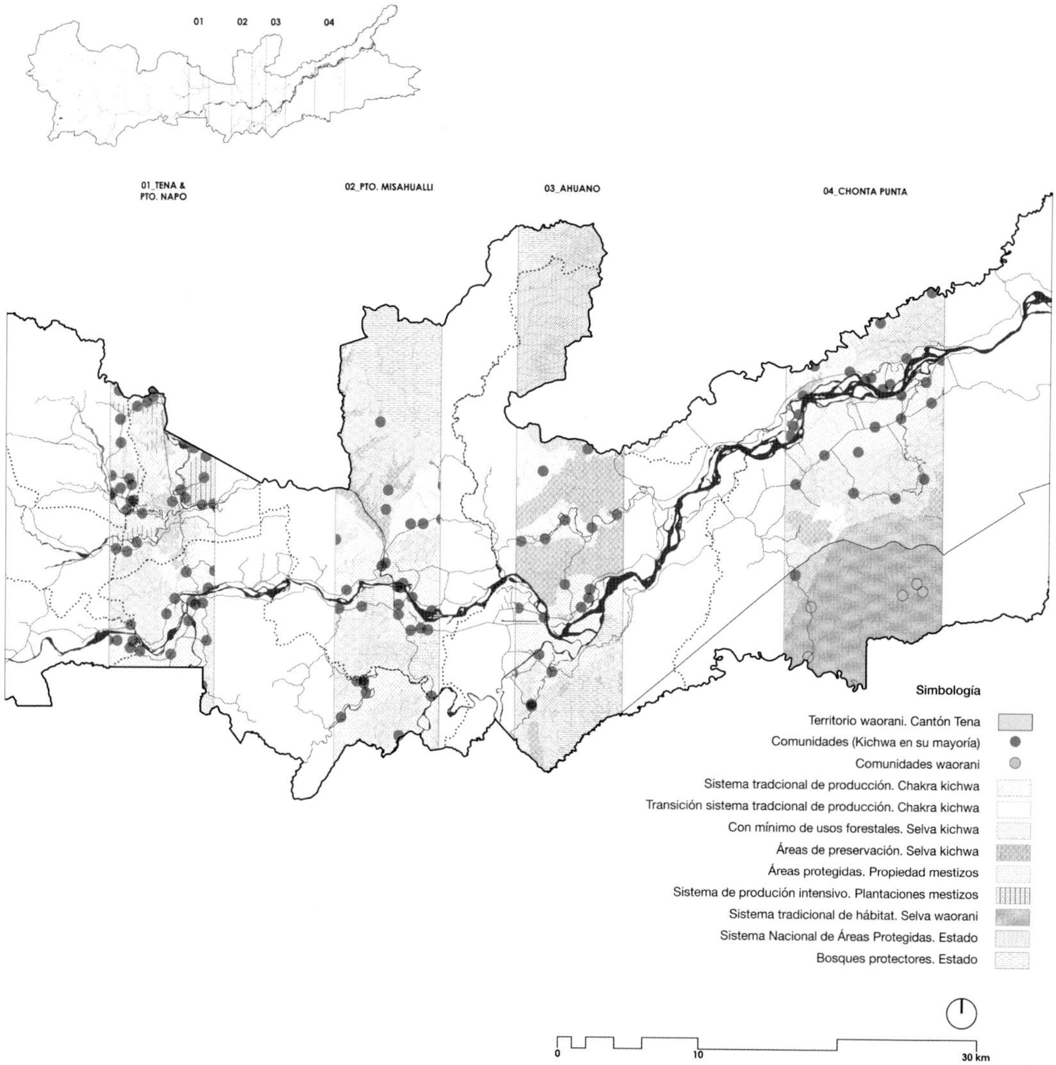

Fig.3
Tena Canton. Chakra. Source: Fernanda Luzuriaga Torres.

(mestizos) were first distributed along the main roads, the distribution subsequently extended towards the back regions according to the order of arrival.[23] Kichwa community settlements can number from a few dozen to 150–200 inhabitants, claiming their own cultural specifity eventually based on particular rural economies (cultivation of cocoa, coffee, bananas, sugar cane) or on forms of community tourism. In case of conflicts within the community or situations of overcrowding, part of the inhabitants separate and establish a new community. The community 'sprouting' process is very intense and corresponds to the occupation of parts of the forest.

The objective of territorial redistribution implied the expansion of the agricultural and demographic frontier, but above all the objective was to provide labor for the oil activity. Then, it could be affirmed that the logic of the colonial/modern system extended to these territories. The enclosure or capture of the bodies on this occasion was directed for the benefit of men, the body of the woman was excluded, being questioned by the alleged absence of force, both for agricultural activities (monocultures) and oil. But it is precisely the body in question, under a patriarchal perspective, which paradoxically returns the doubt to the system by showing the presence of cracks, revealing the fragility of power in its claim of absolute totality,[24] exposing the value of the bodily knowledge in the territory. In effect, this act of exclusion has strengthened the role of Kichwa women in the territory, giving way to ecologies, devices, and spatial practices as *other* expressions under a (specific) feminist perspective. In addition, this *escape* made it possible to organize social and economic networks, which, although they arose from gender demands, are articulated with demands from their communities, from indigenous feminisms under construction.[25] These actions emerge as a necessary exercise of ethnic self-recognition based on gender.[26] However, as María Lugones notes, the struggles of 'women of color' have been particularly indifferent to those of men who "continue to be victims of racial domination, of the coloniality of power, interiorised by global capitalism."[27] For Lugones, this is the first plane of invisibility.

Chakra. The first lifeline

An example of these spatial devices in the Kichwa territories, in the areas of contact between cultivated areas and the forest, is the so-called *chakra*. It is a particular 'forest garden' structured within the farm (40/50 hectares), in which a diversity of crops is produced, arranged according to an apparently random assembly where all species are in biotic exchanges with each other.[28] The presence of birds or animals in this environment is also part of this ecology. These spaces are cared for, assisted by women and their bodily knowledge, the so-called *Chakramamas*. It is they who know how to control ecological cycles and associations between forest species, thus defining their own ecology. The *chakra* is, therefore, a space whose dispositions and measures refer to women's bodies, their manual skills, and the ways in which actions and stimuli are handled and incorporated on the territory of those places. This capacity should not be considered as a property of a subject that acts on an object, but as a whole system of relationships in each environment, on a large scale.

On a smaller scale, the image of the *chakra* invokes the trophic structure of the forest, which, from an ecological point of view, functions as a place of transition between the rural environment and the jungle. But it is also a 'knot,' a connection between the two different ecologies. This space is linked to subsistence economies, but it is also an element that allows income integration and the possibility of intertwining local economies with transnational ones. One of the most widely cultivated products is cocoa, which is sold to local cooperatives and then exported as a semi-finished product to the large foreign chocolate producers.

Fig.4
Tena Canton. Multi-sited dwelling (Esthela Cerda): dwelling in the farthest chakra and dwelling in the chakra at an intermediate distance. Photographs by Fernanda Luzuriaga Torres.

Throughout the Alto Napo valley, there are around 150 families involved in the production, processing, and marketing of cocoa produced in the *chakras*.[29]

The number of *chakras* that the *Chakramamas* can take care of varies and can be up to three.[30] In some cases, the *chakras* are found on both sides of the Napo River, sometimes on the islands formed by the river. Actions of care for these spaces are scheduled every week. Generally, there are *chakras* that are more distant from the others, thus making it necessary to build houses within these spaces, which is another particularity of the *chakra*.[31] We could define this situation as a second spatial strategy, a multi-situated dwelling that responds to a process of 'colonial difference,' to a friction between the present Western and ancestral imaginaries.

The movements between these situations define short-term forms of inhabiting. These movements, mainly linked to economic and subsistence reasons, make it possible to understand housing not as a domestic space in the Western sense (as a place for the family) but as an infrastructure to support the economies of the community. For this reason, the Kichwa lodgings are spatially highly articulated to accommodate a diversity of users. In recent years, the *Ministry of Urban Development and Housing* (MIDUVI) has intervened in the Kichwa territory, mainly in the populated centers, with the construction of houses of 4 × 5 meters. Unlike the houses on stilts built in the *chakras*, which are ecologically comfortable buildings, the houses built by the MIDUVI are in many aspects uninhabitable. Although they do not allow modifications to make them more comfortable to inhabit, these houses are in some cases suitable as places of work (repair of fishing nets, artisan activities), thus adding one more space in their movements.

It should be noted that although multi-site dwelling is characterized by short-term movements, it can also sometimes be long-term. This movement is triggered when it is necessary to go to homes located in the capital or in the main Andean cities for a few months. These movements are essentially also linked to economic and subsistence reasons.

Spatial membranes. The second lifeline

The territorial restructuring or colonization of the Amazon was marked by frictions between colonists and native populations. Kichwa communities are primarily agricultural in their spatial and economic activities, whereas the Waorani communities have different lifestyles. Their settlements, small hamlets with approximately 30 to 100 inhabitants, are located deep within the forest.[32] Waorani territories are autonomous, access to their spaces is not free.[33] The Waorani are basically a semi-nomadic people; for work reasons, they move for short periods between various peoples of their ethnic group living in the Ecuadorian and Peruvian Amazon jungle or in the Andean cities. Compared to those of the Kichwa, the economies of the Waorani are more fragile, based on hunting, handicrafts, and tourism. The parts of the Amazon rainforest managed by the Waorani, although presented as forests in their original state, correspond to controlled ecologies on a large scale, in which an attempt is made to encourage the growth of species useful for the community's food and production needs. Compared to the Kichwa-controlled forest, the Waorani forest is vegetatively denser and climatically cooler.[34]

In the course of time, the territories of these communities have caused a series of frictions and tensions that have been able to unleash episodes of violence. However, the two groups are in intense social exchange with each other, thanks to mixed marriages and tightly intertwined economies. What spatially regulates these exchanges is a particular device, a membrane or contact zone between these territories of different logics.[35] One of these spatial membranes can be identified in the space between the centers of Ahuano and Gareno, in Alto Napo. Ahuano has about 3,000 inhabitants and is one of the main rural parishes of the Kichwa territory; with a total area of 41,776 hectares, it comprises about 42 smaller communities.[36] This territory is in contact with the Waorani community of Gareno, made up of about 200 inhabitants, which manages its own territory of about 23,000 hectares.

However, between these two environments, it is possible to identify a particular spatial device, which is the expression, again, of processes of "colonial difference." It is a large swath of territory that functions both as a space for distancing between the two communities and as a place for social exchange. This band is articulated according to a sequence of five lines that follow almost exactly the traces of the agrarian colonization promoted by IERAC. Proceeding from the Kichwa settlement towards the Waorani settlement, the first strip of territory, about 1 kilometer wide, corresponds to a stretch of forest within which tourist reception infrastructures, the so-called eco-lodges, managed directly by the community, are located. The second strip, about 2 kilometers

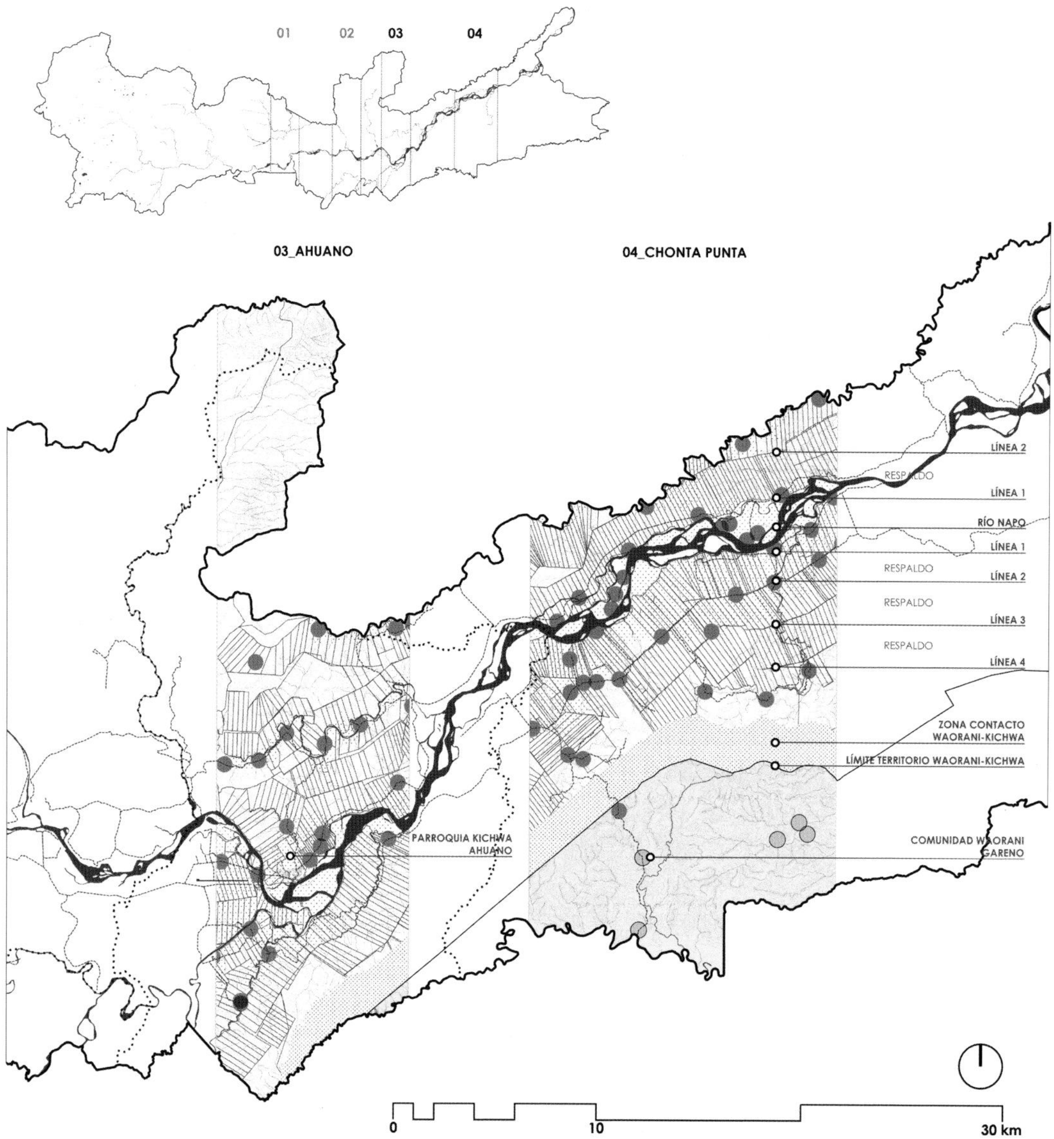

Fig.5
Tena Canton. Contact Zone, Relational Separation. Source: Fernanda Luzuriaga Torres.

wide, comprises stretches of forest, forest gardens (*chakras*), and lines of mestizo settlements. The third strip, about 2.5–3 kilometers wide, is a stretch of protected forest. The Napo River separates the third from the fourth strip, a stretch of forest reserve, 3–4 kilometers wide. Beyond this last strip, the Waorani settlements begin. The dividing lines of these bands coincide with roads, rivers, and colonization routes defined by IERAC. The overall width of this 'contact area' is about 10 kilometers for a total length of about 9 kilometers.[37]

These membranes are effectively devices for a relational separation. What happens inside them are forms of socio-economic exchange that can be defined as examples of 'Silent Trade' through which the Kichwa obtain supplies of meat and forest products, while the Waorani get fabrics, tools, rice, and food of industrial origin. It takes a day of walking to get from the Waorani community in Gareno to the Kichwa community in Ahuano. Once the Waorani have crossed the first two bands, they get dressed, deposit their products in some precise points, and leave. The Kichwa collect these products, leaving their own at the disposal of the Waorani. All these exchanges take place in absence. An important role is also played by the location, this contact area within mestizo settlements, which function as a "free zone" for the mediation and provision of services between the two groups. This spatial membrane functions as a place of "relational separation" or "inclusive disjunction,"[38] which nurtures an exchange between "differences" distant from Western imaginaries based on concepts of mixité, fluidity, and porosity. At the same time, it can be considered an expression of a specific "local spatial thought," or it can be conceptualized as an expression of a particular border thought and, by analogy, of an Amazonian border design,[39] which alludes to the possibility to define design and planning strategies for Amazonian territories as sets of "local spatial thoughts."[40]

Border thinking. Border design

The objective of identifying these processes, ways of living, ecologies, lifelines, and spatial devices is to define relational logics that offer conditions for coexistence and for practices of care and social exchange, incorporating, metabolizing, and negotiating Western patterns. In the three cases identified in the study area, there are not so much hybrid conditions but rather the expression of spaces and processes of relational separation.

In addition, part of this effort refers to a reflection on decolonizing planning practices and discourses for the contemporary Amazon, surpassing traditional Amazonian discourses, generally focused on the issues of environmental protection or passive protection of nature. It has also been an effort to understand the question of 'gender' within spatial production processes. As María Lugones[41] argues, in Latin America modernity/coloniality has been imposed through specific articulations of race and gender, producing hierarchies and value systems in which the female dimension has been diminished to precise limits. Therefore, a decolonial redefinition of Amazonian planning strategies must be made through the incorporation of gender and race issues in the urban discourse.[42] The recognition of a decolonial feminist perspective, in opposition to western patriarchal paradigms and rigid principles of abstraction, rationalization, systematization, could favor the identification of useful spatial knowledge and practices to define, as shown by the case of the *chakra* that represents a socio-spatial structure based on matriarchal organization models, an embedded spatiality, based on the measures and operational potentials of the bodily knowledge of the *Chakramamas*.

Therefore, innovative plans and policies for Amazonian territories and societies can only be defined by imagining other forms of projects, which are not conceived as modernizing projects. In this sense, talking about the spatial configuration of the *chakra*, the relationship of caring for the body with the territory, is to make visible a process that is difficult to identify, since the usual thing in the Amazon is to explore an environment of extractive practices, based on an patriarchal organization that conceives the body of all inhabitants, not only of indigenous communities, as a machine capable of producing force, where body movements are conceived as linear automated processes, processes in which there is no relationship, only domination.
Similarly, the identification of the so-called spatial membranes defined through the recognition and appreciation of differences, as an act of diplomacy, deeply necessary in a pluri-national state, allows us to reflect on other ways of spatial production, such as lifelines that demand respect towards the ethics of care, given the differences and given the connection of the body with the territory, a fabric of interrelations, which connects local spatial thoughts as a declination of the Amazonian border thinking/design.[43]
Then, identifying these processes, ecologies, and spatial devices that are woven, as processes of 'colonial difference' from the relationship with the territory, we could interpret them as ecologies opposed to the modern order and, therefore, decolonial. This type of space requires a different look, since it is not only about other relationship processes, but it is also about explaining other lifelines from a relational, feminine perspective, ecologies built from the woman's body. Lifelines are representing 'failures' and cannibalistic metabolizations of colonial modernization projects.
Inhabiting the Amazon consists of weaving relationships through incorporations, knotting, distancing: lifestyles and forms of spatial production that have nothing to do with patrimonial identity discourses. Therefore, talking about a decolonial project has this meaning: living in the Amazon is somewhat hesitant, based on relationships that are neither domination nor apprehension but rather concealment, penetration, mimesis. By dissolving the distinction between nature and culture, the inhabitant is not a subject that acts from the outside on the space, but is 'interwoven,' is incorporated into it. Within these processes, the contribution of indigenous feminisms, useful spatial knowledge, and practices in opposition to the paradigms of the modern capitalist order of colonial patriarchy, typical of a Western matrix, is important.

Endnotes

1 Quijano, "Colonialidad del poder y clasificación social."
2 Colonial difference, i.e., the friction between local knowledge and western paradigms. The concept does not refer to an attempt to focus on "authentic" or ancestral knowledges, rather it operates in the regeneration of the different forms of local knowledge as they are filtered by alien values. Well, it is precisely in the registry of these states that there is a series of forms of relationship, meager colonial differences, that are difficult to identify. In this sense, the colonial difference is a borderline thought that operates as an epistemological decolonization machine.
3 Scholars such as Walter Mignolo, Enrique Dussel, Edgardo Lander, Zulma Palermo, Arturo Escobar, Catherine Walsh, Santiago Castro Gómez, María Lugones, and Adolfo Albán Achinte are main references.
4 The struggles and claims of Amazonian women are a starting point for the recognition of the configuration of local expressions from bodies that denounce patriarchal structures naturalized by the family, community, state, and transnational nucleus.
5 As a bet to change the productive matrix, the government of Rafael Correa named Tena as the 'living laboratory,' a place to experiment with new economies based on the enhancement of botanical and biopharmaceutical emergencies. Thus, in 2013, the National Assembly announced the creation of the Ikiam Regional Amazon University (forest in the Shuar language) in Tena; contradictorily, its construction was the privilege of the economic surplus, generated mainly by the exploitation of oil, (El Telégrafo 2013), just after the cancellation of the Yasuní-ITT Initiative (Wilson et al. 2015). The initial project contemplated the construction of two campuses, in El Eno, Sucumbíos, in the north of the Amazon region, center of the oil industry, and in El Pangui, Zamora, in the extreme south of the country, center of mining extractivism (El Telégrafo 2014). Initiatives were suspended due to lack of economic resources.
6 SENPLADES – Secretaria Nacional de Planificación y Desarrollo, *Plan Estratégico 2014–2017.*
7 Of these, only the Tena parish is urban.
8 Of the 61,000 inhabitants, 62% live in the rural area and 38% in the urban area of Tena. 38% of the inhabitants are mestizo, 57% Kichwa; 5% Waorani (INEC 2010; PDyOT GAD Tena 2011).
9 Created in 1964 by the Junta Militar de Gobierno, that same year the first Agrarian Reform and Colonization Law was enacted, as well as the Barren Lands and Colonization Law (Ley de Reforma Agraria y Colonización); the objective was to establish a policy of land distribution, but above all not all have affected the large estates of the highlands and in turn expanded the demographic and agricultural frontier (Grijalva et al. 2004).
10 The Waorani population of about 3,000 inhabitants is organized in communities within the Amazonian provinces of Orellana, Napo, and Pastaza, between the Napo and Curaray Rivers. In the province of Napo, the inhabitants of this nationality are located in the parish of Chontapunta. Its territory is divided by the so-called "uncontacted" indigenous peoples. Of these, there are two types. Indigenous groups that never really came into contact with the settlers and those who came into contact at the beginning of the twentieth century and decided in the 1960s to isolate themselves for reasons of low resistance to the diseases introduced by the new inhabitants. An example of the latter are the Taromenani, a group of about 300 individuals, who initially formed a single group with the Waorani and the Tagaeri, a population of about 100 people.
11 In 1908, the liberal president Eloy Alfaro dictated the Law of Beneficence (Ley de Beneficencia), better known as the Law of "Dead Hands" (Manos Muertas), which consisted in the expropriation of the haciendas (latifundios) that were in the hands of religious orders since colonization. The indigenous people worked this land without receiving remuneration, and they lived within the hacienda in a reduced space called Wasipungo. When these properties were confiscated, they passed into the hands of tenants; however, the labor relations that the tenants (new bosses) of the haciendas tried to impose were the same practices as those of the previous owners. This led to an armed strike in 1919 (which lasted over a month).
12 Dolores Cacuango, Tránsito Amaguaña, Rosa Cachipuela, Mercedes Catucumba, and Angelita Andrango, women who worked on farms located in the north of the country.
13 The hacienda was a spatial device of domination and control of the territory, which made possible the consolidation of an economic system; and it was also the indicated place for the enclosure of bodies, by constituting the main work force, thus establishing the body as the first essential machine in capitalism. Tránsito Amaguaña stated: The jobs assigned to both women and girls varied according to age. If they did not comply, heavy sanctions were applied, despite the fact that the work was free and

the hours varied according to the requirements of the owner of the farm. 'We all had to work hard to be allowed to live on the hacienda (Rodas 2007a; 2007b)'.

14 "Concerned, above all, the ways of knowing, of producing knowledge, of defining perspectives, images and systems of images, symbols, meanings. On the ways of considering resources, patterns, and intellectual or visual instruments of formalized and objectified expression." Quijano, "Colonialidad y Modernidad/Racionalidad."

15 Not only to prevent any type of production but also as effective instruments of control when repression weakens in its systematic constancy; see: Quijano, "Colonialidad y Modernidad/Racionalidad," 11–20.

16 Rodas, *Dolores Cacuango: Pionera en la lucha por los derechos indígenas*; Rodas, *Tránsito Amaguaña. Su testimonio*.

17 Federici, *Calibán y la bruja: mujeres, cuerpo y acumulación originaria*.

18 Gondard and Mazurek, "30 Años de reforma agraria y colonización en Ecuador (1964–1994): dinámicas espaciales."

19 Jordán, "Reforma agraria en Ecuador."

20 The process started with the so-called Shushufindi Field in 1969. The economic boom of the 1970s and the financing of approximately half of the state budget during the last four decades had been sustained with the extraction of crude oil, mainly in the provinces of Sucumbíos and Orellana, with five hydrocarbon fields located in Shushufindi, Sacha, Libertador, Auca, and Lago Agrio. In addition, the Amazon region was the appropriate place to host other migratory processes, a consequence of natural events such as droughts, registered in Manabí and Loja, which caused the migration of inhabitants in search of other territories. This is how the northeast became one of the areas with the highest colonizing intensity in the country (Fontaine 2003). Finally, oil activity controlled the organization of space, even influencing the reconfiguration of old urban areas in the Amazon foothills, which are linked to agricultural and livestock activities and situated on soils of volcanic origin, as are the cities Quijos, Tena, Archidona, Puyo, Macas, Sucúa, and Zamora. These last cities and towns were mostly established by native populations due to the natural fertility of the soils (Eberhart 1998; Altmann 2013). In a broad framework, these actions consolidated the process of empowerment of the State over the Amazonian territory, which until the mid-1990s continued to be in dispute with its Peruvian counterpart.

21 In 1970, Texaco built both first-order roads (Quito-Lago Agrio) and second-order roads.

22 The Kichwa territories in the canton cover about 157,000 hectares.

23 Rudel, *Tropical Deforestation. Small Farmers and Land Clearing in the Ecuadorian Amazon*; Gondard and Mazurek, "30 Años de reforma agraria y colonización en Ecuador (1964–1994): dinámicas espaciales."

24 Albán, *Prácticas creativas de re-existencia: Más allá del arte... el mundo de lo sensible*.

25 The principles of caring for the benefit of the community are, we could say, quite close to community feminism, to current experiences in Guatemala and Bolivia, designated as such by intellectuals and decolonial feminist indigenous activists such as Lorena Cabnal (2010, 2014) and Julieta Paredes (2010). For example, in the case of Kichwa women from the Tena Canton, the formation of associations, which represent legal instruments protected by the advantages and benefits of the Popular and Solidarity Economy (EPS), has enabled the public recognition of the values and principles of other ways of doing economics. These acts can be seen as an expression that precisely the administration of care that is responsible for indigenous women enables their legal recognition and with it the possibility of commercializing their agricultural products, in this case, in points administered by the Autonomous Decentralized Municipal Governments. In this sense, being part of an association is a dignified and efficient way for people to combat marginalization, avoiding evictions and retention (loss) of their products. In addition, being part of associations gives them access to other opportunities that allow them to be part of training with national and international organizations.

26 Fernández and Moreno, *Las guardianas de la lengua: mujeres indígenas y educación intercultural bilingüe en Ecuador*.

27 Lugones, "Colonialidad y género."

28 Around 65 plant species, many of which are native. From annual root and tuber crops such as cassava (Manihot esculenta), semi-permanent crops of fruit trees such as bananas, naranjilla (Solanum quitoense), and permanent fruit trees such as cacao, coffee, chonta (Juania Australis), naranjo, guayusa (Ilex guayusa) to forest trees and medicinal and ornamental species.

29 Cerda, interview.

30 According to what has been verified, generally due to the inheritances received, the area can therefore also be divided.

31 The houses are built with the support of the community (labor) through the practice of the *minga*. The houses are infrastructures of limited duration due to their materiality and the climatic conditions, especially when they are located on the banks of the Napo River.

32 An example is the community of Komipare, close to the urban center of Chontapunta, east of Tena. This settlement is made up of 14 families with a total of 63 inhabitants. Each family lives in houses on stilts, arranged on several levels, with parts closed and others protected only by a roof. The buildings are divided into several sections placed side by side or separated by spaces in between and linked by small bridges. This type and way of life was defined and imposed from the middle of the twentieth century. Previously, each community lived in a large common house capable of housing up to forty people.

33 The owner of the community land is the Waorani Nation, recognized by the State as a legal entity.

34 Inside the forest are small forest gardens called *kewenkore*. Compared to the *chakra*, the Kichwa horticultural-jungle cultivation system, the *kewenkore* is smaller, generally measuring between half a hectare to one hectare and is cultivated in rotation to promote soil regeneration through the regrowth of spontaneous vegetation. The cultivated species are corn, yucca, green banana, and cocoa.

35 The concept of 'contact zone' derives from the work of Mary Louise Pratt (1991), who uses it to describe the place where different cultures confront each other through relationships, interaction, coexistence, and conflict.

36 The total population is 5,579 inhabitants, of which 96% are Kichwa citizens (GAD Ahuano 2015).

37 This route system is now accepted by the communities. There are no previous indigenous forms of delimitation.

38 Bene and Deleuze, *Sovrapposizioni*.

39 Anzaldúa, *Borderlands – La Frontera: The New Mestiza*.

40 The concept of Border Thinking was used for the first time by Gloria Anzaldúa in her book *Borderlands/ La Frontera: The New Mestiza* (1987) and was later developed by decolonial thinkers, especially by Walter Mignolo (2001). It is based on the idea that the theoretical and the epistemic must have a lived dimension, and that there are theories that are on the borders of the colonial matrix of power. Border Thinking does not occur independently of modernity, but in response to it, as part of the struggles against the oppressive apparatus of the colonial power matrix. Then Border Thinking is the epistemology of exteriority, that is, of the exterior created from within (Mignolo and Tlostanova 2006). Border Thinking is thinking from the outside, using alternative languages to knowledge traditions.

41 Lugones, "Colonialidad y género."

42 The concept of gender, like that of race, Lugones argues, is a colonial construction that produces precise socio-spatial relationships. According to Lugones, before the arrival of the colonizers to America, there were gender positions other than the hierarchical and dichotomous ones imposed by the colonizers.

43 Ecuador was the first country to recognize the Rights of Nature. This recognition is above all a step forward to understand that a diversity of ecological assemblages involves people intimate with one of the most complex and fragile ecosystems in the world; an ecosystem woven from a variety of different types of beings; see: Anzaldúa, *Borderlands - La Frontera: The New Mestiza*.

Bibliography

Albán, Achinte. *Prácticas creativas de re-existencia: Más allá del arte... el mundo de lo sensible*. México: Del Signo, 2017.

Altmann, Phillip. "El Sumak Kawsay en el discurso del movimiento indígena ecuatoriano." *Indiana*, Vol. 30 (2013): 283–299.

Anzaldúa, Gloria. *Borderlands - La Frontera: The New Mestiza*. San Francisco: Aunt Lute Books, 1987.

Bene, Carmelo and Gilles Deleuze. *Sovrapposizioni*. Macerata: Quodlibet, 2002.

Cabnal, Lorena. "Acercamiento a la construcción de la propuesta de pensamiento epistémico de las mujeres indígenas feministas comunitarias de Abya Yala." *Feminismos diversos: el feminismo comunitario*, edited by ACSUR-Las Segovias and Lorena Cabnal, 11–25. Spain: ACSUR-Las Segovias, 2010.

Cabnal, Lorena. *Despatriarcalización del territorio cuerpo, un acto político y cosmogónico para descolonizarnos*. Guatemala: s/e, 2014.

Cerda, Esthela. "Entrevista." Interview by Fernanda Luzuriaga, Ahuano, July 28, 2019.

Eberhart, Nicolás. *Transformaciones agrarias en el frente de la colonización de la Amazonia ecuatoriana*, Quito: Abya-Yala, 1998.

Federici, Silvia. *Calibán y la bruja: mujeres, cuerpo y acumulación originaria*. Madrid: Traficantes de Sueños, 2004.

Fernández, Blanca S., Adriana Victoria Rodríguez Caguana, and Paola Vargas Moreno. *Las guardianas de la lengua: mujeres indígenas y educación intercultural bilingüe en Ecuador*. Quito: Universidad Andina Simon Bolivar, 2019.

Fontaine, Guillaume. *El precio del petróleo: conflictos socio-ambientales y gobernabilidad en la región amazónica*. Quito: FLACSO/Instituto Francés de Estudios Andinos, 2003.

GAD Ahuano. *Actualización del Plan de desarrollo y ordenamiento territorial de la Parroquia Ahuano 2015–2030*. 2015. https://odsterritorio-ecuador.ec/wp-content/uploads/2019/04/PDOT-PARROQUIA-AHUA-NO-2015-2030.pdf (last accessed: June 18, 2021).

Gondard, Pierre and Hubert Mazurek. "30 Años de reforma agraria y colonización en Ecuador (1964–1994): dinámicas espaciales." *Estudios de Geografía*, Corporación Editora Nacional, Vol. 10 (2001): 15–40.

Grijalva, Jorge, Venus Arévalo, and Charles Wood. *Expansión y trayectoria de la ganadería en la Amazonía*. Quito: INIAPI, 2004.

"Ikiam tendrá laboratorio natural." *El Telégrafo*, December 5, 2013. www.eltelegrafo.com.ec/noticias/sociedad/6/ikiam-tendra-laboratorio-natural (last accessed: June 18, 2021).

INEC – Censo de Población. 2010. "PDyOT GAD Tena, 2011, Datos Estadísticos de Tena." https://tena.gob.ec/index.php/tena/datos-estadisticos (last accessed: January 18, 2021).

Jordán B., Fausto. "Reforma agraria en Ecuador." *Proceso agrario en Bolivia y América Latina*, edited by John D. Vargas Vega, 285–317. La Paz: Plural Editores, 2003.

Lugones, María. "Colonialidad y género." *Tabula Rasa*, No. 9 (2008): 73–101.

Mignolo, Walter. "The Geopolitics of Knowledge and the Colonial Difference." *South Atlantic Quarterly*, Vol. 101, Issue 1 (2001): 57–96.

Mignolo, Walter. *El vuelco de la razón: diferencia colonial y pensamiento fronterizo*. México: del Signo, 2011.

Mignolo, Walter. *Local Histories/Global Designs: Coloniality, Subaltern Knowledges, and Border Thinking*. Princeton: Princeton University Press, 2012.

Mignolo, Walter and Madina V. Tlostanova. "Theorizing from the Borders. Shifting to Geo- and Body-Politics of Knowledge." *European Journal of Social Theory*, Vol. 9, No. 2 (2006): 205–22.

Paredes, Julieta. *Hilando Fino. Desde el feminismo comunitario*. México: El Rebozo; Zapateándole; Lente Flotante; En cortito que's palargo; AliFem AC, 2010.

Pratt, Mary Louise. "Arts of the Contact Zone." *Profession* (2011): 33–40.

"Proceso de inscripción para interesados en estudiar en Ikiam." *El Telegrafo*, February 18, 2013. www.eltelegrafo.com.ec/noticias/sociedad/4/proceso-de-inscripcion-para-interesados-en-estudiar-en-ikiam (last accessed: June 18, 2021).

Quijano, Anibal. "Colonialidad y Modernidad/Racionalidad." *Perú Indígena*, Vol. 13, No. 29 (1992): 11–20.

Quijano, Anibal. "Colonialidad del poder y clasificación social." *Journal of World-System Research*, No. 2 (2000): 342–86.

"Rafael Correa tildó a Guadalupe Llori como 'una mujer tremendamente violenta'." *El Universo*, May 17, 2021. https://www.eluniverso.com/noticias/politica/rafael-correa-tildo-a-guadalupe-llori-como-una-mujer-tremendamente-violenta-nota/ (last accessed: June 18, 2021).

Rodas, Raquel. *Dolores Cacuango: Pionera en la lucha por los derechos indígenas*. Quito: Comisión Nacional Permanente de Conmemoraciones Cívicas, 2007.

Rodas, Raquel. *Tránsito Amaguaña. Su testimonio*. Quito: Comisión Nacional Permanente de Conmemoraciones Cívicas, 2007.

Rudel, Thomas K. *Tropical Deforestation. Small Farmers and Land Clearing in the Ecuatorian Amazon*. New York: Columbia University Press, 1993.

SENPLADES – Secretaria Nacional de Planificación y Desarrollo. *Plan Estratégico 2014–2017*. Quito: SENPLADES, 2015.

Wilson, Japhy, Manuel Bayón, and Henar Diez. "Naturaleza: Ikiam." *Biopiratería: La biodiversidad y los conocimientos ancestrales en la mira del capital*, edited by Alberto Acosta and Esperanza Martínez, 267–279. Quito: Abya-Yala, 2015.

Misappropriation and occupation: lifelines and artistic practices for the city of Beirut

Federica Doglio,
Camillo Boano

In a tentative catalogue of case studies that assist in sustaining, bringing out, and making visible lifelines, this essay seeks a dialogue with a very open definition of lifelines that, in this research, has been used to indicate everything that sustains life and that has a reflection in space. The definition is very open and crosses different practical, cognitive, and political dimensions. In other words: lifelines indicate even very different things.[1]

The hypotheses investigated in this research are different: the spaces of artistic practices bring out lifelines; those artistic practices are forms of resistance; and the figure of the ruin serves to visualize lifelines.

The space and the network of spaces in which Beirut artists work are the starting point for this paper on the relationships between artistic practices and the city itself in some key periods of its recent history, as a particular scenario for bringing out some lifelines.

The city of Beirut, with its conflicts, crises, and vulnerabilities, is at the center of this reflection on the topic of infrastructures in support of life, investigated within the spatial practices implemented by artists and activists, seen as spatial forms of resistance: a cultural resistance, formed by the presence of cultural activities and practices within a hostile context in which it is difficult to create space for oneself.[2]

The words spoken in 2018 by Tania El Khoury, an internationally renowned Lebanese artist, describe the cultural resistance in Lebanon, a history made up of minorities: "The culture of resistance is a culture in which every member of the community – artist or not – uses their work to challenge the centralization of power. [...] In the Lebanese context, there is certainly an intersection between artists, those who work in the cultural sector, and activists: we are all involved in issues linked to gender equality, social justice, spatial justice, and representativeness in local politics. [...] Despite a major effort and widespread popular support, these people are still a tiny minority in Lebanese society, and we are therefore far from being able to create a culture of resistance. We can, however, say that the independent cultural sector in Lebanon is taking steps to develop various strategies of resistance."[3]

In a place made up precisely of resistance and resignation,[4] in its folds, in its fractures, and in its ruins, lifelines – albeit imperfect, ephemeral, and fleeting – spatialize and emerge in a scenario of repeated destructions and rebirths, controversial colonial legacies, divisions, and endemic crises that all overlap.

In this sense, the figure of the ruin can be a key for interpreting the city and, at the same time, its lifeline. First, precisely because this has been repeatedly transformed into ruin as a continuous redesign of an operational space: consider the long fifteen years of the Lebanese Civil War (1975–1990) – as described, for example, by Gabriele Basilico's photographs of 1991 on the skin of the city[5] –, the war of 2005–2008, and the recent port explosion in August 2020. But also because the city itself, with its inhabitants, tells of resistance to the ruin, which is in the folds of the city, in the lives of the people who resist – in various ways – neglect, financial crises, and the negligence of the political class.

Fig.1
Artist Yaza Halwani's mural of the Lebanese singer and actress Sabah. Photograph by Amhad Samhan.

Furthermore, the ruin, sometimes repeatedly portrayed (not only in Beirut – but there are also other contemporary cases such as Detroit, Chernobyl, Fukushima, or Nassiriya), becomes an almost obsessive image (there has been talk of 'Ruin Porn'), which stops at the skin of the city, with the risk of forgetting what lives inside, what still inhabits the substratum of the city, in a layer brutalized by conflicts.
The ruin, precisely because it is – at once – life and death, memory and future, full and empty, is a very broad territory that finds in different art forms the possibility of resistance, which, in some way, is resistance to neglect, to decadence, precisely because ruins are – at once – spaces of imagination and action, that concurrently maintain an expression of loss, of mourning, and of melancholy, as will be seen in some narrations offered below. In the unfinished, in the voids, in the spaces of possibility, free from completeness and finiteness, different forms of art creep in, giving new meanings. Here, lifelines have spatial repercussions. They spatialize precisely. They are created in the fissures of those complexes lacerated by the historical time of destructions, liberalism, and conflicts. The theme of the ruin in these terms is linked to the theme of lifelines. The perspective investigated here is the one already highlighted by Kaelen Wilson-Goldie in 2009, who claims that sometimes the (temporary) absence of spaces of different nature for artistic production (institutions, non-profit organizations, collectives, artistic residences, etc.) has

encouraged artists to work even more closely with the city itself.[6]

In a precarious assemblage, predatory and functional, colonial and security-focused, but also fertile European and American institutions coexist in Beirut, fragments of a negligent and corrupt State, activists who mainly perform actions that start from the folds, from the conflict zones, from the ruins of the city. This is the point of view that is favored in this essay and, at the same time, its narrative choice, in a tale made up of minute episodes originating from non-artistic institutions, from significant actions positioned in some places, chosen because they are spatial representations of our lifelines. The *non* that precedes the words artistic institutions is not intended as a negation but reprises the use made of it by Fluxus artists (fathers of the practice of performance) from the 1960s, as described by Jon Hendricks, "[Fluxus] challenged preconceived notions about art, the function of art, and the role of the artist in society, promoting a *non*-art."[7]

In the belief, therefore, that lifelines have a performing nature, that they are actions, that they are infrastructures, sometimes tangible and sometimes intangible, we attempt here to select some pieces of a broader story: minute phenomena, cultural resistances that emerge in Beirut to object to neglect, to the complete ruin of the city. It is possible, therefore, to interpret a system of urban ecologies, through which the inhabitants constitute an industrious community (able to build, maintain, and repair its spaces),[8] which, through performing occasions, trigger processes and aim to ensure a higher level of livability of a complex, intricate, changing reality such as that of Beirut, continually negotiating crises and vulnerabilities.

The tale proposed here is therefore made up of moments, spots, fragments, precisely because, faithful to the identity of the city, in a very small (about 20 km^2) and fragmented (there is no *unicum* in Beirut) territory, it is the legacy of a not just contemporary history made up of conflicts, separations, divisions, different ethnic interests, districts, religions, cultures, sovereignties.

Artists in the Lebanese capital have often contributed to molding an image – to building a future – and to establishing a connection with memory – the past –, building intangible bonds and lines.

This chapter upholds that in the context of Beirut some artistic practices cannot be distinguished from a clear root of activism and that they are a citizenship movement, in which the right to the city (and, as a consequence, the right to the sea, as we will see) becomes an indistinguishable cause for appropriation (or re-appropriation) of spaces of the city previously misappropriated by different powers. These spaces are subsequently occupied precisely by artistic productions organized in different practices, whether they are actions for the symbolic Martyr's Square or actions to reclaim access to the water, denied by a colossal privatization operation of the seafront and the sea itself that began in 2010.

From the multiple possible fragments, three have been chosen, proposed here as an attempt to visualize lifelines. These cases are precisely minute, not the best available, but they represent an initial attempt to

approach a definition of infrastructures of cultural resistance within the very complex and critical framework of the Lebanese capital.
The first reflection, very problematic here, concerns the public space and the right to the city, expressed in the right to the sea.
In telling of the reasons and ways in which a series of actions were organized from 2012, *The Sea is Mine* presents itself as a journey along the seafront of Beirut, as an attempt to provide a different and more profound comprehension of the requirements of that public space but also as an invitation to re-imagine the city and to demand the right to it.[9]
The issue of public space in Beirut, of its widespread absence, is inevitably a consequence of individual opportunism linked to corruption and negligence, to an absence of the State (in which the State is classically seen as a centralized bureaucratic and sovereign apparatus in matters of internal security).[10] At the same time, however, it is a consequence of the desire for its control which, denying the public space and increasing privatization since the time of tempo Solidere (Société Libanaise pour le Développement et la Reconstruction du Centre-ville de Beyrouth, a private company with the task of rebuilding the capital, which received substantial funding from the Gulf nations), in the name of rebirth after the civil war, leads to the example of Zaytouna Bay, the umpteenth proof of failure, precisely because Solidere, through ethically and legally questionable practices, was the bearer of a development in favor of the large international capital spent in Lebanon, rather than a promotion for a recovery working on social dynamics with the legacies of the civil war.
In the words of its creators, "*This Sea Is Mine* aims to explore our understanding of the notions of 'public' and 'private,' and the ways in which they apply to Beirut's seafront."[11]
The issue of privatization of that part of the city which overlooks the sea, the *seafront* we will call it, was already present in the early 1990s immediately after the end of the civil war. In fact, in 1997, a report commissioned by the World Bank and by the Lebanese Government highlighted a concerning percentage (81%) of private entities in possession, legally and illegally, of parts of the city overlooking the sea (in the areas between Jounieh Bay and Beirut International Airport, a total of about 51km in length).[12] However, the matter was further exacerbated and came to its *climax* in the second decade of the 2000s, when privatization of access to the sea was further pushed, almost completely denying it to the city's inhabitants, refusing them access to this public space.
In particular, *This Sea Is Mine* was a collaborative project, which manifested in a performance organized by the Dictaphone Group[13] in the coastal waters of Beirut aboard a fishing boat, which left from the port of Ein el-Mreisse towards Ramlet el-Baida beach, in an attempt to explore from the sea the nature of ownership of the Beirut seafront, the laws that govern it, and the practices of its users. It was an action questioning the public space and re-imagining the city. The performance lasted 10 days, taking place on two trips per day with five people on each trip in the small boat. These repeated actions were described by the media as 'protests'.

Fig.2
'The Sea is Mine,' performance in Beirut, 2012. Courtesy of Dictaphone Group

Such actions organized by the *Dictaphone Group* – a group established out of the interest in combining urban research and live artistic performances – are spatial forms of resistance; they are actions that, by binding and connecting groups of people – not just artists but activists and common citizens – in the name of the right to the city, build weaves of intent, bonds in support of better quality of living, resisting neglect but not ruin; in these cases, resisting capitalist forms of control of the city. These actions are not isolated performances but, precisely because they occupy a timeframe (from the data found online from 2012 to 2016), are organized in an archive within a platform called *Hands Off Our Commons*, still reinforcing the sense of all the work of artists and citizens aimed at raising awareness and protecting something that is for everyone, not just the public space but the entire city and its access to the sea.[14]

The protests against the privatization of the seafront continued in 2013 with the campaign for free access to the sea in the Dalieh area, named *Civil Campaign to Protect the Dalieh of Raouche* (CCPDR), supported by a coalition of residents, activists, architects, and legal representatives (*Nahnoo*, *Greenline*, *Cedars for Care*, *Public Works*, *Legal Agenda*, *Dictaphone Group*, *We Want Accountability*, amongst others) fighting to preserve a common good; and in 2014 when a new project was advertised

Fig.3
'The Sea is Mine,' performance in Beirut, 2012, pp. 158–159. Courtesy of Dictaphone Group

هذا البحر
لي

15

for a tower designed by OMA, again in the Dalieh, a historical beach warmly remembered in the memories of generations of Lebanese, an iconic location with its white cliffs characterized by their luxuriant nature and, at the same time, a biodiversity reserve (6% of Lebanese flora is found here, and it is a very important site as it is home to the coast's last native plants).[15] The actions produced in this case differed: maps were drawn up of the city's coast (broken down into coastal areas of interest), indicating precisely the ownership and exploitation by private entities within the regulatory framework applicable to the city; public discussions were organized in the academic environment; demonstrations were held in an attempt to raise awareness of the problem, with guided tours of the areas demonstrating the difficulty/impossibility of access, and the risks of cultural, natural, and biodiversity losses in the coastal area.

The protests became more acute when areas were cordoned off for privatization, and other resistance actions emerged, such as Christian Zahr's painting *The Angry Dolosse Army* created on the breakwater rocks.

Here, lifeline becomes an infrastructure of knowledge, of condemnation, of disclosure of important information, of mapping, in some way, of building an image.

Fig.4
Ruin of 'The Egg,' unfinished cinema used as a center of aggregation during the protests of 2019/2020. Photograph by Riccardo Conti, November 2019.

From this perspective, the works of the artists (performances, monumental temporary works, murals, awareness-raising campaigns, mapping, etc.) suggest a different way of establishing relationships, of creating infrastructures, which used to be intellectual and then become real possibilities of occupying the spaces of the city because, as we have said, the public space in Beirut has often been denied, cancelled, violated, many times even made non-existent due to the failure of the State. They are spaces that constitute, within a fragmented and unstable city, a network of 'possibilities' that facilitate the reclaiming of rights and only consequently, a very diversified artistic production. It is a cultural infrastructure that supports the network of these spaces, but it is also the absence of infrastructures that drives artists to work in direct contact with the city itself. It is like navigating and constructing possibilities in the absence of spaces, defending and occupying by assembling precarious alliances. They are artists who represent an international community, not just Lebanese, who contribute to triggering this citizenship movement, constituted by many different voices emerging from Beirut's complex and very rich contemporary artistic scene.

The paradigm of misappropriation and occupation of ruins enunciates spaces and possibilities in the cracks of the city, which escape neglect with spurts of vitality and alliances.

A network of murals which, through participation and protest actions, contributes to giving new meanings to precise parts of the city and, at the same time, weaving a web of memories. Sometimes ephemeral, they are works that have achieved permanence through the digital network infrastructure which allows them to be visible even after having been removed from the physical space in which they were created.[16]

By carefully observing the vast graffiti spread across the capital, you can hear the voices that embody social discontent. An example of this is the work of the Lebanese artist and activist Yazan Halwani[17] who, from 2010, began to paint huge portraits on blank walls in strategic locations of the city overlooking spaces that are, or should be, public. Having grown up in a Beirut immersed in political propaganda as the legacy of the civil war, with portraits of politicians very present in the city spaces, the artist creates, conversely, portraits that allow us to reflect on the cultural identity of the country and propose, above all, the possibility of a different narration of history. They are portraits of poets, musicians, and artists (for example, the teacher, journalist, and activist Samir Kassir who was assassinated in 2005; the painter Khalil Gibran; the singer Fairouz, the actress Sabah). The process of creating the works is once again fundamental: Halwani involves the community before creating the painting, believing that: "The city can be changed, making it belong to citizens instead of politicians or economic power, because citizens have a right to the city."[18]

These murals are examples of intangible forces that mold a process of growth and awareness in extreme conditions, with the aim of constructing narratives that differ from the dominant political one.

The condition of Beirut is an extreme one and it cannot only be ascribed to a condition of crisis, albeit incremental, structural. What

emerges is an exhausted territory, brutalized and vandalized by the preclusion of an imaginable future.[19]
Ruin is the state to which the Grand Théâtre des Mille et Une Nuits has been reduced, a majestic building constructed in the 1920s in the center of Beirut and abandoned for over forty years, a reminder of the ruin of the Lebanese Civil War. This sacred location for Middle Eastern culture had hosted several very famous shows such as the Comédie Française, the Ballet des Champs-Elysées, and the Egyptian Ramses Group, before being converted into a cinema.
In 2020, the directors Aya Atoui and Anthony Sahyoun staged *Shabah El Rih* (*Second Wind*) here, a performance that projects an opera by the singer Mona Hallab into the dilapidated structure, evoking the sensations of Beirut of the past.[20]
The space previously taken away from the community is thereby temporarily occupied by artists who use it as a setting for a reflection on the city of the past but, above all, the present. This work establishes a series of ideal lines between the past and the future, triggering a series of reflections on identity and on the use of that space with a cultural vocation, a space that has been waiting for long decades.
These actions and the powerful propagation of this video with *Nowness* weave a series of lifelines into Beirut's sense of culture and identity.
The relationship between art and the city is very close with a long and articulated history, from the city depicted by futurist painters in the period of early twentieth-century avant-garde to the initial experiments of the Landartists in the 1960s who were driven to work on the city, with the city, beyond the institutional walls of museums and galleries.
In the case of Beirut, the connection between art and the city materializes in the folds of the city, in its ruins, against the backdrop of an industrious community that repairs its spaces, that takes care of its spaces, through different actions.
In this context, taking care can be interpreted through the filter of the words of Pascale Moliner, Professor of Social Psychology at the Sorbonne in Paris, who focuses on the analysis of care as action, or a series of actions, against indifference, in favor of a capacity to listen to the differences of others.[21] In this sense, lifelines, spatialized through artistic practices, can be interpreted as forms of care against indifference, but in favor of differences within the city.
In a very broad and intricate panorama of unresolved issues, ranging from waste management in the capital (*You Stink Movement* of 2015) to the support of LGBTQ rights, to rights of access to work, to the management of Syrian refugees and so on, even in the recent period, the last three years of Beirut's history (which saw the economic collapse, the devaluation of the national currency, the Covid-19 pandemic, and the devastating port explosion), a wave of activism, of collective self-organization, has been defined, from a grassroots mobilization never seen before in the country's modern history, demonstrating that all these practices in some way contribute to creating infrastructures in support of life, to improving critical livability conditions, sometimes extreme in this city.
These actions are at the center of the research project *Beirut Shifting*

Grounds, curated by Sandra Frem and Boulos Douaihy, on display at the 17th Venice Architecture Biennale in 2021, a project that examines "How we will live together," focusing on the spatial practices that started from the bottom in the city of Beirut, which allow people to adapt to uncertainty and to change.[22]

In an open reflection on what lifelines are and on how they find space, on how they emerge in a fragmented, extreme framework of ruin of the Lebanese capital, "lifelines are ecologies of an imperfect possible." Unlike infrastructural thought, of the landscape and in some way of design, the thought of lifelines does not enclose these spaces, these relationships. It does not enclose them in synthetic forms but in an ecology of the possible.[23]

Endnotes

1 Bianchetti, "Cartographies of protection."
2 Carpi and Fogliata, "La resistenza culturale nel Libano contemporaneo. Le sfide di artiste locali e profughe," 7.
3 Ibid.
4 Cristiano, *Beirut, Libano. Tra assassini, missionari e grands café.*
5 Internazionale, "Sotto la pelle di Beirut."
6 Wilson-Goldie, "On the Politics of Art and Space in Beirut."
7 Hendricks, *Fluxus Codex*, 21.
8 Boano, "Beyond violence. Toward the politics of inhabitation," 43.
9 See: https://dictaphonegroup.com/portfolio-item/this-sea-is-mine/.
10 Carpi and Fogliata, "La resistenza culturale nel Libano contemporaneo. Le sfide di artiste locali e profughe," 1.
11 Dictaphone Group, *This Sea is Mine.*
12 ECODIT and Institut d'Aménagement Urbain de la Région d'Ile de France, *Regional Environmental Assessment Report on the Coastal Zone of Lebanon.*
13 *Dictaphone Group* creates live art performances based on findings and stories produced through multi-disciplinary research on space and oral history. The aim of these projects is to question our relationship to the city, with a focus on public space and the goal of its redefinition.
14 See: https://reclaimthesea.org/tag/the-sea-is-mine/.
15 See: https://dalieh.org/en/landscape.
16 Luger and Ren, *Art and the city. Wording the discussion through a critical artscape*, 10.
17 See: https://yazanhalwani.com/about.
18 Bravo, "Beirut, urbanism and me: framing the city through space, identity and conflict," 222.
19 Boano, "Beyond violence. Toward the politics of inhabitation," 41.
20 Piccinini, "Una performance nel grande teatro abbandonato di Beirut."
21 Marzi, "Pascale Molinier, nel corpo smisurato della cura."
22 Frem and Doouaihy. "Beirut Shifting Grounds."
23 Boano, "Lifelines: the stakes of life in the project."

Bibliography

Bianchetti, Cristina. "Cartographies of protection." *Lifelines. Politics, ethics, and the affective economy of inhabiting*, edited by Cristina Bianchetti and Camillo Boano. Berlin: JOVIS, 2022.

Boano, Camillo. "Beyond violence. Toward the politics of inhabitation." *Lo Squaderno*, No. 59 (July 2021): 41–45.

Boano, Camillo. "Lifelines: the stakes of life in the project." *Lifelines. Politics, ethics, and the affective economy of inhabiting*, edited by Cristina Bianchetti and Camillo Boano. Berlin: JOVIS, 2022.

Bramley, Ellie Violet. "How a Beirut graffiti artist is using his murals to try to unite a fragmented city." *The Guardian*, September 22, 2015. https://www.theguardian.com/cities/2015/sep/22/beirut-graffiti-artist-yazan-halwani-lebanese (last accessed: July 15, 2021).

Bravo, Luisa. "Beirut, urbanism and me: framing the city through space, identity and conflict." *Art and the city. Wording the discussion through a critical artscape* edited by Jason Luger and Julie Ren. London and New York: Routledge, 2017.

Carpi, Estella and Stefano Fogliata. "La resistenza culturale nel Libano contemporaneo. Le sfide di artiste locali e profughe." *Archivio antropologico mediterraneo*, Anno XXIII, No. 22 (2) (2020).

Cristiano, Riccardo. *Beirut, Libano. Tra assassini, missionari e grands café*. Turin: Utet, 2008.

Dawson, Aimee. "Beirut art spaces close en-masse as huge anti-government protests take over the city." *The Art Newspaper*, October 21, 2019. https://www.theartnewspaper.com/news/beirut-art-spaces-close-en-masse-as-huge-anti-government-protests-take-over-the-city (last accessed: July 15, 2021).

Dictaphone Group. *This Sea is Mine*. 2013. https://dictaphonegroup.com/wp-content/uploads/sites/90/2018/12/SIM-booklet-compressed-1.pdf (last accessed: July 15, 2021).

ECODIT and Institut d'Aménagement Urbain de la Région d'Ile de France. *Regional Environmental Assessment Report on the Coastal Zone of Lebanon*. Beirut: Council for Redevelopment and Reconstruction, 1997.

Frem, Sandra and Boulos Doouaihy. "Beirut Shifting Grounds." *La Biennale di Venezia*, 2021. labiennale.org/en/architecture/2021/co-habitats/sandra-frem-boulos-douaihy (last accessed: July 15, 2021).

Hendricks, Jon. *Fluxus Codex*. New York: The Gilbert and Lila Silverman Collection, 1988.

Leclair-Paquet, Benjamin, Camillo Boano, and Andrew Wade. "The Recovery of Beirut in the aftermath of the Lebanese Civil War: the value of urban design." *Participatory design and appropriate technology for disaster reconstruction* edited by Gonzalo Lizarralde, Rohit Jigyasu, Rabindra Vasavada, Susane Havelka, Jennifer Duyne Barenstein, 80–95. Conference proceedings. 2010 international i-Rec conference. Ahmedabad, India. Montreal: Groupe de recherche IF, GRIF, Université de Montréal, 2010.

Luger, Jason and Julie Ren, eds. *Art and the city. Wording the discussion through a critical artscape*, London and New York: Routledge, 2017.

Marzi, Laura. "Pascale Molinier, nel corpo smisurato della cura." *Il Manifesto*, September 10, 2021.

Petroni, Marco. "Silence a Beirut." *Domusweb*, September 22, 2016. https://www.domusweb.it/it/design/2016/09/22/silence_beirut.html (last accessed: July 15, 2021).

Piccinini, Camilla. "Una performance nel grande teatro abbandonato di Beirut." *Artslife*, January 4, 2021. https://artslife.com/2021/01/04/performance-teatro-beirut-video/ (last accessed: July 15, 2021).

Pignatti, Lorenza and Tony Chakar. "Beirut, l'incertezza come immaginario." *Il Manifesto*, September 1, 2020. https://ilmanifesto.it/tony-chakar-beirut-lincertezza-come-immaginario/ (last accessed: July 15, 2021).

Proctor, Rebecca Anne. "Huge explosion in Beirut decimates city and leaves art scene in disarray." *The Art Newspaper*, August 8, 2020. https://www.theartnewspaper.com/news/beirut-explosion (last accessed: July 15, 2021).

Saksouk-Sasso, Abir. "Making Spaces for Communal Sovereignty: The Story of Beirut's Dalieh." *Arab Studies Journal*, Vol. XXIII, No. 1 (2015): 296–319.

Sinno, Wael. "How People Reclaimed Public Spaces in Beirut during the 2019 Lebanese Uprising." *The Journal of Public Space*, Vol.5, No.1 (2020): 193–218.

Wilson-Goldie, Kaelen. "On the Politics of Art and Space in Beirut." *Tate Papers*, No. 12, Autumn 2009. https://www.tate.org.uk/research/publications/tate-papers/12/on-politics-art-and-space-beirut (last accessed: July 15, 2021).

Autonomous spaces in Berlin: cynical resistance tactics in the neoliberal city

Lorenza Manfredi

In the thirty years since the fall of the Berlin Wall in 1989, the financialization of urban land has triggered a sharp acceleration in densification and gentrification processes, leading, amongst other things, to the expulsion of many autonomous projects from the internal areas of the city. Facing these processes with disenchantment, some projects developed resistance tactics, managing to grasp the new possibilities with great timing and to identify the most suitable way of maintaining the autonomous use of some central spaces despite the growing competition in a now saturated city. These projects help to reach a difficult balance between autonomy of appropriation tactics and the inescapable rationality of economic processes which regulate the neoliberal city.

Autonomy, originally deriving from the physical, normative, and ideological isolation of temporary activities that were able to appropriate the numerous urban *Brachen*,[1] is now limited to self-determination and self-management of the use of spaces which, in order to continue to exist, are strongly dependent on hegemonic political and economic dynamics in the surrounding city. In an attempt to resist the hyper-development of urban land, autonomous projects thus define new lifelines: despite reacting to the surrounding context, they are able to guarantee intrusions in market logics. While capitalism means creating profit, the resulting spaces are, on the other hand, oriented towards non-profit: their raison d'être is the direct expression of the needs and desires of minorities.

In the contemporary city, these lifelines thus guarantee the survival of spaces for the coexistence – conflicting but dynamic – of different entities. The deliberate cynicism of the tactics developed to maintain the autonomous use of the spaces derives from an acceptance of the neoliberal city's structures and provokes a loss of revolutionary and ideological values of these projects, which thereby provoke ambiguous dynamics. The reflection on ambiguities and vulnerabilities of lifelines being experimented in Berlin emerges and is in dialog with the PhD research that the author is developing at the TU Berlin and IUAV Venice[2] universities, investigating the emergence of new meanings of autonomous spaces in the contemporary city.

The luxury of voids: the Berlin urban transformation of the last thirty years

Fig.1
Development dynamics in the Spreeraum Ost area from 1990 to 2021, pp. 168–169. Autonomous, temporary and subcultural projects confront unregulated densification of buildings. Source: Lorenza Manfredi and Luis Martin Sanchez.

The reunification of Germany and the decision to return the German capital to Berlin meant for this city the start of a period of extreme interest in urban planning: the urgency of re-establishing and restructuring joint urban development between East and West Berlin led to the assignment of new duties and complex roles both in the planning and in the management area.[3] The urban issues that emerged during the post-reunification years, just like the issues that were, on the other hand, not addressed or were intentionally ignored, defined today's city and are still at the center of an urban discourse in Berlin which finally

1
3
The Berlin Wall
The Berlin Strip
Spreeraum Area
Industrial Area
Green Area
Buildings blocks
Buildings between

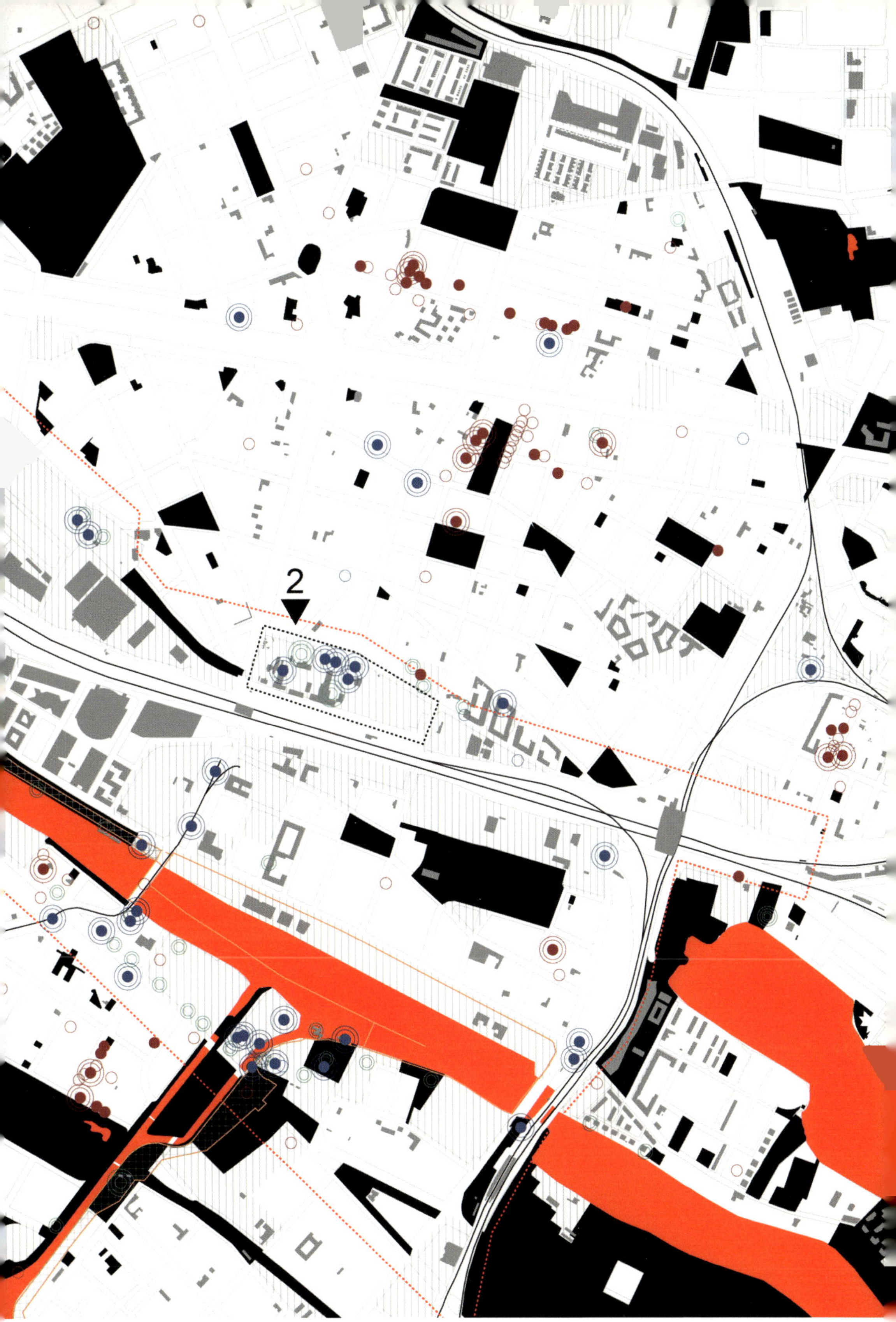

Squats 1990 - 2021/ evicted/legalized
Temporary uses 2007/ still there 2020
Nightclubs 2013-2020/ closed 2021
1 Holzmarkt
2 RAW Gelände
3 Teepeeland

seems to be able to pause and reflect on what has happened in these three decades of impetuous transformation.

The ideological and formal matters that initially dominated the *architectural dispute* in Berlin[4] overshadowed a discussion around the issue of land, which could have monitored and given direction to a spatial development that took place almost uncontrollably.

In the 1990s, the city, as is known, was characterized by voids[5] caused by a series of simultaneous causes: the wartime destruction, the dismantling of a large part of the socialist apparatus that came to be obsolete in united Germany, a reconstruction strategy based upon widespread demolition (*Kahlschlagsanierung*), and finally the presence/absence of the Berlin Wall. The incredible abundance of voids was seen as a luxury[6] by post-urban photographers and aesthetes, but also by activists and pioneers,[7] who quickly colonized these disused spaces to carry out their activities. These ranged from small informal and temporary businesses to cultural and social spaces created *ad hoc* for the occupied spaces, making the city a great *Experimentierfeld*, a testing ground for the most varied ideas.

In this context, land seemed to be an inexhaustible resource and the various temporary appropriations were, at least from the 2000s, seen positively or tolerated both by the administration and by the owners. In fact, the *Zwischennutzungen*, managing to initiate processes in areas currently not usable economically,[8] not only facilitated a re-coding of the urban voids as social spaces[9] but offered an image to the *vacant spaces*, ultimately contributing to further capitalization of the occupied land.[10]

While Berlin was filled with a spirit of euphoric optimism – *Wachstumseuphorie* – in the early years after the reunification, it soon became clear that the forecasts for demographic and economic growth were not being achieved, and indeed the city's financial crisis was worsening[11] and the population was continuing to decline.[12] This meant that the *interim state*[13] of abundance of voids and accessible spaces was able to continue for decades. The expansion of temporary and highly creative activities thus reached dimensions such as to become studied even by inter-European disciplinary research,[14] only then to be used by the administration as a *marketing tool*[15] and by some owners and investors to make their land or the surrounding area more attractive and therefore to increase its value.[16]

The 'Boom'

The absence of available land began to become a cause for concern in recent times. From 2007 at the latest, Berlin finally experienced the construction boom that had been expected, further reinforced by Germany's economic stability in the aftermath of the 2007 global financial crisis, which – distinguishing itself from other more fragile European economies – was able to attract financing, particularly on the real estate market. The reception of this change was, of course, particularly slow by the political and administrative bodies, who continued to favor major investors exploiting the available spatial resources. The massive sell-off of many of the plots owned by the Berlin *Land* was not justifiable by the limited revenues that these sales achieved[17] and proved unsuccessful in the lack of opportunity to develop public real estate assets to create long-term spatial strategies.

Furthermore, the presence of episodes of corruption and illegal transfers of capital and of favoritism, particularly facilitated by the momentary lack of controls during the early years of reunification,[18] introduced private interests into the political and spatial strategies. The dramatic consequences can be recognized in some of the most significant interventions in the privatized central areas in the 1990s, such as on Potsdamer Platz and on Friedrichstrasse. While the sell-off of the former represents a scandalous loss for the city,[19] the amalgamation of entire urban parcels of *Filetgrundstücke* on Friedrichstrasse, divided through the temporary instrument of the KOAI – whose very legitimacy has been heavily criticized[20] – led to a homogeneous development of spaces for offices and retail, excluding any small-scale development which would have guaranteed a mix of uses and ownership structures.[21]

Today, the question of land is the most strongly felt and clearest urban problem in the Berlin debate, manifested with great force on the city's streets. The sell-off of public land, the creation of major projects oriented towards maximizing profits, and the gradual relocation of autonomous projects from the city center are criticalities that are now broadly recognized. Protests against gentrification, rising rents, and misadministration are the order of the day, shifting from year to year between the most affected districts.[22] The expulsion of the low-income part of the population from the city center is perceived by many citizens as a threat to the stability of the housing situation, understandably: in Berlin, in fact, apartment owners numbered just 11% of inhabitants in 2018, the lowest percentage of owners among the various German *Länder*.[23]

Three micro-stories

This chapter[24] analyzes the reconfiguration of three autonomous projects, which have developed survival mechanisms to enhance and increase competition on urban land. The concepts of ownership, common good, and temporariness each time become the fulcrum of their drive to find their own role in the altered context. In order not to be marginalized and expelled from the central areas of the city and to maintain direct and independent control over the use and design of the occupied spaces, cynical tactics are developed – lifelines – which led to the re-signification of the projects themselves.

Holzmarkt arose from the experience of Club25, the space of which it occupies. Club25, a techno music venue, rented the disused area owned by BSR[25] from 2003 to 2010 by way of short-term contracts. In these seven years and in the years that followed, when the club had to move to the other side of the Spree because the contracts were not renewed,

once again temporarily occupying a disused factory, the Club25 music program became known internationally, becoming one of the symbolic projects of techno culture and, although initially established as *Zwischennutzung*, managing to take root in the Berlin context. When BSR put the land up for sale, the cooperative *Holzmarkt25* created a development project for the area that was "free from the pressures of the real estate industry and urban planning from above,"[26] implemented together with the "community,"[27] guaranteeing free access to the banks of the Spree.

Fig.2
Berlin: a garden at Holzmarkt. Implementing cynical tactics, some projects have succeeded in obtaining ownership of the area and are now seeking to encourage public use. Photograph by Lorenza Manfredi.

Not having obtained the necessary support from the administration, the cooperative turned to *Abendrot Stiftung*,[28] which provided the initial capital required to purchase the land and with which a leasehold agreement was signed. A complex network with numerous supporters was to guarantee the capacity to develop the project and repay the debt contracted with the Swiss foundation by way of a rent corresponding to approximately one million Euros per year.[29]

Although the original idea of keeping the riverbank accessible and providing an autonomous space for cultural and social uses was still the main objective of the project, the need to create economic efficiency to repay the debt led to a series of practical consequences, making the project controversial and exposing it to criticism. The aesthetics of the spaces were clearly inspired by temporary projects, whose strong

Fig.3
RAW Gelände is a dismissed infrastructure area whose spaces have been in 'temporary' use for about thirty years. The development plans of the current owners actively involve users but still remain true to valorization goals, creating an ambivalent situation. Photograph by Lorenza Manfredi.

symbolic nature was exploited with broad use of economic and easy-use materials, such as wooden pallets and spray cans.

The events that are organized have continued to build a rich cultural and musical program, known both on the international level and in Berlin. Some factors, however, brought about a radical change to the soul of the project: the increasing involvement and investment of time and energy (as well as capital) by members of the cooperative, complications deriving from a democratic decision-making process with many participants and interests, and finally a gradual diversification of use which, to generate higher revenues, was oriented towards gastronomy and the rental of spaces for ateliers, offices, or hotels. This led to a change of users: the gradual dissolution of the neighborhood 'community' that was initially promoted as the main receptor of the whole initiative[30] corresponded to an increasing presence of young professionals in the cultural field, start-uppers, and young tourists coming from all over Europe.

RAW Gelände is an area located less than two kilometers from *Holzmarkt*. With its 71,000 m², it is the last abandoned large-scale industrial site not yet converted within the perimeter of Berlin's suburban railway system. From 1999, the various buildings that form part of the complex were occupied and rented with short-term contracts by artists and activists. The *RAW Gelände* area – isolated from the rest of the district by the presence of the tracks on one side and by the boundary wall on

the other – encompasses people with very different needs and interests: clubs, concert halls, sports centers, restaurants, education and teaching facilities, galleries and artist's studios occupy the buildings and attract users as varied as the uses they offer. Despite the communication and representation difficulties, the various players present in the area form part of a common project and have found themselves on several occasions in clashes with the owners of the land, trying not to be removed from the area and to be included in the development plans.[31]

Since 2001, when the real estate branch of *Deutsche Bahn, Vivico Real Estate GmbH*, placed this and other disused properties on the market, the greatest difficulties for activists and users of the spaces arose due to repeated transfers of ownership and the presence of some investors who were not very clear about the development strategies for the area. The current owners[32], on the other hand, have participated or initiated discussion and interaction processes with the activists and the citizens affected, involving experts in participatory planning and political representatives of the Friedrichshain-Kreuzberg District.

For the area owned by the Kurth Group, the current agreement is that, in exchange for an increase in the percentage of building volume and the approval of the construction plan by the district authorities, the uses of the 'socio-cultural L' – namely those settled in some buildings arranged in an L-shape in the area, some of which are under protection as historical buildings – will not be exploited. These buildings will be entrusted to the GSE, a state-related body that deals with the management of non-profit spaces within the city.[33] Thanks to monitored rents, users would therefore receive the spaces from the owner through GSE and could continue to use the facilities to develop a social and cultural offer aimed particularly at minorities.

In addition to the thirty-year limitation of the agreement's validity (which leaves uncertainties open for a not-too-distant future), the great problem for these spaces will be adapting to a hugely transforming context which will inevitably also entail new users here, risking the removal of those who, until now, have mostly used the spaces. The socially and economically more fragile brackets of the population, artists and cultural players with low income and the various users of the night entertainment offered here by the clubs and bars, risk being expelled indirectly by the transformation that is underway – despite the agreement and the administration's commitment to allow development attentive to the existing situation. It will only become clear in the coming years if the development projects, still being negotiated, will not only be able to exploit the 'creative' image of the area profitably but also to actually involve the current players and users of the area in the future program realistically and co-productively.

Fig.4
Temporary constructions and tents in the Teepeeland camp in Berlin Mitte. Teepeeland's existence is increasingly threatened by investment sites under construction in the immediate vicinity. Photograph by Lorenza Manfredi.

In the last story analyzed, which occupies a small area of approximately 1,000 m^2 in an inlet between the banks of the Spree and the former *Eisfabrik* area and is currently undergoing redevelopment, no real solution has been found to maintain the use of the occupied spaces on a lasting basis. The *teepee* tents and small wooden constructions (one construction inspired by a Tibetan temple, a group of seats around a bonfire, a

small stage, and a bar) create a sort of camp-village, semi-hidden and well-organized, with indications of behavioral rules to follow (no consumption of drugs or drinks with an alcohol content of more than 15%, etc.),[34] and with a signage system that assists orientation.
The founder of *Teepeeland* calls himself *Flieger* and was previously one of the first tenants of the *Cuvrybrache*, the tent city that occupied a *Brache* located a short distance away from the major hub of Warschauer Strasse until 2014.
Complaining of the dangerousness of some events that occurred in the *Cuvrybrache*, where there were no rules, *Flieger* sought to develop a different project with *Teepeeland*. As well as the regulation, the constitution and the recurring plenums at which assignments and specific responsibilities are entrusted, some of the tents are offered through the *couchsurfing* program, and the stage is used for debates, theatrical and musical events proposed by visitors or neighbors in the district, creating a more inclusive and welcoming atmosphere towards the surrounding city. The buildings constructed by the *Baugruppe Spreefeld* at the neighboring site protect *Teepeeland* from direct access from the road, acting as a filter and permitting alliances between the two projects which, albeit in different ways, both try to test unusual and shared methods of inhabiting the city.
The *Teepeeland* activists, proud of what they have built in their more than seven years of settlement in this area, trust in the tolerance of the *Bezirk Mitte* administration, with which they are in dialogue and with which there is a sort of tacit agreement.[35] The temporary nature of the camp is therefore sealed with a strategy that guarantees its ephemeral permanence, with lightweight tents that may one day – possibly – be dismantled and rebuilt in another niche of the urban fabric.

Lifelines that guarantee contamination of the homogeneous city through plural spaces

These cases briefly illustrated tell of the search for solutions by actors and activists who in recent years have clashed with the Berlin urban transformation and in particular the increased pressure on the land. Their resistance in the neoliberal city demonstrates an attempt to guarantee lifelines that, through autonomous use of the spaces, pay great attention to social and civic issues. These projects create accessible spaces, where the cultural and social offer becomes an opportunity for meeting, expression, and discussion for those who remain excluded from more conventional spaces, that for social or economic reasons are inclusive spaces for diversity.
Berlin, where a few decades ago these spaces had been elevated to the symbol of the entire city,[36] is now dealing with the consequences of the strenuous effort to exploit urban land to create surplus value and profit, ignoring a possible discourse on the land issue. Now that this is an essential topic of the Berlin debate, it seems important to note that not only living as a residence but also living in a public space consisting of

a variety of minority spaces requires the attention of scholars, researchers, and designers. A shared reflection could stimulate new solutions and unprecedented coalitions with the administration, with investors and/or with partners and allies.

The stories of *Holzmarkt*, *RAW Gelände*, and *Teepeeland* raise questions precisely thanks to the contradictoriness and ambiguity of their results. The cynical tactics employed to obtain a role (or a space) in the neoliberal city actually risk leading to the loss of support by the *users* at which these spaces were originally targeted, but in any case, raise interesting issues to be investigated and debated.

Firstly, the *role of government bodies* is called into question. In recent years, it appears that Berlin institutions are more interested in intervening and mediating in favor of autonomous projects, both in the case of safeguarding socio-cultural projects and in that of testing alternative methods to private ownership for the purposes of guaranteeing the right to housing. An increasing demand for intervention by the State is loudly demanded by some citizens.[37] The expansion and growing trust offered to state-related entities such as GSE offer prospects for greater administrative and managerial support aimed at individual spaces and projects followed case by case.

Despite this, it is still unclear which visions are held at the political level and if it is possible to implement a true change of course in terms of State intervention. The test experience of the *Mietendeckel*[38] is a prime example of the scarce possibilities of taking forward new experimental strategies for as long as there is no structural strategic cohesion at national level.

Secondly, the analyzed projects demonstrate the contradictions that emerge from the desire for permanence and stability of autonomous and non-profit projects: the need to compete with the market or to collaborate with financial players requires the search for compromises with investors willing to contribute to maintaining these spaces but not to waive their profits. At what point do these negotiations limit the autonomy and independence of the analyzed cases?

The gradual entrenchment of initially temporary projects involves the establishment of complex managerial and organizational decision-making structures, as well as the diversification of the offer to create greater economic efficiency. The same aesthetic characteristics of temporary and low-cost projects are transformed into a visual identity or a brand, cancelling out any ideological or political meaning of the same. The typical spontaneity of the autonomous projects of the 1990s and early 2000s is replaced by cynical tactics, in an attempt to pragmatically resolve the difficulties that have emerged in more recent years. The re-signification that this entails puts at risk the capacities of inclusion and accessibility that make these projects fundamental for a plural urban space.

The *role of space* in the city still seems to be a fundamental issue today. The interest in and strength of the analyzed projects are in fact guaranteed above all by their position and accessibility. These spaces are and intend to remain in the central areas of the city. They are large spaces but also minimal spaces, which do not act concomitantly with each other. The richness and variety of their offer of uses, and the multiple origins (geographic, social, cultural, and age-related) of the persons actively involved, reveals the great capacity of these spaces to accommodate demands and desires that are not answered in the conventional city. Gathering all autonomous energies in a single project, thereby cancelling the great offer of minimal and diversified spaces, along with the creation of new spaces in the outermost areas of the city, do not seem to be solutions able to maintain these qualities and the values they represent.

The stories briefly narrated in this chapter show us a series of lifelines made of minimal, adaptable, interstitial, situated spaces.

Urbanity is not made up of just residences. The cranes used in constructing the area surrounding the tents of *Teepeeland* are coming closer and closer, reminding Berlin of the urgency of reflecting on how these lifelines keep alive their plural spaces, guaranteeing their autonomy in designing their uses and activities.

Endnotes

1 Wastelands – disused spaces – whose peculiar accessibility in Berlin from the second post-war period to the first decade of the 2000s has seen the major development of spontaneous appropriation practices, from the *squatting* movement to the more recent *Zwischennutzung* phenomenon. "The *Brachen* of Berlin are unique. Emerging from wartime destruction, economic malaise, and geopolitical division, these ostensibly empty sites evolved into laboratories for botanists, artists, and ordinary people seeking respite from the city." In: Gandy, *Natura Urbana: The Brachen of Berlin*.
2 The PhD is developed as a joint project between the TU Berlin and IUAV Venice universities under the working title: "Disruptions. Spreeraum Ost, Berlin, 1990–2020." Doctoral dissertation defense is scheduled for September 2022.
3 Kunst and Deutsche Akademie für Städtebau und Landesplanung Berlin-Brandenburg, eds., *Berlin & Berlin. Stadtplanung und Städtebau nach dem Mauerfall im Gespräch*.
4 Hertweck, *Der Berliner Architekturstreit. Architektur, Stadtbau, Geschichte und Identität in der Berliner Republik 1989–1999*.
5 Among others: Huyssen, "The voids of Berlin"; Huyssen, *Present Pasts. Urban Palimpsests and the Politics of Memory*.
6 Kil, *Luxus der Leere: vom schwierigen Rückzug aus der Wachstumswelt. Eine Streitschrift*.
7 Howard and Gröschner, "Luxus der Leere."
8 Overmeyer, "Raumpioniere in Berlin."
9 Krauzik, "Zwischennutzung als Initiator einer neuen Berliner Identität?".
10 Colomb, "Pushing the Urban Frontier: temporary uses of space, city marketing, and the creative city discourse in 2000s Berlin."
11 It reached its peak with the financial collapse of the *Bankgesellschaft Berlin* in 2001, of which the Berlin *Land* was one of the major shareholders.
12 Since 1993, when a population of about 3 and a half million was registered, there was a continuous decrease in the number of inhabitants until the early 2000s. It was only from 2004 that the population steadily started to grow again, returning to 3 and a half million in around 2011. Source: Amt für Statistik Berlin Brandenburg.
13 Till, "Interim Use at a Former Death Strip? Art, Politics, and Urbanism at Skulpturenpark Berlin_Zentrum."
14 Like the EU-funded project "Urban Catalyst," the results of which are contained in the publication: Oswalt, Overmeyer, and Misselwitz, *Urban Catalyst. The Power of Temporary Use*.
15 While, initially, the voids were cut off from the promotional imagery of the city as they were seen as remnants of an undesired past and the result of the 'failure' of the dominant place marketing narrative, they were later recognized as fertile ground and a possible resource for promoting a marketable urban image. In: Colomb, *Staging the new*, 239–245.
16 Colomb, "Pushing the Urban Frontier: temporary uses of space, city marketing, and the creative city discourse in 2000s Berlin."
17 Schüschke estimates that the total earnings over 29 years of mass privatization (covering a total surface area of 21 km^2) amounted to roughly 5.2 billion euros. When considering that in 2018 alone, Berlin's budget corresponded to 28 billion euros, the gains from privatizations cannot be justified as a remedial tool for the city's poor finances. In: Schüschke, "Ausverkauft. Die Privatisierung von landeseigenem Grundbesitz in Berlin," 76–85.
18 Krätke, "City of Talents? Berlin's Regional Economy, Socio-Spatial Fabric and 'Worst Practice' Urban Governance."
19 Mainly financial: sold in four parts by the Senate in 1991 for approximately 80 million DM, the part that was purchased by Daimler-Benz was then resold in 2007 for 1.4 billion euros; but also in terms of urban planning and programming, representing what Gregotti defines as "excitement without prospects." In: Gregotti, "La grande bonaccia."
20 The KOAI (*Koordinierungsausschuss für innerstädtische Investitionen*) was a committee that included representatives of the senate, the senior finance directorate, and the *Treuhandanstalt* (privatization agency) and was responsible for deciding which investors were to be given the go-ahead to buy. It was an informal organization that, without a legal basis and without the prescribed mechanisms of parliamentary control, essentially acted in a sort of legal void. KOAI acted from 1991 to 1993 and dealt with at least 50 large projects, structuring the plots, the ownership system, and their intended use, also allowing investments even where there were pending restitution processes or decisions in favor of a previous owner.

21 Lenhart-Roth, "Der Koordinierungsausschuss für innerstädtische Investitionen. Eine Blackbox als Macht- und Entscheidungszentrale."
22 The online archive Umbruch Archiv contains the main events linked to the Berlin protests dating back to the 1970s: https://www.umbruch-bildarchiv.de/willkomm1.html.
23 See: https://de.statista.com/.
24 Reasoning in parallel to the PhD thesis, already cited at the start of the chapter.
25 Entity that deals with waste collection in Berlin.
26 Statute of *Holzmarkt25*, available on the association's website: https://www.holzmarkt.com/ueber-den-holzmarkt.
27 Ibid.
28 The *Abendrot Stiftung*, founded in 1984, is one of Switzerland's largest pension funds.
29 The information dates back to a conversation between the author, the researcher Natalia Kvitkova, and Konstantin Krex, spokesman of *Holzmarkt25*, in July 2020.
30 For example, the *Mörchenpark e.V.* association, which was initially to have 25% and to take care of the public spaces, gradually disappeared from the scene of activities and was less and less actively involved.
31 The events were narrated by Kristine Schütt, alias Mikado, in a conversation with the author in September 2020. Mikado was one of the first people active on the site and is still today involved in self-organized educational and artistic projects in some spaces of the area.
32 In particular, the *Kurth Group*, a family company based in Göttingen, and *International Campus AG* based in Munich, which owns the two largest parts of the area.
33 In 1995, a trust contract from the Berlin *Land* assigned GSE the task of forming and managing the trust assets aimed at creating a public asset. This has involved taking over, administering, managing, and renting entire properties in order to be able to offer residential and commercial spaces on a long-term basis to requesting groups.
34 Information presented on the webpage dedicated to couchsurfing requests to stay overnight temporarily in an area free of charge: https://teepeeland.wordpress.com/couchsurfing/.
35 The activists' point of view was narrated by Niko Rollmann, an activist who often takes on the role of spokesperson for the group, in a meeting with the author and researcher Natalia Kvitkova in July 2020.
36 Be Berlin campaign. "The place to be for change" (2009). Cited in Colomb, *Staging the new Berlin. Place marketing and the politics of urban reinvention post-1989*, 261.
37 As shown by the initiative *Deutsche Wohnen & co enteignen!* which calls for the withdrawal from the market and remunicipalization of 12% of the apartments currently rented by large real estate groups. The initiative organized a popular referendum that took place on September 26, 2021, in which 56.4% of voters were in favor of expropriation.
38 The *Mietendeckel* is a law on the reorganization of legal provisions on rental restrictions proclaimed by the Berlin Chamber on January 30, 2020. The law envisaged the freezing of rents, the regulation of maximum rents, the monitored reduction of rents, and the restriction of the modernization fee. On March 25, 2021, the Federal Constitutional Court established that the *Mietendeckel* is incompatible for legislative competence reasons and that the law promulgated by Berlin is void.

Bibliography

Colomb, Claire. "Pushing the Urban Frontier: temporary uses of space, city marketing, and the creative city discourse in 2000s Berlin." *Journal of Urban Affairs* 34, No. 2 (2012): 131–152.

Colomb, Claire. *Staging the new Berlin. Place marketing and the politics of urban reinvention post-1989*. Oxfordshire and New York: Routledge, 2012.

Gandy, Matthew. *Natura Urbana: The Brachen of Berlin*. DVD booklet. UK and Germany: Sarah Dockhorn and Esther Niemeier, producers, 2019.

Gregotti, Vittorio. "La grande bonaccia." Casabella 595 (November 1992).

Hertweck, Florian. *Der Berliner Architekturstreit. Stadtbau, Architektur, Geschichte und Identität in der Berliner Republik 1989–1999*. Berlin: Gebr. Mann Verlag, 2010.

Howard, Michelle and Annett Gröschner. "Luxus der Leere." *Frankfurter Allgemeine blog*, Ich. Heute, 10 vor 8, May 23, 2014. https://blogs.faz.net/10vor8/2014/05/23/luxus-der-leere-1509/ (last accessed: December 15, 2021).

Huyssen, Andreas. "The voids of Berlin." *Critical Inquiry* 24, No. 1 (Autumn 1997): 57–81.

Huyssen, Andreas. *Present Pasts. Urban Palimpsests and the Politics of Memory*. Stanford, CA: Stanford University Press, 2003.

Kil, Wolfgang. *Luxus der Leere: vom schwierigen Rückzug aus der Wachstumswelt. Eine Streitschrift*. Wuppertal: Müller+Busmann, 2004.

Krätke, Stefan. "City of Talents? Berlin's Regional Economy, Socio-Spatial Fabric and 'Worst Practice' Urban Governance." *The Berlin Reader. A Compendium on Urban Change and Activism*, edited by Matthias Bernt, Britta Grell, and Andrej Holm. Bielefeld: Transcript Verlag, 2013.

Krauzik, Maren. "Zwischennutzung als Initiator einer neuen Berliner Identität?" *ISR Graue Reihe*, No. 7 (2007): 13.

Kunst, Friedemann and Deutsche Akademie für Städtebau und Landesplanung Berlin-Brandenburg, eds. *Berlin & Berlin. Stadtplanung und Städtebau nach dem Mauerfall im Gespräch*. Berlin: JOVIS, 2021.

Lenhart-Roth, Karin. "Der Koordinierungsausschuss für innerstädtische Investitionen. Eine Blackbox als Macht- und Entscheidungszentrale." *ARCH+* 241, Berlin Theorie. Politik des Raums im neuen Berlin (2020): 86–95.

Manfredi, Lorenza. "Autonomous spaces reconfiguring themselves to survive in the neoliberal city: the case of Berlin/Spreeraum Ost in the years 1990–2020." PhD diss., Università Iuav di Venezia, forthcoming.

Oswalt, Phillipp, Klaus Overmeyer, and Phillip Misselwitz. *Urban Catalyst. The Power of Temporary Use*. Berlin: DOM Publishers, 2014.

Overmeyer, Klaus. "Raumpioniere in Berlin." *Stadtforum Berlin 2020 – Dokumentation der Veranstaltung am 15. April 2005 "verschenken? bewalden? zwischennutzen?"*, edited by Stadtforum Berlin. Berlin: SenStadt, 2005.

Schüschke, Florine. "Ausverkauft. Die Privatisierung von landeseigenem Grundbesitz in Berlin." *ARCH+* 241, Berlin Theorie. Politik des Raums im neuen Berlin (2020): 76–85.

Till, Karen E. "Interim Use at a Former Death Strip? Art, Politics, and Urbanism at Skulpturenpark Berlin_Zentrum." *The German Wall: Fallout in Europe*, edited by Marc Silberman. New York: Palgrave Macmillan, 2011.

Taranto: a system of necrotized spaces protecting life

Cristina Bianchetti,
Alessandra Cusanno,
Agim Kërçuku

In the Fordist era, the factory and the city were tied together structurally: the former constructed the latter, the latter was the former. The city was, without mediation, the factory. In the 1980s, the ties loosened and then broke. The factory abandoned the city, and the latter mourned its absence. As Freud explained, mourning is not merely a circumscribed loss but a reaction to any loss, including that of liberty or of an ideal or one's identity. And so, the factory and the city once again hybridize in the optimistic assumptions of the period following the 2008 economic crisis. They touch each other differently; they are each other's internal horizon. One involves and crosses the other.

Within this dialectic of relationships between factory and city, Taranto's situation takes an extreme, entirely particular position. One of Europe's biggest steel mills was opened in Taranto in 1965. The factory aimed to sustain the city but is, in fact, incompatible with it. The last sixty years of history of the city of Taranto have been a history of this incompatibility, played out in the fields of health, employment, ecology, and living. In other words, the last sixty years of history of the city of Taranto have been the story of the *cannibalization* of the city by the factory.

Cannibalization implies a death-life relationship; it crosses bodies, creates things, models spaces, forms knowledge, and produces discourse. It is, in its own way, a mesh that stretches across the whole social body of the city: a relationship that generates effects and produces identities, behaviors, and interests. In Foucauldian terms, it is a productive network, an expression of the microphysics of power.

In this condition, building greater distance between the factory and the city perhaps becomes the only possible protective move. A move that is both protective and critical in relation to the many precise devices brought into play over the years, aimed at separating the factory and the city, to remedy, to protect: hills, walls, shells. In other words, thinking of the cannibalization process of the city by the factory leads us to consider lifelines as *a broad spatial system* that confronts the factory, is on the same scale, and links the city to the territory. It is a system of necrotizing or progressively abandoned spaces, which has a symbolic, narrative, dreamlike component but at the same time conveys a very material, physical, and spatial idea of a distance that protects life: something radically different from the arrangement of public spaces.[1]

Taranto and Ilva

When, in 1959, the Italian Government, IRI, and Finsider decided to base the Ilva steel plant in Taranto, the city had 182,000 inhabitants. Twenty years later, the plant (which covers an area of 15.5 km^2) employed 43,000 workers, including the related industries,[2] and the city numbered 228,841 inhabitants. Those twenty years of lightning growth saw the Pope (Paul VI, 1968), extreme left-wing political groups (Primi Fuochi di Guerriglia in the 1970s), and the President of the Republic (Sandro Pertini, 1980) all pass through the plant.

Fig.1
The factory cannibalizes the city. Source: Alessandra Cusanno.

This was the phase in which, amidst workers' struggles, the initial steel crises, and the increase in related industries, the plant was defined as the future of the city. This phase would be followed by others marked by chemical and epidemiological findings, plant seizures, public referenda, and judicial wrangles. Meanwhile, the factory had also gained public attention thanks to the numerous historical reconstructions, films, and documentaries.[3]

Until the late 1980s, a handful of major players (Ilva, Eni, Cementir, and Marina Militare) were behind the rapid growth: the city was modelled and oversized on their requirements, and its survival was inextricably

linked to their presence. The local area's environmental and social resources had become a stock from which to extract value.
Then, in the 1990s, things changed: the city's economy entered a state of crisis and the horizons of growth reduced. The population gradually declined, ultimately falling below the threshold of 200,000 inhabitants (196,702).[4]
Today, Taranto is a fragmented city, consisting of rigid pieces: the industrial activities of the former companies Ilva, Cementir, and ENI, the military areas of the Military Maritime Arsenal, the Buffoluto Arsenal, and the New Military Naval Station, the port system, the Old Town, the Porta Napoli plant, the New Town, the Tamburi and Paolo VI residential districts, the illegal cities of San Vito, Lama, and Talsano, the agricultural areas, and the two seas (Mare Piccolo and Mare Grande). It is an extremely complex city that is always traced back to the constant juxtaposition of these different 'pieces.'
The city's fragmented layout identifies physical and perceptive boundaries. The arsenal wall conceals the view of the Mare Piccolo, the two seas isolate the Old Town, the agricultural fabric separates Paolo VI from the rest of the city, and the large avenue Viale Magna Grecia distances the Salinella District from the New Town. The distance between these fragments is not progressive, gradual, or uncertain, despite them having traits in common: when walking around the city, you can see the transition from one to the other. The limits are tangible and perceptible through the succession of urban fabrics, building types, and practices of using space. As a repercussion, the separation creates a strong sense of belonging to the individual places.

A hyper-designed city

As is the case for many Italian cities, for Taranto, the urban planning history of the modern era sees the succession of numerous plans and projects in a crescendo that has in recent years reached a paroxysmal rhythm. From the defenses against the factory (the hills of Pietro Porcinai, the wall, the shells)[5] to the competitions for urban redevelopment and regeneration, to the strategic plans of recent years (Taranto Futuro Prossimo of 2018) and the numerous design competitions. If there is one thing that appears to be plentiful in Taranto, it is plans that are, in most cases, ineffective.[6]
Within this vast repertoire, it is, for the purposes of our discourse, worth briefly focusing on a single case: that of the environmental project requested from Pietro Porcinai at a time when the steel activity was still booming but its serious health implications were already being detected. In 1972, the ITALSIDER Company contacted the architect to seek a solution to the problem of the 'slag' dust, namely the mountains of raw materials stored in the factory's mineral park which, lifted by the wind, were spreading over the city and particularly over one of the districts (Tamburi) located just a few meters from the industrial chimneys and minerals.

Fig.2
How to breathe in Tamburi: graphs of the direction of the winds and concentration of PM10 identified on windy days, pp. 186–187. Source: Alessandra Cusanno.

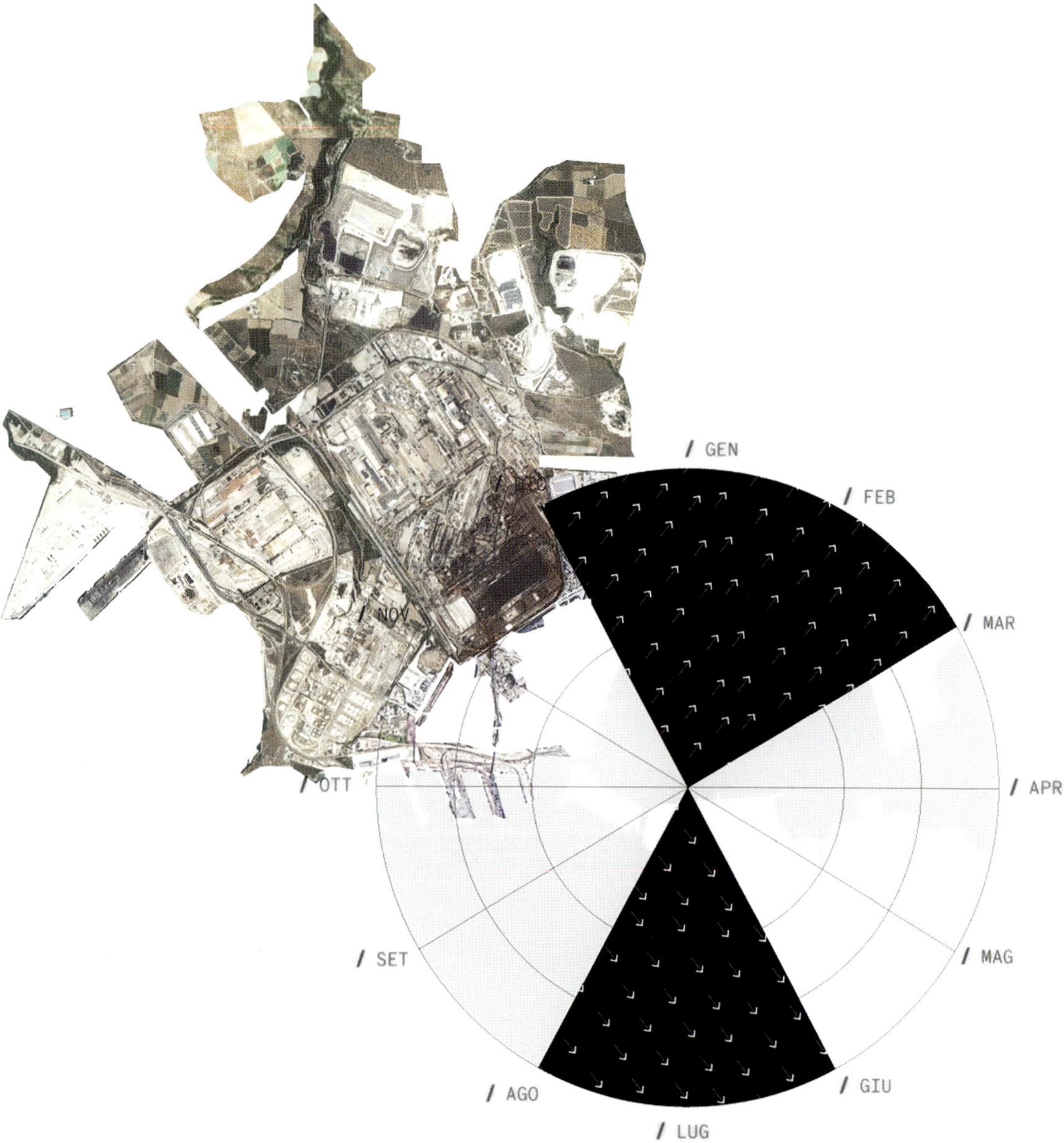
/ GEN
/ FEB
/ MAR
/ APR
/ MAG
/ GIU
/ LUG
/ AGO
/ SET
/ OTT
/ NOV

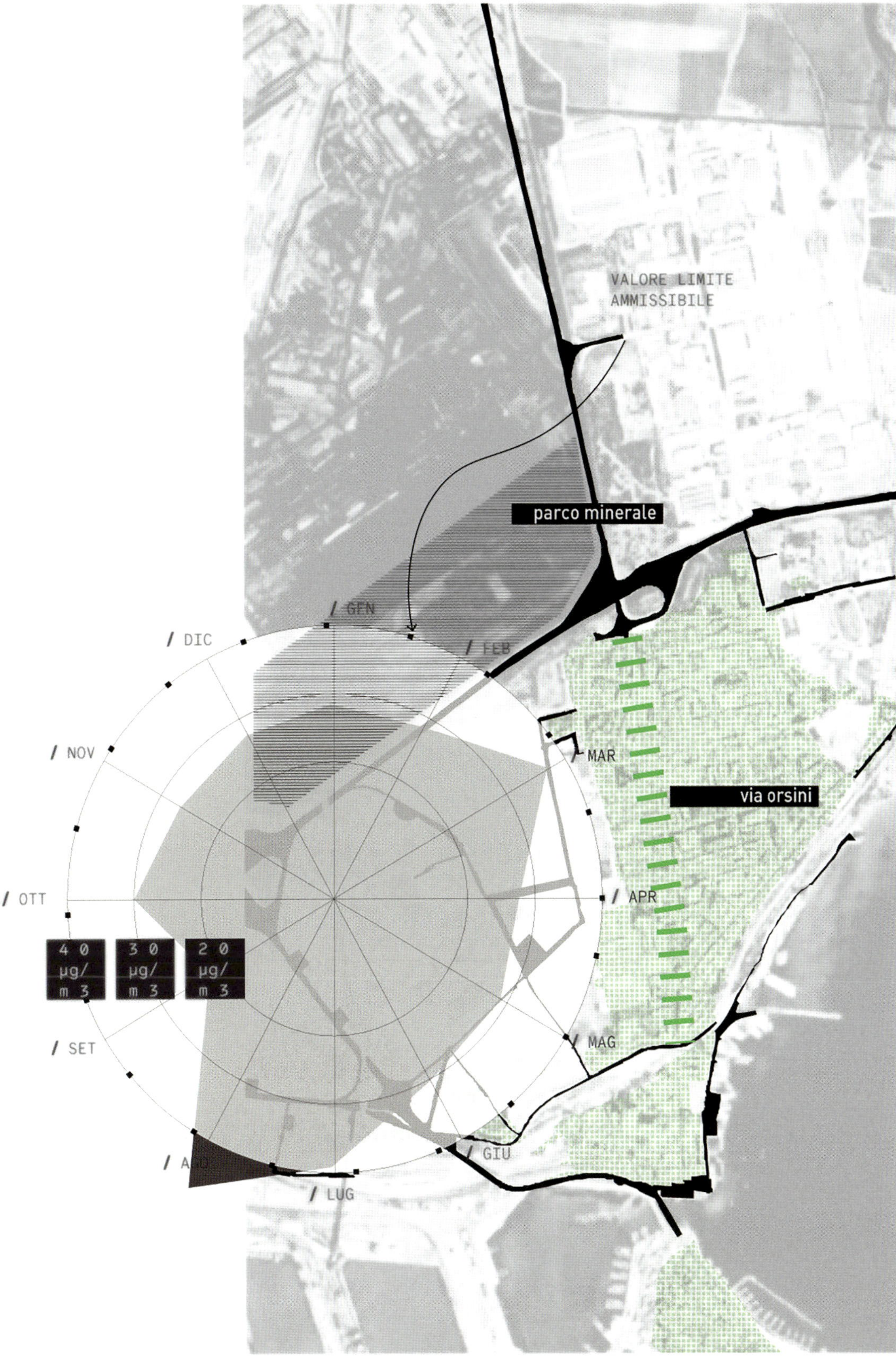
VALORE LIMITE
AMMISSIBILE
parco minerale
via orsini
/ GEN
/ FEB
/ MAR
/ APR
/ MAG
/ GIU
/ LUG
/ AGO
/ SET
/ OTT
/ NOV
/ DIC
4 0 µg/ m 3
3 0 µg/ m 3
2 0 µg/ m 3

Porcinai, using the experience he had already gained in the Ruhr area, proposed hills 30–35 meters high, including the height of the trees that would act as windbreaks to divert the airflow coming from the plant upwards. They would be similar to dunes, he wrote, referring to the experience gained during his consultancy in transferring the Abu Simbel temples in Egypt. Dunes covered by vegetation. Porcinai was inspired by nature and experimented with new soil consisting of slag (compacted and almost impermeable), blast furnace dross, and soil that made it porous. He designed these dunes to be covered by tall trees, guaranteeing adequate conditions for the development of the root system and identifying the most suitable species of trees for the soil and air conditions. The area to be made into hills covered 50 hectares, and the planned expenditure was 1.5 billion lire.[7]

The universal right to breathe

Isn't toxicity, asks Achille Mbembe, i.e., the multiplication of chemical substances and hazardous waste, a structural dimension of the present?[8] These substances and this waste not only attack nature and the environment (air, soil, water, food chain) but also bodies. And he adds: "as much as you try to get rid of it like a dead weight, in the end everything returns to the body."

Mbembe is obviously not talking about Taranto but about what we are experiencing as a result of the Covid-19 pandemic. However, it is all too easy to think of Taranto.

The emissions originating from industry and the dust carried by the winds have led to an increasing risk for populations located close to and within the spread of pollutants. Those environmental fragilities were also very clear in 1964 when the Italia Nostra Association raised the issue, but it was not until 2000 that the area was designated as a Site of National Interest (SIN), that dealing with the environmental problems caused by the steel plant became a matter of national urgency.

Against this background of national and community urgency, research and reports attempting to demonstrate a link between deaths due to infections of the airways and the actual figures relating to emissions produced by the steel industry have multiplied over the years. In all the research observed, the Tamburi District and its buildings with their facades colored red by ferrous dust became a symbol of environmental pollution in Italy. According to OECD figures, over 30,000 inhabitants live in this place with the highest mortality rates in the country.[9] The public open spaces which, in some cases, are located less than 500 meters from the Ilva iron and steel parks have reached soil contamination levels so high that in 2010 a municipal order prohibited children from playing in unpaved green areas.

Today, we can interpret in the spaces of Tamburi the networks of places made inaccessible on days marked by critical air conditions, including schools and public parks; the networks of places of condemnation, marked by plaques naming those who have died from pollution; and

Fig.3
Spaces that aggregate in the new infrastructure between factory and city. Photograph by Agim Kërçuku.

finally, the networks of places of protest where people have voiced their concerns over the conditions making them uninhabitable.

Lifelines

The hills that Porcinai wanted to design could have been higher, up to 60 meters,[10] but for hills so high it would have been necessary, wrote the designer, to have a much larger base area than was available. Such intuition can help in reviewing the problem of the relationship between Ilva and Taranto.

Even the body of the city, like all living bodies, is exposed to physical exhaustion and to all types of biological risk. Around Ilva, towards Tamburi, there are numerous spaces exposed to exhaustion. It is risky to live there, sometimes lethal, and not only on windy days when the dust turns everything red. They are spaces that are forsaken or remain suspended: threatened by suffocation. Places where you can see what the right to breathe actually means:[11] breathing beyond purely biological aspects. Presence marks life, absence marks death; it is what we have in common. It is a universal right.[12] The locations around Ilva are an emblem of the contrary, of the absence of this right that affects humans and the environment: a right to existence.

What places are we talking about? The large white shells, sarcophagi that cover waste materials so that they are not exposed to the wind; Porcinai's hills, designed as living soil and now reduced to very little, with scarce vegetation, also suffering; the large road infrastructures that disappear into the subsoil of the factory; the cemetery, a place used to accommodate the bodies of the dead; the large necrotized spaces where nothing will presumably happen; the very District of Tamburi condemned to be emptied, house by house, road by road, where children can no longer play outdoors and the schools are closed on the worst days. These are all spaces contaminated by dust, minerals, pollen, spores, and molds. Everyone talks about death that is not just environmental. This is a vast necrotized territory that is halfway between the factory and the city. It includes part of one and part of the other: parts that can no longer be used. In a reversal of meaning, we can see these necrotized spaces as a dilated lifeline that declares the right to live in the broadest sense of the term: that of making forms of living possible. The right to recompose a habitable city that can offer us all the possibility of a breathable life.

Against the good intentions of urban regeneration aimed at repairing the individual locations, bringing order, and improving open spaces, the only path to take is to distance yourself. To establish a rupture with a space that is on the same scale as that of the factory. To take a radical stance. This space (this large territorial infrastructure) is interposed between the factory and the city. It removes the city from Ilva and at the same time connects it to the external territory. It brings together places and devices of the territory, proposing a network of spaces that assumes an extension comparable to that of the factory. It is an infrastructure that works to the contrary: it does not connect but separates. It can be claimed that an infrastructure of this nature is still an infrastructure of yesteryear: a sanitary cordon, as in the social hygiene movement. The counter-objection is that it is no longer a classic infrastructure, the pride of a high public concept[13], "supply and transmission machine" with the formidable symbolic power of the modern infrastructure. These are necrotized spaces, in which *the protection of life is expressed by demonstrating its death*. These spaces dissuade, they do not promote. They declare the act of withdrawal, of distance. And distance is never an empty space. Distance that exists between bodies is what allows bodies to feel, act, and live.[14]

Fig.4
A fragmented city consisting of rigid pieces, pp. 192–193. Photograph by Agim Kërçuku.

Endnotes

1 This chapter reports some outcomes of the research carried out between September 2020 and July 2021 on Taranto by Alessandra Cusanno for her Master's degree thesis in the Architecture City Construction Course, *Tra le pieghe di Taranto*, a/y 2020–21, Politecnico di Torino.

2 Istat, "Population census of the city of Taranto 1861–2011."

3 The most significant include: *Mondocane*, 2021, Alessandro Cell, 110 min; *Ilva. A Denti Stretti*, 2019, Stefano Maria Bianchi, 66 min; *In viaggio con Cecilia*, 2013, Mariangela Barbanente and Cecilia Mangini, 80 min; *Marpiccolo*, 2009, Alessandro Di Robilant, 93 min; *Il miracolo*, 2003, Edoardo Winspeare, 93min; *White Pop Jesus*, 1980, Luigi Petrini, 94 min; and the novella by Cosimo Argentina in C. Argentina, Orso Tosco, *Dall'inferno. Due reportage letterari*, minimumfax 2021.

4 Istat, 2020.

5 In 1983, Italsider executives proposed the design of a *large wall* 20 m high and 1,500 m long with the intention, on one side, to limit the dispersion of polluting agents and, on the other, to limit the visibility of the plant. However, the intervention never came to fruition as engineering studies demonstrated its ineffectiveness in mitigating pollution originating from the mineral parks or absorbed by the soil. The *shells* are the roofs that cover the mineral parks of the plant. The project was commissioned by Ilva s.p.a under extraordinary administration in 2018. The design and execution was entrusted to Cimolai S.p.A. in the same year. The project involves covering the mineral park and the fossil park, consisting of a total area of 355,600 m^2, using metal structures 700 m long and 254 m wide.

6 Through the Preliminary Planning Document, the administration is currently working on projects that, considering themes of regeneration and urban redevelopment, propose the redesign of the roads, the implementation of green areas, the insertion of catalyzing public buildings. The most significant include *The Tamburi regeneration plan* (2019); *Atleti Azzurri d'Italia* (2020); *Waterfront Mar Grande and Mar Piccolo* (2021); *Taranto – Oasi Urbana* (2021).

7 Attino, *Generazione Ilva. Gli ulivi, le industrie, il boom, il declino, l'inquinamento. La tragica parabola di una terra illusa dall'acciaio, tradita dallo Stato.*

8 Mbembe, "Il diritto universale di respirare."

9 OCSE, *ACTORS Italia – Cultural attractors for tourism and education in Southern Italy. Report on the city of Taranto and the National Archaeological Museum of Taranto.*

10 Attino, *Generazione Ilva. Gli ulivi, le industrie, il boom, il declino, l'inquinamento. La tragica parabola di una terra illusa dall'acciaio, tradita dallo Stato.*

11 Mbembe, "Il diritto universale di respirare."

12 Ibid.

13 Rouillard, *Public: Infrastructure, architecture, territoire.*

14 Nancy, *Corpus.*

Bibliography

Adorno, Salvatore and Simone Neri Serneri, eds. *Industria, ambiente e territorio. Per una storia ambientale delle aree industriali in Italia*, Bologna: il Mulino, 2009.

Assennato, Giorgio. "Un nano per un gigante, arduo il controllo all'ILVA." *Ecoscienza* 6 (2012): 20–23.

Attino, Tonio. *Generazione Ilva. Gli ulivi, le industrie, il boom, il declino, l'inquinamento. La tragica para-bola di una terra illusa dall'acciaio, tradita dallo Stato*. Nardò: Besa Editrice, 2013.

Bellifemine, Onofrio. *Una nuova politica per il Meridione. La nascita del quarto centro siderurgico di Taranto 1955–1960*. Bologna: Il Mulino, 2018.

Biasi, Paola and Salvatore Romeo. "Taranto e l'Ilva. Dipendenza economica ed emergenza ambientale." *Le politiche per l'ambiente in Italia*, edited by Gabriella Corona and Riccardo Realfonzo, 87–109. Milan: Franco Angeli, 2017.

Borri, Dino and Domenico Camarda. "Degrado e resilienza nella transizione postindustriale. L'atipico profilo di Taranto." *CRIOS - Critica degli Ordinamenti Spaziali* 14 (2017): 17–28.

Calafati, Antonio, ed. *Città tra sviluppo e declino. Un'agenda urbana per l'Italia*. Rome: Donzelli, 2015.

Castel, Robert. *L'insicurezza sociale. Cosa significa essere protetti?* Turin: Einaudi, 2004.

Colucci, Fulvio. "Taranto." *Il Mulino*, No. 6 (2017): 230–233.

Colucci, Fulvio and Giuse Alemanno. *Invisibili. Vivere e morire all'Ilva di Taranto*. Calimera: Kurumuny, 2011.

Coppola, Alessandro and Marianna d'Ovidio. "Embedded economic practices in the city of Taranto." *Territorio* 87 (4) (2019): 98–104.

Curci, Francesco and Chiara Geroldi. "La Città Vecchia e i grandi sistemi urbani di Taranto: evoluzione, spazi e paesaggi." *Territorio* 94 (2020): 48–58.

Cusanno, Alessandra. "Tra le pieghe di Taranto." Master diss. Master Degree Architecture Construction City, Politecnico di Torino, 2021.

Galuzzi, Paolo and Piergiorgio Vitillo. "Trame resilienti per territori della contemporaneità. Il caso della Città Vecchia di Taranto." *Planum. The Journal of Urbanism*, Vol. 04, XXIII Conferenza Nazionale SIU, 2021.

Guida, Irene. *L'acciaio tra gli ulivi; Il caso Ilva di Taranto dalle origini a oggi*. Milan: Linkiesta.it, 2013.

IESIT 2 – Indagine Epidemiologica del Sito Inquinato di Taranto. "Le mappe della salute a Taranto: IESIT investigation 2." https://www.sanita.puglia.it/documents/890301/2267941/REPORT_IESIT_2_FINALE_290618/45c57481-b6aa-467d-889e-2d0aa57f6e15 (last accessed: July 14, 2021).

Istat. "Population census of the city of Taranto 1861–2011." https://www.tuttitalia.it/puglia/64-taranto/statistiche/censimenti-popolazione/ (last accessed: July 14, 2021).

Jakob, Michael. "La mia Taranto: una passeggiata critica." *Domus*, 1018 (2017): 12–16.

Kërçuku, Agim. "Ambiente: l'impresa parassita. Il caso di Taranto tra nuove e vecchie ossessioni nel rapporto tra impresa e ambiente." *iQuaderni di U3 rivista di studi urbani*, No. 22 (2019): 61–69.

Leogrande, Alessandro. *Dalle macerie, cronache sul fronte meridionale*. Milan: Feltrinelli, 2018.

Mbembe, Achille. "Il diritto universale di respirare." *il lavoro culturale*, April 22, 2020. https://www.lavoroculturale.org/il-diritto-universale-di-respirare/achille-mbembe/2020/ (last accessed: September 19, 2021).

Mbembe, Achille. "The Universal Right to Breath." *Critical Inquiry*, April 13, 2020. https://critinq.wordpress.com/2020/04/13/the-universal-right-to-breathe/ (last accessed: September 19, 2021).

Nancy, Jean Luc. *Corpus*. New York: Fordham University Press, 2008.

OCSE. *ACTORS Italia – Cultural attractors for tourism and education in Southern Italy. Report on the city of Taranto and the National Archaeological Museum of Taranto*. Paris: OECD Publishing, 2016.

Pignatelli, Francesca. *Il progetto dello scarto. Taranto Shrinking City*. Milan: Maggiori Editore, 2012.

Piovene, Guido. *Viaggio in Italia*. Florence: Bompiani, 2019.

Prandi, Adriano. *In Terra di Taranto*. Milan-Rome: Carlo Bestetti, 1970.

Rinella, Antonella. *Oltre l'acciaio. Taranto: problemi e progetti*. Bari: Progedit, 2002.

Romeo, Salvatore. *L'acciaio in fumo. L'Ilva di Taranto dal 1945 a oggi*. Rome: Donzelli, 2019.

Rouillard, Dominique. *Public: Infrastructure, architecture, territoire*. Paris: Ensba, 2021.

Santandrea, Rocco Vincenzo, ed. "L'abbandono scolastico in Puglia." *IPRES Nota tecnica* 13/2017, 2017.

Sgobio, Cristina. *La Taranto dell'Ilva. Veleno salute e lavoro*. Martina Franca: Artebaria, 2015.

Vignola, Marta. *La fabbrica. Memoria e narrazioni nella Taranto (post)industriale*. Milan: Meltemi, 2017.

Fracture and resistance lines of modern designed spatial infrastructures

Elisabetta M. Bello,
Maria Teresa Gabardi

In the last thirty years, urban transformations have been subjected to strong economic market pressures, accompanied by the gradual erosion of the urban welfare apparatus, namely public and collective spaces as well as Public Housing Construction (ERP) districts, which have provided, over time, physical support to fragility and economic and social vulnerability of various generations of inhabitants. Looking at the ERP districts today raises questions about the persistence of spatial and social protection systems in the contemporary city and, above all, reflections on how these have changed and on what it now means to be protected. Our hypothesis[1] argues that ERP districts still constitute an infrastructure for the care of fragilities and vulnerabilities of certain groups of the population through new practices of use. Often, innovations of practices and design originate precisely from these locations, which are then echoed more generally at urban and institutional level. The observation of practices of the "public city"[2] (the reuse of its underused or unused spaces) offers an interpretation on two levels: the methods of physical reuse of buildings and open spaces and the capacity of spaces brought back into play to satisfy social needs of population groups considered most fragile and vulnerable. The investigation observes practices of signification of spaces and the differences that emerge depending on the populations that use them; the more or less strong alliances that are created between inhabitants and other entities in the relevant context. Based upon these observations, we consider how these infrastructures are still useful for caring for and overcoming fragility and vulnerability.

The privileged location in which it was decided to observe this process is the city of Milan and, more precisely, the San Siro ERP District – hereafter just San Siro – where, in recent years, reuse initiatives have been implemented, attempting to combine the demand and supply of spaces and social needs in innovative ways. Through appropriations, protocols, understandings, and alliances between the various players involved in the reuse process, new strengths and numerous relationships are being created between various entities at different scales, which condition the spaces and uses and contribute to generating a sense of security, belonging, and affectivity to the location. Some initiatives observed originated from proposals by public institutions, which are trying to encompass in them the tricky task of indicating objectives, finding new tools and protocols involving the different stakeholders also considering the situation that has been generated as a result of the pandemic.

The San Siro investigation helps us to understand how the ERP district can itself be seen as a lifeline or interpreted as an infrastructural space both in the physical sense (within which even the compositional materials permit or deny some actions) and in the social perspective as a means of generating relationships, as already discussed in Keller Easterling:[3] reciprocal relationships between inhabitants of the district and between the inhabitants, managers, and local associations. In paraphrasing (and partly adapting) Easterling, it is a sort of *intra-statecraft*: no longer external but well within the State. It is a space that produces a perception of security or social insecurity – depending on the points of view

– and re-produces new forms of living that see the physical space itself acquire another form of value, compared to its original value, generated by different forms of recognition: affective, social, and legal, not necessarily antagonistic or mutually exclusive.[4]
Seen from this angle, the ERP still constitutes a socio-spatial infrastructure of care and support to daily living and of possible mitigation of the various forms of fragility and vulnerability. As it has been in the past, it is still a space of protection despite being degraded, underused, and repopulated in various ways. It is a space which, through new practices of use, generates new relationships of belonging and attachment to the place, triggering, in turn, a feeling of security for some, although this is not the case for all social groups present.

Spatial characters and social articulation of the district yesterday and today

San Siro was built between 1935 and 1947 through a rationalist project and in the absence of a general architectural design, but with a clear articulation of the infrastructural network and the subdivision of lots. Consisting of 6,135 houses spread over a surface area of 240,000 m^2 in the west of the city of Milan, it now has a total population of about 12,000 inhabitants.
Its spatial layout is characterized by a rhomboid-shaped composition split into two very recognizable sectors known as *Milite Ignoto* and *Baracca* which reflect the succession and overlapping of separate parts, expressing the change of different criteria and conceptions of public housing intervention over time.[5] Within it, there is some architectural experimentation and a broad articulation of artefacts which reflect – at least as regards the original project – the different categories of population for which the various houses were intended (weak groups and middle classes).
The two sectors referred to above are split physically by the infrastructural road axis of Via Mar Jonio and Viale Aretusa. It was precisely the road arteries, split into primary and secondary, which contributed to the division of the district into parts.
Currently, the housing space differs greatly between the various sectors, with the presence of additional forms of internal polarization partly due to practices of use and redevelopments of housing that have further fragmented the district.
Over time, San Siro has seen its assets sold, although a large part of them, still remaining publicly owned, have been redeveloped by way of a District Contract.[6] However, some buildings are still in conditions of severe decay. This leads to spatial fragility of the entire area which, despite being incorporated for some time within the consolidated city, remains in certain respects isolated from the surrounding spaces in relation to the development dynamics of the surrounding areas.
San Siro is inhabited by individuals and families belonging to different social groups, with different backgrounds and origins.[7] Quite a large

Fig.1
Population and use practices. Source: Elisabetta M. Bello, Maria Teresa Gabardi, Luis Martin Sanchez.

Elderly people
Immigrant men
Immigrant women
Young people
Kids

group of inhabitants is constituted mainly by elderly Italians who have lived in San Siro for many years, often in the same residence.[8]
A second group, ethnically more heterogeneous, is made up of foreign citizens of different nationalities who arrived in the district more than twenty years ago, characterized by two different situations: on one side, individuals and families with better economic conditions (families with children, heads of families active in the labor market, originating mainly from Egypt and Morocco); on the other side, young men with precarious working conditions, who arrived in more recent times from countries in crisis.
A third group consists of an Italian and foreign mobile population which, at different times and in different ways, illegally occupy ERP housing or informally share houses used by other inhabitants.
Finally, a fourth group is made up of resident citizens, who arrived more recently in the district through the rankings for Public Residential Construction or through tenders of the so-called *Fuori ERP*.[9]
In summary, the district, no longer entirely public and now central to the urban context, presents a high level of building degradation, which is widespread and broadly perceived, together with problems of asset management and demands related to rights to quality of life expressed by inhabitants who differ greatly.
An ambivalent picture of San Siro emerges: on one side, we can see the specific traits of an ERP district (serious social and economic fragility: numerous low-income and handicapped tenants, high presence of single elderly people); on the other, a certain distance from the image of inertia[10] and passive dependence of inhabitants on public institutional aid, which coexists, however, with lively dynamism of third-sector and self-promoted initiatives.[11]

Spatial, relational, and recognition infrastructures

The space of the ERP district in its grammar and syntax allows for the establishment of relationships between the various parts, along with the alternation of different practices and uses. At the same time, it clearly reflects relationships of privilege or vulnerability between the different social components and the different players operating in the territory. For these reasons, it can be assimilated to a spatial infrastructure that simultaneously serves social recognition which repairs and protects but also lays itself open to conflict situations.
From the spatial point of view, San Siro's roads and squares represent welcoming outdoor places for escaping the minimal housing, often characterized by overcrowding. From the social point of view, they provide support to relationships between the different individuals or groups of inhabitants; and they constitute a set of locations where to meet with others similar to oneself.
Young people belonging to different ethnic groups use them for various activities such as sports,[12] play,[13] music,[14] artistic and recreational activities, to get together and simply pass time outside of the flat. They are

Fig.2
Piazzale Segesta. Photograph by Luis Martin Sanchez.

connoted spaces (murals and street art), and visibility and recognition are increasingly connected to such connotations. It is not only symbolic connotation: these interventions themselves form part of a relational system which finds 'outlets' in the space.[15]
It is a densely inhabited space: families with small children get together for play activities mainly in the equipped areas located in the center of San Siro and in the public spaces (parks and gardens) situated on the outskirts of the district.[16]
Immigrant women use them to get together and socialize. These spaces are considered more welcoming, looked after, and protected than others in the district, allowing inhabitants to limit their 'self-exposure' and practices.[17]
Furthermore, immigrant women often meet at the Luigi Cadorna School and the Lombardo Radice School[18] to take advantage of Italian courses and other support activities and to start a working profession. In fact, associations work in the district to allow women to build integration paths and to achieve greater economic and personal autonomy. All these activities constitute forms of action aimed at "caring for others."
The elderly often get together in the district's recreational centers or on its margins, places which allow them to maintain social relationships and to avoid isolation and loneliness by spending several hours of the day together.[19]

Fig.3
Piazzale Selinunte, pp. 202–203. Source: Google Street View.

The space of San Siro is also the space of courtyards belonging to the buildings that encourage or negate social relationships. In the case of children or adolescents, these spaces act as a direct extension of the houses and as support for interaction and play activities, but they also generate conflicts in the case of adults. This occurs when situations of closure, intolerance, and verbal aggression arise between individuals due to "misrecognition"[20] of the living habits of some which are in conflict with the rules imposed by the manager as a standard for the use of common and associated spaces. For example, courtyards become places for the improper disposal of waste or places where to claim rights to legal recognition and realization in terms of equality.
The infrastructural space also helps us to understand the phenomena that Honneth calls "recognition or misrecognition." In this author's opinion, recognition by young people with respect for these spaces is placed under an affective lens of their relationship with the location. Young people feel proud of living in the district[21] and they openly declare it: they claim that those who live outside of San Siro consider it a ghetto; in fact, for them, it is a place as "beautiful as Disneyland" and they consider it a value.[22] Sometimes, this expectation of recognition generates in these persons anticipations of social redemption and broader claims: this occurs in locations that assume the capacity to express not only degradation, marginality, vulnerability but also protest, claim, and conflict as in the recent news case, cited in note 13 above. It is the *déplacement du public* incarnated in the order of movements that are formed around the infrastructure.
Other forms of recognition in places are expressed by immigrant women and by the elderly. For the former, the connotation of recognition is educational; for the latter, it is nostalgic.

Lifeline that supports and protects

This interweaving of ways of perceiving, using, and getting together in the space produces the capacity to not only recognize oneself as belonging to a small group within the district but also horizons with plural meanings. Namely, it redefines the way in which persons perceive the experience of their being in the world within interweaved forms of cooperation, play, solidarity, and conflict. In all this, space plays a crucial role: that of a fully fledged lifeline that supports and protects; even when it is a space designed and created for a different society, within different policies of social protection. It highlights almost an inter-generational and inter-temporal disposition that goes beyond the same intentions that originally defined its characteristics. In other words, a case such as the one discussed here calls into question the relationship between systems of protection and temporality.

Endnotes

1 Although the essay is the result of common work, the introduction and the paragraph "Lifeline that supports and protects" were written by both authors; the paragraph "Spatial characters and social articulation of the district yesterday and today" was written by M.T. Gabardi, while the paragraph "Spatial, relational, and recognition infrastructures" was written by E.M. Bello.

2 The wording 'public city' means parts of cities created by public institutions, following particular procedures aimed at regulating the relationships between public and private. See, in that regard: Di Biagi, "La costruzione della città pubblica," 8–27.

3 Easterling, *Extrastatecraft. The Power of Infrastructure Space*.

4 For Honneth (1995) there are three forms of recognition: 'affective' in reference to family relationships and friendship; 'social' where the sense is that of contributing to the realization of a collective good or purpose; 'legal' where every individual is endowed with equal rights, ratified by law. For the author, there is human dependence on inter-subjective recognition. Individuals can only live a good human life when they are guaranteed a context of reciprocal recognition. In the absence of recognition and self-realization, social struggles will occur, which may lead to an expansion of recognition actions and will constitute a normative advancement of society as a whole.

5 For further analyses on the history of the district, see: ALER MILANO, *100 anni di edilizia residenziale pubblica a Milano*; Bruzzese, "Scomporre la città pubblica: configurazioni, posizioni, materiali urbani," 52; Cognetti and Padovani, *Perché (ancora) i quartieri pubblici. Un laboratorio di politiche per la casa*.

6 This is a District II Contract approved by the Regional Council of Lombardy in 2003 and subsequently by the Lombardy Joint Committee in 2006. The main objective was to break the isolation in which "San Siro" was found, despite the dense public transport network, which reaches and crosses it, and its position at the center of large areas of transformation or in neighboring projects: the "Portello" project, the reconversion of the *Nuova Fiera*, the former *Piazzale dello sport* and, prospectively, the disposal of the *Perrucchetti* barracks, as well as the redevelopment of the former Piazza d'Armi adjacent to it. Close to the district there are also the urban parks of Trenno, Parco delle Cave, and Monte Stella. The planned interventions included: extraordinary maintenance works, renovation and recovery for many district buildings (not yet fully completed); primary infrastructure works and interventions on existing public equipment (completed); the construction of a new underground car park (including the redevelopment of the central *parterre*, completed but partly of very poor urban quality); numerous social actions in support of the elderly, mentally ill, or other fragile sections of society. The public open spaces of the district have been redeveloped and converted into areas for play, sports, and greenery. Interventions have also been carried out on the roads: Via Zamagna has been pedestrianized; other roads have been transformed for one-way traffic.

7 Cognetti and Padovani, *Perché (ancora) i quartieri pubblici. Un laboratorio di politiche per la casa*.

8 One-third of the inhabitants of this group have, in many cases, occupied the same residence for more than thirty-three years.

9 *Fuori-ERP* are the so-called "under-threshold houses," namely those with an area of less than 28.8 m^2, in accordance with Lombardy Regional Regulation no.1/2004. These residential units cannot be included in the rankings of traditional ERP tenders.

10 Inertia due mainly to the absence of policies on the part of the owners.

11 These arise as the effect of exogenous processes promoted by different players and with particular purposes: micro-actions and interventions implemented by third sector entities working on issues of community welfare and social cohesion; public institutions and associations, by way of the *Custodi Sociali* service, the projects *Tempo per le famiglie Centro Diurno* and *Porto*; the Cooperatives *Tuttinsieme* and *Dar Casa*. There is also a broad network of humanitarian and religious associations such as Caritas, Emergency, and *Associazione Alfabeti* (established within and in service of the district), which promote forms of support to fragility and orientation to basic services and issues of the right to health and education. Finally, there is the presence of some tenants' representations, both organized by block and at district level.

12 Close to Piazza Selinunte, they get together to play sports in the equipped area of the square redeveloped under the District Contract of 2003.

13 The pedestrianized area of Via Zamagna is used for that purpose.

14 The district's streets have been used to film music videos. A recent news story focused on a clash between young people who had gathered for the video and the police. Due to the heated conflict, the district was closed off around Piazzale Selinunte by armored police and Carabinieri vans, with police arriving in riot gear.
15 A similar argument, albeit with radical differences with respect to the context and the effects, is found in the case of Beirut discussed by Camillo Boano and Federica Doglio in this volume.
16 They meet mainly in Piazzale Selinunte and close to subway line 5 at Piazzale Segesta, where there are equipped areas.
17 Bianchetti, "Intimité, extimité, public. Riletture dello spazio pubblico," 7–17.
18 Respectively located on Via Carlo Dolci and on Via Paravia.
19 For example, close to Via Carlo Dolci or Piazzale Velasquez.
20 Honneth, *The struggle for recognition. The moral grammar for social conflicts*.
21 Cognetti, interview.
22 Neima, "Perif (Documentario)"; Cognetti, interview.

Bibliography

ALER MILANO. *100 anni di edilizia residenziale pubblica a Milano*. Milan: Litogì, 2008.

Bianchetti Cristina. "Intimité, extimité, public. Riletture dello spazio pubblico." *Territorio* 72 (2015): 7–17.

Bianchetti, Cristina. *Bodies. Between Space and Design*. Berlin: JOVIS, 2020.

Bruzzese, Antonella. "Scomporre la città pubblica: configurazioni, posizioni, materiali urbani." *Dal recinto al territorio. Milano, esplorazioni nella città pubblica*, edited by Francesco Infussi, 52. Milan: Bruno Mondadori, 2011.

Cognetti, Francesca. "A San Siro, nel quartiere più giovane e multietnico di Milano dove mancano prospettive e si sogna la vita di CityLife." Interview by Luca De Vito, *La Repubblica*, April 17, 2021. https://milano.repubblica.it/cronaca/2021/04/17/news/a_san_siro_nel_quartiere_piu_giovane_e_multietnico_di_milano_dove_mancano_prospettive_e_si_sogna_la_vita_di_citylife-296843690/ (last accessed: November 18, 2021).

Cognetti, Francesca and Liliana Padovani. *Perché (ancora) i quartieri pubblici. Un laboratorio di politiche per la casa*. Milan: Franco Angeli, 2018.

Di Biagi, Paola. "La costruzione della città pubblica." *Urbanistica* 85 (1986): 8–27.

Easterling, Keller. *Extrastatecraft. The Power of Infrastructure Space*. London: Verso Books, 2014.

Ezza, Neima. "Perif (Documentario)." Video: 16.14. https://www.youtube.com/watch?v=ci2vYQieK9c (last accessed: November 18, 2021).

Honneth, Axel. *The struggle for recognition. The moral grammar for social conflicts*. Cambridge, MA: The MIT Press, 1995.

Laino, Giovanni, ed. *Quinto Rapporto sulle città. Politiche urbane per le periferie*. Bologna: Il Mulino, 2020.

Nomisma-Federcasa. *Dimensione e caratteristiche del disagio abitativo in Italia e ruolo delle aziende per la casa. Sintesi*. 2016. https://www.federcasa.it/wp-content/upload-s/2017/03/disagio_abitativo.pdf (last accessed: November 18, 2021).

Contradictions in housing: lifelines in Santiago de Chile

Valentina Saavedra Meléndez,
Emanuel Giannotti

In Chile, housing policies have a long tradition.[1] Recently, they have been celebrated internationally for having reduced the housing deficit by providing millions of units, and they have been proposed as a model for other countries.[2] The actual policies are inspired by a neoliberal and mercantilist idea, established by some reforms approved during the Pinochet's dictatorship (1973–1990), according to which the State provides a subsidy that covers a large part of the cost of a house.[3] In four decades, they have enabled a considerable number of low-income families to acquire a house and become owners, securing a permanent shelter to protect life. In this sense, Chilean social housing could be understood as lifelines.

Nevertheless, this seemingly successful story has been widely criticized. According to several authors, the neoliberal Chilean policies have produced housing complexes with more than one problem. The houses, which are very small and of poor quality, offer limited opportunities for adapting to family needs. Public spaces and services are deficient. The housing complexes are located on the periphery, far from employment opportunities and previously used support networks. The housing assignees were burdened with credit and other expenses, whereas family income was limited.[4]

The burden generated by domestic inadequacies of the habitation falls mainly on women due to socially assigned gender roles. In a patriarchal society, domestic and care tasks are associated with female responsibilities. Moreover, the public institutions offer only very limited support as care is mainly left to families.[5] Those factors imply an increase both in responsibility for the care of dependent persons and in distances to services and work centers, often forcing women to postpone their autonomy to solve family tasks.

As seen from this perspective, Chilean social housing seems the opposite of a lifeline and resemble the "oppressive house" described by John Turner.[6] According to this author, housing should be judged for what it does and not for what it is. Social housing, despite having certain standards of comfort, often hinders the development of the inhabitants.[7]

The Chilean assignees are fully aware of the difficulties that living in low-quality housing in peripheral and stigmatized neighborhoods generates. However, they also appreciate having a home with a bathroom and a kitchen, especially since many of them came from precarious housing situations, such as informal settlements or *allegamiento*.[8] In the face of this ambivalent evaluation and despite all the problems, in most cases the assignees accept the housing units they have been offered, as they see it as the only alternative to reach a permanent and stable dwelling and, in this way, to better integrate into the society.[9] In contrast to other similar cases, such as Mexico,[10] Chile has a low rate of abandonment of social housing.

This acceptance is what makes Chilean social housing a lifeline, and it is also what exposes its contradiction. Social housing is meant to support family development, but in fact it oppresses several aspects of it. It offers certain protection to life but, at the same time, exposes it. To the extent that dwellings and neighborhoods do not respond to the needs of the inhabitants, their acceptance often triggers processes of organization and mobilization, which may be collective or individual. In general, collective processes are oriented to improve the neighborhood and take more institutional routes, while individual responses tend to be informal and are geared towards adapting the environment more directly to family life. These processes and strategies can be also understood as lifelines, because they allow to improve the physical environment and built social structures that sustain life.

The transformation processes lead to considerable heterogeneity in the results, as they depend on many factors, such as the urban context, the degrees of organization of the inhabitants, the support received from the state and other actors. We can find cases where these actions lead to a significant improvement, and other cases where the neighborhoods have slowly transformed into ghettos. Despite the differences, the participation of women is a recurrent characteristic. Although women not always lead neighborhood organizations, they always make up the majority of them, as the process of improving housing and neighborhood conditions is associated with the care for the family and the community, which is usually undertaken by women.

In the following pages, we will analyze the processes of constructing lifelines that started with the provision of two social housing complexes and continued in the following years through several improvement projects led by the inhabitants, both collectively and individually. We will describe the contradiction of those processes, highlighting the difficulties created by the dwellings and the neighborhoods for the development of inhabitants and, especially, of women.

The two neighborhoods were analyzed on the basis of 52 interviews, which included marking on a map the spaces that were perceived as good or bad in terms of security and identity. In addition, detailed interviews were conducted with experts, municipal officials, neighborhood leaders, and two women from each neighborhood. The interviews with the women included a temporal map of their daily life, which allowed them to recognize aspects of the houses and neighborhoods that favored or hindered their daily life.[11]

Housing as lifelines: emerging from some cases

El Refugio and *El Labrador* are two neighborhoods realized as part of the Basic Dwelling Program (*Programa de Vivienda Básica*), which was launched during the dictatorship and modified in the early 1990s, when Chile returned to democratically elected governments. This program was intended for people in a situation of 'marginality,' that means with little income and assets.

Both neighborhoods have been completed in the 1990s and are located in Puente Alto, the municipality of the Santiago Metropolitan Region that received the highest rate of social housing in that decade. The complexes provide around 700 dwellings, with *El Refugio* consisting of one-story terraced houses and some slab-shaped, four-story buildings; and

El Labrador consisting of two-story houses. All the flats are approximately 40 square meters, and the neighborhoods have similar connections to local public transport.

El Refugio was allocated to several previously organized housing committees, as the assignees were selected through collective application. The houses in *El Labrador*, on the contrary, were assigned by individual applications. People living in these two neighborhoods are aware of the difficulties their home and physical environment generate, but the way they deal with them differs according to the level of organization.

In *El Refugio*, the fact of obtaining the houses in a collective manner has produced closer ties among the residents, the willingness to improve their environment, and a good appreciation of their neighborhood. This comes from previous organizational experiences and the feeling that their habitation is the result of collective work. Most people say they want to stay and feel to be in a relatively better space than in surrounding neighborhoods. *El Labrador* had a different trajectory. Individual application has generated a break in the previous networks of the assignees. According to the interviewees, there have been lower degrees of trust and collective organization among the inhabitants. They do not show much willingness to take care of their own environment and want to leave it, which they do not do because of the material difficulties involved in getting a new and better house. This has created a feeling of insecurity and less attachment to the neighborhood.

The development of community spaces and associated care burdens

In the two neighborhoods, the houses were completed before the residents arrived. In the case of *El Refugio*, the buildings were distributed in the perimeter, leaving an empty lot in the center for future community services. In *El Labrador*, the vacant space for community uses were placed in the marginal zones in the north and in the south-eastern sectors.

In both cases, the spaces for community programs were left empty for future development and remained in the hands of neighborhood organizations. In *El Refugio*, the community decided to use the space for a school, a kindergarten, a primary care clinic, a football field, a community meeting room, and a public square. Each of these programs was implemented as a stand-alone project, in negotiations with public institutions or in collaboration with private institutions, through applications for public funds. In *El Labrador*, the community decided to realize a public square, three football fields, and a community meeting room, all implemented through public institutions.

In both cases, the communities placed their trust in a formal institutional process to improve their neighborhoods. This shows the ability to manage and deal with state bureaucracy and to take into account the time required for such projects. The biggest difference between the two neighborhoods is related to the selection of programs, which is

TOMÉ
PROFESOR ALCAÍNO
EDUARDO CORDERO
CALLE UNO

TOMÉ
PROFESOR ALCAÍNO
EDUARDO CORDERO
CALLE UNO

associated with the management capacity and the level of participation of residents in the process.

In *El Refugio*, social cohesion enabled a more active participation. The programs decided by the community responded to the needs expressed by families and the concern for collective care. According to community leaders and neighbors, the presence of educational and health institutions facilitate the autonomy of women, who continue to oversee reproductive tasks but can decrease the time needed for them as the social services are nearby. Moreover, the selected programs, such as schools and kindergartens, promote daily interactions among neighbors that enable collective recognition and strengthen neighborhood networks. This is essential for women, who can create support networks, which contribute to increase safety and share the load of care tasks. One of the women interviewed has highlighted the importance of having support networks – in her case family ones – and nearby educational services for her daughter. This has allowed her personal and professional development, as she currently works as a secretary in a municipality office.

In *El Labrador*, the community decided to use the available space mainly for football pitches. Although the decision was taken by the inhabitants, the low social cohesion resulted in a process that was not very reflective of community needs. The idea that spaces dedicated to sports could increase outdoor activities, and thus safety, have prevailed, but this has not happened. Right now, neighbors think that football pitches are mainly used for drug and alcohol trafficking and consumption. Moreover, there is a critical view about the masculinization of these places, as football is associated with men, which reinforces the exclusion of women from the few public spaces in the neighborhood. According to one woman interviewed, the absence of support networks and nearby care services for her children forced her to drop out of school and now prevents her from being able to get a formal job.

The development of public spaces and facilities projects is related to the management capacity of the community. In *El Refugio*, the facilities were built in partnership with private institutions, which helped to apply for public funds for construction and subsequently took over the administration and management of the educational and health centers. On the one hand, this is proof of the community's good management capacity owing to its higher level of organization. On the other hand, it unveils the inadequacy of public institutional channels to respond to the needs of the community beyond certain standardized solutions. This limitation of state programs could lead to different responses from the community. However, the two cases show that the community tends to accept the alternatives provided by public and private entities.

Fig. 1
Original plan of the neighborhood *El Refugio* with the layout of the respective community space (above) and changes in private space made by households (below). Source: Valentina Saavedra Meléndez.

Individual actions to improve cramped houses

The consciousness of residents about the space they are living in is also expressed in various individual actions to improve their domestic environment. The most evident of these is the expansion of their houses,

which is a necessity due to their tiny dimensions. These extensions do not follow institutionally regularized mechanisms or processes but rather are informal efforts that each family made on their own.
One of the women interviewed in *El Labrador* points out the cramped space and believes that the reasons are to be found in the State's lack of confidence in their ability to improve their social and economic conditions, for example, by being able to expand the house without giving up the yard or being able to have a parking space for a private car.
The extensions have similar shapes: they are built towards the front garden, the backyard, or the second floor. The slab-shaped buildings present a different situation, as it is more difficult to realize extensions there. The only extended flats are on the ground floor, facing the street. It is in any case striking that most of these extensions observe limits, such as respecting the official property boundary.
The lack of space is a fact, since the houses were designed for families of four, whereas in most cases the number of inhabitants is higher. In one case we studied, there were twelve people living in the same dwelling, where a mother has housed her daughters with their children. The lack of space generates overcrowding and a greater urge to leave in order to improve one's living conditions. This was the motivation of our interviewee, who some years ago went to live with her ex-partner, because she thought that her daughter would be better off than in an overcrowded house. However, after becoming a victim of domestic violence, she returned to her mother's house.
Lack of space definitely affects women's lives when, for instance, they carry out various small-scale economic activities, such as confectionery or embroidery, but have no space to do so. One of the interviewees was planning to make an extension in order to have a workshop in which to work without disturbing family life. However, this extension implies giving up the side yard where they also do domestic activities such as hanging laundry.
Individual actions to transform the space sometimes take place outside the dwellings. An example of this is front gardens of houses or flats, which can be found in *El Refugio* and are a sign of appropriation and care for the public space of the neighborhood. In *El Labrador*, on the contrary, we only find graffiti that normally delimit an area for specific groups of people.

Final remarks

The two cases analyzed show the processes that began after the provision of social housing in two different complexes. When the assignees moved in, the dwellings and the neighborhoods were deficient in many respects. They caused difficulties for the residents, exacerbated the asymmetries present in families and communities, and reproduced inequalities, including gender ones. The housing programs paid little attention to the care work provided in the neighborhoods, assuming that it is the women within each family who take care of them. This is reflected in the lack of public programs for care services or the reduced space available for them in the homes.

This means a daily effort of resistance and adaptation on the part of women to comply with the care for the family, the home and the neighborhood; hence women often postpone their interests and possibilities of autonomy. In addition, the collective and private processes of adapting and improving the domestic and community environment are often led by women, which is explained by the fact that they are the ones who assume responsibility for domestic life and are therefore the first to detect its shortcomings.

A greater degree of organization in the neighborhoods has shown that the use of community space can lessen this burden and improve living conditions, mitigating the 'oppressive' aspects of housing policies. In *El Refugio*, a strong organization allowed to build facilities that helped daily life, especially taking care of children and dependent persons. In this way, the load of women was alleviated. In *El Labrador*, where the community was not very cohesive, the decisions made were less effective: the public spaces that were realized did not help to build a sense of community and safety.

Regardless of the results, the capacity to organize and act shows the agency of the inhabitants, who developed a good knowledge of the mechanisms for applying for and taking advantage of the public and private resources available, depending on the degree of community articulation. A similar agency can be found in the processes of improvements of the dwellings, although these ones are individual and often informal.

In either case, the inhabitants have opted to improve their neighborhoods through the available institutional tools. This could be surprising if we consider that the same institutions are the ones that generate housing policies. Between the State and the residents there is a contradictory relation, or, to use Caldeira expression, there are transversal logics.[12] Residents don't refuse the institutional programs and often resort to them, but, at the same time, they are aware of their limits and critical of them. The State does not encourage the participation of the inhabitants in the housing programs very much,[13] but, at the same time, if compared to other Latin American countries, we should recognize the number of resources allocated in programs for social housing and for the improvement of peripheral neighborhoods.

These transversal relations between institutional programs and inhabitants provide support for life, but, at the same time, reproduce inequalities and create difficulties to that same life. They can be understood as lifelines, but as contradictory ones.

Endnotes

1 Hidalgo, *La vivienda social en Chile y la construcción del espacio urbano en el Santiago del siglo XX.*
2 Gilbert, "Helping the Poor through Housing Subsidies: Lessons from Chile, Colombia and South Africa;" Gilbert, "Ten Myths Undermining Latin American Housing Policy."
3 Fuster, "Las políticas de vivienda social en Chile en un contexto de neoliberalismo híbrido"; Giannotti and Roja, "Un 'sistema destinado a perdurar': el subsidio habitacional y las políticas de vivienda durante la dictadura pinochetista"; Gilbert, "Power, Ideology and the Washington Consensus: The Development and Spread of Chilean Housing Policy"; Sugranyes, "La política habitacional en Chile, 1980–2000: un éxito liberal para dar techo a los pobres."
4 Ducci, "Chile: el lado obscuro de una política de vivienda exitosa"; Farha, "End-of-mission Statement, Special Rapporteur on adequate housing, Santiago, Chile, 28 April 2017"; Rodríguez and Sugranyes, *Los con techo. Un desafío para la política de vivienda social*; Rolnik, *Urban warfare: housing under the empire of finance*; Sabatini, Wormald, and Rasse, *Segregación de la vivienda social: ocho conjuntos en Santiago, Concepción y Talca*; Tironi, *Nueva pobreza urbana: vivienda y capital social en Santiago de Chile, 1985–2001.*
5 Carrasco and Díaz, *Economía Feminista. Desafíos, propuestas y alianzas.*
6 Turner, *Housing by People. Towards Autonomy in Building Environments.*
7 Ibid.
8 *Allegamiento* is a situation common in Chile and Latin America, in which more than one family lives in the same department, house, or urban lot.
9 Aravena and Sandoval, "El diagnóstico de los pobladores "con techo"; Cáceres, "¿La construcción de un barrio? Villa Nueva Resbalón, de Cerro Navia, y villa San Arturo, de Maipú."
10 Nicolai, "Vivienda en abandono. Análisis socio especial de la vivienda abandonada en México."
11 The case studies are part of the results of research conducted for a Bachelor's and Master's thesis. See: Saavedra, "Desarticulación social y espacial como efectos de la política habitacional focalizada. Santiago de Chile 1980 a 1997" and Saavedra, "Reproducción de la desigualdad de género como efecto de la política urbano-residencial subsidiaria. Santiago de Chile 1990–1997."
12 Caldeira, "Peripheral urbanization: autoconstruction, transversal logics, and politics in cities of the global south"; for the Chilean case: Murphy, *For a Proper Home. Housing Rights in the Margins of Urban Chile, 1960–2010.*
13 Castillo, "Competencias de los pobladores: potencial de innovación para la política habitacional chilena."

Bibliography

Aravena, Susana and Alejandra Sandoval. "El diagnóstico de los pobladores "con techo." *Los con techo. Un desafío para la política de vivienda social*, edited by Alfredo Rodríguez and Ana Sugranyes. Santiago de Chile: Ediciones SUR, 2005.

Cáceres, Teresa. "¿La construcción de un barrio? Villa Nueva Resbalón, de Cerro Navia, y villa San Arturo, de Maipú." *Los con techo. Un desafío para la política de vivienda social*, edited by Alfredo Rodríguez and Ana Sugranyes. Santiago de Chile: Ediciones SUR, 2005.

Caldeira, Teresa. "Peripheral urbanization: autoconstruction, transversal logics, and politics in cities of the global south." *Environment and Planning D*, 35 (I) (2017): 3–20.

Carrasco, Cristina and Carme Díaz. *Economía Feminista. Desafíos, propuestas y alianzas*. Barcelona: Entre Pueblos, 2017.

Castillo, Maria José. "Competencias de los pobladores: potencial de innovación para la política habitacional chilena." *Revista INVI* 29–81 (2014): 79–112.

Ducci, María Elena. "Chile: el lado obscuro de una política de vivienda exitosa." *EURE* XXII (69) (1997): 99–115.

Farha, Leilani. "End-of-mission Statement, Special Rapporteur on adequate housing, Santiago, Chile, 28 April 2017." https://www.ohchr.org/en/NewsEvents/Pages/DisplayNews.aspx?NewsID=21544&LangID=E (last accessed: November 20, 2021).

Fuster, Xenia. "Las políticas de vivienda social en Chile en un contexto de neoliberalismo híbrido." *EURE*, 45–135 (2019): 5–26.

Giannotti, Emanuel and Javier Roja. "Un 'sistema destinado a perdurar': el subsidio habitacional y las políticas de vivienda durante la dictadura pinochetista." *Santiago 1977–1990. Arquitectura, ciudad y política*, edited by Daniel Telesnik. Santiago: ARQ ediciones, 2021.

Gilbert, Alan. "Power, Ideology and the Washington Consensus: The Development and Spread of Chilean Housing Policy." *Housing Studies*, 17(2) (2002). 305–324.

Gilbert, Alan. "Helping the Poor through Housing Subsidies: Lessons from Chile, Colombia and South Africa." *Habitat International*, 28 (2004): 13–40.

Gilbert, Alan. "Ten Myths Undermining Latin American Housing Policy." *Revista de Ingeniería*, 35 (2011): 79–87.

Hidalgo, Rodrigo. *La vivienda social en Chile y la construcción del espacio urbano en el Santiago del siglo XX*. Santiago: Centro de investigaciones Barros Arana, 2005.

Murphy, Edward. *For a Proper Home. Housing Rights in the Margins of Urban Chile, 1960–2010*. Pittsburgh, PE: University of Pittsburgh Press, 2015.

Nicolai, Arturo. "Vivienda en abandono. Análisis socio especial de la vivienda abandonada en México." *Territorios en Formación*, No. 12 (2017): 41–54.

Rodríguez, Alfredo and Ana Sugranyes, eds. *Los con techo. Un desafío para la política de vivienda social*. Santiago: Ediciones SUR, 2005.

Rolnik, Raquel. *Urban warfare: housing under the empire of finance*. London: Verso, 2019.

Saavedra Meléndez, Valentina. "Desarticulación social y espacial como efectos de la política habitacional focalizada. Santiago de Chile 1980 a 1997." Bachelor diss., Universidad de Chile, 2017.

Saavedra Meléndez, Valentina. "Reproducción de la desigualdad de género como efecto de la política urbano-residencial subsidiaria. Santiago de Chile 1990–1997." Master diss., Universidad de Chile, 2018.

Sabatini, Francisco, Guillermo Wormald, and Alejandra Rasse. *Segregación de la vivienda social: ocho conjuntos en Santiago, Concepción y Talca*. Santiago: Colección Estudios Urbanos UC, 2013.

Sugranyes, Ana. "La política habitacional en Chile, 1980–2000: un éxito liberal para dar techo a los pobres." *Los con techo. Un desafío para la política de vivienda social*, edited by Alfredo Rodríguez and Ana Sugranyes. Santiago de Chile: Ediciones SUR, 2005.

Tironi, Manuel. *Nueva pobreza urbana: vivienda y capital social en Santiago de Chile, 1985–2001*. Santiago: RIL editores, 2003.

Turner, John. *Housing by People. Towards Autonomy in Building Environments*. London: Marion Boyars Publishers, 1976.

Zibecchi, Raúl. *Territorios en Resistencia. Cartografía política de las periferias urbanas latinoamericanas*. Buenos Aires: Lavaca, 2007.

Zibecchi, Raúl. *Territories in Resistance: A Cartography of Latin American Social Movements*. Chico, CA: AK Press, 2012.

Part 3
The dark side of protection

The concept of lifelines contains a structural ambivalence: something that can neither be expelled nor eliminated. A coming to terms with the idea of contamination that allows us to think of "vulnerability and contamination" as the outcome of a metamorphosis of fear. A reflection of situations in which lifelines are themselves part of vulnerability, feeding it: they protect against and at the same time nourish mechanisms of exclusion.

Borgo Mezzanone: vicious circles that keep informality together

Cristina Bianchetti,
Antonio di Campli,
Camilla Rondot

This paper reports the results of some research carried out between September 2020 and July 2021 on Borgo Mezzanone in the province of Foggia:[1] an extreme case on which we wanted to test our notion of lifelines. It may seem paradoxical to go in search of "something that sustains life" in a context of this nature, in which the intensity of the migrant presence poses the question of the relationship between rurality, ethnicity, and racial conflict. What are lifelines in Borgo Mezzanone? We tried to keep the question open; the paper below describes what we found. The text is split into three parts: the first describes the location; the second constructs a direction of reflection towards the notions of "rural others" and "black space"; and the third identifies the vicious circle of illegal recruitment as what holds the system together and allows us to discuss the uniquely positive meaning of lifelines. The case of Borgo Mezzanone helps us to focus on the fact that we take care of others also to benefit ourselves, to exercise power, and to perpetuate unfair practices and behaviors.

Borgo Mezzanone

The space

On one side, there is the village, and on the other, about twenty minutes away by foot, one of the biggest informal settlements in Puglia. On satellite images, Borgo Mezzanone appears to be a fragmented territory, consisting of very recognizable spaces, with their uses, shapes, dimensions, and temporal trajectories, remnants of stories interrupted for some time. Urgency, necessity, desire, and redemption become negotiable when reduced to material possessions. Spatial and social radicalism confront each other on the two-platform stage in Borgo Mezzanone: the fascist village and the airstrip, which has now become a fully fledged city. In Borgo Mezzanone, it is not just the residences that are rigged up, but here, moral and affective concepts find the space and different methods to express themselves.

Known also as Borgo La Serpe, in honor of the fascist squad member Raffaele La Serpa, Borgo Mezzanone is part of the reclamation project of the fascist period. Designed by engineer Giovanbattista Canevari and architect Domenico Sandrì, it was built in a short period of time, begun in July 1934 and completed in April 1935,[2] and is characterized by a rather simple layout. The state road divides the village into two separate areas, one to the north, in which the public functions were concentrated, and one to the south, filled with residences and commercial services. Still today, the gravitational center of the village is the square in front of the church dedicated to the Madonna del Grano, with the old fascist house and the school next to it and, on the other side of the road, a fountain, now the only really useful system for those passing by the church or waiting at the bus stop for the shuttle to Foggia.

Some commercial businesses are still going today; a supermarket, a bar/tobacconist, and some principal services, including two schools, a

Fig.1
Satellite image of Borgo Mezzanone. Top left the village, bottom right the informal settlement, pp. 222–223. Source: Google Earth.

clinic, a parish, and two associations, Caritas and Auxilium,[3] occupy the spaces.

Developed on the site of the former NATO airport runway, behind CARA,[4] the Borgo Mezzanone settlement provides shelter to about 1,500 people every summer (2020 figure). Its spatial layout is defined by two parallel axes about three kilometers long, interrupted by the succession of three gates, installed in the center's early years of development in a largely unsuccessful attempt to contain it, and by an asphalted platform. Shacks built from waste materials alternate with old containers and actual houses built from brick and concrete. Everyone lives on the ground floor, taking advantage of the verandas leaning against the already existing shacks or containers that blur even further the threshold between public and private space. Public places, such as mosques, churches, and brothels, are mostly accommodated in containers where collective activities take place.

Established close to the old military runway, CARA, which remained operational until about a year ago, was built in 1999 as an emergency facility for Kosovo refugees and converted into a permanent asylum center in 2005. For years, the situation of coexistence between the institutional asylum center and the informal settlement behind it, which has developed over the last ten years, generated very complex management conditions; currently, with the center officially closing in 2019 and the walled area being converted into a Covid center, even the modules of the platform have been occupied.

Since 2018, the non-governmental humanitarian association INTERSOS has been the only external organization in the settlement.

Cultivate, harvest, extract

Borgo Mezzanone is part of a circuit of informal settlements in the province of Foggia, hidden among the expanses of wheat fields, which support both the province's rural production infrastructure and a series of orbital, fluid, and unstable paths, which workers follow within the national and regional area.

Our analysis of the type of economy, its development, and the dynamics involved in production, transformation, and movement processes (of products, bodies, and values) allowed us to observe the way in which those production forms construct the space and transform it, combining them with the power relationships that they manage to trigger. This is not due to the type of cultivation, to environmental aspects, or to production procedures but due to how an articulated machine, only partially visible and legal, is built around this rural condition. It is precisely in the folds of those productive actions, in their spatial and residential repercussions, that the systems of protection and care of life emerge, nestled in informal practices and spaces.

In the province of Foggia you *cultivate*, you *harvest*, you *extract*. Three analytical levels that describe and define the production machinery. Three areas of action that allow us to interpret the spatial impacts of the exploitation dynamics in this area. It is a descriptive analytical breakdown that allows us to relate the productive dimension of the observed territory with migratory phenomena.

According to what is shown in the PPTR,[5] describing in detail the development and methods of land use in the province of Foggia, people *cultivate* mainly non-irrigated and irrigated arable land, vineyards, and olive groves.

The *harvest* of the products is strongly influenced by the change that the cultivation cycles have had to address. This has changed from a monoculture to a rotational plan that involves the alternation of different crops and affects the seasonal nature of the work required.[6]

The *extraction* dynamics that affect these territories mainly generate two outcomes in terms of environmental aspects: on one side, they contribute to a phenomenon of homogenization of the ecological and landscape value of the territory, which has followed the progress of the development of a type of intensive economy; on the other, they contribute in increasingly widespread ways and spaces to the development of uses related to the production of alternative energies.

Swarms

It is precisely in the folds of those production dynamics that swarms of men and women move, following the seasonality of the products they cultivate and harvest. The movement of workers can be interpreted as one of the main cornerstones on which the entire system of exploitation of the agricultural sector is based, an element that identifies the fluid and dynamic nature of the observed territory, and a theme that connects some of the meanings of the term lifelines. The movements of migrant bodies do not occur in a fixed scenario but precisely in the folds of Foggia's production system. Attempting to outline the dynamics that describe the movements of workers clarifies the conditions that affect the rural space and the bodies that support it. The interpretation of such movements is made very complex by the expression of the same at different scales: that of international, national, regional, and provincial migration overlapped by the circuit of micro-mobility, which describes the movements of day laborers to reach the fields in which they work.

Obvious, semi-hidden, and hidden mobility are crucial variables for the success of the type of economy found in these spaces, based mainly on operations of exploitation of bodies and lands that require the use of poor, precarious, mobile, and low-cost labor, to be used only cyclically in very limited periods.[7] The rhythms of the movements of bodies within the country are marked by the ripening times of the produce to be harvested, in a cycle that repeats itself year after year. From potatoes to vegetables, from citrus fruits to tomatoes and olives, the rural areas of Calabria, Sicily, Puglia, Basilicata, and Campania are crossed throughout the year by men and women in search of work.[8]

The Foggia countryside becomes the backdrop to cyclical movements of exploited bodies; the fluidity of economic dynamics that force workers

Fig.2
Cultivated land use map of the province of Foggia, pp. 226–227. Source: Camilla Rondot.

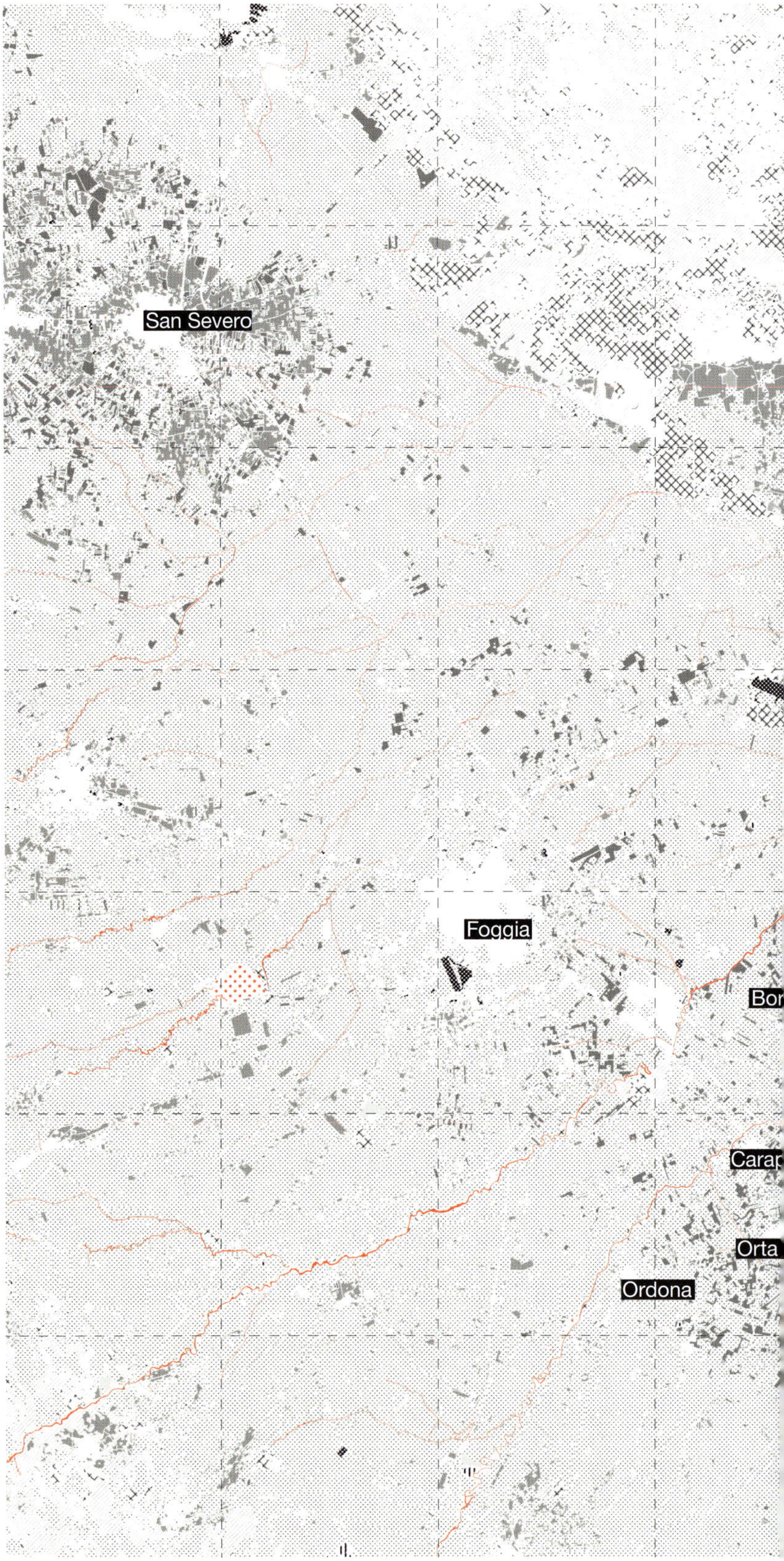

- colture permanenti
- aree a pascolo naturale
- aree agroforestali
- bacini idrici
- boschi misti
- canali e idrovie
- fiume e torrenti
- colture orticole in serra
- uliveti
- vigneti
- saline
- seminativi semplici
- laghi, lagune, paludi
- prati e pascoli alberati
- suoli rimaneggiati

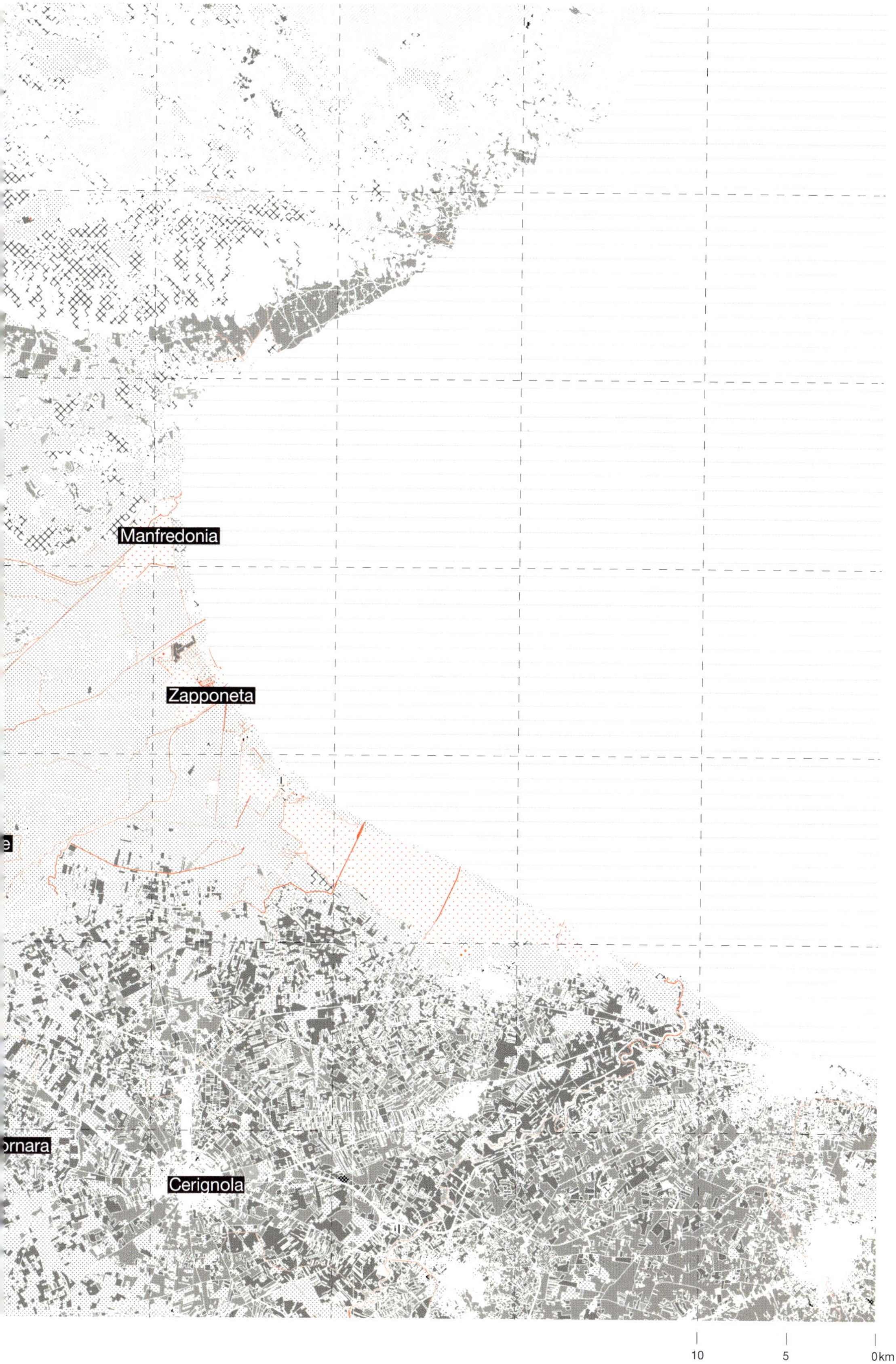
Manfredonia
Zapponeta
e
ornara
Cerignola
10
5
0 km

to move comes up against the fragmentary nature and opacity of the territory and the practices through which they move.

Rural spaces

"Rural others"

For at least thirty years, Italian rural spaces have been experimenting with a radical redefinition of their social structures, undermining the traditional image of a 'white' place.[9] The recent flows of refugees and asylum seekers from conflict zones on the Mediterranean shores have swelled the ranks of foreigners willing to work in our countryside. This phenomenon is particularly evident in areas of intensive agriculture, as well as in mountain areas. In many regions, agricultural, forestry, or pastoral work is mostly carried out by foreign workers.[10] The intensity of the presence of migrants poses the question of the relationship between rurality, ethnicity, and racial conflict.

In the collective imaginary of Italians, places such as Borgo Mezzanone, Rosarno, or San Ferdinando are seen as annoying toponyms indicating the presence of racism within rural societies. New population groups, mainly African, have taken root in these towns in a more or less stable manner, engaging in a wide variety of agricultural jobs. In some cases, migrant communities have defined settlement strategies of community nature and developed self-support networks.[11]

In the common rural image, these migrants and their places of living are out-of-place figures; their spaces and living practices have no place in our representation of the landscape. Their very presence is an act of transgression that challenges the consolidated idea of rural living as something rooted, sedentary, and naturalized. The presence of migrants in our rural spaces, their orbital and unstable forms of living, their activities linked to extractive economies redefine the soil of the Italian countryside as something fluid, unstable, and precarious.

Investigating the "rural others" helps us to build a mosaic of situations that are much more articulated than what is seen when simply focusing on the idea of the average rural person that Philo calls *Mr. Average* or, more implicitly, by supposing that the condition of rurality is more or less the same for everyone. There is no single "rural rule" but many differences, often in conflict with each other. As stated by Murdoch and Pratt,[12] "the point is there is not one but there are many." However, the recognition of this plural dimension remains sterile from the planning perspective if attention is not paid to the question of power, to how the different rurality situations conflict and interweave, expressing power relationships.

We must consider which images and rural subjects are dominant at a given time and in a particular location and how such domination is produced. In this sense, recognizing the "rural others" is not sufficient; it is not just a matter of identifying a multitude of perspectives.[13]

The places of others, of the "less fortunate" of Cloke, must be seen as sets of situations, of ecologies linked between them, within processes articulated according to variations of 'light' and of 'dark.' In this sense, it may be more apt to speak of "rural others," placing at the center of planning attention the issue of coexistence, cohabitation, composition between differences in rural contexts, considering the power relationships that are produced.

In contemporary disciplinary debates, rurality is an element that constantly oscillates between 'otherness' and 'identity'; it is not a simple geographic space but a sort of political 'position.' When analyzing and planning rural spaces and landscapes, which "rural others" do we consider? Women? Ethnic minorities? Residential tourists? Gay community? Religious minorities? *Psychos*? The homeless? Communities that choose to isolate themselves? Poor farmers?

Recognizing "rural others" implies a basic question, which is: who is the beneficiary of our research and our planning processes? Does the emphasis on the issue of "rural others" simply reflect a sense of dissatisfaction as to the outcomes of governance instruments of the traditional rural territory or is it part of an aesthetical stance that tends to celebrate diversity without considering the power relationships that structure interactions between "rural others"? Looking at the rural space by placing 'others' at the center of the matter aims to both identify diversity of ecologies, forms of living, and spatial production that connote contemporary rural spaces and landscapes, and, above all, their composition, imagining weaving operations between differences.

A black space

The migrant camp of Borgo Mezzanone is in effect a piece of an African city planted in the middle of Tavoliere. The territory is that of the fascist reclamation of the 1930s. From the 1980s, the collapse of that complex colonial infrastructure resulted in the abandonment of that settlement model and triggered complex extractive phenomena linked to the production of vegetables – both intensive and large-scale at the same time – to be used as raw materials in northern Italy's food industries. As stated, those processes are linked to the work of migrants and their enslavement. Borgo Mezzanone is therefore one of the main places of crisis and rural conflict in the West.

Borgo Mezzanone is a dense place, equipped with its own sensorial life, produced by the muscular tensions of the migrants. Outdoor butchers, discos, vegetable gardens, shared toilets. Meat is the matter that characterize the landscape. Meat subjected to extraction and pressure. Here, more than anywhere else, color is what supports and contrasts those persons with other colors from other social groups. Black, it can be said, is an infrastructure that gives shape to the space. Blackness, says Fanon, is the will to be in the space that was abandoned by colonialism, by the norm, by order. Perhaps this is also why many of the houses in Borgo Mezzanone are distinguished by a very marked visual regime: the

Fig.3
Zenith image of the patterns of the rural territory of Foggia, 230–231. Photograph by Camilla Rondot.

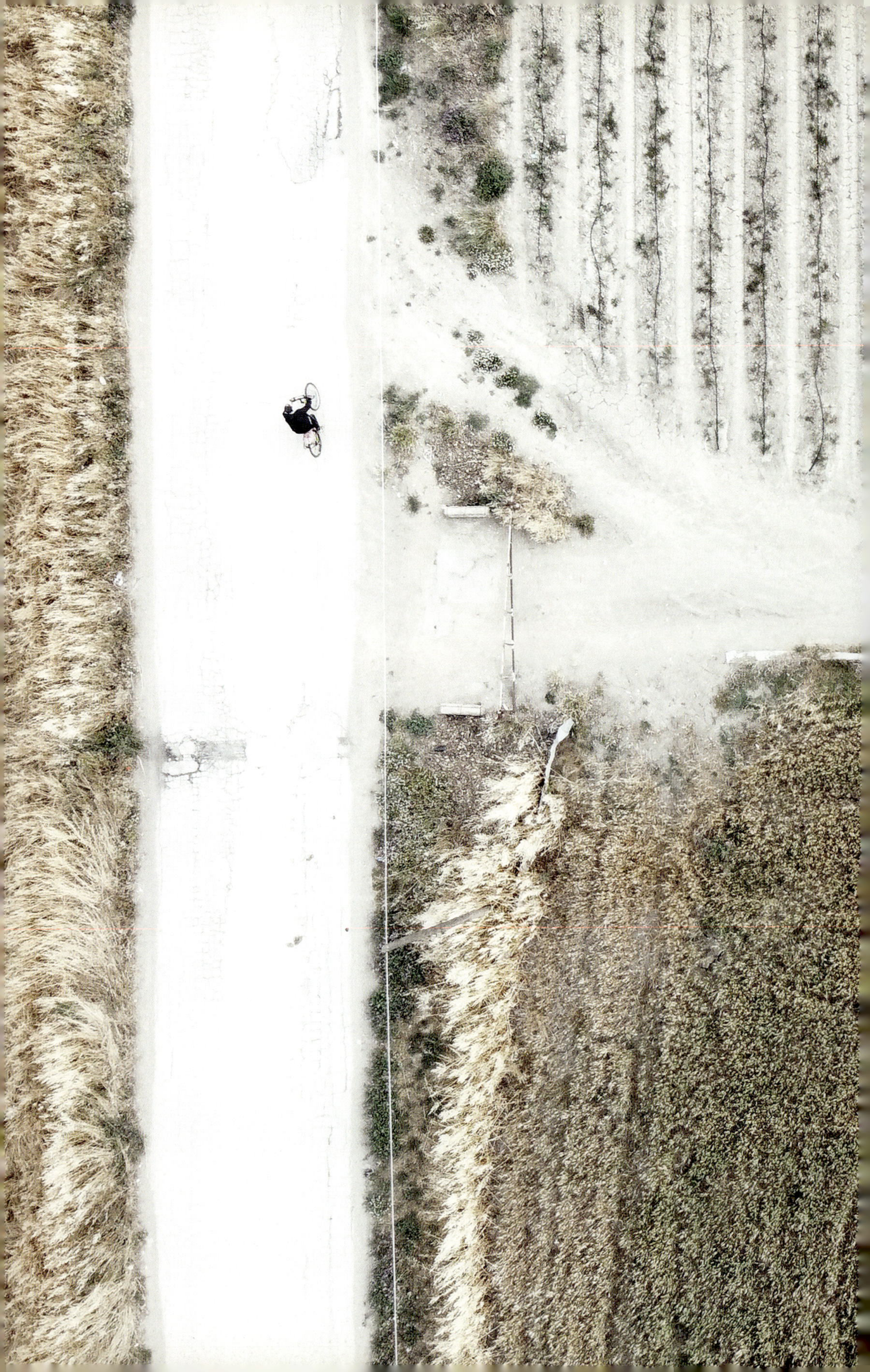

excess of language is a strategy that allows you to think with blackness. Borgo Mezzanone is a place of repetition. The circular movements of migrants between numerous work areas, the regular scans of the times of day, the grooves of bicycles on dirt roads, the very production of spaces of living is repetitive, linked to the dissemination of the spatial prototypes themselves.

The camp is the outcome of extractive logics in which strategies of resistance to extraction manifest: community self-support networks, informal economies, mobility between several locations, a great deal of irony in the ways in which migrants speak to each other and about themselves. As always, the informal space is both dystopian and utopian.

Borgo Mezzanone is a settlement nestled within a rural space partly shaped by extractive industries, a space separated from neoliberal logic and logistics, from deeply rooted rural inhabitants who occupy stable places and positions. The relationships with the surroundings are defined by sequences of production locations that become, on nearing the camp, increasingly scarce. Those sequences are ruled spatially by networks of broken, interrupted paths. You move forward with uncertainty and then, all of a sudden, you are inside it, you are already in there. The path towards the camp crosses an opaque place, paved with the local society's rejection of the camp's presence, as well as with waste. This space can be interpreted as a sequence of uncertain, overlapping lines, as if it were the coast of an island. Such fluidity and instability mean that it can be interpreted as a contact zone, a concept that Gloria Anzaldúa developed in her work *Borderlands/La Frontera: The New Mestiza*.[14] For Anzaldúa, the contact zone is the place where dualistic thought enters a crisis, where contradictions and ambiguities reign, where multiple subjects clash and collide, where a single territory houses multiple and mutually implicated worlds. The Borgo Mezzanone coast is a threshold marked by incessant negotiations, a figure of proximity, division, and endless movement. It is a place of arrivals and departures, of hostile intrusions. Here, both the vulnerability of migrants and of other social groups that interact in this part of the Foggia countryside is most evident. The Borgo Mezzanone coast is a place from which to learn and to consider the difficulties of coexisting in the rural space. Observing this location allows you to think ecologically, which means understanding the fluid relationships that exist between a vast range of agents. Sometimes, these relationships are harmonious; more often, they are characterized by discord and violence.

Borgo Mezzanone, Felicity Scott would say, is an *outlaw territory*, the result of a desire for the outside, for being outside, for productions of difference beyond consolidated normative structures. It is an example of an *undercommon*, a place for the unstructured, for those always on the move.[15] Inhabiting the *undercommon* means experiencing a feeling of 'being at home' where the comprehension of home is a constantly negotiated process within infinite landscapes rather than an object.

Borgo Mezzanone, a place of collision between race and production processes in a rural space governed by the regime of fear, can be a place of

shelter. How can we trigger processes of self-production of difference, how can we eliminate repetition? How can we coexist? If the battle between races is what defines the colony, how can we make the spaces of the 'racial scene' a place for re-assembling the broken bonds, the amputated parts? How do we define a thought of living outside, away from the system of interiors produced by principles of abstraction, classification, selection, and division that dominate Western thought today?
That effort is not intended to put an end to the exploitation but to articulate, from that location, an antagonism able to undermine the racial hierarchies of that rural space.

Lifelines

Killjoy

Lifelines mean spaces of survival. Symbolic, narrative, dreamlike spaces and at the same time very tangible spaces that support life. What is a lifeline in an extreme situation such as that described in the above paragraphs? It is several things, one would immediately respond. Very different things. Infrastructures of support and care in the protective and public sense, in which different associations participate, supporting or replacing institutional policies and projects.[16] Attentive actions of observers who document a situation on the fringes of imagination and seek to construct fragments of public opinion. Lifelines are definitely the informal fabric of mutual help between individuals who, in the migrant condition, find themselves facing processes of incapacitation.[17]
It is also the succession of colonial spaces, isolated houses, containers, shacks: the fragmented set of shelters. Depending on how Borgo Mezzanone is seen, a lifeline is each of these chains and spaces (relational or material) of protection, or the set of them. Lifelines are therefore many players, many spaces, many actions. What holds them together is the focus on the bodies present in those spaces and their relationships to other bodies, space, and power.
The disturbing lifeline on which we want to focus is rooted in the illegal system of recruitment. Paradoxically, illegal recruiters of day laborers are perhaps the most efficient group in dealing with interdependences between the needs of workers: employment, movement, procurement, financial support, and the space in which they move repeatedly, find shelter, work, and interact. In a way, it can be said that illegal recruitment constitutes the *vicious circle that holds the system together*: the *connecting joint* on which Borgo Mezzanone stands. A joint that both marks and facilitates the specific logics of value extraction that we have described in the above paragraphs.
The lever of this mechanism is debt. A very clear example, albeit specific and partial, is the intermediation offered to workers to transform undeclared work into regular employment and the issuance of temporary residence permits, as laid down by Article 103 of the so-called "Re-Launch Decree" of 2020. This process, which we cannot describe here

in detail,[18] is interesting from several aspects. Firstly, it fictitiously puts workers into the domestic work sector (even those employed in agriculture), as it is easier to find 'fake' employers who have the formal requirements to support (for a fee) an application to transform undeclared work into regular employment. Secondly, it implies a complex mobilization network of different people that leads immigrants to get into debt with illegal recruiters of day laborers, front names, usurers, intermediaries, agencies that deal with submitting applications (a task attributed by law to Tax Assessment Centers): this process is extremely crowded with people and skills. Thirdly, the process takes on the nature of fraud and scam: it is a pretense that stages fake jobs, workers, and employers. It leads to the transformation of undeclared work into regular employment in work sectors different from those in which the individual is employed. Finally, it is a process that uses a measure aimed at transforming undeclared work into regular employment to extract economic value from situations that are already, in themselves, unsustainable; up to 5,000–7,000 euros per application are demanded from workers, who obtain this money by getting into debt. This is all covered by a cloak of silence due to the inestimable value of the residence permit for immigrants.
The transformation of undeclared work into regular employment is certainly not the only aspect of this cynical role of 'care' performed by illegal recruiters of day laborers. It is, however, the most evident in the snares of recent legislation. And it is expressed thanks to the capacity to cross-cut specialist languages (bureaucratic, administrative, economic, biological, racial ...), bringing them back to the same crux that *chains together protection and power*. A protective response that transforms and corrupts: the articulation of the entire production system.
This example alone demonstrates that the system is able to manipulate dependence and absence (of documents, home, work, possibility of moving, services, cash, etc.) and make people even more dependent than they already are. It induces *further incapacitation*. Paradoxically, it is the provision of services that accentuates the dispossession of those who use these services, increasing their dependence on them. Thus, illegal recruitment becomes a visible expression of a domination that is exercised over the bodies, lives, and desires and the way in which these are molded and interact in work. The crucial game revolves around illegal recruitment not only on the production field but also on the biological and, specifically, political one.
We have mentioned that Borgo Mezzanone raises for us a question about what a lifeline is, about its political role, its opacities. Placing the vicious circle of illegal recruitment at the center of our interpretation helps us understand the problem better: the illegal recruiter is a killjoy[19] as he overturns a uniquely positive meaning of lifelines. The illegal recruiter erodes the repeated accolades given to care activities that are marked only by empathy, compassion, justice. There is an enormous debate on the way in which care summarizes ethical and regulatory responses to social pathologies; it is definitely an important debate both due to the push to affirm a positive voice in the face of inequality,

Fig.4
House built inside the informal settlement of Borgo Mezzanone. Photograph by Camilla Rondot.

exploitation, humiliation, and poverty, and due to the urgency with which to address atomism, indifference, erosion of the social bond, and neglect. Taking care seriously is important. What our case helps us to highlight is that we often also care for others to benefit ourselves, to exercise power, to perpetuate unjust practices and behaviors. This is obvious but should perhaps be reiterated.

Endnotes

1 Research carried out by Camilla Rondot for her Master's thesis project in the Architecture City Construction Course at the Politecnico di Torino. Tutors: Cristina Bianchetti and Antonio di Campli. The text was discussed by the authors throughout. Camilla Rondot is the author of the first part; Antonio di Campli of the second; Cristina Bianchetti of the third. The photographs are by Camilla Rondot.
2 Piemontese, *Urbanistica ed architettura nel Tavoliere delle Puglie. L'esperienza dei centri rurali 1929–1942*.
3 Caritas, a confessional body of the CEI for charity promotion, works in Borgo Mezzanone, offering some initiatives to promote the integration of migrants. It operates in the premises of the Parish of Santa Maria del Grano. The association *Auxilium* is an association for social promotion established in the village in 2013. It deals mainly with promoting training initiatives with a particular focus on sports, leisure, art, school, tourism, human and social solidarity.
4 CARA is the *Reception Centre for Asylum Seekers*, now closed for several years across Italy.
5 Regione Puglia – Assessorato all'Assetto del Territori, ed., *Piano Paesaggistico Territoriale Regionale*.
6 "We start with courgettes, asparagus, artichokes, beans, and peas, only then to move on to tomatoes in August, but also onions, for which the area of Foggia is renowned and, finally, from September onwards, to olives, grapes, and potatoes." (Medici Per I Diritti Umani 2019).
7 Tarsi, "Quando la mobilità è il parametro dello sfruttamento: migrazione e agricoltura."
8 The Strategic Immigration Dossier of 2018 attempts to provide some explanations on this type of dynamics, explaining the clear correlation between movements internal and external to the regions and the seasonality of products. See: IDOS – Centro Studi e Ricerche, *Dossier Statistico Immigrazione 2018*.
9 Corrado, Castro, and Perrotta, *Migration and Agriculture. Mobility and Change in the Mediterranean Area*; Macrì, Cardillo, Vanino, Perito, Coderoni, "Lavoratori stranieri nell'agricoltura italiana. Dove sono e cosa fanno secondo le cifre ufficiali."
10 Caruso, "Al ghetto agli alberghi diffusi reinserimento abitativo dei braccianti stagionali nei contesti dell'Europa meridionale."
11 Tarsi, "Quando la mobilità è il parametro dello sfruttamento: migrazione e agricoltura."
12 Murdoch and Pratt, "Rural studies: modernism, postmodernism and the 'post-rural'," 425.
13 Barrell (1980, 33) saw a similar hazard with regard to the presentation of the poor in landscape paintings: *one version of the Pastoral... simply replaced another, and the rural poor were no worse off when at the end of the eighteenth century they were continually obliged to express their gratitude and obedience, than when in the middle of the nineteenth their chief virtue was to be seen but not heard.* Failing to address power when exploring rural others runs the risk of replacing one rural representation with another that is equally selective. More or less doing what we did before. The figure of the average rural subject, *Mr Average*, remains the protagonist and *others' are bit part actors in this scene* (Cloke 1997, 375).
14 Anzaldúa, *Borderlands/La Frontera: The New Mestiza*.
15 The *undercommons* are a concept, a practice, and a scenario: they are territories that escape surveillance, spaces that have not yet been colonized by normalization, communities that have refined a logic of subterfuge as a survival strategy against the dynamics of global capitalism. In *The Undercommons. Fugitive Planning and Black Study*, Stefano Harney and Fred Moten theorize a political approach, a way of being and learning together, which identifies and benefits from the 'criminal escape' opportunities that exist in the substratum of any institutional organization governed by a corrective apparatus.
16 The associations operating within the airfield are Caritas and INTERSOS, which maintain relations with the inhabitants of the airfield throughout the year, and the non-profit organization *Io Ci Sto*, which organizes voluntary initiatives promoted by the Archdiocese of Manfredonia-Vieste-San Giovanni Rotondo and the *Scalabrinian Missionaries*.
17 There is broad literature: the loss of capacity, linked to the migrant's condition, is, for example, well expressed in the interviews of Franco Alasia with migrants from the south who moved north in the 1950s: it is the loss of trades, languages, forms of protection. See: Alasia and Montaldi, *Milan, Corea. Inchiesta sugli immigrati negli anni del "miracolo."*
18 Art. 103 of Law no. 77 / 2020, published in Official Journal dated July 17, 2020: conversion law, with modifications, of Decree Law no. 34 of May 19, 2020 (known as "Re-Launch Decree"), containing urgent measures on health, support to employment and to the economy, and social policies connected to the Covid-19 epidemiological emergency.
19 For the positive use of the term, see: Casalini, *Il femminismo e le sfide del neoliberismo*.

Bibliography

Alasia, Franco and Danilo Montaldi. *Milano, Corea. Inchiesta sugli immigrati negli anni del "miracolo."* Milan: Feltrinelli, 1960.

Anzaldúa, Gloria. *Borderlands/La Frontera: The New Mestiza*. San Francisco: Aunt Lute Books, 2012.

Barrell, John. *The Dark Side of the Landscape: the Rural Poor in English Painting 1730–1840.* Cambridge: Cambridge University Press, 1960.

Caruso, Francesco Saverio. "Al ghetto agli alberghi diffusi reinserimento abitativo dei braccianti stagionali nei contesti dell'Europa meridionale." *Sociologia urbana e rurale*, No. 116 (2018): 78–92.

Casalini, Brunella. *Il femminismo e le sfide del neoliberismo*. Rome: IF Press, 2018.

Cloke, Paul. "Country backwater to virtual village? Rural studies and 'the cultural turn'." *Journal of Rural Studies*, Vol. 13 (1997): 367–375.

Cloke, Paul and Jo Little. *Contested Countryside Cultures: Otherness, Marginalisation and Rurality*. London: Routledge, 1997.

Corrado, Alessandra. "Migrazioni, processi di rururbanizzazione e lavoro." *Rivista online di Urban@*, No. 12 (2018): 2–20.

Corrado, Alessandra, Carlos de Castro, and Domenico Perrotta, eds. *Migration and Agriculture. Mobility and Change in the Mediterranean Area*. London: Routledge, 2016.

Harney, Stefano and Fred Moten. *The Undercommons. Fugitive Planning and Black Study*. New York: Minor Composition, 2013.

IDOS – Centro Studi e Ricerche, ed. *Dossier Statistico Immigrazione 2018*. Rome: IDOS, 2018.

Macrì, Maria Carmela, Concetta Cardillo, Silvia Vanino, Maria Angela Perito, Silvia Coderoni S. "Lavoratori stranieri nell'agricoltura italiana. Dove sono e cosa fanno secondo le cifre ufficiali." *Agriregionieuropa*, No. 55 (December 2018).

Medici Per I Diritti Umani, ed. *La cattiva stagione. Rapporto sulle condizioni di vita e di lavoro dei braccianti nella Capitanata*. 2019. https://mediciperidirittiumani.org/medu/wp-content/uploads/2019/10/rap_ottobre_medu_2019_web.pdf (last accessed: November 25, 2021).

Murdoch, Jonathan and Andy C. Pratt. "Rural studies: modernism, postmodernism and the 'post-rural'." *Journal of Rural Studies*, Vol. 9 (1993): 411–27.

Piemontese, Gianfranco. *Urbanistica ed architettura nel Tavoliere delle Puglie. L'esperienza dei centri rurali 1929–1942*. Foggia: centro FG/32, 2010.

Regione Puglia – Assessorato all'Assetto del Territori, ed. *Piano Paesaggistico Territoriale Regionale*. 2015. http://paesaggio.regione.puglia.it/PPTR_2015/2_Norme%20Tecniche/02_Norme%20tecniche%20di%20attuazione.pdf (last accessed: November 25, 2021).

Rondot, Camilla. "Abitare l'opacità. Gli spazi rurali di Borgo Mezzanone." Master diss., Master Degree Architecture Construction City, Politecnico di Torino, 2021.

Tarsi, Elena. "Quando la mobilità è il parametro dello sfruttamento: migrazione e agricoltura." *Contesti città progetti e territori*, No. 1 (2019): 136–153.

Tarsi, Elena and Diletta Vecchiarelli. "Una lettura critica degli insediamenti informali dei lavoratori stagionali: il caso della piana di Gioia Tauro." *Archivio di Studi Urbani e Regionali,* No. 27 (2020): 100–125.

Turner, John. *Housing by People: Towards Autonomy in Building Environments,* London: Marion Boyars, 1976.

The ambivalent nature of productive lifelines: values without waste and landscape without inhabitation

Ianira Vassallo,
Luis Martin Sanchez

The Langhe territory, located south of Piedmont between the provinces of Asti and Cuneo, although not corresponding to specific administrative boundaries, is clearly recognizable both in the media and in terms of landscape and morphology.[1] It is a hilly landscape made up of vineyards, farmhouses and *ciabots*, castles, and small and medium-sized towns, shaped by an important and deeply rooted local winemaking tradition. As early as from the 1980s, this territory underwent a major repositioning process of its economic system – historically linked to agriculture and manufacturing – towards what Boltanski and Esquerre[2] call the construction of an "economy of enrichment": namely, a project to increase the value of local production.

On June 22, 2014, during the 38th session of the UNESCO Committee in Doha, Langhe, together with the areas of Roero and Monferrato, was officially included on the list of World Heritage Sites.[3] This event represented the culmination of the capitalization process which made the agri-food space the very value of the heritage. In the last thirty years, the food and wine industry has therefore become a great infrastructure that supports life in these locations between production and living.

The promotion of local agricultural products (primarily, but not only, wine) was built mainly around the project aimed at valorizing the product origin (certified in Italy by labels or classifications such as DOC, DOCG, etc.) which, in turn, generated immeasurable growth in the market value of agricultural land, the need for an increase in land productivity but also the intensification of tourist interest. Tourism, in fact, then became a great ally for the sale of local products, which are exhibited at festivals, fairs, and shows of various types. Even manufacturing, previously in crisis, has been enriched thanks to these processes and is increasingly oriented towards the high-end market (agri-food is growing rapidly – driven also by the presence of Ferrero –, while other local manufacturing sectors – rubber-plastic and clothing-textiles – are in crisis).

This process demonstrates emblematically another side "of the political use of memory" which, as recounted by François Herzog and Jacques Revel,[4] leads to the commodification of territorial identity by virtue of the "staging of consumerist entertainment."[5]

This complex and exhibited "*fabrique du patrimoine*"[6] is sustained by dark and opaque spaces, interstices, and folds made up of invisible people, fragile individuals, temporary workers, mostly immigrants (initially from Eastern Europe but recently replaced by groups of sub-Saharan origin). They are populations made invisible as they are extraneous to the narration and imagery of a 'picture-postcard' territory; they represent the dark side of capitalization, a fragile but at the same time unavoidable infrastructure, without forms of protection and support but capable of demonstrating that this process, which aims to valorize the identity of the territory, is actually exclusionary and elitist, as opposed to the very concept of authenticity that these projects often recount and stereotype. There is strong ambiguity in which lifelines are renegotiated between visibility and invisibility, production and extraction, relegated to act within the limits imposed by consumption of the landscape

and frictions between hostile and reassuring environments, on sale but in some way in reserve, in excess. In the Langhe spectacle, as we argue in this chapter,[7] lifelines are spaces that produce value, compressing relationships and exposing the instability of value production by making invisible the very infrastructures that produce it, as if there were no waste, no surpluses.

Production and capital

Until the early decades after the Second World War, Langhe was mainly an agricultural territory with high rates of emigration, mainly to the industrial areas of Northern Italy, primarily to nearby Turin. The situation began to change with an inversion of the trend as early as the 1960s, when major industries were established in the area, such as Ferrero and Miroglio,[8] constituting the first line of a consolidated system of manufacturing and craft businesses linked mainly to the sectors of agri-food, clothing-textiles, and rubber-plastic, which came to characterize the areas in the following years.[9] During those years, the entire Province of Cuneo saw its industrial fabric strengthened, particularly in the engineering and agri-food sectors, alongside its traditional specialization in the primary sector (agriculture and livestock). As noted by Gioacchino Garofoli, the strengthening of the manufacturing sector had the merit of maintaining in the local area "a considerable amount of the population by supplementing insufficient agricultural incomes (mainly earned by cultivating vines and hazelnuts) with income from factory work without allowing the houses and hills to be abandoned."[10] All this ensured that a sufficiently articulated demographic structure by age was maintained and could be sustained over time, avoiding the phenomenon of progressive aging and the lack of a workforce that is generally seen in rural and peripheral areas that have a high rate of dependence (proportion of non-active people in the active population).

However, as early as the late 1980s, a process of repositioning the local wine production system into the luxury and high-end sectors began, which, in subsequent years, had a major impact on the entire region, its economy and society. This economic repositioning process – affecting many Western territories since those years – built the foundations for what Boltanski and Esquerre term the "economy of enrichment."[11] In the economy of enrichment, goods do not have a value so much in terms of their use or their durability, as in the case of mass production, but in relation to their intrinsic preciousness, their uniqueness, or their price. They are often products associated with areas recognized to have particular 'knowledge' or specific environmental qualities that should guarantee that they are 'authentic,' 'traditional,' and 'singular,' The extreme version of this case is represented by the various "Made in" (in which the "Made in Italy" holds a particularly central position), thus becoming a guarantee of exceptionality which "can also be used to show the ethical commitment of social responsibility of the producers," thereby contributing to increasing the added value of the product.[12] Importance is

Fig.1
Langhe: morphology of the soul and territorial sections. Source: Domiziana Morelli, Antonino Grasso, Sara Giudice, Laura Larocca, Eric Antohi, Paolo Francesco Marino, Chiara Ianniciello, Emidio Alabrese, Miriam Taormina, Cristina Centoni, Angelica Occhiena, Martina Riva, Antonio Niccolì, Ayoub Anebarou, Omar Alaoui Chrifi, Karim Abdel Magid.

not just attributed to the product in itself, but also to the 'universes' in which these objects are designed and in which they circulate: persons, knowledge, skills, spaces, places, and communication thus build the mythographies of the new goods.

The transformation process of the Langhe economic system towards an economy of enrichment occurred mainly through the gradual orientation towards quality wine production, with a crucial role being played by some innovative leaders who pushed towards greater agro-industrial integration and a repositioning strategy of local production towards luxury and high-end products with strong attention to the promotion of image and communication. In the 1990s, studies revealed the centrality of the topic of internationalization of local excellences through different policies strongly supported by public operators who, in just a few years (also thanks to the Winter Olympic Games being held in nearby Turin in 2006), would give impetus to the start-up and consolidation of wine tourism. In recent years, the local production system has become even more complex as tourism has grown, no longer only linked to wine but also to gastronomy, culture, cities of art, major events, and the environmental characteristics of the area. This process stimulates "the degree of inter-sector production integration, promoting new opportunities for enterprises in service sectors and in the supply of complementary goods and services, integrating in the production system different segments of crafts, commerce and services."[13]

As in other similar territories, in Langhe the process of developing production is carried out through measures aimed at certifying and regulating its uniqueness through registration on a list, often guaranteed by a public body. In Langhe, about 86% of the agricultural area used is listed in DOC and DOCG registers.[14] A large portion of commercial farms practice organic farming, reaching the highest share at regional level. The Slow Food association was founded in this very area in the second half of the 1990s. As already noted, these strategies to valorize the production system have also had major repercussions on the local tourism system, with roughly 339,000 tourists being welcomed in 2017. As in Langhe, luxury production and food and wine, cultural and environmental tourism have become closely related sectors in a gradual expansion process of the value chain, so that some scholars speak of an "agro-tertiary" or "agro-politan" system[15] when defining the area's particular economic system.

The strengthening and diversification of the new local economies has also had demographic repercussions and affected ways and forms of living. For example, in Bassa Langa there was a +516% increase in foreigners (seasonal workers) between 2002 and 2010, in Roero +421%, in Alta Langa +404%, all figures exceeding the provincial average (+390%). Migratory flows constitute an essential resource for the production system which, also given the very low rates of unemployment, requires an available exogenous workforce.

For Boltanski and Esquerre,[16] it is not only the development of the production system towards high-end markets that contributes to the construction of this new economy of enrichment but also territorial capitalization processes. The territory does not contain production lifelines, but it exposes them by flattening them in their entirety for consumption and use, hiding their intimacies, details, waste, and surpluses. In Langhe, in fact, capitalization is an actual technique which has been able to reveal assets that have so far been ignored, exposing them to consumption by combining agriculture, manufacturing, the tertiary sector, and tourism. Lifelines made of a 'dormant' and, in some respects, obsolete legacy in reserve have opened up to the growing demand for productivity of land and products, activating themselves, stimulating the capacity of players to "take ownership of history, even at the cost of transforming it."[17] So heritage, history, tradition, identity, past, and memory, lifelines precisely of the Italian territory, are stripped of any complexity and become devices for increasing the (capital) value of goods and services so as to "specify" and "differentiate the products and services from their competitors."[18] Thus, the lifelines of memory, once embellished and reduced to consumer goods, manipulated into a marketable reduction, become capital – architecture, city, or farmhouse – in the form of "marketing of memory or the training ground for infinite commemorations."[19] Over the last thirty years, Langhe has experienced a process of this nature, which culminated in its inscription on the UNESCO World Heritage List in 2014 together with Roero and Monferrato.

In the last thirty years, the binomials of production-capitalization and assets-territory have constructed an indistinguishable and profound intertwining. Assets use the territory as an element of development, and the territory is represented and promoted through its assets. The lifelines of wine production, food and wine, tourism, manufacturing, and the tertiary sector are mutually reinforced, being enhanced by the new mythographies of local heritage in a territory that does not appear to be experiencing any crisis. And everything that is beyond this glossy narrative is disguised, hidden, or expelled.

The dark side of heritage

Fig.2
Langhe: heritage, tourism, manufacturing, and agricolture, pp. 244–245. Source: Domiziana Morelli, Antonino Grasso, Sara Giudice, Laura Larocca, Eric Antohi, Paolo Francesco Marino, Chiara Ianniciello, Emidio Alabrese, Miriam Taormina, Cristina Centoni, Angelica Occhiena, Martina Riva, Antonio Niccolì, Ayoub Anebarou, Omar Alaoui Chrifi, Karim Abdel Magid.

"Territorial heritage" is a relatively recent concept which has been broadly debated in the disciplines of Italian territorial planning[20] and urban geography, particularly in the Francophone context, proposing a useful contamination between the terms heritage,[21] territorial capital,[22] and territorial resource.[23] In this context, it is defined as a "co-evolutionary historical construct, the result of reifying and structuring anthropic activities that have transformed nature into territory"[24] in which material, socio-economic, cultural, and identity sediments converge. The territory, in fact, is the outcome of a continuous process of negotiation and assessment on what is to be capitalized and what must be excluded. The identification of a place as capital thus implies its "economic development"; an operation that is social, cultural, political, and economic at the same time.[25] The risks of this path are clear. While, on one side, the validation of the process reaches its culmination precisely with

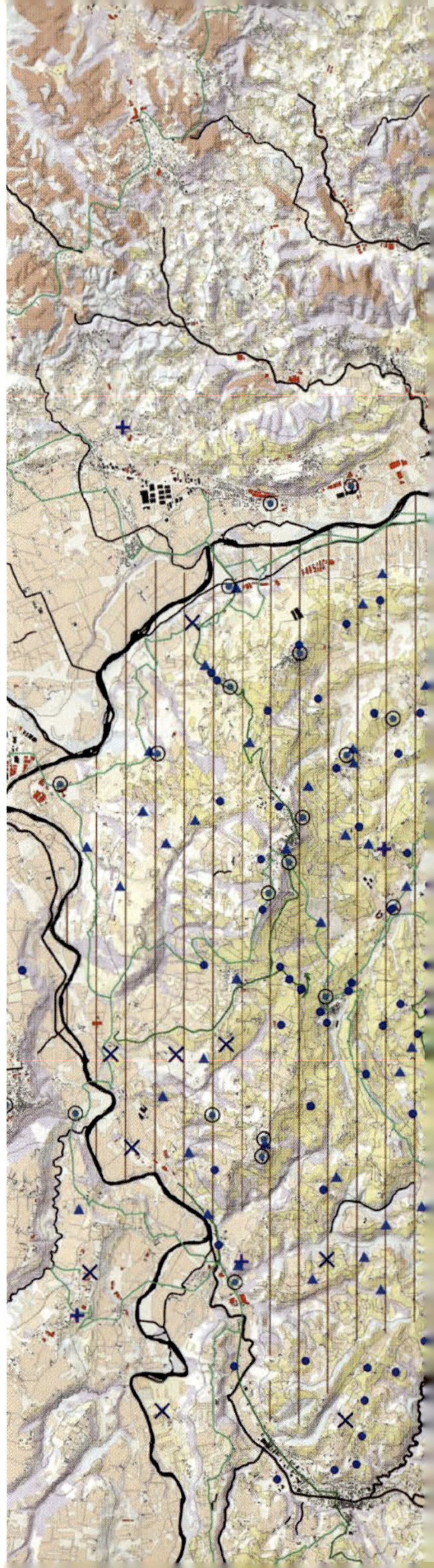

- ▲ Alberghi
- + Chiese
- ● Cantine
- Edificato
- Rete sentieristica
- Superficie forestale
- Percorsi panoramici
- Robinieti
- × Cascine
- Castagneti
- Industrie
- Terreno agricolo seminativo
- Idrografia
- Frutteti
- ◉ Ristoranti
- Vigneti
- | | | Langhe (Patrimonio Unesco)

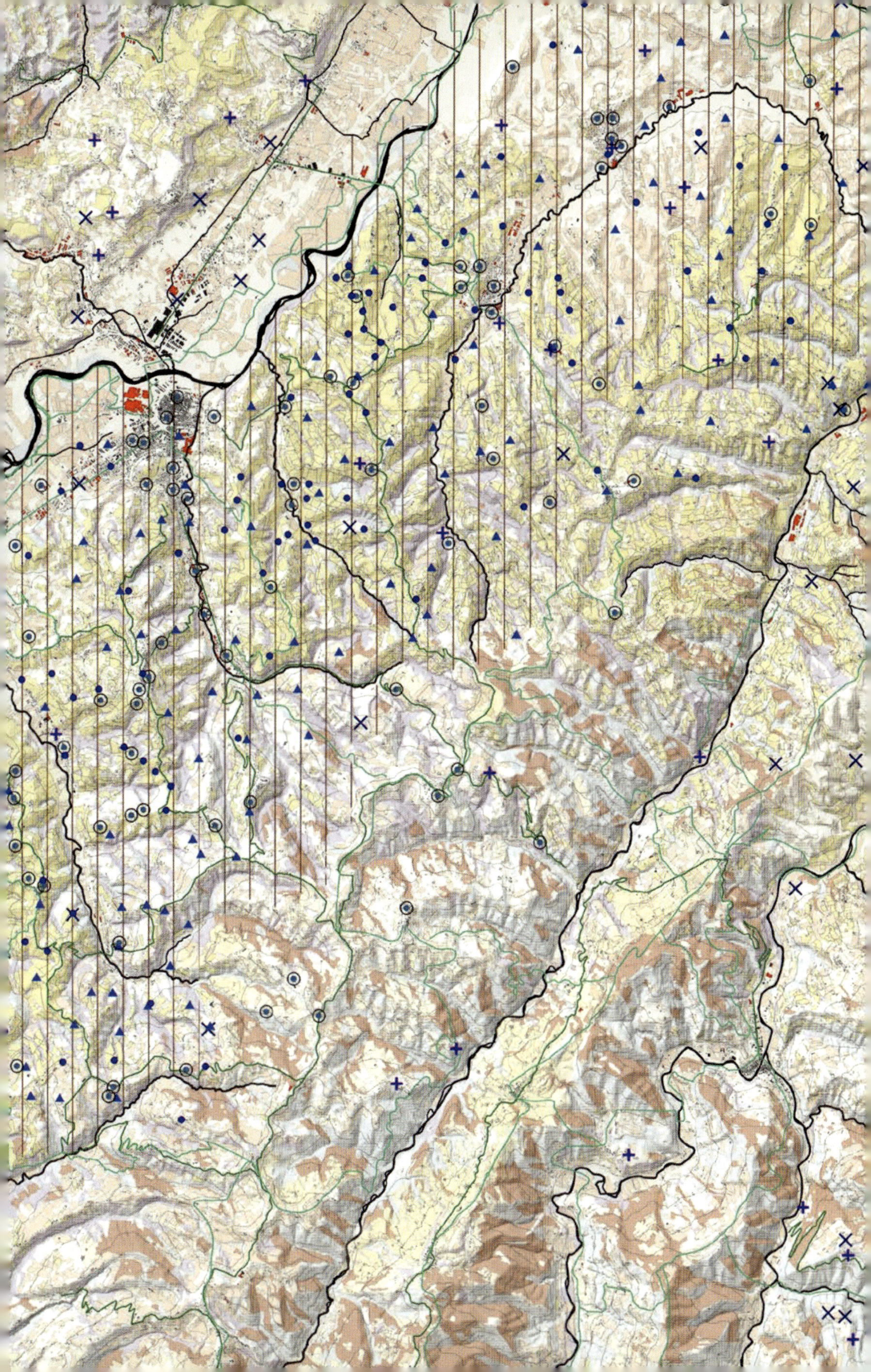

the recognition by authoritative bodies (primarily UNESCO but also the presence of the Slow Food brand and the various local consortia), it is undeniable that, at the same time, this labelling leads to an "iconic reduction"[26] of the territory and therefore its homologation by virtue of the standardization of the services in the name of greater tourist accessibility.[27] On the other side, the management of the protocols eliminates any possible practice of collective construction of the territory as a common good for the production of social wellbeing, subjecting it to the malfunctioning of the global economy and the conditioning of neoliberalist policies. In the last thirty years, therefore, the capitalization system of Langhe is the main political, economic, and spatial lifeline that innervates the production and living processes of these locations.

It therefore seems clear that, in order to sustain the continuous growth demands of the capital factory in recent decades, Langhe, like the whole of Cuneo Province, has experienced a phenomenon of immigration, both seasonal and permanent, of workers willing to follow the rhythms and requirements dictated by agricultural production and international tourism. Thus, in a short space of time, a relationship of synergy and symbiosis between the land, capital, and labor has been defined, so clear as to dictate forms and new norms to its society. It can therefore be said that the economy of enrichment has generated a rigid system of Fordist matrix, in which the capitalization infrastructure has generated an efficient consumption and "territorial branding" machine.[28] As had already happened in *les Trente Glorieuses* of the previous century,[29] the workforce had to be increased to guarantee the operation of the territorial machine; therefore, in the agricultural epicenter of Piedmont – which alone accommodates 40% of primary sector enterprises and about 48% of laborers active at regional level – the number of workers grew in line with the regional average over the decade 2009–2018, whereas the increase in non-EU workers was decidedly more marked (+84%).

The phenomenon is confirmed by the data on new employment of foreign citizens in the agricultural sector: in 2017, Cuneo Province absorbed 64% of recruitments in Piedmont, with even higher levels for non-EU citizens (69.2%). The nationalities of most workers are Albanian (2,981 recruitments), Malian (1,559), Macedonian (1,341), Indian (1,288), Ivorian (1,168), Senegalese (1,132), and Chinese (1,011). With respect to the ways and times of this important growth in labor demand, at a historically negative time for the national labor market, it can be said that in 2018 the vast majority of non-EU agricultural workers employed in Cuneo Province (95%) were recruited on temporary contracts. Those who worked for periods shorter than fifty days during the year make up about 46%, with the implications cited above. Women represent 22.5% of the labor force: these are mainly Chinese women employed in harvesting small fruits and/or Eastern European women involved in the harvest. These figures highlight a complex and dynamic social picture, far from the simplification and stereotyping outlined in wine culture, built around the image of the historical family-run company but, at the same time, able to restore the fragmented contours of a continuously changing economic system. While on the one hand, the

scenario presented important opportunities for social and economic integration of the most fragile populations, generally excluded from urban processes of intensification of the economy of knowledge, it denies, on the other hand, the capacity to accommodate migration flows of seasonal workers as an opportunity to build for them the prospect of a better life (in the typically Fordist utopian idea of the factory as an instrument of regulation and redistribution of economic and cultural capital).
When observing this territory by putting capitalization lifelines to work, what emerges is a rigid picture of senseless exploitation of environmental and human resources in contrast with the manifesto of quality, landscape, and environmental authenticity outlined by the tourism industry and by the economy based upon local excellence.

Lifelines: the return to mutualism

In this context, the Municipality of Canelli[30] is an interesting place of observation to precisely and tangibly identify the relationship of dependence and dissonance between a virtuous and intangible economic system and a fragmented and fragile social structure, which connotes the ambivalence of productive lifelines: spaces of ready-to-eat dishes, apparently waste-free, which can, however, be glimpsed in the Canelli hills.
Albeit sporadically, this municipality, more than others, has been the epicenter of various resistance actions and conflicts between these two dimensions in the past decade: in fact, in the face of a production system centered on increasing the value of territorial resources, it has become very evident that the social capital that allows it to function is devoid of any form of protection, attention, and form of living. The situation shows an ideal model of 'producing without living.'
The problem of accommodating seasonal workers to support the frenetic period of the Muscat (and others) harvest is actually a phenomenon that has existed for some time, highlighted by the local press, associating it mostly with political issues concerning spatial safety, urban decorum, and the emerging need to contain the spread of Covid-19. Between 2010 and 2016, some local newspapers (La Nuova Provincia, La Stampa locale, La Gazzetta di Alba)[31] reported on numerous occasions on the illegal camps scattered around the area, prompting the Municipal Administration of Canelli to respond to the demand to accommodate the seasonal workers. Faced with the public condemnation of this phenomenon, the Municipality therefore implemented a project with Caritas to welcome and support these populations (a temporary residence for twenty-five workers in Piazza Gioberti), and an 'official space' was then prepared for tents, mostly improvised, to respond to the emergency.
Furthermore, in 2018, on the initiative of the seasonal workers for the harvest (about forty people) in collaboration with operators of the social cooperative Crescere Insieme, in the absence of any other arrangement, a cleaning action was started on the former railway station to convert it into a bivouac and socializing area.

Despite these manifestations, which demonstrate the extreme fragility and inadequacy of the political response to a very significant social and economic problem, during the night of September 1, 2020, the Carabinieri cleared a room of the railway station in which about a dozen seasonal workers had taken refuge. And again, the same year, the Carabinieri of the Compagnia di Alba and the guards of the State Forestry Corps raided a farmhouse in Mango, where seventy seasonal workers were found crammed into rooms that would struggle to accommodate a dozen. Subsequently, other checks were carried out in the municipalities of Barbaresco and Neive, where twenty or so laborers were found in another farmhouse, also living in very poor sanitary conditions. Producing without living, consuming without stopping, working without resting, these seems to be appropriate phrases to outline how much the so celebrated productive lifelines that have 'made' the Langhe model have attempted to hide any trace of its infrastructures. The turning point of this process occurred in the face of a request from Caritas and from CRI to set up a new tent area (with 12 spaces to alleviate the demand of about 50 homeless workers), a proposal for which the local administration, however, denied consent.

Therefore, faced with this scenario, Caritas (together with the various endorsements of the Piedmont Catholic social network active in the area) denounced the inefficiency of a government focused on denying and concealing the evidence (in Canelli and in the wine-making municipalities there is enormous demand for seasonal laborers), delegating to the voluntary sector a solution that, based upon the numbers faced, it is unable to provide, but which above all is not its responsibility given that it is part of the issues of the area's main economic supply chain.

The violent short circuit between the glossy image of a pleasant and authentic territory, rich in historical identity, and that of a dark place where the growing phenomena of expulsion of seasonal workers, treated as illegal immigrants, reveals an emergency that risks bringing the system to its knees. It is then that Confcooperative manifests all its solidarity towards the problem. The issue of labor protection was recently addressed by Confcooperative Cuneo, which, together with Consorzio Barolo Barbaresco, Coldiretti, Cia, and Confagricoltura, signed a shared housing contract for seasonal workers to provide a lease to workers not recruited directly by commercial farms during the harvest. The aim is to ensure that those who work in the vineyards and perform essential work for the agri-food district are given security and dignity. The contract, therefore, arose from the need to offer accommodation to workers who are recruited by the cooperatives (and not directly by the commercial farms). The wineries, in fact, often sign contracts with cooperatives to manage this service, and the presence of the latter in the area represents a concrete response to its production requirements.

The mediation work carried out by cooperatives thus transforms into substantial support for building a process to enhance the quality of living. The agreement signed in Cuneo represents a step forward in building an inclusive and ethical supply chain against the ongoing dynamics of illegal recruitment but, above all, an opportunity to identify in the Third Sector a player capable of restoring the complex and multifaceted dimension generated by a hegemonic capitalization process in the territory. In this sense, Langhe is an emblematic case study: it is a manifestation of how capitalization processes of the territory, in their most extreme forms, constitute a rigid infrastructure that aims to exclude and mask everything that supports its functioning (and is essential in that sense) but that is not part of the construction of a "selected storytelling."[32]

Endnotes

1 The territory is, in turn, subdivided into three internal sub-areas: Alta Langa, Bassa Langa, and Roero. Alta and Bassa Langa include the territories located on the right bank of the Tanaro, while Roero includes those on the left. Furthermore, Bassa Langa comprises the hilly area (with altitudes of less than 600 meters) between the Tanaro river to the north and the Belbo river to the south. Alta Langa is, on the other hand, the part of territory on the border with Liguria, where the hills reach altitudes of 750 meters to almost 900 meters in Mombarcaro (Fondazione CRC – Centro Studi 2014).

2 Boltanski and Esquerre, *Enrichment: A Critique of Commodities*.

3 In June 2014, the project "The Vineyard Landscape of Piedmont: Langhe-Roero and Monferrato" won UNESCO recognition: it mainly involves nine municipalities of Bassa Langa and two of Alta Langa, over 15 centers of the province of Asti and three of Alessandria. The reasons for the candidacy are based upon the recognition of value of the Langhe-Roero and Monferrato territories, lying not only in the strong and undisputed social and economic role of the current wine production but also and above all in the landscape of these areas, shaped over the centuries by wine culture and the wine-making industry, by this wealth of knowledge, expertise, feelings linked to the vineyards, to the harvest, to production and daily consumption of wine (Fondazione CRC – Centro Studi 2014).

4 Hartog and Revel, *Les usages politiques du passé*.

5 Olmo, "Sull'uso (politico) della memoria, tra consumismo e tragedia."

6 Heinich, *La fabrique du patrimoine. De la cathédrale à la petite cuillère*.

7 The reflections offered in this text arise from the outcomes of the City and Territory Planning Workshop of the academic year 2020–2021 at the Politecnico di Torino coordinated by Cristina Bianchetti, Ianira Vassallo, and Armando Baietto with the following collaborators: Luis Martin Sanchez, Giacomo Mulas, and Emiljan Prenga. The "Inhabit the distance (No Distance Living)" workshop attempted to investigate the territory of Cuneo Province during the pandemic crisis through three main topics: the project of care, the different forms of living, and the complex relationship between production and capitalization. With respect to this last topic, the group consisting of Domiziana Morelli, Antonino Grasso, Sara Giudice, Laura Larocca, Eric Antohi, Paolo Francesco Marino, Chiara Ianniciello, Emidio Alabrese, Miriam Taormina, Cristina Centoni, Angelica Occhiena, Martina Riva, Antonio Niccolì, Ayoub Anebarou, Omar Alaoui Chrifi, and Karim Abdel Magid developed an interesting project on Langhe from which the hypotheses of this work arose.

8 Ferrero is an Italian multinational specializing in the confectionery industry. The company, which now has its administrative and fiscal headquarters in Luxembourg, was founded in 1946 by the Ferrero family (Giuseppe and Piero), originally from Alba (Cuneo). Miroglio is an Italian clothing and textile company, established in 1947 by Giuseppe Miroglio, the son of textile traders of the previous century. Today, the brand is an international group (Miroglio Group) consisting of about 35 companies in 20 different countries. The brand, in addition to production, has over 900 flagship stores across the world.

9 Four industrial districts are present in the area: the agri-food districts of La Morra and Cortemilia, the food and wine district of Canelli e Santo Stefano Belbo, and the paper and wood district of Dogliani (Fondazione CRC – Centro Studi 2014).

10 Garofoli, "La 'Governance' dello sviluppo locale nelle Langhe."

11 Boltanski and Esquerre, *Enrichment: A Critique of Commodities*.

12 Ibid.

13 From research conducted locally (Garavaglia 2009), based upon the active enterprises (those registered) in the list of the Chamber of Commerce of Cuneo, the agri-food district of Langhe and Roero reaches a considerable dimension, surpassing 10,600 production units. Even without considering the over 8,700 commercial farms, about 2,000 enterprises belonging to the industrial transformation and services sectors related to the agri-food industry operate in the local system. The number of enterprises in the food processing sector is high (about 700 companies) as well as in the commercial intermediation sector (retail – many of which are specialist stores – and wholesale) of agricultural and agri-food goods (with over 1000 companies), but there is also a large number of agricultural services companies (almost 150 companies) and enterprises in the machinery manufacturing sector for agriculture and the agroindustry (over 70 companies). This is therefore a complex, articulated, and interactive system which is at the basis of entrepreneurial dynamics and the production of innovative ideas that have vastly changed the position relating to the Langhe production system in the national and international context.

14 Cuneo Province boasts, in particular, a leading position in the wine sector, with a good 37 DOC and

seven DOCG wines – Controlled and Guaranteed Denomination of Origin: Barolo, Barbaresco, Roero, Roero Arneis, Asti, Dolcetto di Dogliani Superiore, and Dolcetto di Diano d'Alba. Aside from the wine sector, Cuneo Province boasts other products that have obtained European certification: eight with PDO and three with IGP labels, particularly for cheeses but also hazelnuts.

15 Garofoli (2014) defines the local production system as "agro-tertiary" or "agro-politan," citing Friedmann and Weaver (1979) emphasizing the high degree of interaction between the different sectors.

16 Boltanski and Esquerre, *Enrichment: A Critique of Commodities*.

17 Ibid.

18 Ibid.

19 Olmo, *Città e democrazia. Per una critica delle parole e delle cose*.

20 Magnaghi, *Il progetto locale: verso la coscienza di luogo*.

21 Choay, *L'allegoria del patrimonio*.

22 OECD, *The Well-being of Nations. The Role of Human and Social Capital Centre for Educational Research and Innovation*.

23 Corrado, "Introduzione. Il concetto di risorsa territoriale"; Gumuchian and Pecquer, *La ressource territoriale*.

24 Magnaghi, *Il progetto locale: verso la coscienza di luogo*.

25 Lazzarotti, "Tourisme et patrimoine: ad augusta per angustia / *Tourism and heritage: ad augusta per angustia*."

26 D'Eramo, *The World in a Selfie. An Inquiry into the Tourist Age*.

27 Ibid.

28 Rossi and Vanolo, *Urban Political Geographies: A Global Perspective*; McNeill, *The Labor Movement: The Problem of To-Day*.

29 Polanyi, *The Great Transformation*.

30 This is an ancient medieval village, which is part of the set of territories included on the UNESCO World Heritage List in 2014 as part of the Langhe and Roero wine landscapes thanks not only to the presence of native Muscat vines that produce the famous sparkling wine but also to its famous underground cathedrals. Its strategic position has, in fact, allowed this territory to become the preferential place for the establishment of a system of native vines and a production system built on a network of wine cellars and underground paths useful for processing wine in all its stages. The historic town center is still home to some of the most famous Italian wineries such as *Coppo, Contratto and Bosca*.

31 Fiori, "Settanta lavoratori stagionali stipati in una cascina di Langa"; Germano, "La stazione-dormitorio è pulita dai braccianti"; La Nuova Provincia, "Canelli, Caritas critica sul 'no' del Comune ad installare due tende per ospitare braccianti stagionali"; Ferraris, "Stazione di Canelli rifugio di vendemmiatori. I carabinieri sgomberano un locale occupato abusivamente"; Pinaffo, "Le voci dei lavoratori stagionali accolti nelle strutture albesi."

32 Sandercock, "Out of the Closet: The Importance of Stories and Storytelling in Planning Practice."

Bibliography

Boltanski, Luc and Arnaud Esquerre. *Enrichment: A Critique of Commodities*. Cambridge: Polity Press, 2020.

Caccia Gherardini, Susanna and Carlo Olmo. *La Villa Savoye. Icona, rovina e restauro (1948–1968)*. Rome: Donzelli, 2016.

"Canelli, Caritas critica sul 'no' del Comune ad installare due tende per ospitare braccianti stagionali." *La Nuova Provincia*, August 29, 2020. https://lanuovaprovincia.it/attualita/canelli-caritas-critica-sul-no-del-comune-ad-installare-due-tende-per-ospitare-braccianti-stagionali/.

Choay, Françoise. *L'allegoria del patrimonio*. Rome: Officina Edizioni, 1995.

Comune di Alba – Comunicato Stampa. "Si è riunito il Tavolo di lavoro dedicato al tema degli stagionali del comparto agricolo." *Comune di Alba*, June 10, 2021. https://www.comune.alba.cn.it/comunicati-stampa/4946-si-è-riunito-il-tavolo-di-lavoro-dedicato-al-tema-degli-stagionali-del-comparto-agricolo (last accessed: December 12, 2021).

Confcooperative Piemonte. "Confcooperative in prima linea per una vendemmia più giusta." *Confcooperative Piemonte*, April 27, 2021. https://www.piemonte.confcooperative.it/LA-COMUNICAZIONE/LE-NOTIZIE/ArtMID/482/ArticleID/2135/ Confcooperative-in-prima-linea-per-una-vendemmia-pi249-giusta (last accessed: December 12, 2021).

Corrado, Federica. "Introduzione. Il concetto di risorsa territoriale." *Le risorse territoriali nello sviluppo locale*, edited by Federica Corrado, 15–38. Florence: Alinea Editrice, 2005.

D'Eramo, Marco. "Unescocide." *New Left Review*, Vol. 88 (Jul/Aug 2014).

D'Eramo, Marco. *The World in a Selfie. An Inquiry into the Tourist Age*. London: Verso Books, 2021.

Ferraris, Gaia. "Stazione di Canelli rifugio di vendemmiatori. I carabinieri sgomberano un locale occupato abusivamente." *La Stampa*, August 31, 2020. https://www.lastampa.it/asti/2020/09/01/news/stazione-di-canelli-rifugio-di-vendemmiatori-i-carabinieri-sgomberano-un-locale-occupato-abusivamente-1.39252310 (last accessed: December 12, 2021).

Fiori, Roberto. "Settanta lavoratori stagionali stipati in una cascina di Langa." *La Stampa*, September 18, 2016. https://www.lastampa.it/cuneo/2016/09/18/news/settanta-lavoratori-stagionali-stipati-in-una-cascina-di-langa-1.34806870 (last accessed: December 12, 2021).

Fondazione CRC – Centro Studi. "Langhe e Roero. Tra tradizione e innovazione." *Quaderni della Fondazione CRC*, No. 22 (2014).

Friedmann, John and Clyde Weaver. *Territory and Function: Evolution of Regional Planning*. London: Edward Arnold Publishers Ltd, 1979.

Garavaglia, Luca. "Cluster produttivi e traiettorie di sviluppo nei territori del cuneese." *Quaderni della Fondazione CRC*, No. 5 (2009).

Garofoli, Gioacchino. "La 'Governance' dello sviluppo *locale nelle Langhe." La governance come fattore di sviluppo*, edited by Francesco Mantino, 199–216. INEA: Studi e Ricerche, 2014.

Germano, Lorenzo. "La stazione-dormitorio è pulita dai braccianti." *La Gazzetta d'Alba*, September 30, 2018. https://www.gazzettadalba.it/2018/09/la-stazione-dormitorio-e-pulita-dai-braccianti/ (last accessed: December 12, 2021).

Gumuchian, Hervé and Bernard Pecquer. *La ressource territoriale*. Paris: Anthropos, 2007.

Hartog, François and Jacques Revel. *Les usages politiques du passé*. Paris: Édition de l'EHESS, 2001.

Heinich, Nathalie. *La fabrique du patrimoine. De la cathédrale à la petite cuillère*. Paris: Éditions de la Maison des sciences de l'homme, 2009.

IRES Piemonte and Osservatorio Rurale del Piemonte, eds. *Piemonte Rurale 2020. Rapporto annuale dell'osservatorio rurale*. 2020. http://www.piemonterurale.it/images/documenti/PiemonteRurale2020.pdf (last accessed: December 12, 2021).

Lazzarotti, Olivier. "Tourisme et patrimoine: ad augusta per angustia / *Tourism and heritage: ad augusta per angustia." Annales de géographie* 629 (Année 2003): 91–110.

Magnaghi, Alberto. "Le dimensioni del progetto infrastrutturale nella costruzione dei luoghi e nella valorizzazione dei paesaggi: la pedemontana." *Territori regionali e infrastrutture*. curated by Attilio Belli, Giuseppe De Luca, Sandro Fabbro, Anna Mesoiella, Simone Ombuen, Piero Properzi. Milan: Franco Angeli, 2008.

Magnaghi, Alberto. *Il progetto locale: verso la coscienza di luogo*. Turin: Bollati Boringhieri, 2010.

McNeill, George E., ed. *The Labor Movement: The Problem of To-Day*. New York: The M.W. Hazen Co, 2009.

"Nelle Langhe, anche le cooperative di contoterzismo dovranno garantire alloggio agli stagionali." *WineNews*, April 22, 2021. https://winenews.it/it/nelle-langhe-anche-le-cooperative-di-contoterzismo-dovranno-garantire-alloggio-agli-stagionali_440662/ (last accessed: December 12, 2021).

OECD. *The Well-being of Nations. The Role of Human and Social Capital Centre for Educational Research and Innovation*. 2001. https://www.oecd.org/education/innovation-education/1870573.pdf (last accessed: December 12, 2021).
Olmo, Carlo. "Sull'uso (politico) della memoria, tra consumismo e tragedia." *Il Giornale dell'architettura*, February 24, 2016. https://ilgiornaledellarchitettura.com/2016/02/24/sulluso-politico-della-memoria-tra-consumismo-e-tragedia/ (last accessed: December 12, 2021).
Olmo, Carlo. *Città e democrazia. Per una critica delle parole e delle cose*. Rome: Donzelli, 2018.
Pinaffo, Francesca. "Le voci dei lavoratori stagionali accolti nelle strutture albesi." *Gazzetta d'Alba*, September 6, 2021. https://www.gazzettadalba.it/2021/09/le-voci-dei-lavoratori-stagionali-accolti-nelle-strutture-albesi/ (last accessed: December 12, 2021).
Polanyi, Karl. *The Great Transformation*. New York: Farrar & Rinehart, 1944.
Rossi, Ugo and Alberto Vanolo. *Urban Political Geographies: A Global Perspective*. New York: SAGE, 2012.
Sandercock, Leonie. "Out of the Closet: The Importance of Stories and Storytelling in Planning Practice." *Planning Theory and Practice*, Vol. 4, No.1 (March 2003): 11–28.
"Vendemmia. Nelle Langhe e Barolo nasce il contratto condiviso di alloggio per stagionali." *Agricoltura.it – Giornale dell'agricoltura italiana*, April 21, 2021. https://www.agricultura.it/2021/04/21/vendemmia-nelle-langhe-nasce-il-contratto-condiviso-di-alloggio-per-stagionali/ (last accessed: December 12, 2021).

The Beik infrastructure of loyalists: Sawfar's fragmented lifelines

Hanadi Samhan,
Hoda Mekkaoui

Introduction

The old village of Sawfar, hidden in the mountains of the Aley District, is located on the Damascus international highway, 35 kilometers from the capital city of Beirut. It overlooks the beautiful mountains of the Metn region and the Hammana Lamartine Valley: Sawfar owes its existence to the railway built by the Ottomans in 1880, which linked Beirut to Riyaq in the Beqaa Valley. At an altitude of 1,300 meters above sea level, Sawfar has always been a touristic destination for Lebanese and Arab visitors escaping the moisture and summer heat, while enjoying its stone villas, hotels, and beautiful sceneries. Although located along the Beirut-Damascus road infrastructure, Sawfar resisted being a road stop due to its undeniable charm, along with its strategic location. Because of its easy access, pure air, and remarkable location overlooking the beautiful Hammana Lamartine Valley, Sawfar quickly became popular among Beirut's *'haute bourgeoisie'* who made it their favorite summer destination.

The residents of Sawfar are mainly Lebanese belonging to the Druze religious sect, with a majority supporting the PSP (Progressive Socialist Party) founded in 1949 by the leader Kamal Junblat and run by his son, Walid Jumblatt, the '*Beik*' (meaning the master), since 1977. Ever since, the *Beik*,[1] has been taking care of his loyalists, wisely and eagerly defending their rights in the Lebanese cabinets, acting assertively whenever he feels that their privileges might be jeopardized by any other Lebanese constituents.

Although permanent residents of Sawfar don't exceed 3,000,[2] up to 15,000 people live here during summer, including Beiruties and other tourists from all Arab countries, to enjoy the lovely summer breeze, cold fresh water, and seasonal tasty fruits.

Sawfar is considered Lebanon's historical hub of luxury since the nineteenth century. Unfortunately, this privileged position started to fade out due to the late crises and the harsh economic circumstances endured in Lebanon. With the deteriorating infrastructure services and the absence of the government and an effective welfare system, Lebanese are struggling through their daily lives. The community in Sawfar was mobilized by the call of their leader, Walid Junblat, to trust his judgment and to launch individual and collective initiatives of lifelines to "defend and protect" the community and the village from hunger.

Fragmented lifelines

Historically, Sawfar experienced many crises since the 1980's. The village, due to its strategic location, was the separation line between the Israeli armies and the Syrian troops during the Israeli invasion of Lebanon in 1980. In addition, it experienced a lot of destruction and dislocations during the Mountain War of 1984; and with the total collapse of public services, the region, in addition to many other Druze regions, witnessed the emergence of diverse institutions created by the *Beik* and

the PSP to ensure the resilience and sustainability of their people. In Lebanon – in particular in the post-war era – the patron-client relationship remained dominant between the state and its citizens. Infrastructure and service provision required the patron to serve as intermediary between government and community, channeling whatever resources and favors were needed and available. In Sawfar, throughout the crises experienced since 1980, the conservative Druze appeared to have established lifeline models to deal with their needs. With recent emerging crises, the community's attachment to and dependency on the leader became stronger and evident. The *Beik's* helping hands seemed to be present everywhere, and loyalty to the leader is strengthened. "The *Beik* bought the center for us so that we don't have to pay a monthly rent. I used to do a dinner gathering each year in order to get donations to be able to pay the monthly rent," assures Samiha. "He always works to provide the best for his community, and without his wisdom and assistance, we would not have been able to overcome any crisis." Her very humble house displays her sincere loyalty to the Junblat family through a photo of Walid (the current leader) and another huge photo of his belated father Kamal adorning her living room.

The Lebanese Druze[3] are a minority in Lebanese society; they are believed to constitute about 5.2% of Lebanon's total population.[4] Being a minority, they have always felt the need to build internal solidarity:

Fig.1
Aerial view of Sawfar village (Photo taken from a poster at the Municipality, dated year 2000). Photograph by Hoda Mekkaoui.

"repeatedly they have compensated for a lack of numbers with solidarity and a military prowess that have permitted them to play important political roles, often to the discomfort of the governments under which they have lived."[5] For this reason, they are tied to their lands and thus do not properly belong to the cosmopolitical urbanite, with little aspirations to politics, state, and supremacy in Lebanese society.[6] The solidarity and connections in Sawfar become the lifelines of a community. They are the main keys where envisioned lifelines became a series of nods that co-respond (a term proposed by Ingold) and interact with one another, relying mainly on sectarian affiliation and sectarian correspondence. As explained by Ingold,[7] for life to carry on, it has to be commonly shared and articulated with others.

In the Druze region of Sawfar, solidarity, loyalty, and trust are well pronounced given the private and independent nature of its confessional group. Helping each other and co-responding with one another is not a matter of choice, it is the obligation of each community member to show loyalty to their leader and to trust him in order to provide support for the community whenever needed. Maintaining life means being strongly engaged in close relationships, in a close network, in a series of protective relationships.

In the following sections, several community-based initiatives and volunteer-run associations in Sawfar village are showcased. These initiatives and associations succeeded in helping people survive the crises, despite the absence of government plans. They were promoted and launched by the *Beik's* call to fight hunger. In the national newspaper, Mr. Junblat declared "the hunger revolt will come and we have no answer."[8] In a virtual panel organized by the Beirut Institute, he also anxiously stated: "It started. Every chief of tribe, every chief of community is trying to satisfy his own people." Following the *Beik's* instructions, individuals in Sawfar were encouraged by the municipality to build a special network of connections. It included Lebanese emigrants or people from foreign, mainly Arab, countries who have relatives in the village or own properties in Sawfar, and who care about providing support for the families there during the crisis. The initiative intended to provide continuous, uninterrupted funding for the municipality, whose main role was to ensure food and medical supplies (especially during Covid-19) to the community and residing families. With the help of associations and NGOs, the municipality was able to provide medical and food supplies for many families, following a specific database with information about needy families in Sawfar and the outskirts, its neighboring villages of Bedghan, Charoun, and Majdel Baana.

Misk association

Misk is the first association in Sawfar to take care of people who lost their job after the Beirut port explosion and the subsequent economic and financial crisis that hit the country. Its assistance is extending to families or elderly people who do not receive financial support from a family member working outside of Lebanon. Only 20% of the families in Sawfar have a family member working abroad. Misk emerged to ensure livelihood opportunities by soliciting donations from generous expatriate donors willing to help families in need. Mounira[9] calls them the 'loyals' to Sawfar, with 'white hands.' She explains that "without their support we wouldn't be able to help our families. They have gained the trust of many generous donors from different countries around the world. They know that we volunteered to work for our people without any personal profits." The late recurrent crises pushed Sawfar residents to think of alternative solutions and measures to support families and community members in need. Many associations have emerged, establishing links between donors and needy families. Mounira confirmed that within a few months they were able to distribute food parcels and medical supplies to about 300 families. Mounira is also a member in another association that helps orphans complete their postgraduate studies. This year, they were in charge of 28 students, paying their tuition fees and providing them with pocket money to help in the absence of parental support. "We will seek additional funding for our association to be able to help more orphans in completing high school. We believe that ensuring education for our people is essential for the community," she said.

The dispensary of Secours Populaire Libanais

The Secours Populaire Libanais is a dispensary[10] that provides medical services for the community at affordable fees. The building, once a hospital (eighteen years ago), was abandoned and in a much-deteriorated condition. Nine volunteers from Sawfar and the neighboring villages gathered to find ways to provide the region and the community with a dispensary at affordable fees given the unbearable and persistently harsh economic conditions. They agreed to refurbish the abandoned hospital because the building was already there and only needed refurbishment with the help of external funding. They arranged a project and submitted it to the City Council of Barcelona, which had launched a competition for similar projects. Among eleven entries, the project won the competition, and the committee received 45,000$ to renovate the building, prepare the examination rooms, and equip the center. Hosting several clinics with the majority of medical specialties, the center was inaugurated on August 3, 2020, one day before the Beirut port explosion. Amin, a volunteer in the dispensary, identified "the geographical location of the center, the potential number of beneficiaries, the building shape, the surrounding environment, and the community needs" as the key success factors that contributed to winning the competition. He assured that "the dispensary is self-funded, we don't receive any financial support from anyone." Mounira (she is also a member in the volunteer-run committee) and Amin added that "what makes them happy and proud is that 90% of the patients we serve are Lebanese, contrary to the other dispensaries in Beirut, where 90% are Syrian refugees and

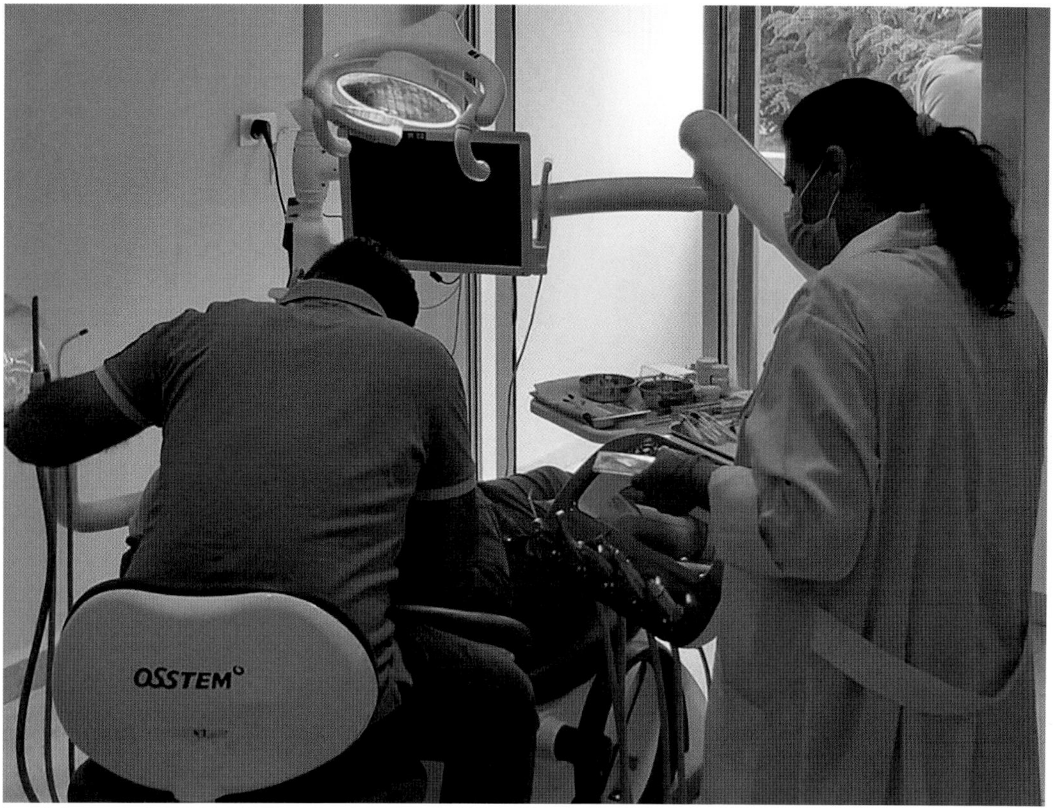

Fig.2
The Secours Populaire Libanais, June 2021. Photograph by Hoda Mekkaoui.

10% Lebanese. This means that our community is satisfied with the services that we are offering them."

The Charitable Association for Bedghan Ladies – '*Mounet*'

The Charitable Association for Bedghan Ladies was originally initiated in 2017 to support the women of Bedghan village, particularly widows or single mothers. The association launched a special project – supported and funded by the FAO – aiming to empower 40 women by supporting their specialized food production for the winter season, called '*mounet*,' and later selling it competitively in the local market. They produce more than 45 *mounet* types, including jams, olives, vinegar, tomato paste, cornichons, and else. Moreover, the association provided food, milk for babies, medical supplies, seeds for planting, and sometimes money in cash for the families in need. The funding for the association comes from generous donors and from numerous charitable activities. They recently organized an activity for children in collaboration with UNICEF. In order to expand their charitable work, they arranged to refurbish a small-size center (100–120 m^2), where women can produce the *mounet*. The center is made available by the religious Druze charity '*machayekh*' and is continuously funded by the FAO, which is

responsible for paying the equipment and salaries of the 40 women participating in the project. Samira, a founding member and the official representative of the association, enthusiastically revealed that the association "applied for a project funding from the FAO, won the project and got the fund." She explained that "the submitted project was convincing and proved to be a necessity for the Bedghan community in general and for women in particular."

Although Samira is living in very harsh social and economic conditions, she believes that social and charitable work is the duty of every human being to ensure solidarity and cohesion within the community. To secure her personal and family income, she relies on preparing and selling various *mounet* products. Her big asset is a berry tree in her backyard. Her husband was seriously ill and has not fully recovered to this day; she also lost her elder son five years ago. However, she continues serving her people, whether as a member and representative of the charitable association or with her charity work in the dispensary: "we must stand strong for our people, because when the government is not supporting the families, then it is our responsibility. We have many elderly people in the village who cannot be transferred to Beirut for treatment and medication." She recalls [crying] a cold winter day when she had no money for fuel to operate the heaters at her house and slept in despair, when the next morning a stranger knocked on her door and bought

Fig.3
Winter food provision: 'Mounet items' (left) and prepared at Samira's house in Bedghan (right), June 2021. Photograph by Hoda Mekkaoui.

some items of the *mounet* she prepares. She felt that she is being rewarded for the good work she does for her community.

Entrepreneurs in the countryside – "Sewing/Khiyata"

Sewing is a skill that most women in Sawfar learned during their childhood. The skill is thought to empower young women and can be developed further. In collaboration with the UNDP, the *Entrepreneurs in the countryside* initiative was established in a municipal building to develop women's sewing skills. Out of 700 candidates, only 10% were selected following very specific criteria: social status, economic status, and age. Not only do these women learn *khiyata*, but they also receive a monthly allowance to help them sustain themselves until they are able to work and be self-sufficient. After the Covid-19 outbreak, they began to produce facemasks and sell them in the local markets at competitive prices. Nagham, who completed her training, confirmed that the initiative was so successful that it started to expand to neighboring villages in the Chouf area.

Framing the *Beik* lifelines

The *Beik's* call for Druze to mobilize, network, and launch initiatives to support their community is a form of lifeline, a social infrastructure to provide support for a community in time of crisis and in the absence of state services. It establishes a progressive understanding of urban infrastructures that moves away from the common conceptualization of infrastructures as transmission and supply machines and towards one intended as a support for living, even though in Sawfar it is restricted to a community with a specific religio-political affiliation in a limited geography. Lifelines became a sectarian societal support with strong political connotations, designed and implemented by small circles of trust and loyalty, shared and articulated among individuals in a community to ensure mutual sustainment and to emphasize the pride in the Druze society. The continuity of the life process is therefore not individual, not social, but rather politico-religious and buttressed by loyalists of the *Beik* party. It responds to limited internal community rights and is restricted to local, sectarian support designed for a specific community.
Knowing the specificity of the Druze in the region as a minority and their closed confessional nature, their survival lifelines tactics become understandable, coupled with the struggle of their leaders (the Junblat family) to preserve their elite family position and thus their power in Lebanese society. "But the younger Junblat's main concern was to secure the semi-autonomous position of the Druze and to develop their communal institutions."[11] For the weakening of the Druze community will naturally also diminish the power of the Junblat family as the leaders of the community. Lifelines thus became a tool to support, preserve, and maintain the power of the leader, rather than only serving as a vital

survival tool for the community. Lifelines are no longer only an instrument of emancipation and socio-corporative tool, but rather a politico-religious scheme, a form of protection that preserves political and family ties through associations and welfare establishments on which the community is strongly dependent.
An important element, as the experience of the *Beik* in the Druze village of Sawfar emphasizes, is not to think of living as separate from cultivation and care. Living always has to do with otherness, with the surplus of an otherness that is not constructed but preserved. Samira is a good example: she herself lives in very harsh social and economic conditions, but still, she fulfils her role in life – helping needy persons in her community. Care and maintenance of relationships, mutual support and attention become characteristics of an inhabitant life in Sawfar. In Sawfar, individuals and collectives developed a "creative process through which inhabitants withdraw from death in order to escort it, constituting an industrious community capable of building, maintaining and repairing its living space."[12]

The '*Beik*' and his 'loyalists': an ecological relationship

The *Beik*, in its ambivalent condition and its perverse aim, is not simply a vitalism, but a complex, intersecting, interweaving of inclinations, dissociations of displacements when life is understood as an obstinacy leaving space for the other, for the situation, for contingency. According to Merleau-Ponty, life is fragile and obstinate precisely because it is not something affirmative of givenness that is to be cared for or simply abandoned, something that "is if nothing opposes it" and that sees the cohabitations and composability that are given in space.[13]
On his way to dominance in the Druze community, the *Beik* has persistently and deliberately dissolved any form of democracy or egalitarianism. He is the ultimate responsible leader, the 'protector' channeling to the Druze community whatever services and resources are needed. In return, the 'loyalists' have to show a complete form of respect, appreciation, and obedience, and even sometimes admiration for the *Beik's* wisdom and strategic decisions. For them, the community is under continuous threat and in a constant need for protection from the rest of the Lebanese society, underscoring a communitarianism with religio-political connotations and a long history of entrenchment.
In this context, life then becomes a relationship, certainly, but not as an exchange between distinct inseparable entities, a subject and an environment, a body and a space, a territory and an infrastructure. The *Beik* is not a thing but a relationship, a circle, and practices of protection, a lifeline, a tangle of spaces, actions, intuitions that "come to terms with the environment,"[14] emerging where life is played out in the limitedness imposed by the surroundings and the occasions, therefore in a perpetual ambiguity, situated in this tension between life and nature where nature, the environment is not an original endowment but the place of a contingency. Unlike infrastructural thoughts, Sawfar does not enclose spaces,

relations, it does not enclose in synthetic forms but an ecology of the possible where resistances cause friction and create conditions of existence that allow existence, life, even if precarious and vulnerable, architectural details that configure space, determine lines of escapes, and construct different horizons of hope.

Endnotes

1 Hazran, "How Elites Can Maintain their Power in the Middle East: The Junblat Family as a Case Study."
2 See: https://stad.com/index.php?city_id=268097.
3 The Druze are concentrated in the rural, mountainous areas east and south of Beirut. They live in various villages in Hasbaya, Rachaya, Chouf, Aley, Marjeyoun, and in Beirut, and they constitute the majority of the population in Aley, Baakleen, Hasbaya, and Rachaya. They make up more than half of the population of the Aley District, about a third of the residents of the Rachaya District, and about a quarter of residents of the Chouf and Metn Districts.
4 Minority Rights Group International, "World Directory of Minorities and Indigenous Peoples – Lebanon: Druze."
5 Harik, "Perceptions of Community and State among Lebanon's Druze Youth."
6 They also follow a lifestyle somehow characterized by isolation and independency; conversion both to and from their faith is forbidden.
7 Ingold, "On human correspondence."
8 Oweis, "Lebanon crisis: Druze leader Walid Joumblatt warns of hunger revolt."
9 Mounira is in her mid-50's and a former member of the municipal board, now in charge of two volunteer-run associations, one being Misk, to help students.
10 The dispensary does not provide laboratory tests or scanning. The committee is seeking funding from people with "white hands" to equip the center as the basement is still not used, many of its rooms are still empty and need to be equipped.
11 Hazran, "How Elites Can Maintain their Power in the Middle East: The Junblatt Family as a Case Study."
12 Boano, "Beyond violence. Toward the politics of inhabitation."
13 Merleau-Ponty, *Phenomenology of Perception*.
14 De Fazio, *Ecologie del Possibile. Razionalità, Esistenza, Amicizie*.

Bibliography

Boano, Camillo. "Beyond violence. Toward the politics of inhabitation." *Lo Squaderno*, No. 59 (July 2021): 41–45.

De Fazio, Gianluca. *Ecologie del Possibile. Razionalità, Esistenza, Amicizie*. Verona: Ombre Corte, 2021.

Harik, Judith P. "Change and Continuity among the Lebanese Druze Community: The Civil Administration of the Mountains, 1983–90." *Middle Eastern Studies*, Vol. 29, No. 3 (July, 1993): 377–398.

Harik, Judith P. "Perceptions of Community and State among Lebanon's Druze Youth." *Middle East Journal*, Vol. 47, No. 1 (Winter, 1993): 41–62.

Hazran, Yusri. "How Elites Can Maintain their Power in the Middle East: The Junblat Family as a Case Study." *Middle Eastern Studies*, 51:3 (2015): 343–369.

Ingold, Tim. "On human correspondence." *Journal of the Royal Anthropological Institute*, Vol. 23 (1) (2016): 9–27.

"Jumblatt: A food starvation revolt is on the verge, and the Lebanese people are the most affected by the sanctions against Hezbollah." *Al Anbaa Electronic Newspaper*, May 20, 2020. https://anbaaonline.com/news/66576 (last accessed: June 12, 2021).

Kadi, Samar. "Sofar: Lebanon's historic hub of luxury." *The Arab Weekly*, October 10, 2018. https://thearabweekly.com/sofar-lebanons-historic-hub-luxury (last accessed: June 12, 2021).

Merleau-Ponty, Maurice. *Phenomenology of Perception*. London: Routledge, 2010.

Minority Rights Group International. "World Directory of Minorities and Indigenous Peoples – Lebanon: Druze." https://minorityrights.org/minorities/druze-2/ (last accessed: December 20, 2021).

Oweis, Khaled. "Lebanon crisis: Druze leader Walid Joumblatt warns of hunger revolt." *The National News*, May 20, 2020. https://www.thenationalnews.com/world/lebanon-crisis-druze-leader-walid-joumblatt-warns-of-hunger-revolt-1.1022491 (last accessed: June 12, 2021).

Viral politics: protection lifelines granting differentiated conditions of vulnerability during the Covid-19 outbreak in Brescia, Italy

Marco Alioni

Introduction

By May 2021, the Covid-19 pandemic had caused 125,000 casualties in Italy,[1] and 3.5 million ones globally. Since March 2020, scholars, politicians, and activists have been arguing that this pandemic is heightening already existing inequalities in several domains of social life.[2] In such a context, one emerging question is whether lockdown policies and their spatial strategies, forms, and effects, could be interpreted as an operative space of *protection*. This space is made up of many different things and is featured by its own ambiguities and ambivalences, granting differentiated conditions of vulnerability. Indeed, it has been widely argued that these lockdowns have contributed to the unequal distribution of households' financial stability,[3] safe working conditions,[4] opportunities to move,[5] different exposure to risk and infection,[6] among other conditions of socio-spatial inequalities.[7]
By conceptually following the argument according to which the Covid-19 pandemic is not acting as a "great equalizer,"[8] this chapter aims to construct a preliminary account of specific protection spaces in the context of Brescia, Italy. It is exploring whether and how they influenced policies of (im)mobility implemented in the last year and a half. Examining the pandemic operative spaces of protection means to navigate through the contested connections and fractures between movements, (im)mobilities, privileges, and vulnerabilities[9] as well as their infrastructures of power relationships and forms of socio-spatial inequalities. Epidemiological data, lockdown policies, and media contents are used as preliminary examples to explore the hypothesis according to which the pandemic policies have assumed the form of ambiguous and unequally accessible infrastructures of protection, depending on the specific (im)mobility regimes implemented in Brescia.
An ambivalent condition of life saving and risk exposure is here considered as what characterizes the operative formations, in that they are assemblages of precarious conditions of vulnerability featuring strategies and circumstances of living together in the time of Covid-19, as discussed by Boano and Bianchetti earlier in this volume.[10] The main assumption sustaining this interpretation is that the pandemic conditions of (im)mobilities have been redefining the relationships between movements and privilege, vulnerability and immunity, mobility and security.[11] The goal of the chapter is to discuss whether such conditions of (im)mobilities, that have guaranteed economic and personal safety to specific segments of population, could be conversely interpreted as conditions and movements of exposure and precarity for others.

Chronology of a lockdown

At the end of February 2020, it became clear that Covid-19 infections were booming in Italy, especially in the Lombardy region. Starting from the first fully locked-down epicenter in Codogno (Lodi), several other epicenters in the municipalities of Bergamo and Brescia soon appeared

Fig.1
The JFK fly-over in Brescia during the 2020 March-May lockdown. Courtesy of Nicola Zambelli, from the exhibition "What Makes Us Weaker, Makes Us Closer" at Centro CARME, Nov. 5, 2020–Jan. 10, 2021.

on the map.[12] In a couple of weeks, these municipalities reported around 7,000 infections combined, which represented half of the cases in the same region and a quarter of the national ones.[13] On March 7, the mayors of the twelve Lombard cities requested Attilio Fontana (President of the region) and Giuseppe Conte (Italy's Prime Minister) to implement draconic policies to slow down the spread of the infection.[14] On March 9, the national government implemented a lockdown policy involving the entire country, the so-called #iorestoacasa decree (#Istayathome). This norm involved only a limited range of activities, such as: reduced individual opportunities to go out in one's spare time; limitations to interregional movement; limited access to bars, theatres, and music halls; closure of non-essential shops and malls on the weekends; closure of swimming pools, gyms, and cultural centers; stop of professional and amateur sport championships; closure of schools and universities; stop to cultural, gastronomic, and religious fairs. No norm did really include the industrial sector. On March 11, the President of the region stated in an interview that no factory would have had been closed through an "act of authority," and that any decision would have had been taken by Confindustria Lombardia, the regional section of the Italian federation of industrial employers.[15] Consequently, on March 12, many workers in the Northern regions went on strike against the opening of thousands of factories, supported by the main national trade unions.[16] Only few factories remained temporarily closed or reduced their production in Lombardy,[17] and even in those few cases they made this decision against the politics of "nobody stops" followed by Confindustria Lombardia.[18] On March 17, the Mayor of Brescia witnessed that the local hospital was going to collapse, that an adequate number of health personnel was lacking, and that morgues did not have enough space for other corpses.[19] He told a local newspaper that the influence of the industrial lobbies on the regional and national politics was too strong and that factories should have had been closed long before. On March 18, national press agencies released grisly pictures of military trucks loaded with coffins to be transferred from the hospital of Bergamo to other regions less affected by the epidemic.[20] In 2021, the Italian parliament declared March 18 as the national day in memory of the casualties of the Covid-19 pandemic.[21] While on March 22, the Italian government released a list of 'essential activities' that were allowed to avoid stopping their productive processes,[22] around 3,000 requests for exemption from closure were presented at the *prefettura* of Brescia.[23] As reported by several newspapers, 317 request came from factories involved in the industrial-military complex.[24] In a few words, hundreds, if not thousands, of factories remained open during the first wave of the Covid-19 pandemic in Brescia. In mid-April, many of the factories closed in the previous weeks were fully re-opened, including the biggest ones such as AlfaAcciai, Iveco, and Beretta.[25] Research coordinated by the University of Bergamo found significant correlation between the infection tolls in these specific areas of the region and the level of air pollution in the areas situated along the Brescia-Bergamo-Milan highway.[26] It also found possible correlations between infection rates and, on the one hand, the territorial organization of the health care system and on the other, with the commuting rates of these highly industrialized municipalities.[27] Local political discourses were less devoted towards blocking the productive system and more focused on reducing opportunities for social contacts and blaming individual behaviors and habits. Despite the implementation of lockdown policies, the regional authority in Lombardy kept complaining that "too many people [were] still on the streets": on March 17, the regional Vice-President Sala reported that 45% of the Lombard population was still moving about, as revealed by an analysis of the data of cell towers scanning mass-scale movements on the regional scale.[28] Although the Vice-President admitted that presumably most of these people moving about were workers allowed to commute, he argued that it was not acceptable that so many people were still out and about despite the pandemic. He was echoed by Fontana: the regional chairman lamented that Lombard people were moving too fast towards "coming back to normality," and that rules should have been reinforced as the only remaining way to fight against the pandemic outbreak.[29] After the release of the cell tower report cited above, on March 20, the Regional Minister of Health, Gallera argued that "people [did] not understand the gravity of the situation."[30] For this reason, he announced that the local public transit facilities were going to be decreased, non-essential shops' hours were going to be reduced, and hundreds of soldiers were going to be deployed in Milan and in the other cities in order to block any gathering. These measures have been implemented through the new policy issued by the Regional Government on March 21. This new order also included new important measures: the total ban on sport activities, even individual ones; total closure of public spaces such as parks, gardens, natural reserves, and playgrounds; total closure of non-essential shops and malls; total suspension of human services activities; total closure of bars, restaurants, hotels; total stop to non-essential construction sites. The closure of public spaces and gathering places echoed a strong rhetoric against individual behaviors, doing individual sports like running, that had been developing in the first half of March 2020.[31] As doing individual sports was the only reason allowing people to move beyond the limit set at 200 meters away from their home, it soon became the target of politicians, celebrities, and scientists, who started to discursively portray runners as infectors, who were exposing other people to the risk of being infected.[32] The President of the Italian Federation of Sports Physicians, a citizen of Brescia, declared that running was "a habit that needs to be temporarily forgotten," because it was considered a "threat for ourselves and for our communities as well"[33] – a declaration justified by the skyrocketing infection rates and death tolls experienced by the city during March 2020.

An ambiguous interplay

The assemblage of policies, discourses, and events described above seems to suggest that the infrastructures of protection implemented in Brescia could be perceived as transforming relations between risk and movements, (im)mobility and immunity, privilege and vulnerability.[34] The main element sustaining this interpretation lies in the ambiguous interplay between the discourses portraying moving outdoors as a stigmatized behavior with the positive values associated to immobility by national and regional policies. It seems that this interplay retraced the existing class relations of power in the city. While industrial workers were forced to expose themselves to the risk of being infected at the workplace due to the pandemic policies, their movements were negatively labeled by discourses that produced definitions of blame through individualizing narratives on risk. Furthermore, as hundreds of factories remained fully operative during the first pandemic wave in Brescia, it is still necessary to discuss whether differentiated kinds of (im)mobility regimes have been encouraged and which forms these conditions have been taking in the city. The next paragraphs develop a preliminary discussion sustaining the hypothesis according to which the (im)mobility regimes implemented in Brescia took the form of ambiguous infrastructures of protection, which granted specific conditions of vulnerability or immunity following the class cleavages of this highly industrialized municipality.

The (im)mobile 'geographies of risk' in Brescia

One question is to understand whether (im)mobile 'geographies of risk' have been defined in terms of the conditions of vulnerability produced by the pandemic infrastructures of protection. The concept of 'geography of risk' originates from epidemiological literature, and it has been developed for analyzing data about the socio-spatial distribution of exposure, susceptibility, and adaptation to epidemiological and environmental threats.[35] However, it is here applied to discuss if and how specific segments of the city's population have been exposed to the risk of being infected by the Covid-19 virus. In this case, the term is used in a conceptual sense to observe how the 'geographies of risk' have been developing and transforming during the pandemic wave in March-May 2020. In other words, the 'geography of risk' is not used in this case to show how the exposure to infection has been spatially distributed in Brescia. Rather, it is here connected to the discussion on the pandemic (im)mobility regimes in order to develop a preliminary interpretation of the pandemic infrastructures of protection at the socio-political level.
The chronology of the lockdown policies implemented in Brescia are used as empirical examples to discuss the renovated linkages and fractures between immunity and immobility, moving and vulnerability.
There are three preliminary hypotheses sustaining this argument, that are going to be discussed later. One hypothesis is that the Covid-19 pandemic has transformed the relations between (not) moving and the multiple privileges usually associated with owning a high mobility capital.[36]
In the case of Brescia, it could be argued that those who kept moving the most despite the pandemic outbreak were forced to do so by the specific (im)mobility regimes implemented by national and regional lockdown policies. The second hypothesis is that these movements carried in themselves the risk of being infected.[37] In other words, immobility and being locked down came to represent a privileged position of immunity, while moving became an avenue for risk to be unequally distributed among those who did not have the choice not to move, making them vulnerable subjects to the circulation of the virus. The third hypothesis is that the relations between immunity, vulnerability, and (im)mobility are not straightforward ones. For example, it will be argued that certain risk exposed movements were considered as essential for other conditions of life-saving (im)mobility regimes to be imposed. This is one of the critical ambivalences of the 'risky lifelines' that is preliminarily discussed in this chapter, one element that could be interpreted as a signal of the emergence of specific class-based geographies of risk in Brescia in 2020. Indeed, it seems that the systematic inequalities of exposure to risky conditions have been rewritten by the interlocking conditions of (im)mobilities that determined who moved and who did not; who had to move and who did not; when, how, and where one was expected to move, and who was able to choose the whens and hows of one's movements.[38]
The ability to (not) move is considered a key area for observing the new geographies of risk implemented in Brescia discussed in this chapter.

This concept is used to observe the transformations in the patterns of exposure to risky living and working conditions in terms of how individuals and groups have been constrained in conditions of forced (im)mobility by the pandemic infrastructures of protection.[39] In this sense, the 2020 Covid-19 outbreak has not only disrupted human (im)mobility at the global level, but it has also intensified and polarized the "existing, uneven relations of (im)mobilities."[40] Indeed, stigmatizing or privileging values and meanings associated to those movements are being polarized and intensified by the pandemic conditions. Furthermore, as (not) moving has always been a matter of life and death, some groups' mobilities have come to be perceived as "threatening the biosecurity of others."[41]

Spaces of (im)mobility in Brescia

One crucial (im)mobile geography that emerged during the first 2020 wave in the context of Brescia is related to the opening of factories during the outbreak. This reveals some of the ambivalences that characterized the implementation of the infrastructures of protection in Brescia. It could be argued that there are at least two main ambivalences that are worth highlighting:

1. The chronology has revealed that regional and national policies have been enforced through non-linear and ambiguous processes. These conditions allowed the industrial federation and the private sector to make crucial decisions with important outcomes in terms of public health and safety. Furthermore, it could be argued that policies and discourses defining what could be legitimately considered as risk-worthy activities have been developed according to specific political and economic interests. This rhetoric emphasized more the excessiveness of economic losses from potential lockdowns and less the social and individual costs of keeping factories and production sites running. By downplaying the socio-individual costs of health-related externalities of the production processes in that precise moment, the industrial federation produced two juxtaposed mobile 'geographies of risk.' Policies that garanteed the hyper-mobility of capitals, commodities, and workforce acted as life-saving infrastructures for the industrial elites, allowing them to avoid penalties and costly delays by keeping plants and facilities fully operative. Conversely, the same policies acted as infrastructures exposing risks for workers who were forced to work in those environments. Despite regulations forcing employers to update biosecurity procedures in case of epidemiological threats, the Italian government, in the decree issued March 11, 'recommended' employers implement safety protocols specific to the pandemic situation, such as daily hygiene measures, cleaning, and social distancing.[42] Furthermore, although work-related infections were equated to occupational injuries by the 42nd article of the decree issued by the national government (*Decreto 'Cura-Italia'*) on March 17, the Secretariat of State declared that existing norms would have made it really complex to ascribe juridical responsibilities for

Fig.2
A view of the city center of Brescia during the 2020 March-May lockdown. Courtesy of Nicola Zambelli, from the exhibition "What Makes Us Weaker, Makes Us Closer" at Centro CARME, Nov. 5, 2020–Jan. 10, 2021.

infections to work environment conditions, in particular in cases where employers had strictly followed the guidelines set by the government.[43]
2. The infrastructures of protection implemented in Brescia in 2020 have deeply transformed and reconfigured the relationships between 'being (im)mobile' and conditions of privilege and immunity, exposure and vulnerability, that used to exist before the pandemic.[44] The conditions of (im)mobility produced by the pandemic infrastructures in Brescia defined specific geographies of risk, composed by novel entanglements of meanings and values attached to (not) moving. On one hand, industrial workers were forced to move around the city in order to get to the factories and production sites that remained operative. However, as explained before, moving itself has been targeted by stigmatizing discourses that blamed moving bodies and individuals that were supposedly disobeying the lockdown policies implemented by national and local authorities. Local newspapers released several articles about the congestion of highways and orbital roads, asking the readers: "are we really locked down?"[45] Indeed, the rhetoric according to which the 'main roads look[ed] trafficked as usual,' contributed to the structuring of an anti-movement rhetoric of blaming. Moving bodies were therefore identified as the main infectors, as the vectors used by the virus to move around and threat the existence of individuals and communities. The anti-movement rhetoric was rooted in the lockdown policies, which

specified precisely who, what, where, when, and how was allowed to move around. These definitions aside, in public discourses, 'moving' retained a stigmatizing value, completely detached from the reasons justifying the necessity of moving. Conversely, 'being immobile' became the symbol of the civic effort, a metaphorical sacrifice for the public good in the resistance against a common threat. This system of positive immobility was enforced by the deployment of policemen and soldiers around the city. At the end of March, Brescia started to be patrolled by drones and helicopters of the Carabinieri corps.[46] Furthermore, a study on private enterprises in Brescia revealed that only 75% of them were able to implement teleworking regimes, and only for limited and specific departments and units.[47] This meant that immobility has been rewarded by public discourses and promoted by the deployment of patrolling police forces. Conversely, moving has been constantly subjected to a rhetoric of suspicion and blaming. In this sense, those who kept moving despite the outbreak, no matter the reason, were defined as threats to the community, promoting the construction of 'blame' and 'responsibility' through individualizing discourses that did not consider the structural conditions of inequality, disparity, and authority forcing people to move during the pandemic.

Final remarks

By defining the hyper-mobility of capitals and commodities as 'risk-worthy,' the pandemic infrastructures of protection relegated industrial workers to conditions of risky movements, justifying this situation through the development of a pandemic "state of acceptance."[48] Furthermore, the negative/positive values attached to (not) moving sustained this state of acceptance that defined what could be legitimately considered as risk-worthy (im)mobility, based on specific interests and power relationships. These interests promoted a rhetoric that strongly encouraged and pursued the hypermobility of capitals and commodities, while rebuking and condemning the conditions necessary for the mobility of industrial workers. The power relationships underlying these dynamics involved Confindustria Lombardia, the national government, the regional authorities, and the industrial workers themselves. The latter were forced into conditions involving risk-prone movements by the infrastructures of protection in their form as policies exposing people to risk. Conversely, Confindustria Lombardia had the power to make decisions based on its own agendas, benefiting from national policies acting as life-saving infrastructures for its own interest. However, these life-saving infrastructures were activated by weighing the individual risk of being infected at the workplace against the costs of stopping the entire industrial productive system of the municipality.

The pandemic infrastructures of protection seem to have been implemented through the generation of risk-exposing spaces and movements for powerless sections of the population by public authorities and economic elites. As argued by Boano and Bianchetti,[49] this ambivalence seems to reveal one of the 'dark sides' of lifelines – they are conditions and dispositifs that create spaces where life and death, immunity and risk, privileges and vulnerability are bound together, confused, negating and reinforcing each other. The pandemic infrastructures of protection emerged not only in their material and discursive forms. Rather, they have been supporting the emergence of new forms of living together, as fragile conditions of membership in the national community. These forms are characterized by ambivalences and ambiguities that affect temporalities, ecologies, materiality of the relationships between the social and the infrastructural, permeated by unequal distribution of power and authority. The pandemic infrastructures have been reconfiguring and reorganizing both life and the vital forces of society. Several agencies, distinguished by their own degrees of power, have been constituting new links and connections between life and infrastructures, creating new life-saving and risk-exposing strategies for individuals and groups. The pandemic risk-prone lifelines become practices, meanings, values, alliances, entanglements between different subjectivities, spaces, materiality, and institutions, that have defined what it means to live collectively in contemporary society. Furthermore, the biopolitical functions of these lifelines were not limited to the protection against/exposure to risk of a 'life in general,' as discussed by Boano and Bianchetti. Rather, they produced a juxtaposition between a certain life and a certain death, spaces that operatively revealed the forms of violence generated by the infrastructures of protection through the sovereignty and authority of the State in the time of Covid-19. In other words, death was the 'cost of life,' a condition that allowed the emergence of ambiguous immobile spaces of (in)visibility and protection, of immunity and vulnerability.

Endnotes

1 See: https://www.salute.gov.it/portale/nuovocoronavirus/.
2 Sandset, "The necropolitics of COVID-19: Race, class and slow death in an ongoing pandemic."
3 Ahn and Norwood, "Measuring food insecurity during the COVID-19 pandemic of Spring 2020."
4 Yun, Wei, Hsu, Christiani, and Kales, "Work-related COVID-19 transmission in six Asian countries/areas: A follow-up study."
5 Sheller, "A mobility justice lens on mobility poverty."
6 Hamidi and Hamidi, "Subway ridership, crowding, or population density: determinants of COVID-19 infection rates in New York City."
7 Sandset, "The necropolitics of COVID-19: Race, class and slow death in an ongoing pandemic."
8 Bowleg, "We're not all in this together: On COVID-19, intersectionality, and structural inequality."
9 Sheller, "A mobility justice lens on mobility poverty."
10 Boano, "Lifelines: the stakes of life in the project"; Bianchetti, "Cartographies of protection."
11 Sheller, "A mobility justice lens on mobility poverty."
12 Brescia Today, "Coronavirus: 143 casi nel Bresciano, i dati Comune per Comune."
13 Eco di Bergamo, "Coronavirus, 2.864 casi a Bergamo La più colpita insieme a Brescia - I dati."
14 Varese Noi, "I sindaci dei capoluoghi lombardi: 'Subito regole chiare e inequivocabili da trasferire ai nostri cittadini'."
15 Il Fatto Quotidiano, "Coronavirus, la serrata di Fontana non comprende le fabbriche: 'Deciderà Confindustria'. Che non intende chiudere."
16 Amato, "Emergenza coronavirus, la rabbia nelle fabbriche aperte. Scioperi spontanei: 'Non siamo carne da macello'."
17 Brescia Today, "Coronavirus, gli altiforni si fermano: chiude Alfa Acciai, 1.000 dipendenti a casa."
18 Querzè, "Bergamo e Brescia: da lunedì si ferma il cuore industriale della Lombardia."
19 Giornale di Brescia, "Coronavirus, Del Bono: 'Le fabbriche andavano chiuse prima'."
20 ANSA, "Coronavirus: colonna mezzi militari a Bergamo con feretri."
21 See: https://www.salute.gov.it/portale/nuovocoronavirus/dettaglioNotizieNuovoCoronavirus.jsp?lingua=italiano&menu=notizie&p=dalministero&id=5386.
22 Giornale di Brescia, "Le aziende che cambiano il codice Ateco per continuare a produrre."
23 Zanca, "Il Nord non chiude: boom di deroghe per le imprese."
24 Crespi, "Emergenza Coronavirus: Leonardo, braccio di ferro sullo stop."
25 Quibrescia.it, "Coronavirus, tre fabbriche bresciane riprendono (graduale) l'attività."
26 Casti, Adobati, and Negri, *Mapping the epidemic. A systemic geography of COVID-19 in Italy.*
27 Ibid.
28 See: https://tg24.sky.it/milano/2020/03/18/coronavirus-spostamenti-lombardia-fabrizio-sala.
29 Il Fatto Quotidiano, "Coronavirus, la diretta – Fontana: 'Contagi non si riducono. State a casa o dovremo chiedere misure più rigorose'. La stretta dell'Emilia-Romagna: 'Spostamenti in bici o a piedi solo per lavoro, salute e spesa'."
30 Il Messaggero, "Coronavirus Lombardia, A Milano esercito in strada. Gallera: 'Stop al trasporto pubblico'."
31 Acolla, "Runner, untori e il bisogno di odiare chi esce da casa."
32 Sempione News, "Ancora troppi runners al Parco Sempione. Fontana 'sacrifici per salvare vite umane'."
33 De Bac, "Coronavirus, il medico sportivo: 'No alla corsa anche da soli. È un rischio'."
34 Sheller, Adey, Hannam, and Tyfield. "Pandemic (im)mobilities."
35 Jerrett, Gale, and Kontgis, "An Environmental Health Geography of Risk."
36 Sheller, Adey, Hannam, and Tyfield, "Pandemic (im)mobilities."
37 Ibid.
38 Sheller, "A mobility justice lens on mobility poverty," 13.
39 Ibid.
40 Sheller, Adey, Hannam, and Tyfield, "Pandemic (im)mobilities," 4.
41 Ibid, 9.
42 Guarinello, *La sicurezza sul lavoro ai tempi del coronavirus.*
43 Ibid.
44 Sheller, "A mobility justice lens on mobility poverty."
45 EliveBrescia, "Coronavirus, solo a Brescia il contagio non decresce. Perché? Forse perché siamo ancora così?"

46 RAS, "Coronavirus, vietato riunirsi e uscire di casa. A Brescia ora ci controllano pure i droni."
47 Giornale di Brescia, "Covid e smart working: a Brescia si passa dal 10% al 75%."
48 Sandset, "The necropolitics of COVID-19: Race, class and slow death in an ongoing pandemic."
49 Boano, "Lifelines: the stakes of life in the project"; Bianchetti, "Cartographies of protection."

Bibliography

Acolla, Dario. "Runner, untori e il bisogno di odiare chi esce da casa." *Linkiesta*, March 24, 2020. https://www.linkiesta.it/2020/03/blog-post-2020-03-19-runner-untori-e-il-bisogno-di-odiare-chi-esce-da-casa-28891/ (last accessed: June 12, 2021).

Ahn, Sunjin, and F. Bailey Norwood. "Measuring food insecurity during the COVID-19 pandemic of Spring 2020." *Applied Economic Perspectives and Policy*, 43 (1) (2021): 162–168.

Amato, Rosaria. "Emergenza coronavirus, la rabbia nelle fabbriche aperte. Scioperi spontanei: 'Non siamo carne da macello'." *La Repubblica*, March 11, 2020. https://www.repubblica.it/economia/2020/03/12/news/fabbriche_scioperi_coronavirus-251055353/ (last accessed: June 12, 2021).

"Ancora troppi runners al Parco Sempione. Fontana 'sacrifici per salvare vite umane'." *Sempione News*, March 19, 2020. http://www.sempionenews.it/cronaca/ancora-troppi-runners-al-parco-sempione-fontana-sacrifici-per-salvare-vite-umane/ (last accessed: June 12, 2021).

Bianchetti, Cristina. "Cartographies of protection." *Lifelines. Politics, ethics, and the affective economy of inhabiting*, edited by Cristina Bianchetti and Camillo Boano. Berlin: JOVIS, 2022.

Boano, Camillo. "Lifelines: the stakes of life in the project." *Lifelines. Politics, ethics, and the affective economy of inhabiting*, edited by Cristina Bianchetti and Camillo Boano. Berlin: JOVIS, 2022.

Bowleg, Lisa. "We're not all in this together: On COVID-19, intersectionality, and structural inequality." *American Journal of Public Health*, 110 (7) (2020): 917–920.

Casti, Emanuela, Fulvio Adobati, and Ilia Negri. *Mapping the epidemic. A systemic geography of COVID-19 in Italy*. Elsevier, 2021.

"Coronavirus, la serrata di Fontana non comprende le fabbriche: 'Deciderà Confindustria'. Che non intende chiudere." *Il Fatto Quotidiano*, March 11, 2020. https://www.ilfattoquotidiano.it/2020/03/11/coronavirus-la-serrata-di-fontana-non-comprende-le-fabbriche-decidera-confindustria-che-non-intende-chiudere/5733147/ (last accessed: June 12, 2021).

"Coronavirus, 2.864 casi a Bergamo La più colpita insieme a Brescia - I dati." *Eco di Bergamo*, March 14, 2020. https://www.ecodibergamo.it/stories/bergamo-citta/coronavirus-in-lombardiatutti-gli-aggiornamenti-video_1345101_11/ (last accessed: June 12, 2021).

"Coronavirus, Del Bono: 'Le fabbriche andavano chiuse prima'." *Giornale di Brescia*, March 17, 2020. https://www.giornaledibrescia.it/brescia-e-hinterland/coronavirus-del-bono-le-fabbriche-andavano-chiuse-prima-1.3467623 (last accessed: June 12, 2021).

"Coronavirus: colonna mezzi militari a Bergamo con feretri." *ANSA*, March 18, 2020. https://www.ansa.it/lombardia/notizie/2020/03/18/coronavirus-colonna-mezzi-militari-a-bergamo-con-feretri_3b4e3a18-8467-4185-ad72-2939cc607f66.html (last accessed: June 12, 2021).

"Coronavirus, solo a Brescia il contagio non decresce. Perché? Forse perché siamo ancora così?" *EliveBrescia*, March 24, 2020. https://www.elivebrescia.tv/coronavirus-solo-a-brescia-il-contagio-non-decresce-perche-forse-perche-siamo-ancora-cosi/ (last accessed: June 12, 2021).

"Coronavirus, la diretta – Fontana: 'Contagi non si riducono. State a casa o dovremo chiedere misure più rigorose'. La stretta dell'Emilia-Romagna: 'Spostamenti in bici o a piedi solo per lavoro, salute e spesa'." *Il Fatto Quotidiano*, March 18, 2020. https://www.ilfattoquotidiano.it/2020/03/18/coronavirus-la-diretta-fontana-contagi-non-si-riducono-state-a-casa-o-dovremo-chiedere-misure-piu-rigorose-la-stretta-dellemilia-romagna-spostamenti-in-bici-o-a-piedi-solo-per-la/5740368/ (last accessed: June 12, 2021).

"Coronavirus Lombardia, A Milano esercito in strada. Gallera: 'Stop al trasporto pubblico'." *Il Messaggero*, March 20, 2020. https://www.ilmessaggero.it/italia/coronavirus_lombardia_milano_gallera_trasporti_ultime_notizie_news-5122562.html (last accessed: June 12, 2021).

"Coronavirus, tre fabbriche bresciane riprendono (graduale) l'attività." *Quibrescia.it*, April 11, 2020. https://www.quibrescia.it/economia-4/2020/04/11/coronavirus-tre-fabbriche-bresciane-riprendono-graduale-lattivita/560179/ (last accessed: June 12, 2021).

"Covid e smart working: a Brescia si passa dal 10% al 75%." *Giornale di Brescia*, April 14, 2020. https://www.giornaledibrescia.it/economia/covid-e-smart-working-a-brescia-si-passa-dal-10-al-75-1.3570113 (last accessed: June 12, 2021).

Crespi, Lorenzo. "Emergenza Coronavirus: Leonardo, braccio di ferro sullo stop." *Il Giorno di Varese*, March 24, 2020. https://www.ilgiorno.it/varese/cronaca/leonardo-coronavirus-1.5079438 (last accessed: June 12, 2021).

De Bac, Margherita. "Coronavirus, il medico sportivo: 'No alla corsa anche da soli. È un rischio'." *Corriere della Sera*, March 20, 2020. https://www.corriere.it/cronache/20_marzo_20/coronavirus-medico-sportivo-no-corsa-anche-soli-rischio-cf83ec62-6a70-11ea-b40a-2e7c2eee59c6.shtml (last accessed: June 12, 2021).

Guarinello, Raffaele. *La sicurezza sul lavoro ai tempi del coronavirus*. Wolters Kluwer Italia, 2020.

Hamidi, Shima and Imam Hamidi. "Subway ridership, crowding, or population density: determinants of COVID-19 infection rates in New York City." *American Journal of Preventive Medicine*, 60 (5) (2021): 614–620.

"I sindaci dei capoluoghi lombardi: 'Subito regole chiare e inequivocabili da trasferire ai nostri cittadini'." *Varese Noi*, March 7, 2020. https://www.varesenoi.it/2020/03/07/leggi-notizia/argomenti/attualita-17/articolo/i-sindaci-dei-capoluoghi-lombardi-subito-regole-chiare-e-inequivocabili-da-trasferire-ai-nostri-c.html (last accessed: June 12, 2021).

Jerrett, Michael, Sara Gale, and Caitlin Kontgis. "An Environmental Health Geography of Risk." *A Companion to Health and Medical Geography*, edited by Tim Brown, Sara McLafferty, and Graham Moon, 418–445. Hoboken: Blackwell, 2010.

Kuttler, Tobias and Massimo Moraglio. *Rethinking mobility poverty. Understanding users' geographies, backgrounds, and aptitudes*. London: Routledge, 2021.

"Le aziende che cambiano il codice Ateco per continuare a produrre." *Giornale di Brescia*, March 24, 2020. https://www.giornaledibrescia.it/economia/le-aziende-che-cambiano-il-codice-ateco-per-continuare-a-produrre-1.3469013 (last accessed: June 12, 2021).

Mimi, Sheller, Peter Adey, Kevin Hannam, and David Tyfield. "Pandemic (im)mobilities." *Mobilities*, 16 (1) (2021): 1–19.

Querzè, Rita. "Bergamo e Brescia: da lunedì si ferma il cuore industriale della Lombardia." *L'Economia*, March 13, 2020. https://www.corriere.it/economia/aziende/20_marzo_13/bergamo-brescia-lunedi-si-ferma-cuore-industriale-lombardia-c5f08492-6545-11ea-86da-7c7313c791fe.shtml (last accessed: June 12, 2021).

RAS., B. "Coronavirus, vietato riunirsi e uscire di casa. A Brescia ora ci controllano pure i droni." *Il Giorno*, March 27, 2020. https://www.ilgiorno.it/brescia/cronaca/coronavirus-droni-1.5083578 (last accessed: June 12, 2021).

Sandset, Tony. "The necropolitics of COVID-19: Race, class and slow death in an ongoing pandemic." *Global Public Health*, Vol. 16 (8–9) (2021): 1411–1423.

Sheller, Mimi. "A mobility justice lens on mobility poverty." *Rethinking mobility poverty. Understanding users' geographies, backgrounds, and aptitudes*, edited by Tobias Kuttler and Massimo Moraglio. London: Routledge, 2021 (last accessed: June 12, 2021).

Yun, Fang Yung, Chih-Fu Wei, Yu-Tien Hsu, David C. Christiani, and Stefanos N. Kales. "Work-related COVID-19 transmission in six Asian countries/areas: A follow-up study." PLoS ONE 15(5) (2020).

Zanca, Paolo. "Il Nord non chiude: boom di deroghe per le imprese." *Il Fatto Quotidiano*, March 31, 2020. https://www.ilfattoquotidiano.it/in-edicola/articoli/2020/03/31/il-nord-non-chiude-boom-di-deroghe-per-le-imprese/5754769/ (last accessed: June 12, 2021).

Inhabiting *Tell* Serhoun: holding places operated to confront the uninhabitable

Joana Dabaj,
Camillo Boano,
Ramona Abdallah

While displacement evokes a sense of movement, uprootedness, violence, and impermanence in Lebanon and elsewhere, refugees who stay for protracted periods of time are making space, thereby generating a highly complex spatial language that questions the very nature of what is "uninhabitable."[1] Not because such conditions are making it impossible for people to reside, to find shelter, rather because what remains is just matter of life. *Tell* Serhoun in Bar Elias, a Lebanese town located close to the Syrian border, is a territory that exceeds consideration of human inhabitation and manifold modalities of livability. It is exceptional because the very possibility of living and inhabiting has always been inextricably intertwined with agriculture and mobility but also, lately, with destruction, disappearance, displacement, which occur regularly and unalterably. *Tell* Serhoun makes evident lifelines as structures that hold and support different ways of living in extreme but not exceptional situations generated between temporalities that are experienced differently, spaces that are continuously rewritten, and conditions of refuge constantly negotiated with cycles of debt, labor exploitation, power imbalances. A form of urbanism generated by displacement, which is a spatial process that implies a continuous shaping of the urban and that reveals its agency. It is made up of acts that create friction within an existing system of oppression and opportunities.
The influx of displaced Syrians to Bar Elias since 2011 has resulted in a rapid population growth. Since 2011, Bar Elias hosts a mixed community of 60,000 to 70,000 Lebanese; 7,000 Palestinian refugees arrived in Lebanon in the 1950s and almost 45,000 Syrians have been displaced since 2011.[2] In late 2020, Bar Elias still recorded the highest number of 29,802 registered Syrian refugees in the Zahle District.[3] Bar Elias' rural and agricultural forms of inhabiting adapt to a new urban future[4] through the dispositive emergence of refugee informal tented settlements (ITSs) that have sprung up as a response to the high influx of Syrian refugees and the government halting any decision of establishing formal camps. At the time of writing, six ITSs with more than 450 families[5] – the very possibility of inhabiting and reshaping space – are the spatial device governed by the *shawish*, a powerful mediator who manages contracts, relations, and debts, reproducing and complicating matters with regulatory and fiscal actions. A form of informality somehow governed by models, key figures, defined prices, generating a landscape of opportunities.

Tell Serhoun's spatial evolution

According to the local historian Ahmad Moussa,[6] *Tell* Serhoun is one of the four key archaeological *tell*[7] dating from the Late Chalcolithic age, located at the north-eastern border of Bar Elias, amidst agricultural fields along the main road between Bar Elias and Riyaq that links to the Beirut-Damascus highway. It was established in 1970 and remained unchanged until 1989 when the first house was built and has since been used as a military base. In 2005, the Syrian army withdrew from

Fig.1
Diagramming spatiality and housing transactions in Tell Serhoun, 2020, pp. 282–283. Source: CatalyticAction.

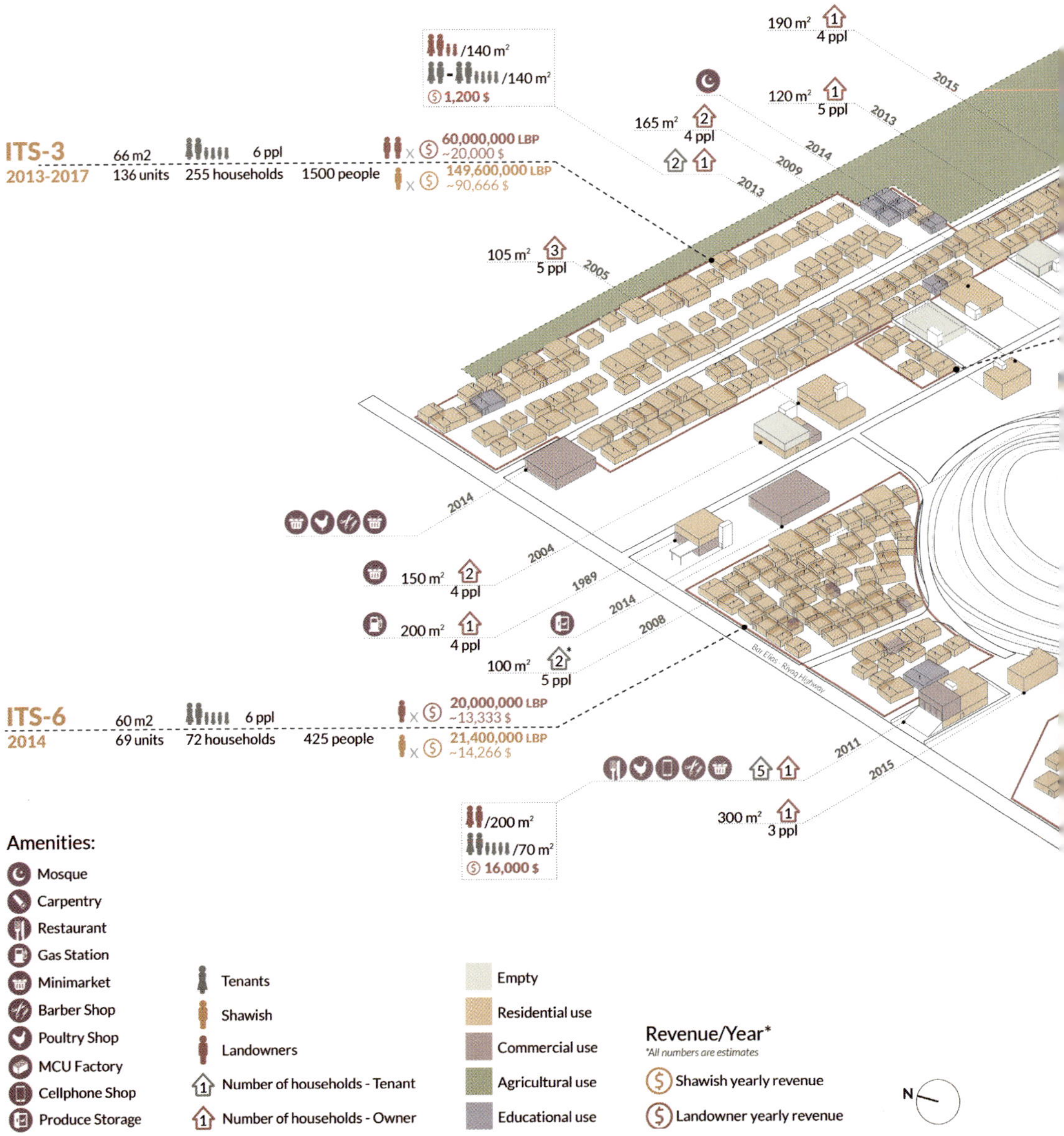

ITS-3
2013-2017
66 m2
136 units
6 ppl
255 households
1500 people
60,000,000 LBP
~20,000 $
149,600,000 LBP
~90,666 $
/140 m²
/140 m²
1,200 $
190 m²
4 ppl
120 m²
5 ppl
165 m²
4 ppl
105 m²
5 ppl
150 m²
4 ppl
200 m²
4 ppl
100 m²
5 ppl
300 m²
3 ppl
2015
2013
2014
2009
2013
2005
2014
2004
1989
2014
2008
2011
2015
Bir Elias - Riyaq Highway
ITS-6
2014
60 m2
69 units
6 ppl
72 households
425 people
20,000,000 LBP
~13,333 $
21,400,000 LBP
~14,266 $
/200 m²
/70 m²
16,000 $
Amenities:
Mosque
Carpentry
Restaurant
Gas Station
Minimarket
Barber Shop
Poultry Shop
MCU Factory
Cellphone Shop
Produce Storage
Tenants
Shawish
Landowners
Number of households - Tenant
Number of households - Owner
Empty
Residential use
Commercial use
Agricultural use
Educational use
Revenue/Year*
*All numbers are estimates
Shawish yearly revenue
Landowner yearly revenue
N

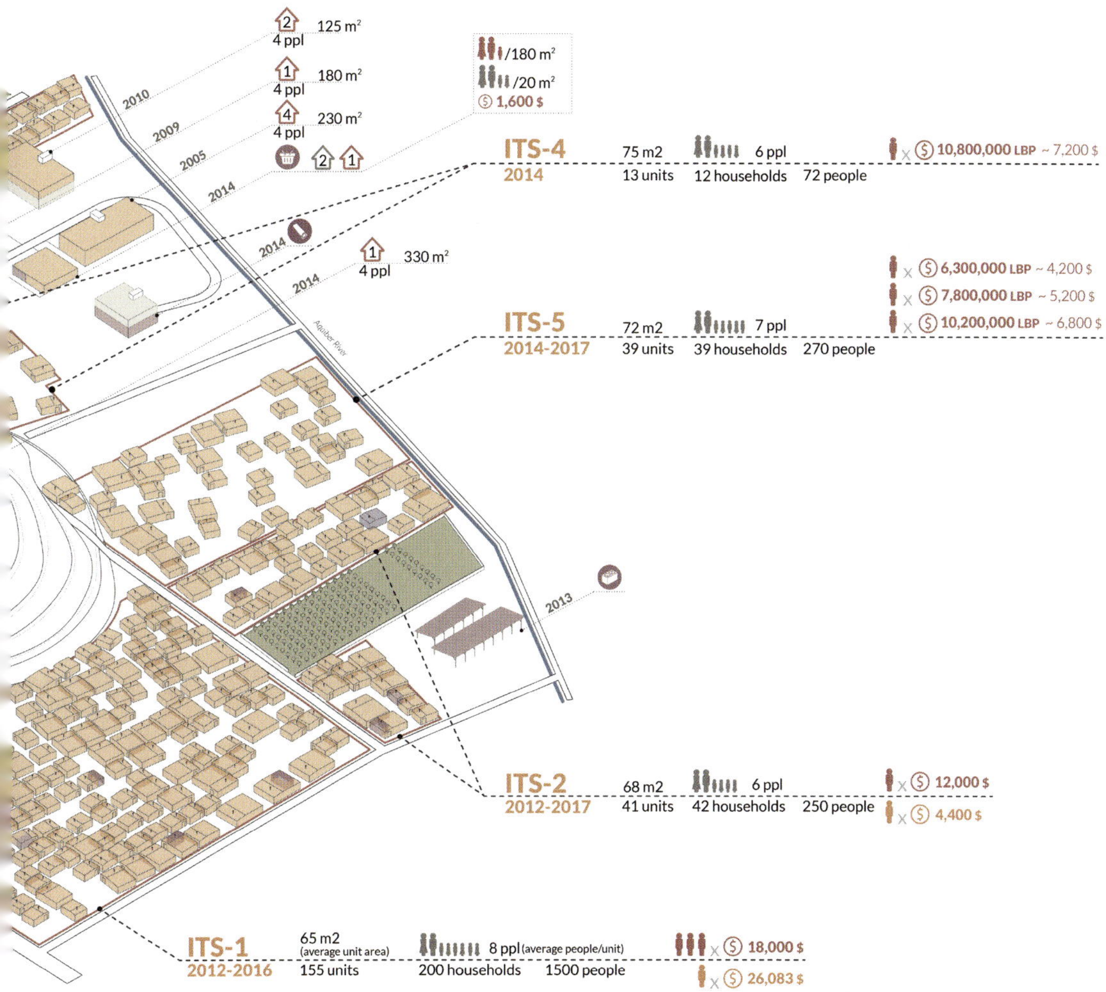
2 125 m²
4 ppl
1 180 m²
4 ppl
4 230 m²
4 ppl
2 1
/180 m²
/20 m²
1,600 $
2010
2009
2005
2014
2014
2014
1 330 m²
4 ppl
Aqaber River
2013
ITS-4
2014
75 m2
13 units
6 ppl
12 households
72 people
x 10,800,000 LBP ~ 7,200 $
x 6,300,000 LBP ~ 4,200 $
x 7,800,000 LBP ~ 5,200 $
x 10,200,000 LBP ~ 6,800 $
ITS-5
2014-2017
72 m2
39 units
7 ppl
39 households
270 people
ITS-2
2012-2017
68 m2
41 units
6 ppl
42 households
250 people
x 12,000 $
x 4,400 $
ITS-1
2012-2016
65 m2
(average unit area)
155 units
8 ppl (average people/unit)
200 households
1500 people
x 18,000 $
x 26,083 $

Lebanon, and *Tell* Serhoun was transformed into a settlement for Syrian agricultural laborers who set up tents seasonally as they migrate following work opportunities. With the beginning of the Syrian Civil War in 2011, displaced Syrians started to move to *Tell* Serhoun and settle there. ITSs started to form gradually, with the protracted nature of the refugee crisis, from two in 2012 with no more than 20 tents, to six with around 450 tents in early 2020. Locals from Bar Elias and its neighboring towns began building up *Tell* Serhoun, the number of permanent buildings doubled post 2011, predominantly housing for rent to Syrian refugees. In addition, a mosque and various shops were set up to serve the needs of the inhabitants (barber, groceries, poultry, cell phone shop, and storage units).
In 2005, a Palestinian family from Bar Elias bought a piece of land in *Tell* Serhoun and moved to their newly built house in 2008. "It was calm and empty, amongst agricultural fields. The land price was cheaper than in the center of Bar Elias. Only a couple of years later (2013), *Tell* Serhoun started to change with the growing number of tents all around."[8] ITSs are a product of the humanitarian inhabitation mode of production in response to crises. In most cases, ITSs are organized on private land, leased directly from a landowner. The rental agreement is either obtained directly with the landowner or rented through the *shawish*. The term *shawish* in Arabic is a masculine word that has been used to refer to a person managing migrant laborers in Lebanon. But since the onset of the Syrian conflict and the influx of 1.5 million displaced Syrians to Lebanon,[9] the word has found a new meaning referring to a person that has been nominated by other refugees as a community leader to act as the supervisor and decision-maker for refugees living there.[10] The role and responsibilities of the *shawish* vary from one ITS to another, however, usually he is the first person to arrive in a location and negotiate the rent agreement with the landowner, and he remains the central point of contact for the residents.

Tell Serhoun's spatial configuration and housing transactions

To understand the complexity of *Tell* Serhoun's spatial configuration and rent transactions, which are making the financial infrastructure of inhabitability materially possible, Figure 4 depicts the six ITSs of *Tell* Serhoun and the permanent units. It provides information on the year of establishment, year of expansion, key actors involved (*shawish*, tenant, landowner), the number of tents, average area of a tent, average family size in a tent, the total number of households and total number of residents living in the ITS, and the yearly revenue of the landowner and/or *shawish*. *Tell* Serhoun's spatial configuration and rent transactions are forging a materially possible financial infrastructure of inhabitability, directly leased by a property owner, mediated by a rental agreement through the *shawish* – a migrant manager of some sort, a good one, a protector, an abusive one but inevitably a master and decision-maker over the lives of refugees.

Agricultural laborers' networks as infrastructural organization

Before 2011, Syrian agricultural laborers in search of work opportunities settled seasonally in *Tell* Serhoun. Karam[11] explained that he was a *shawish* before the Syrian war started. Karam used to establish contacts with Lebanese farmers and manage foreign laborers from Syria prior to the Syrian crisis. The dispositif to organize labor becomes more diffused and can have urbanizing effects. "I did not become a *shawish* because I want to manage the ITS per se, it's a family business originally."[12] When the Syrian army left *Tell* Serhoun in 2005, he moved there to set up a Syrian laborers' settlement to organize agricultural labor for one of the *Araji* landowners. The number of tents at that time used to vary between five tents in winter to seventy tents in summer, when more workforce was needed. With the Syrian crisis, ITS 1 was established on the same lands owned by three *Araji* cousins. Karam looks for work in the fields in the area, he gets paid by the field owners, and pays the workers living in the ITS. Karam highlighted that he only accepts tenants who are able to work, otherwise "they would struggle to pay the rent." ITS 1 is the largest of *Tell Serhoun* with 155 inhabited tents (2020) with an average of eight persons per tent. On the other side, ITS 2 consists of 41 tents (2020) located on two plots of land owned by the *Araji* family; it is managed by a *shawish*, Ahmad, who established the ITS with four tents in 2012 for agriculture business, but the ITS grew between 2014 and 2017. Most of the tenants living in ITS 2 are either directly related to the *shawish* or come from the same village in Syria. ITS 6, by contrast, was set up in 2014 by a *shawish* who has lived in Lebanon since 1981, working as an agriculture and construction *shawish*. "I am not a refugee," Naji stated to differentiate himself.[13] The income from an ITS is considerably greater than that from the agriculture field. There are 69 tents crowded together on the land with hardly any open space. "We don't see the sun because the tents are very close to each other and there's no place for children to play," said a mother.[14] Such high density of tents hasn't allowed tents to be expanded to meet the growing needs of the tenants (marriage, having children, having visitors, etc.), forcing several tenants to move out, but others moved in to take their place. The *shawish* finds agricultural jobs for the tenants, acting as an intermediary between laborers and field owners. There are 17 *shouwesh*[15] in Bar Elias who are his relatives, cousins or brothers; in fact, the *shawish* of ITS 1 is his cousin. *Shawish* have formed an extensive agricultural labor network in Bar Elias that predates the Syrian war and is the basis of these settlements in *Tell* Serhoun.

The shawish's social networks as main drivers for the genealogy of an ITS

Fig.2
Aerial view of Tell Serhoun, 2020, pp. 286–287. Photograph by CatalyticAction.

In 2013, ITS 3 was set up on the northern side of *Tell*, behind the permanent residential units. "The Lebanese families who bought

property here recently do not own any of the lands where the ITS are set up," said the Lebanese owner of a permanent house nearby.[16] Only a few months after moving into his new house, he started seeing the tents grow around him which felt like the whole "neighborhood [was] changing drastically,"[17] with no control whatsoever. Hathem, the *shawish* of ITS 3, was living in an ITS in Dalhamiye, where he used to act as a representative to the *shawish*, but after a conflict with the *shawish*, he decided to rent land in *Tell* Serhoun and set up his own ITS. He moved together with his family and other members from the Dalhamiye ITS. Hathem has a good relationship with the landowner from the Salloum family, who often visits the ITS as he manages the shops built in 2014 at the edge of the ITS. "Syrians pushed the Lebanese economy forward in a significant way, they lifted the economy," said Hathem.[18] He added that these shops would not have been built and running if it wasn't for the Syrians. In 2017, the *shawish* expanded ITS 3, doubling its capacity, to adjacent land that used to be a cultivated field. The owner of the land is a Lebanese from Ksara who assigned a legal representative to collect the rent on his behalf. ITS 3 includes a total of 136 tents, the second largest ITS of *Tell* Serhoun. There are no shops in the ITS 3 but a vocational school run by UNICEF, a kindergarten run by Save the Children, and another one for children 6–8 years old run by Alphabet NGO. However, managing the rent of a plot of land for ITSs can be done without an NGO or the mediation of the *shawish*. It happens in the vacant spaces made available. In 2013 and 2014, ITS 4 and ITS 5 were established between ITS 2 and ITS 3, organized neither by a *shawish* nor by an NGO. ITS 4 is the smallest of *Tell* Serhoun, consisting of twelve tents set up near the Lebanese landowner's house. "*Tell* Serhoun was empty until ten years ago, when people started to buy land here. I am from Bar Elias and so is another family in *Tell* Serhoun, but all the others are Bedouins and Palestinians," said a Lebanese landowner.[19] He is looking to sell his house and move back to live in Bar Elias. ITS 5 was set up adjacent to ITS 2 in 2014 on land owned by three members of the *Araji* family. Each landowner collects money directly from the tenants living on their property. In 2017, the ITS expanded and now includes 39 tents (2020). "I didn't choose to make an ITS, no *shawish* approached me either. It happened naturally, and the number of tents grew without my knowledge as I rarely go there."[20]

Space and informality in ITSs: debts, pressures, and a sense of security

ITSs are such a powerful lifeline in *Tell* Serhoun that even Syrian families renting apartments have an affiliation with them. The ITSs create a sense of security, as one tenant suggests, "despite the bad conditions of the building, I and other tenants would not leave even for cheaper rent in other places in Bar Elias, because of the relationship we have with ITS 1. We feel safe and surrounded."[21] Yet despite their protracted nature, the ITSs that started to emerge and expand have the

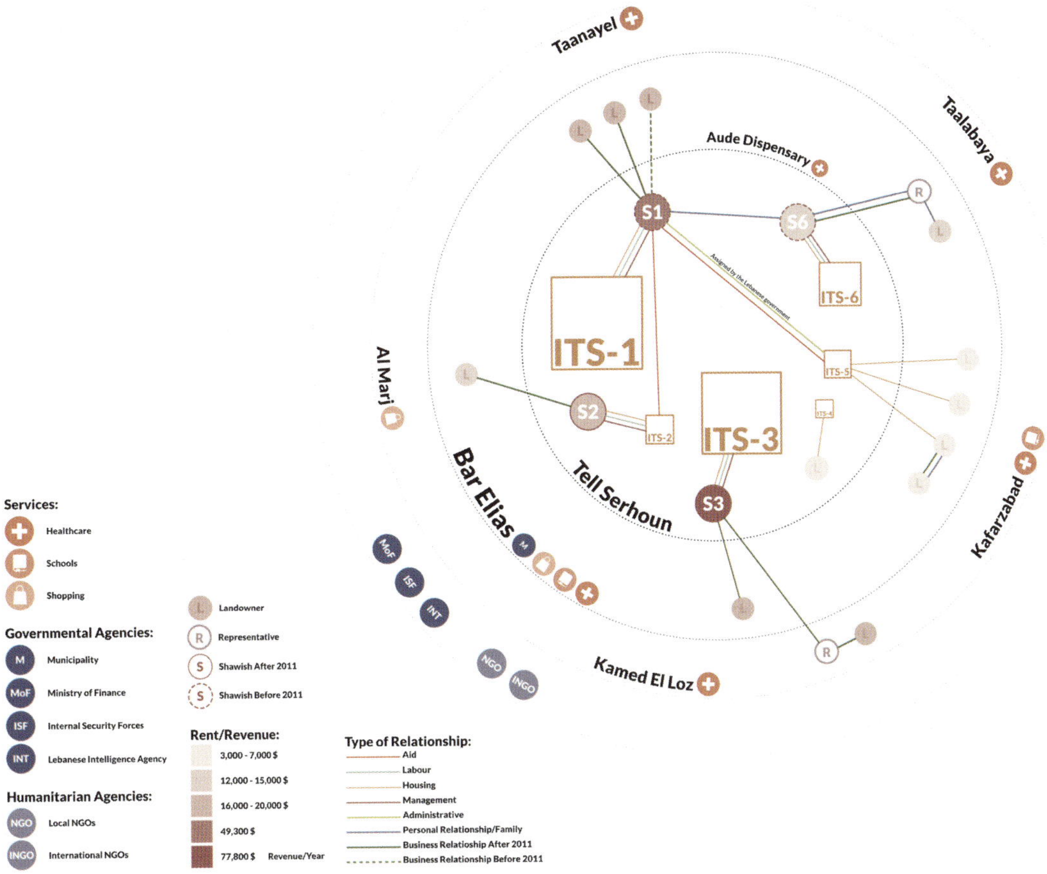

Fig.3
Diagram of relationships and actors organizing Tell Serhoun in 2020. Source: CatalyticAction.

conventional aesthetics and spatial characteristics of precarity and makeshift temporalities. There are two factors affecting *Tell* Serhoun's ITSs and their future modification. Firstly in 2017, the government banned the addition of new tents and prevented newcomers from moving into the ITSs, despite the fact they were already established. Therefore, the *shouwesh* were unable to replace the tenants who were leaving. The Lebanese army also raided the ITSs at least once a year and demolished empty tents. Secondly, the Lebanese Ministry of Finance (MoF) (2020) made a recent decision to tax landowners 10% of the rent per tent over the years of the ITS investment; the MoF estimated the rent per tent at 100,000 LBP per month. The landowner of ITS 6 is worried that the situation in Syria will improve and the *shawish* will run away. That's why he is eager to solve the tax issue quickly before the *shawish* leaves, because, according to him, "the *shawish* is the one who should pay the tax, even if forcibly, as he is benefiting from the tent rental and not me."[22] In 2020, there was a negotiation between the landowners and the *shouwesh* regarding whose responsibility it is to pay the tax on one side, and, on the other side, between the landowner/*shouwesh* and the MoF regarding how the MoF calculated the amount of tax to be paid. In early 2021, ITSs 2, 3, 5, and 6 had already paid the MoF tax to their landowners while Karam, the *shawish* of ITS 1, said that the landowners of ITS 1 halted the negotiation with the MoF due to the country's current economic situation. More recently, in 2020, the Lebanese government's ban on commercial activities from within tents forced Syrians who had shops selling groceries, vegetables, and tailoring to close their businesses. All these events and decisions put into question the future of living in and maintaining *Tell* Serhoun. Agricultural laborers are not allowed to seek out landowners directly or work as agricultural laborers on their own. Agricultural labor is solely managed through the *shawish*. Tenants either work as laborers for the *shawish*, provide skilled labor, or they own a small business such as a tailor or a grocery shop. Either way, what is emerging clearly is a society, a life, and therefore a space governed by the power of the *shawish* who completely controls the tenants, either through family, labor, or debt relations. The ITS is the dispositif of such management.

Debt plays an important role. Most of the tenants in their respective ITSs are indebted to the *shawish* but also to grocery stores, pharmacies, and doctors. "The issue is not the rent that is paid once a year but rather the food prices that go up every month without there being any additional income," said *shawish* Hathem.[23] The soaring prices of food items is the main challenge shared by everyone in *Tell* Serhoun. "Life changed drastically, but people are forced to adapt."[24] Meat, rice, fruits, and even some vegetables are among the items people had to cut back on. During the pandemic, the role of the *shawish* extended beyond housing and labor transactions to health control with safety measures of social distancing. At the beginning of the pandemic crisis, both the Bar Elias municipality and the ISF visited the ITSs in *Tell* Serhoun to check that all shops were in lockdown and to ensure that people were abiding by the curfew. Many people got infected, but no deaths were recorded. To mitigate the spread of the virus, the *shawish* of ITS 1 said that whenever someone was infected, he would inform the entire ITS so they would avoid contact – even though it is extremely hard to quarantine in a tent without infecting the entire family due to proximity and shortage of space.

Since 2018, Syrians running informal businesses have been given 48 hours to either close their shops or legalize them. More restrictive measures were taken in June 2019, when the newly appointed minister of labor launched a crackdown on unregistered or informal foreign workers. During the fieldwork in February 2020, *shouwesh* and tenants in all the ITSs in *Tell* Serhoun spoke about a recent raid carried out by the General Security, giving them two days to close all the shops in the ITSs. This is drastically increasing the vulnerability of tenants who are not agricultural laborers and rely on informal trades or skilled labor jobs. "You can't work unless you have a sponsor, and anyway there aren't any jobs in Lebanon anymore. [...] We're trapped. I'm a trapped man. I never know when there will be a raid and I will be taken away," deplored a tenant who had set up a tailor shop in his tent and was given 2 days' notice to close his business.[25]

Fig.4
Shawish-run ITS 6. Photograph by CatalyticAction.

Lifelines in the making

Tell Serhoun cannot simply be framed within the notion of crisis, even if incremental, connected, overlapping, and structural. What is emerging there is an exhausted territory, predated by the absence of the public, brutalized by the fragility of the common, and vandalized by the preclusion of a thinkable and imaginable future. The kind of organic, incremental micro-practices shaping life in *Tell* Serhoun have created modes and mechanisms of coping with space and its urban surroundings that allow us to understand its history and relations as a process of inhabitation. *Tell* Serhoun's organizational systems and processes are created by multiple actors that constantly make it livable. The *shawish* is a mediator, a broker, and a constructor. A figure that ensures the functioning of such a place and helps to make it possible and livable. The spatial effects of displacement determine the unknown, the uncontrolled, the monstrous, and somehow the urban. The role of the *shawish* recalls what Mezzadra and Neilson called the "assemblages of power and the different forces of capital through which they are fragmented, recombined and produced,"[26] that resist "dispossession,"[27] making space and producing a site, inextricably intertwined with the promise of death and disappearance (regularly and invariably fulfilled) and the incomplete, unfinished possibility of inhabiting. *Tell* Serhoun tells a story of life that inhabits what cannot become 'home' but what, nonetheless, is livable, to paraphrase Nasser Abourhame.[28] It is a terrain beyond emergency from which to think and act, a politics that seeks nothing more than to overcome the primacy of life. The value of *Tell* Serhoun is the value of the place for those who live there: feeling safe, the opposite of what it would seem; feeling protected, the opposite of being simply a workforce but still a place for a "trapped life."

The delicate and precarious entanglements between different spatial arrangements, incremental aesthetics, and rent transactions have contributed to making a plastic experiment where the ITS is the dispositif of both salvation and oppression, exhaustion, and extraction. *Tell* Serhoun suggest that the circle of debt, labor exploitation, and power imbalances construct an infrastructure that urbanizes Bar Elias: a territory that exceeds consideration of human emplacement and proposes manifold modalities of livability. *Tell* Serhoun is at the same time a space of exception and an unfinished project. *Tell* Serhoun is exceptional because the very possibility of living and inhabiting has always been inextricably intertwined with violence: the promise of death, destruction, disappearance, displacement, and eviction that all occur regularly and unalterably. However, the inhabitable is also a continuous creative process through which inhabitants withdraw from death in order to escort it, constituting an industrious community capable of building, maintaining, and repairing its living space. The inhabitable is a tenacious struggle to resist the violent subtractions of future, of space, of possibilities by creating space and forms of life. A struggle, in complete anonymity and opacity, it is continually inventing an inhabiting life and practice exceeding inhabitability and the politics of inhabitation. The intelligence of the urban, when seen beyond the absolute centrality of its violence, is the ability to express politics, culture, and self-organization that indicates these spaces as a place of possibility, a plural becoming that marks the triumph of the contemporary urban world.[29] A power that should certainly not be romanticized as it is always constituted by the form of violence as a generative matrix.

Endnotes

1 Simone, *Improvised Lives.*
2 UNDP, *Below the Surface: Results of a WhatsApp Survey of Syrian Refugees and Host Communities in Lebanon.*
3 UNHCR Inter-Agency Information Management Unit, "Syria Refugee Response: Lebanon - Syrian Refugee Response, Bekaa & Baalbek-El Hermel Governorate, Distribution of the Registered Syrian Refugees at the Cadastral Level, as of 30 September 2020."
4 Dabaj, Boano, and Al-Harithy, "Learning to be a City: Emerging Practices for Housing the Displaced in Bar Elias (Lebanon)."
5 With the protracted nature of Syrian refugees' displacement in Lebanon, residents from host and refugee communities negotiate and produce an urban environment that reflects their challenges. After almost a decade, Lebanon continues to host the highest number of displaced Syrians per capita in the world (LCRP 2021). As of November 2020, the Lebanese government estimates that Lebanon currently hosts 1.5 million displaced Syrians, including 879,598 registered Syrian refugees (ibid.). The Lebanese government has reasserted over the past decade that it is not a country of asylum, a final destination for refugees, or a country of resettlement. This is reflected by the limited protection and rights refugees are afforded by the Lebanese government (LCPS 2021). Displaced Syrians are treated as 'economic migrants' and seen as a 'security threat' (ibid.), an attitude which not only impacts their everyday lives in Lebanon but also perpetuates their prolonged situation of limbo. Since 2019, the needs, vulnerabilities, and tensions of both the host and refugee communities in Lebanon have been exacerbated by the economic crisis, the outbreak of Covid-19, and the Beirut port explosions.
6 Interview with Ahmad Moussa, local historian, Bar Elias, 2019.
7 The other three are *Tell* Bar Elias around which the town of Bar Elias grew, *Tell* Dalhamiye, and *Tell* Deir Zanoun.
8 Interview with Salem, Palestinian property owner, *Tell* Serhoun, 2019.
9 LCPS – Lebanese Centre for Policy Studies, "Legal Limbo: Who is a Refugee in Lebanon?"
10 Mawad, "Syrian refugee challenges traditions in community leader role."
11 The *shawish* of ITS 1, pseudonyms are used.
12 Interview with Karam, *shawish* of ITS 1, *Tell* Serhoun, 2020.
13 Interview with Naji, *Shawish* of ITS 6, *Tell Serhoun*, 2020.
14 Interview with Soumaya and Hamid, tenants at ITS 6, *Tell* Serhoun, 2020.
15 *Shouwesh* is plural of *shawish.*
16 Interview with Samir, Lebanese landowner, *Tell* Serhoun, 2019.
17 Interview with Samir, Lebanese landowner, *Tell* Serhoun, 2019.
18 Interview with Hathem, *shawish* of ITS 3, *Tell* Serhoun, 2020.
19 Interview with Wassim, Lebanese landowner of ITS 4, *Tell* Serhoun, 2020.
20 Interview with Jamil, Lebanese landowner in ITS 5, *Tell Serhoun*, 2020.
21 Interview with Hussam, tenant in a permanent unit, *Tell* Serhoun, 2020.
22 Interview with Khaled, Lebanese landowner of ITS 6, *Tell* Serhoun 2020.
23 Interview with Hathem, *shawish* of ITS 3, *Tell* Serhoun, 2021.
24 Interview with Hathem, *shawish* of ITS 3, *Tell* Serhoun, 2021.
25 Interview with Nidal, tenant in ITS 1, *Tell* Serhoun, 2020.
26 Mezzadra and Neilson, *The Politics of Operations: Excavating Contemporary Capitalism*, 236.
27 Butler and Athanasiou, *Dispossessions: The performative in the political.*
28 Abourahme, "The Camp."
29 Boano, "Urbanism of exception: camps and inhabitation."

Bibliography

Abourahme, Nasser. "The Camp." *Comparative Studies of South Asia, Africa and the Middle East*, Vol. 40, No. 1 (2020): 35–42.

Boano, Camillo. "Urbanism of exception: camps and inhabitation." *Revista Jatobá*, 3 (2021).

Butler, Judith and Athena Athanasiou. *Dispossessions: The performative in the political.* Cambridge: Polity Press, 2013.

Dabaj, Joana, Camillo Boano, and Howayda Al-Harithy. "Learning to be a City: Emerging Practices for Housing the Displaced in Bar Elias (Lebanon)." *Urban Recovery. Intersecting Displacement with Post War Reconstruction*, edited by Howayda Al-Harithy. London: Routledge, 2021.

LCPS – Lebanese Centre for Policy Studies. "Legal Limbo: Who is a Refugee in Lebanon?" *Policy Brief*, No. 64 (May 2021). https://www.lcps-lebanon.org/publications/1620803581-policy_brief_64_eng_(c).pdf (last accessed: July 12, 2021).

LCRS – Lebanon Crisis Response Plan. "Lebanon Crisis Response Plan (2017–2021) – 2021 update." Last modified March 12, 2021. https://reliefweb.int/sites/reliefweb.int/files/resources/LCRP_2021FINAL_v1.pdf (last accessed: July 12, 2021).

Mawad, Dalal. "Syrian refugee challenges traditions in community leader role." *UNHCR Lebanon*, June 4, 2018. https://www.unhcr.org/lb/11806-syrian-refugee-challenges-traditions-community-leader-role.html.

Mezzadra, Sandro and Brett Neilson. *The Politics of Operations: Excavating Contemporary Capitalism.* Durham: Duke University Press, 2019.

Simone, AbdouMaliq. *Improvised Lives*. Cambridge: Polity Press, 2019.

UNDP. *Below the Surface: Results of a WhatsApp Survey of Syrian Refugees and Host Communities in Lebanon*. 2018. https://reliefweb.int/sites/reliefweb.int/files/resources/67579.pdf (last accessed: July 12, 2021).

UNHCR Inter-Agency Information Management Unit. "Syria Refugee Response: Lebanon - Syrian Refugee Response, Bekaa & Baalbek-El Hermel Governorate, Distribution of the Registered Syrian Refugees at the Cadastral Level, as of 30 September 2020." https://reliefweb.int/map/lebanon/syria-refugee-response-lebanon-syrian-refugee-response-bekaa-baalbek-el-hermel-0 (last accessed: December 20, 2021).

Part 4
Towards a permanent seminar

The afterlife of Lifelines

To conclude, we feel three aspects deserve to be underlined.
First of all, this research was carried out, as already mentioned, in an extreme difficult period for all. The Covid-19 pandemic has repositioned our bodies in the physical and social space, in the space of control and limitation of certain freedoms, including those of moving around the territory, approaching the objects and places of the research, and talking freely with its protagonists. As we entrust this book to the publisher, there is much talking of a post-pandemic city, a post-pandemic situation, and post-pandemic research. We are hoping for new practices and new obligations, sometimes radical, but which do not seem to involve, at least at first glance, the construction of a new way of thinking about the city, about situations, about research. In order not to fall into mysticism, into fabulation, into wishful thinking, a slow work of reflection on the legacy of this period is necessary. It is necessary to slowly begin to face the construction of a different thought on the points of articulation between natural determinations, social determinations, spatial determinations. We believe that this task is extremely relevant and that reflecting on what has worked and still works concretely at Lifelines can constitute a first, still uncertain attempt in this direction.
This requires – and this is the second aspect – saying something about the uses we imagine this research to have, a point that is emphasized by the current discourse on scientific research and its evaluation guidelines and a much more global discussion on the role and the configuration of academia. Contrary to what the emphasis on the use-impact pair of notions and its mutual reinforcement might lead one to believe, the uses of research can never be defined *a priori*. Not even by those who conducted the research themselves. Not even when the research is considered to produce usable outcomes within some protocol. Because usefulness is not defined by usability and not everything that is usable is useful. Uses are always potential and possible. They are what we would like to or can do with what we have understood. From this point of view, the affective dimension is very important, empathy with the issue, the individuals, the spaces: living in its zero degree and the new morphologies of protection, with reference to space. Affective does not mean elusive, emotional, evanescent. It indicates a way of doing things in which the subjective way of doing research prevails, its experiences, its history, its relationships, and also its limits, which can define short-sightedness, misunderstandings, and stumbling blocks.
Finally, Lifelines as research is not finished. It will develop in the readings that will be made of it, in the criticism, in the dissent that it will generate and, we hope, in some appreciation. As far as we are concerned, we hope that the continuous tension will develop, the permanent dialogical character that it has been given by the various initiatives that have taken place in these two years. There have been cycles of seminars, round tables, discussions on themes and cases during its life. Like a kitchen table, where stories, readings, reflections intersect, outside the logic of the laboratory, rediscovering the dimension of relationship, dialectics, and proximity. A seminar, perhaps a continuous one, which unveils the power of thought, not the instrumental thinking of projects,

which enlarges, moves, widens, disassembles, and re-centers the critical practice of design and territorial thoughts dismantling the binary thinking of architectural and urbanistic criticism. An agenda that becomes a project of criticism of the present, proper to modernity: wonder, care, and yearning that can once again create a supplement of meaning to the triumph of death and neglect in those tensions between consolation and care, exile and escape, calculation and poetics, imaginary and monstrosity. To liberate from the end and the projecting imposition, to produce critical knowledge is not only to confront negativity but is to unmask the complicit role of the project in the natural order of things as an act of suspension to reclaim a certain space to imagine and practice a transformation of society.

The afterlife of Lifelines as we see it would be a space for new practices of imagining resistance, revolt, repair. The answer that Lifelines helps us to give is still that of Spinoza, to "know how to make the right encounters" and therefore reopen the power of encounters. But, as Stefania Consigliere says, it is a matter of making encounters without fear of our own fragility and vulnerability, that is, living radical encounters that are bearers of transformations able to go beyond relativism and universalism and therefore able to build new lines of flight, new alliances and otherwise. An otherwise "require[s] a commitment to not knowing," suggest Lola Oufemi poetically. In her book *Experiment in imagining otherwise* (2021), hidden almost in the fold of an intense topography of thoughts, she thinks design with the words of June Jordan (1995) below:

"I would wish us to indicate the determining relationship between architectonic reality and physical well-being. I hope that we may implicitly instruct the reader in the comprehensive impact of every Where, of any place. This requires development of an idea or theory of place in terms of human being; of space designed as the volumetric expression of successful existence between earth and sky; of space cherishing as it amplifies the experience of being alive, the capability of endless beginnings, and the entrusted liberty of motion; of particular space inexorably connected to multiple spatialities, a particular space that is open-receptive and communicant yet sheltering particular life."

Bibliography

Jordan, June. *Civil Wars: Observations from the Front Lines of America*. New York: Touchstone, 1995.
Olufemi, Lola. *Experiment in imagining otherwise*. London: Hadjar, 2021.

Editors' and authors' biographies

Camillo Boano is full professor in Urban Design and Critical Theory at The Bartlett Development Planning Unit (DPU) and full professor in Architecture and Urban Design at the Politecnico di Torino, Italy. He is co-director of the UCL Urban Laboratory. Camillo's research has centered on the interfaces between critical theory, radical philosophy, and urban design processes. He is working on a series of interconnected research projects in Latin America, Southeast Asia, and the Middle East on urban infrastructures, habitability, and the urban project. He is the author of *The Ethics of Potential Urbanism. Critical Encounters between Giorgio Agamben and Architecture* (Routledge, 2017) and *Progetto Minore. Alla ricerca della Minorità nel Progetto Archiettonico ed Urbanistico* (LetteraVentidue, 2020).

Cristina Bianchetti is full professor in Urban Design at the Politecnico di Torino, where she was deputy dean at the School of Architecture (2007–2012). Her studies deal with themes related to critical theory and urban design. Her participation and coordination of many research projects and more than 250 publications published with Italian and foreign publishers testify to her presence in the contemporary urban debate. She has a wide experience in research evaluation, including serving as coordinator of the Group of Experts for the Evaluation of Research Quality in Architecture (VQR 2011–2014) in Italian universities. Currently, she is President of the Evaluation Board of the IUAV University of Venice.

Ramona Abdallah is an activist, architect, and researcher. She's currently doing her Master's degree in Gender Studies at the University of Gothenburg in Sweden, focusing her research studies on queer migrants' space-making and belonging. Ramona is an architect researcher at *CatalyticAction* charity, working on participatory design and research projects in Lebanon. Her research interests cover inclusive design with a focus on the intersection between gender and ability, human-centered research, and decolonial feminism. Ramona is the co-founder of Architects for Change, a community-based organization in Beirut, working on the *Feminist Architecture Initiative* she launched and that aims to highlight grassroots urban and architectural practices in SWANA.

Marco Alioni is a PhD candidate in Urban and Regional Development at the Politecnico di Torino (Italy). Marco participated as a research assistant in the *Urban Thresholds Working Group* at the Rutgers University – Newark (NJ, USA) in 2019–2020. Currently, his research interests include urban mobility, mobility justice, infrastructural planning processes, and socio-spatial inequalities in Europe and the United States.

Elisabetta M. Bello holds a PhD in Territorial Planning Local Development and is adjunct professor in Urbanism at the Politecnico di Torino. Her research deals with themes such as dwelling, public housing, urban planning, and mobility infrastructures. On these topics she published several essays and two monographs: *Spazi moderni nella città contemporanea. Trasformazioni di quartieri di edilizia pubblica* (FrancoAngeli, 2017) and *Smart cities vs Smart Territories* (Licosia, 2018, with Maria Teresa Gabardi, Nunziante Mastrolia, and Christian Gasparini).

Nadine Bekdache is a practicing designer and urbanist, and co-founder of Public Works Studio. She researches socio-spatial phenomena through multidisciplinary methods, including mapping, imagery, and film as both processes of investigation and representation. As part of her research on urban displacement, she authored *Evicting Sovereignty: Lebanon's Housing Tenants from Citizens to Obstacles*, and co-directed *Beyhum Street: Mapping Place Narratives*. Nadine is also a graphic design instructor at the Lebanese University.

Federico Cavallaro (PhD) is associate professor in Transport at the Politecnico di Torino. From 2010 to 2019, he collaborated with Eurac Research as project manager of several EU-funded projects about transport, and he was senior researcher and head of the research group *Sustainable Mobility*. He has been collaborating with IUAV University of Venice since 2012, first as teaching assistant in Transport and in Transport Planning and as scientific consultant for some European projects, then as aggregate professor in Transport. His scientific interests include the assessment of infrastructural impacts on the territory, transport externalities (mostly GHG emissions), the assessment of transport infrastructures and plans, accessibility, freight transport (with a focus on combined transport), the evaluation of the quality of public transport, and the role of social media in transport planning. His research activity is documented by more than 50 publications, published mostly at international level.

Alessandra Cusanno graduated from Politecnico di Torino in the Architecture Construction City Master's program. Her research is concerned with the irreducible relationship between the factory and the city in a territory where spatial issues are related to the impact of industry on the environment. She is currently working in a building and design firm in Apulia.

Joana Dabaj is the co-founder of CatalyticAction, a charity that works to empower vulnerable children and their communities through participatory built interventions. She holds an MSc in Building and Urban Design in Development from the Development Planning Unit at UCL. She is a Lebanese architect and researcher whose recent work revolves around working closely with displaced and host communities in Lebanon to co-design inclusive educational and recreational places; this includes participatory research, co-design, and community-based implementation of built interventions with a focus on play and the public realm. She collaborated on various research projects with universities such as UCL and AUB. Joana has over eight years of experience in using participatory design and research methodologies, working with a range of diverse groups including children, refugees, and women. Throughout her practice and research work, she embedded intersectionality and diversity into participatory design to address inequalities.

Alberto Dianin. After earning his Master's degree in architecture at the IUAV University of Venice (2017), Alberto worked as research fellow for IUAV in the field of transportation. Then he moved to Bolzano, where he has been working as researcher for Eurac Research since January 2018. Here he develops European and local projects about sustainable mobility, scientific reports and articles for international journals, and presentations for technical conferences. His research focuses on the improvement of transport accessibility in rural areas, especially across regional/national borders; the promotion of cycling as sustainable (tourist) mobility, and the analysis of the implications of autonomous vehicles on accessibility and transport equality, on which he has been writing his doctoral thesis in Transport and Spatial Planning at Vienna University of Technology.

Federica Doglio, architect and scholar, has been teaching in Architecture Design Studios at Nuova Accademia di Belle Arti (NABA) in Milan and Urbanism at the Politecnico di Torino since 2015. She is a visiting scholar at the Canadian Centre for Architecture (CCA) in Montreal and PhD scholar at GSAPP Columbia University in NY. Federica earned her PhD in Cultural Heritage from the Politecnico di Torino in 2013. She authored two monographs (*Shadrach Woods*, *Per una teoria urbana*, 2015; *Paolo Soleri, Paesaggi energetici*, 2013, with Piergiorgio Tosoni) and has published articles in international journals and magazines. Her most recent editorial project is *Loqui*, a series of thematic interviews about the practice and the theory of architecture and design. (The first issue is: Federica Doglio, Mirko Zardini, *Dopo le crisi. 1973, 2001, 2008, 2020*, LetteraVentidue, 2021). Her research focuses on contemporary design theory and criticism in Europe and North America.

Antonio di Campli is assistant professor in Urban Planning at the Politecnico di Torino, Interuniversity Department of Regional and Urban Studies and Planning (DIST), Italy. He has been professor and developed research activities at various universities in Italy, Switzerland, Colombia, and Ecuador. His research interests lie at the intersection of urban studies, urban planning, and social sciences and are concerned with issues of 'coexistence of differences,' of conflicts and interaction between multiple ecologies, dwelling, and spatial production practices. He is currently working on research projects in Amazonia and in other Latin American contexts with a focus on rural restructuring processes. His last book is *La differenza amazzonica. Forme ed ecologie della coesistenza* (LetteraVentidue, 2021).

Maria Teresa Gabardi earned her PhD in Territorial Planning and Real Estate Market and is adjunct professor in Urbanism at the Politecnico di Torino. Her research deals with themes such as local and territorial planning, environmental issues, public services and equipment, and public housing. She has published essays in several books and scientific journals. These papers include the following: Bello E.M., Gabardi M.T. (2019), "Welfare e spazio urbano oggi. Una relazione incerta e frammentata," *Dalla società fordista alla società digitale. Diritti sociali per il XXI secolo*, Mastrolia N. (ed.), Ogliastro Cilento: Licosia, 173–199; and Gabardi M.T. (2018), "Smart Cities e territori. Elementi di governance urbana e territoriale," *Smart Cities vs Smart Territories*, Bello E.M., Gabardi M.T., Gasparini C., Mastrolia N., Ogliastro Cilento: Licosia Eleatiche, 33–50.

Emanuel Giannotti is assistant professor in the Department of Urbanism at the Universidad de Chile. Emanuel is an architect and completed his PhD at IUAV University of Venice. His research interests focus on two main areas: the relationship between housing policies, social movements that have claimed a decent house, and the development of informal neighborhoods; ecological planning and the dynamics of the co-creation of green infrastructures and nature-based solutions. His research has been published in several international journals.

Agim Kërçuku is an architect and urbanist, holds a PhD in urbanism from IUAV University of Venice. Since December 2018, he has been a research fellow at the DAStU Excellence Department of the Politecnico di Milano. His research activity focuses on the dimension of fragility in territories marked by dynamics of demographic contraction and lack of care and maintenance of social fixed capital, and on the spatial implications of the phenomenon of aging population in coastal territories. He edited the publication of *Territory in crisis. Architecture and Urbanism Facing Changes in Europe* (JOVIS, 2015, with other authors), *Tensioni Urbane, Ricerche sulla città che cambia* (LetteraVentidue, 2017, with other authors) and contributed to national and international publications.

Fernanda Luzuriaga Torres is currently a doctoral student at the Polytechnic University of Catalonia, Spain. She was awarded a scholarship at the Department of Urbanism within the Program for the Incorporation of Research Personnel in Training, UPC (FPI-UPC 2020). Her research focuses on spatial production processes in the territories of the Ecuadorian Amazon, adopting a decolonial approach. In recent years, she has researched and taught at different universities in Ecuador.

Lorenza Manfredi graduated in architecture from Politecnico di Milano. She is a PhD candidate with a joint project in Urban Planning at IUAV University of Venice and at the Technical University Berlin. Her theoretical and design research observes and promotes transformations of contemporary public space in European cities. She has published articles for Transcript, Quodlibet, LetteraVentidue, and others. She has been a DAAD scholarship holder. Lorenza currently lives in Berlin, where she works as a freelance architect and manages and curates the project and art space *Officina Neukölln*. She initiated and led design workshops with the team of *Stellepolari* in Spain, Italy, and Lebanon.

Luis Martin Sanchez, architect and PhD, is a post-doctoral research fellow and adjunct professor at the Politecnico di Torino where he is part of the research project Lifelines. Luis earned his PhD in urbanism from IUAV University of Venice and has been a visiting PhD researcher at the Tongji University of Shanghai and at the Xi'an Jiaotong-Liverpool University of Suzhou in 2019. His research focuses on the relationships renewed after the crisis between the territory and production across Italy. On this subject, he curated (with Eloy Llevat Soy) the volume *Mass Production Makes a Better World. Che fine ha fatto l'utopia fordista nella Torino contemporanea* (LetteraVentidue, 2020) and has widely published in journals and magazines.

Clare Melhuish is principal research fellow/director of the UCL Urban Laboratory and a coordinator of the Curating the City research cluster at the UCL/University of Gothenburg Centre for Critical Heritage Studies. Her background lies in architectural history and criticism, anthropology, and cultural geography, drawing on ethnographic and visual research methods to interpret and understand architecture and the built environment as social and cultural setting. Recent publications include *Post-war Architecture and Planning in Italy and the UK: Exchanges and Transcultural Influences* (eds. Ciccarelli and Melhuish, UCL Press, 2021), and *Co-curating the city: universities and urban heritage past and future* (eds. Melhuish, Benesch, Sully, and Martins Holmberg, UCL Press).

Hoda Mekkaoui is an architect and urban practitioner with an emphasis on green solutions and sustainability. Throughout her career, Hoda worked on a diverse variety of projects in Lebanon, Jordan, Ghana, and Algeria. She developed specialized expertise in projects on design fully compliant with environmental and safety-sensitive standards such as sustainable development, energy efficiency, seismic safety, and fire protection regulations. Hoda is a passionate researcher and has an in-depth understanding of the Lebanese context. She is part of a team of researchers working on mapping and archiving spatial violence in Lebanon as part of the *Imagining Futures* project at the University of Exeter.

Isabel Peñaranda Currie is an anthropology major from Columbia University and a PhD student in City and Regional Planning at the University of California – Berkeley. She holds a Master's degree in History from La Universidad Nacional de Colombia, and a second Master's degree in Urban and Regional Planning from the Interdisciplinary Centre of Development Studies – CIDER at the Universidad de los Andes. She has worked as a researcher and context analyst in the Land Restitution Unit, the Truth Commission, and the Universidad de Rosario Rebel Roads project, and as a professional in the field in diverse post-conflict programs. Currently, her research interests are those of peripheral and frontier urbanization in Latin America.

Lorenzo Rabagliati graduated in the Architecture Construction City Master's program from Politecnico di Torino. He was a teaching assistant and after an exchange period at École Polytechnique Federal de Lausanne, he was one of the authors of the master thesis research entitled *Agenda Tropicale*. The research focused on the relationship between urban practices and the phenomenon of climate change, aiming for a climatic coexistence in the city of Turin.

Nina Rappaport is an urbanist, architectural historian, and educator. As director of Vertical Urban Factory, a think tank and consultancy, she focuses on the intersection of production spaces, architecture, and the role of the factory worker. She is author of *Vertical Urban Factory* (Actar 2015, paperback 2020) and curator of the eponymous traveling exhibition (2011–2022). She co-authored *Design for Urban Manufacturing* (Routledge, 2020), and her book on the conference *Hybrid Factory/Hybrid City* at Politecnico di Torino is forthcoming in summer 2022. She has written significant essays on the urban factory. Nina has been a visiting professor at Politecnico di Torino and the University of Sapienza Roma. She is coordinator of the history/theory program at the School of Public Architecture at Kean University, has taught at numerous New York City area universities, and lectures internationally. She is publications director at the Yale School of Architecture, where she edits the magazine *Constructs*, books, and exhibition catalogs.

Giulia Ravera graduated from Politecnico di Torino in the Architecture Construction City Master's program. Her research focuses on the relationship between climate and urban space. She is currently working in the urban design studio 1010au in Brussels.

Camilla Rondot graduated from Politecnico di Torino in the Architecture Construction City Master's program. Her research focuses on the relationship between contemporary rural spaces and migratory flows. She is currently a teaching assistant on urban planning at Politecnico di Torino.

Valentina Saavedra Meléndez is an urbanist, architect, and feminist activist. She's currently a PhD student in Geography at the Universidad Autónoma de Barcelona and works as an academic at the Instituto de la Vivienda of the University of Chile. Her research focuses on housing policy and gender studies. Co-founder of the *Vértice Urbano Foundation* and the *Red de Mujeres por la Ciudad of Chile*, she is also a member of the *Ciudad Constituyente* platform.

Abir Saksouk graduated as an architect in 2005 and later did her Master's degree in Urban Development Planning at UCL. She is co-founder and co-director of Public Works, a research-based organization that addresses spatial inequality in Lebanon. Her primary focus includes urbanism and law, property and shared space, and right to the city of marginalized communities.

Hanadi Samhan is an urban practitioner, PhD candidate at UCL, and a tutor at the Bartlett School of Planning. Throughout her career, Hanadi led key development projects in the MENA region, working in both the private and public sectors in Riyadh, Jeddah, Makkah, Baghdad, Damascus, Doha, and Beirut. She worked as an adviser for the Saudi Ministry of Housing and the Qatari Ministry of Education. As a Palestinian researcher born in Beirut, Hanadi's interest lies in the Palestinian refugee camps while deciphering their intricacy within the violence of the Lebanese context. She is currently investigating the volume of four refugee camps in Beirut, challenging the flatness of camp thinking as a bounded territory and as a distinctive geopolitical urban space.

Andrea Sanguedolce graduated in the Architecture Construction City Master's program from the Politecnico di Torino. His research, Agenda Tropicale, focused on the relationship between urban space and the phenomenon of climate change, aiming for a climatic coexistence in the city of Turin. He currently collaborates with Associates Architecture in Brescia.

Ianira Vassallo, architect and PhD in Regional Planning and Public Policy (IUAV University of Venice), is assistant professor in Urban Planning at DIST (Interuniversity Department of Regional and Urban Studies and Planning), Politecnico di Torino. Her research interests focus on informal and innovative practices of spatial transformation in contemporary cities. On this topic she published several papers and the book *Spatial Tensions in Urban Design* (edited with Michele Cerruti But, Agim Kercuku, and Giulia Setti, Springer, 2021). In 2021, she was visiting researcher at the Institut d'Urbanisme et de Géographie Alpine (IUGA). Currently, Ianira works in the research project Lifelines (2020–2022) and is research coordinator of *STeP – Schools, Territories and Proximity. Towards an educational alliance in the small and medium-sized cities of the Italian province* (winner of the FISR 2020 COVID call).

Colophon

Cover image: © Camilla Rondot, 2021
Copyediting: Bianca Murphy
Design: Susanne Rösler, jovis Verlag
Typesetting: Luis Martin Sanchez
Lithography: Luis Martin Sanchez
Printed in the European Union.

Bibliographic information published by the Deutsche Nationalbibliothek:
The Deutsche Nationalbibliothek lists this publication in the Deutsche Nationalbibliografie; detailed bibliographic data are available on the Internet at http://dnb.d-nb.de

jovis Verlag GmbH
Lützowstraße 33
10785 Berlin

www.jovis.de

jovis books are available worldwide in select bookstores. Please contact your nearest bookseller or visit www.jovis.de for information concerning your local distribution.

ISBN 978-3-86859-753-0 (softcover)
ISBN 978-3-86859-800-1 (PDF)